BOLIVAR

BOLIVAR

BOLIVAR

THE LIBERATOR OF LATIN AMERICA

THE WAR AGAINST THE SPANISH EMPIRE

ROBERT HARVEY

A Herman Graf Book
Skyhorse Publishing

First North American Paperback Edition 2021

Skyhorse Publishing books may be purchased in bulk at special discounts
for sales promotion, corporate gifts, fund-raising, or educational purposes.
Special editions can also be created to specifi cations. For details, contact
the Special Sales Department, Skyhorse Publishing, 307 West 36th Street,
11th Floor, New York, NY 10018 or info@skyhorsepublishing.com.

Visit our website at www.skyhorsepublishing.com.

10 9 8 7 6 5 4 3 2 1

Library of Congress Cataloging-in-Publication Data available on file

A copy of the British Library Cataloguing in
Publication Data is available from the British Library

Hardcover ISBN: 978-1-61608-316-8
Paperback ISBN: 978-1-5107-6065-3
Ebook ISBN: 978-1-62087-663-3

Printed in the United States of America

For Oliver on his 21st birthday

CONTENTS

Part 2: THE LIBERATION OF PERU
(Modern Ecuador, Peru and Bolivia)

Part 3: DOWNFALL

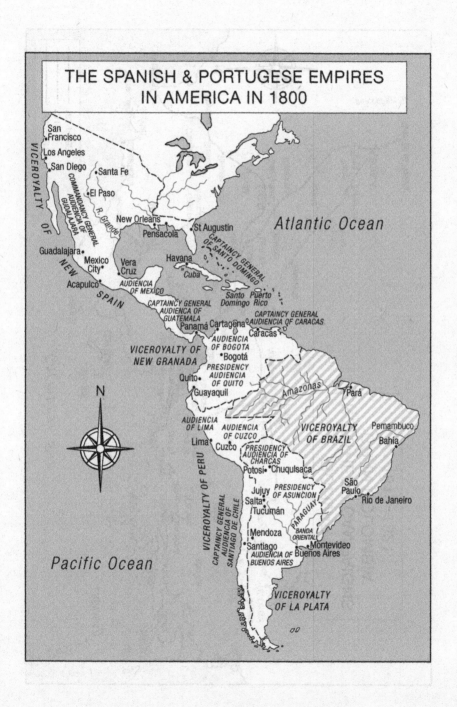

THE SPANISH & PORTUGESE EMPIRES IN AMERICA IN 1800

San Francisco
Los Angeles
San Diego
Santa Fe
El Paso
New Orleans
Pensacola
St Augustin
Guadalajara
Mexico City
Vera Cruz
Havana
Acapulco
Cuba
Santo Domingo
Puerto Rico
Panamá
Cartagena
Caracas
Bogotá
Quito
Guayaquil
Lima
Cuzco
Potosí
Chuquisaca
Jujuy
Salta
Tucumán
São Paulo
Rio de Janeiro
Mendoza
Santiago
Montevideo
Buenos Aires
Pará
Pemambuco
Bahía

VICEROYALTY OF NEW SPAIN

COMMANDANCY GENERAL AUDIENCIA OF GUADALAJARA

R. Grande

AUDIENCIA OF MEXICO

CAPTAINCY GENERAL AUDIENCIA OF GUATEMALA

CAPTAINCY GENERAL OF SANTO DOMINGO

CAPTAINCY GENERAL AUDIENCIA OF CARACAS

AUDIENCIA OF BOGOTA

VICEROYALTY OF NEW GRANADA

PRESIDENCY AUDIENCIA OF QUITO

AUDIENCIA OF LIMA

AUDIENCIA OF CUZCO

VICEROYALTY OF PERU

PRESIDENCY AUDIENCIA OF CHARCAS

PRESIDENCY OF ASUNCION

PARAGUAY

BANDA ORIENTAL

CAPTAINCY GENERAL AUDIENCIA OF SANTIAGO DE CHILE

AUDIENCIA OF BUENOS AIRES

Amazonas

VICEROYALTY OF BRAZIL

VICEROYALTY OF LA PLATA

Atlantic Ocean

Pacific Ocean

N

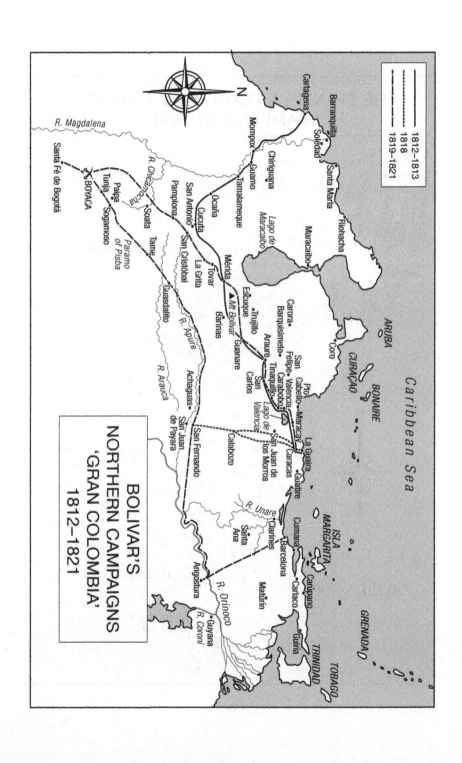

BOLIVAR'S NORTHERN CAMPAIGNS 'GRAN COLOMBIA' 1812–1821

1812–1813
1818
1819–1821

Caribbean Sea

R. Magdalena

Cartagena
Barranquilla
Soledad
Santa Marta
Riohacha
Mompox
Chiriguana
Guamo
Tamalameque
Ocaña
Lago de Maracaibo
Maracaibo
Coro
ARUBA
CURAÇAO
BONAIRE

Santa Fé de Bogotá
R. Chicamocha
Paipa
Tunja
Sogamoso
BOYACA
Soata
Pamplona
Cucuta
San Antonio
La Grita
San Cristóbal
Tame
Paramo of Pisba
Guasdalito
R. Apure
R. Arauca
Achaguas
San Juan de Payara
San Fernando

Mérida
Tovar
▲ Mt Bolívar
Barinas
Esteque
Trujillo
Guanare
Carora
Barquisimeto
San Felipe
Araure
Carabobo
Tinaquillo
San Carlos
Valencia
Lago de Valencia
Calabozo
San Juan de los Morros
Pto Cabello
Maracay
Caracas
La Guaira
Guatire

ISLA MARGARITA
Cumana
Carúpano
Cariaco
Güira
TRINIDAD
TOBAGO
GRENADA

R. Unare
Santa Ana
Clarines
Barcelona
Maturin
Angostura
R. Orinoco
Guyana
R. Coroní

ACKNOWLEDGEMENTS
AND A NOTE ON SOURCES

I am immensely grateful to a host of friends in Venezuela and also in Colombia for the help given to me in the writing of this book, timed to coincide with the 200th anniversary of Latin America's wars of liberation. They include, especially, Alfredo Toro-Hardy and his wife Gabriela, who was for seven years ambassador in London and is a formidable scholar and author of 20 books; the current Venezuelan ambassador to London, Samuel Moncada, a great Venezuelan historian; the former Venezuelan foreign minister, Ambassador Roy Chaderton Matos; the great historian of Francisco de Miranda, Professor Carmen Bohórquez; and the former Venezuelan cultural attaché, Gloria Carneval, who has restored Miranda's house in Grafton Way to its deserved splendour (and also brought Venezuelan music to global attention). In Caracas I had the help of the late Professor J.L. Salcedo-Bastardo, the greatest and most charming of modern Venezuelan historians, who among other things gave me access to the extensive Miranda archives; and I was able to visit Simón Bolívar's beautiful restored house in the capital, as well as the many libraries of works devoted to him. I visited, too, Bolívar's tomb in Caracas and the stunning painted ceiling of the Battle of Carabobo by Tovar y Tovar.

In Colombia, Alfonso López Caballero, as ambassador in London, arranged for a visit which took me not just to the palace in which Bolívar was nearly assassinated, but the beautifully preserved and peaceful *quinta* (country house) under the mountains on the outskirts of Bogotá where he and Manuela Sáenz lived, and Rosario University which contains his office.

Canning House library in London has one of the greatest collections of books about Latin America to be found anywhere in the world, and I remain immensely grateful to its staff for their help in research. I was also fortunate to have been able to travel frequently to all four of the other countries liberated by Bolívar – Peru, Bolivia, Ecuador and Panama.

Apart from Salcedo-Bastardo's books, I would like to draw attention to works which particularly influenced me in the writing of this book – although responsibility for both the writing and the judgments are mine alone. They include Indalecio Liévano Aguirre's superb *Simón Bolívar*, Gerhard Masur's masterly *Simón Bolívar*, Salvador de Madariaga's *Bolívar*, Mariano Picón Salas' *Miranda*, Augusto Mijares' *El Libertador* and, most recently, John Lynch's magnificent academic biography, *Simón Bolívar: A Life*. I am indebted for an insight into his least understood female companion to the beautifully written novelization, *Bolívar y Josefina* by Gladys Revilla Pérez. A splendid recent book following in Bolívar's footsteps is the finely written and carefully observed *Viva South America!* by Oliver Balch.

I remain grateful to the hospitality, in past researches, of the former British ambassador in Caracas Giles Fitzherbert and his wife Alessandra, to Raymond and Mariabianca Eyre, and to Raleigh Trevelyan, whose exploits on the Orinoco helped to inspire this book. I am hugely grateful to my publishers Nick Robinson and Leo Hollis, for their enthusiasm and enormously constructive editorial support and suggestions for the book; to my indefatigably encouraging agent Gillon Aitken; and especially to my courageous and hardworking assistant Jenny Thomas, during what has been a very difficult time, and her brilliant historian husband Geoffrey, who was taken away from us far too soon.

Finally, I owe my biggest debt as always to my mother, and to Jane and Oliver, who have had to put up with the irrational demands and moods involved in writing this book.

PROLOGUE

Tame is even now one of the most remote and isolated towns in the western hemisphere, although endowed with a pleasant enough climate and pasture. It lies in the foothills between the vast Venezuelan llanos – literally plains or steppes, sodden wastelands in the rainy season, an arid dustbowl in the dry – and the steeply ascending cordillera (mountain range) of the Colombian Andes to the west. This sleepy, unremarkable little town in June 1819 for once presented an unusual appearance: it was on the cusp of history. Just outside its one-storey houses and cobbled streets there lay a military encampment of some 3,500 men, made up of four battalions of pro-independence Venezuelan infantry, a rifle battalion, a large detachment of guerrillas and a force of foreign mercenaries – about 1,550 infantry and 750 cavalry altogether. They were encamped alongside a New Granadan force of two infantry battalions and a cavalry contingent.

It was a picturesque scene. A canopy of mist lay like a blanket over the flooded plains below to the east, which extended as far as the eye could see; the prosperous settlement nestled beneath wooded green hills – whose fields, though, could not hope to support so large a body of men; to the west was the shimmering white Andean cordillera in the middle distance – peaks of unimaginable height, intensely strange to the guerrilla horsemen who had experienced only flat lands all their lives. Looking closer, the camp was less than ideal. The soldiers' clothes had been rotted by rain and torn by vegetation, as they recovered from a damp that had seeped into their bones; their horses were exhausted and drained. So starved were they that they had considered eating their beloved steeds – and, if necessary, these desperate grizzled men threatened to kill and eat each other.

Six officers were gathered in a relatively comfortable local merchant's house. They, like their men, were just beginning to recover from the ardours of crossing the llanos, hundreds of miles of which were inhospitable swamp at that time of year. They, their soldiers and their women had endured weeks of dense fog and torrential rains. They had made their way through water and mud, up to chest-deep, across the interminably flooded plains, fording fast-flowing rivers and spending their nights on boggy, sodden hillocks in the ground, while being bitten by innumerable insects and flesh-eating caribe fish. The officers relished their new temperate paradise, above the mists, above the water-saturated hell they had traversed for so many weeks.

One of the six, a small, wiry, balding man with fine brow, a penetrating gaze, intense and fast nervous gestures and an air of command, had just finished speaking. He was dressed in a blue tunic, with gold braid and red epaulettes, the uniform of a Russian dragoon; Simón Bolívar was incongruous among both his 'generals' and troops. Two of the others were shouting at him. One was a stocky, barrel-chested man with a flowing moustache: he wore a simple long tunic with a belt, military boots and a fine cloak as well as a broad-brimmed hat: he was José Antonio Páez, the famed leader of the 'llaneros', the plainsmen cowboys who were some of the greatest riders on earth. His companion, José Anzoátegui, was serious-looking, dressed in more modest standard military attire. The other three men remained silent: one was Colonel James Rooke, a fair-haired man with broad shoulders and an open, honest expression, a former British army major who commanded the mercenary troops. The other European present was Bolívar's personal aide, Daniel O'Leary, a red-faced Irishman with dark, curly hair, baby cheeks and shrewd eyes. Making up the complement was a thin man with a goatee beard, calculating, expressionless eyes and a domed forehead: Francisco de Paula Santander, commander of the New Granadan forces.

The two dissenters – Páez and Anzoátegui – were indignantly shouting because they believed they had been tricked by Bolívar. He had led their men, and his own, across the purgatory of the eastern llano swamps so that they could veer northward across the higher ground towards Cucúta and the plains of Casanare to surprise the Spanish army occupying Venezuela in the rear. That was what Bolívar had told them as they sat on bleached oxen skulls at an historic meeting in the village of Setenta by the mighty Arauca river before they had embarked on the expedition.

But Bolívar had been deceiving them. He intended instead to march the armies straight across the giant Andes mountain chain – the second highest in the world, where the lower passes were 13,000 feet high, overlooked by towering peaks of up to 20,000 feet – through the snows and ice in their ragged, torn clothes, to descend and attack the civilized heartland of Spanish power in South America, the city of Santa Fé de Bogotá in its fertile mountain saucer. He was proposing a venture twice as dangerous as Hannibal's crossing of the Alps with only a tiny army, which had already endured the ferocious hardships of weeks in festering tropical heat and clinging damp. It was pure madness.

Páez stormed out of the room in protest at the deception and at first, with Anzoátegui, sought to secure the support of the other commanders to overthrow the seemingly crazy Bolívar. But Rooke and O'Leary were intensely loyal and approved of the seeming insanity of the strategy Bolívar had proposed, while Santander wanted to liberate his homeland of New Granada, of which Bogotá was the capital. The furious Páez told his llaneros, who were fearful of climbing these high mountains, to desert but over the next two days he decided not to abandon Bolívar in his madcap expedition.

So began the great crossing of the second highest mountains on earth, the most daring attack on the flank of an empire in history. Embarking on a superhuman feat, taking on apparently impossible odds, showing foolhardy boldness, all tinged with deceit and persuasiveness – these were trademarks of Simón Bolívar, but he had never attempted anything on this scale. The outcome was utterly uncertain for a man who had led his men both to triumph and disaster so many times before. Bolívar's army left the mist blanket of the llanos behind it, climbing towards the coned meringue heights with kite-like condors wheeling above them. The 36-year-old desperado had come a long way from his roots as the pampered orphan heir of one of the richest families in Caracas.

INTRODUCTION

Simón Bolívar was a child of the enlightenment, a dedicated follower of Jean-Jacques Rousseau, yet ironically he was to become the world's foremost expression of the romantic hero in the early nineteenth century, a Nietzschean superman on horseback who, sword in hand, slashed his way 20,000 miles across jungle, swamp, desert and the Andes, almost singlehandedly, to liberate his peoples from cruel imperial repression. In romantic style, he often yielded to the tyrannical and murderous undercurrents within his own feverish personality.

Bolívar was one of the shapers of the modern world, leading his ragged band of followers to take on what was then the longest enduring empire, that of Spain, which disposed of some 36,000 troops and 44,000 seamen to preserve an entire continent in its iron grip. He liberated no fewer than six modern countries from the Spanish stranglehold – Venezuela, Colombia, Peru, Ecuador, Bolivia and Panama – in a series of astonishing marches that led his army across Amazonian rainforests, sodden marshes, dizzying mountains, parched outbacks and prosperous highlands to exceed the achievements of the conquistadors, Hernán Cortés and Francisco Pizarro (because the Spanish empire was so much better armed than the Aztecs and the Incas). He commanded his troops in hundreds of engagements on a dozen major campaigns across distances of thousands of miles. He was perhaps the last of the great one-man commanders before the age of industrial warfare and giant mechanized armies. In his continent-spanning achievement his record perhaps even exceeded those of Alexander the Great, Genghis Khan, Tamerlane, Clive of India and Napoleon.

He conquered a land more than 1 million square miles in extent – and then, unlike most conquerors, refused to set a crown upon his head, rejoicing instead in the title of Liberator. There were many other great Latin American liberators – Venezuela's Francisco de Miranda, Colombia's Francisco de Paula Santander and Antonio Nariño, Argentina's José de San Martín, Chile's Bernardo O'Higgins, Brazil's Crown Prince Pedro, Bolivia's General Andrés Santa Cruz and Antonio José de Sucre, Peru's José de la Riva Agüero, Mexico's Padre Hidalgo, José María Morelos and Francisco de Itubide, as well as the Scottish seaman Thomas Cochrane – but Bolívar's military achievements eclipse them all, as does his sophisticated yet decisive political thinking. He remains an object of admiration among educated Latin Americans and quasi-religious veneration among the poor people of the continent alike. Inspired by the leadership of the revolutionary cause in North America – in particular George Washington – in shaking off the British imperial yoke by 1783 (the year of Bolívar's birth), Bolívar stands unchallenged at the head of the romantic revolutionary pantheon.

Bolívar's role was pivotal at a world-defining moment in the history of the Atlantic peoples. With the rebellious colonists' achievement of freedom from Britain, the new United States was anxious to expand into the immense and at that time much richer continent to the south – and at the very least to preserve it from encroachment by the European powers. Spain and Portugal, whose grip was slipping, were capable nevertheless of still putting up a powerful, ferocious and desperate struggle to preserve their empires. The British, who had consolidated their hold on the wealthy Caribbean and Canada, were eager to add the rich pickings of Latin America to their own empire. The French also sought a bridgehead on the American continent, but with Napoleon's defeat by the British navy they were effectively excluded. None of these formidable world powers reckoned on the human whirlwind who was to be unleashed on the continent in the shape of Simón Bolívar, standing for the self-determination and independence of South America.

One of the most misleading names in geography is Latin America, although it provides a useful shorthand for the continent. The greatest paradox represented by this vast landmass (one which

Simón Bolívar directly sought to address, resulting ultimately in his downfall) is that perhaps the most unified stretch of the world in terms of recent culture, language, history and religion, although not ethnicity, should have remained so divided after independence into a collection of big, small and medium-sized states. They remain obdurately separated and irritably nationalist (although wars between them have been mercifully few over the past two centuries compared with, say, Europe). While the United States, Europe and India have managed to evolve a steadily more unified framework, in spite of the huge linguistic, racial, religious, cultural and political differences within them, and Russia and China have done so through imperial conquest, Latin America remains determinedly divided, although to a first-time visitor it may be hard to tell one country apart from another.

The answer to this puzzle is simpler than may at first appear: Latin America evolved as a collection of imperial viceroyalties and subdivisions, established and maintained by an overseas empire. For 300 years an often impenetrable geography of mountains, deserts, jungles and huge distances divided these units of empire, ensuring their evolution into different city-based states united by culture but each with their own particular history, racial mix and different interests.

The same phenomenon has occurred in many mountain regions, for example in the Caucasus, the Balkans (also divided along ethnic lines), Spain (which has some different languages, too), to a lesser extent in mountainous southern Germany and Austria, and above all in Italy, united in culture, language and religion but long divided by its rugged mountain topography into city-states with flourishing individual civilizations. The drive to unity has occurred across the great plains of the United States, the central plain of Europe and the steppes and flats of Russia rather than in mountains with their isolated city-states.

In South America, the jealously guarded independence of these city-states made for a continent that was extremely weak after independence, prostrate at the feet of its unified northern neighbour, the United States, as well as the British empire and, today, the economic co-operation that unites most of Europe. The old Spanish revolutionary slogan, '*un pueblo unido jamás será vencido*' ('a people, united, will never be defeated') applies less to the divided countries of the continent than to almost any other.

The resultant culture of city-states with a common heritage yet little co-operation occupying the most varied topography on earth yielded some of the most singular and spectacularly sited cities in the world. They stood alongside the creations of science fiction. Each had its own special character: cosmopolitan Buenos Aires located beside an inland tongue of ocean and a seemingly infinite extension of grassland; provincial, cheery Montevideo across the water; Asunción, a tropical lost world upriver; Rio de Janeiro, with its magnificent backdrop of mountains straddling an isthmus; La Paz, set in a mountain canyon by an inland sea, Lake Titicaca, 12,000 feet up; Santiago de Chile with its backdrop of the jagged, snow-capped jawline of the second highest mountains in the world, the Andes; Lima, a beautiful colonial city on a parched, cloudy and rainless desert between sea and mountains; Quito, an indigenous city beneath snow-topped conical volcanoes; Bogotá, in its fertile mountain saucer; Caracas, in its deep valley; Panama City, with its Caribbean, wooden city centre; Guatemala City, at the base of picturesque indigenous highlands; Havana, a lovely colonial city on an island of plantations and rugged mountains; Mexico City, beneath the lazy Popocatépetl volcano, high on an upland plateau in a country of mountains and deserts.

It is in six of these subdivisions of empire that this book is primarily set: Venezuela, Colombia, Panama, Peru, Bolivia and Ecuador. But the political earthquake that struck them was to affect the whole continent. In so far as such a huge and complex upheaval as the liberation of Latin America can be given a name, or be identified with a single person, it is with Simón Bolívar.

Latin America is a continent of staggering variety, beauty and geographical extremes, and Venezuela is no exception. Part of the viceroyalty of New Granada until 1776, it was looked down upon both physically and socially by the viceroy and his court in glittering and fertile upland Bogotá. In the west was the extensive sweltering region around Lake Maracaibo, an inland sea whose stilt houses over the water gave the name to the country – Little Venice (the lake would later be the prime source of the country's oil – today it is an eerie landscape of a vast collection of praying mantis oilrigs, their beaks dipping and rising in the water).

To the west and skirting the sun-baked coast was one of the tendrils of the Andes Mountains, centred on the upland city of Mérida, descending to the beautiful and fertile valleys of central Venezuela, eventually towards the cities of Valencia and Caracas. The mountains surrounding these beautiful lands plummeted down to the coast and its ports of Puerto Cabello and La Guaria (the port of Caracas) to which it was connected by a precipitous ribbon road rising some 3,000 feet.

Further along the coast, Barcelona, Cumana and Maturín marked the extremity of the uplands, before they descended to the barely inhabitable Orinoco delta, a kind of dress rehearsal for the vast Amazon delta much further south. This great river, second only to the Amazon in its continental immensity, snaked towards Angostura (now Ciudad Bolívar), the highest navigable port, and then into the emptiness of the Venezuelan llanos (savannah), an unrelentingly flat immensity of alternate dustbowl desert and, in the rainy season, impassable marshland and swollen rivers. Two great tributaries flowed from the Orinoco across the llanos, the Apure and the Auraca. South of the Orinoco basin lay upland Venezuelan Guyana with its landscape of *mesetas* – table mountains – and the nearly 9,000-foot-high Roraima, the location of *The Lost World* of Arthur Conan Doyle. A nearby *meseta* hosts the highest waterfall in the world, the Angel Falls, discovered by an American of that name in the early twentieth century. To the west the llanos ended in the more temperate area around Guanaré, before ascending to the Colombian Andes.

The badlands of Venezuela – the Orinoco, the llanos, the south-eastern regions – were barely inhabited. The population was concentrated along the temperate and fertile mountain valleys of the north and, to a lesser extent, along the Caribbean coastline. Caracas itself lay in a lovely bowl formed by two parallel spurs of mountains, dominated by Mount Avila to the north.

Part 1

THE LIBERATION
OF NEW GRANADA

(MODERN VENEZUELA,
COLOMBIA AND PANAMA)

Chapter 1

YOUNG BOLÍVAR

Simón Bolívar was born on 24 January 1783 to an enormously wealthy and distinguished Venezuelan family that had aristocratic roots in the mountainous and windswept region of Vizcaya (Biscay) in northern Spain. As long ago as the thirteenth century, the Bolívar clan, in the remote walled villages of the region, had resisted the centralizing influence of the Castilian state, and only after sporadic and bitter warfare was the Bolívars' small fortress destroyed in 1470. The family's characteristic independent spirit drove one of their number, Simón, to migrate in 1589 to experience the pioneering hardships of the early settlers of the future land of Venezuela. The family rapidly became one of the most industrious and influential in that beautiful land.

The Bolívars were responsible for fortifying the port of La Guaira, for founding several towns and for helping to secure the wild interior. Juan Bolívar, grandfather of the Liberator, is supposed to have had a relationship with a black slave, which may have accounted for his grandson's slightly negroid features. In 1728 Juan paid the colossal sum of 22,000 golden doubloons to King Philip V to secure the title of Marqués de San Luis. However, the Spanish genealogists sent to ascertain the purity of the Bolívar family tree discovered that one of their female antecedents was of Indian blood. The title was denied him. This ferocious snub by the Spanish crown incensed this already proud family of two centuries' standing as one of the richest and most powerful in Venezuela. For the first time there awoke a sense of apartness in a clan that had always regarded itself as Spanish in origin. Of course, it later became convenient for the Liberator to be able to claim that he was of mixed white, Indian and black extraction – the three racial components of Latin American nationhood.

Juan's son, Juan Vicente, was brought up rich and idle, leading an agreeable life in Caracas, a city set 3,000 feet above sea level some 40 miles inland from the Caribbean coastline in a deep, fertile valley, criss-crossed by rivers, between two medium-sized mountain ranges. The 40,000 inhabitants enjoyed a pleasant climate, at 40°F not too cold in winter and, rising to a maximum of 96°F, not too hot in summer, with a modest rainy season and cool nights.

Juan Vicente lived in a family mansion in Plaza San Jacinto in the centre of this colonial city of long, narrow streets arranged on a classical grid. The house is a lovely, one-storey Spanish colonial villa, set around a large courtyard. The other houses were built of mud or stone, only one or two storeys high, because of the danger of earthquakes in the central highlands. Something of a social lion, he was a womanizer: he was denounced by two sisters, Margarita and María Jacinta, as an 'infernal wolf' imploring them to 'make sin with him', and nearly prosecuted for rape. Juan Vicente did not marry until the age of 46 when he chose María Concepcion Palacios y Blanco, the beautiful 15-year-old daughter of another prominent family.

The teenage girl was by all accounts as lively as Juan Vicente was sensual. Like her famous son, she was dark, vivacious and passionate – and ambitious. But she could also be moody and unsatisfied. Hard-headed and practical, she would complain 'it makes one grieve to pay 300 pesos for slaves which you cannot use for more than eight years, and the black woman could barely bring forth many young'. This socially prominent couple, separated in age by more than 30 years, proceeded to have four children: a boy, then two girls and, last, Simón. Doña María Concepcion, by the time her lastborn had arrived, was more temperamental than ever and, still being very young, was bored by her husband's easygoing indolence. She had begun to suffer from a chest infection – probably tuberculosis – of which she was eventually to die.

It was common for the children of the wealthy to be raised apart from their parents. The infant was cared for from the beginning by two devoted nurses, Ines, from a respectable Spanish family, and a black slave, Hipolita – both devoted to their lively young charge. He loved

Ines and worshipped Hipolita, who sought to give him his every wish. As a slave, she considered it her duty to serve him almost as soon as he could issue commands. Simón grew up bossy and capricious. He was also hyperactive, accustomed to getting his own way and – because life was so pleasant – imbued with a ferocious optimism that was to stand him in good stead through the trials and reverses of his later life.

Bolívar's father, who had died of tuberculosis when Simón was under three years old, obviously had only a limited direct influence on the child's life; but as the boy grew Juan Vicente's views would have had a profound effect, as would his involvement in circles hostile to the Spanish crown. Juan Vicente Bolívar had actually written to the rebel Francisco de Miranda complaining of 'tyrannical measures taken by the intendant [Spanish colonial administrator Bernardo de Gálvez] who treated all Americans, no matter what their class, race or circumstances, as vile slaves'. Miranda, who was in Europe trying to rally support for his mission to free his homeland from the Spanish crown, was to play a hugely important part in Simón's life.

For the moment the boy was spoilt. With the death of Juan and the stillbirth of another child, Doña María Concepción could stand no more of what little she saw of the assertive little boy, and gave him over to the care of the family lawyer, Miguel José Sanz. The infant was trotted out of the cheerful, spacious family home where he used to play with his brother and sisters, and into the bachelor house of this misanthropic pedant. He was determined to improve his charge through a regime of discipline and austerity.

It was the young Simón who won, however. At formal lunches in the house he would interrupt the grownups and on one occasion was told furiously by Sanz to 'keep quiet and keep your mouth shut'. When the boy was observed not to be eating, Sanz asked him sharply why. 'Because you told me to keep my mouth shut,' retorted the four-year-old. Within 18 months the lawyer had had enough, and despatched Simón back to the care of his mother.

The widow, still only in her twenties, sent him to be educated by a succession of tough-minded tutors, including a priest, Father Andújar, a teacher, Guillermo Peligron, a Dr Fernando Vides, and the brilliant young Andrés Bello, later a father of Venezuela's independence and one of Latin America's foremost poets.

Each in turn despaired: they found him boastful, imperious and demanding. Simón's ailing mother had by now given control of the family's affairs to an elderly uncle, Feliciano Palacios. He advised her to hand over the task of educating the child to a remarkable clerk of his, Simón Rodríguez. Externally severe, Rodríguez was to be one of the most unusual pedagogues of his time, eccentric to the point of madness.

At the time Simón was entrusted to Rodríguez's care, he was a man who would today be described as 'born again'. After a miserable childhood he was bitter, anti-social and intellectual, but had alighted, on a trip to France, on Rousseau's *Émile*. To Rodríguez, the book explained perfectly how upbringing, education and political indoctrination were responsible for all his miseries. His emotions released, he determined to fight the system that had caused them. Understandably, these views did not go down well in stuffy, conventional, laid-back Caracas. When he was given the task of looking after the troublesome boy, he accepted with alacrity. Here was a chance to prove his theories: Simón was to be his Émile.

In 1792 Doña María Concepcion died. Rodríguez immediately took Simón to the family's sprawling and remote hacienda at San Mateo, to the relief of his guardian, Palacios. There Rodríguez would have the freedom to experiment with his new educational ideas. Following Rousseau, he believed in giving free vent to the boy's natural inclinations.

Rousseau had written, 'instead of laying down the law, let him obey the lessons of experience or impotence. Do not give him what he asks, but what he needs. When he commands, don't obey, and when others command him, don't let him obey. Accept his freedom of action as much as your own'. The strange tutor supplemented this liberal method of raising a child with a regime of physical exercise that also kept the boy close to nature. Rodríguez believed in teaching 'one's child to protect himself, once a man, to stand the blows of fate, to adapt himself to wealth or poverty, to support life if necessary, in the bitter cold of Iceland or the burning rock of Malta'.

At San Mateo, Simón would be woken early and taken on long walks or rides, subsisting on Spartan rations, while his tutor taught him how to look after himself in the wild, how to overcome the dangers he faced there, how to survive and how to keep clean. Simón learnt to become an excellent swimmer and horseman. Besides all this, Rodriguez indoctrinated the boy with his liberal political ideas about freedom and the rights of man, and recounted the lives of great men to his eager young listener. Rodríguez was a crackpot, but an enlightened one.

To the schoolboy, this mixture of a cowboy existence and philosophical indoctrination was a joy, and he delighted in his new life in the wilds as much as he respected his unconventional tutor. Those five years, between the ages of nine and fourteen, were the formative ones of Bolívar's life. Hobbes, Locke, Montesquieu, Rousseau, Payne and Raynal were Bolívar's principal intellectual influences. Baron de Montesquieu's argument was the most straightforward and inspiring: 'The Indies and Spain are two powers under the same master, but the Indies are the principal one, and Spain is only secondary. In vain policy wants to reduce the principal one to a secondary one; the Indies continue to attract Spain to themselves.'

In 1795 the outside world impinged on this idyllic frontier existence. A revolt against Spanish rule took place in the valley of Curimagua, led by José Chirino, who was beheaded in Caracas. The 12-year-old Simón was brought to Caracas to watch the execution. The sentence on the conspirators read that they should be:

> brought from the jail at dawn, tied to the tail of a beast and dragged to the gallows; that, dead naturally upon this at the hands of the executioner, the head be cut off and the body quartered; that the head be carried in an iron cage to the port of La Guaira and placed at the high extremity of a thirty-foot post fixed in the ground at the entrance to that port from Caracas.

The head and quarters sections of the body were exhibited in iron cages, to keep out the vultures. Bolívar's pleasant, carefree existence for the first time had run up against the cruel reality of the Spanish empire.

Rodríguez himself was implicated in the plot, and in 1797 was forced to leave Venezuela. The teenage Simón was brought back to Caracas and entrusted to the care of his uncles. The boy argued furiously with his guardians, who decided he was quite beyond their powers of control. The solution adopted was to instil some military discipline: he was sent as a cadet to the elite Whites of Aragua corps which had been founded by his grandfather. There his physical prowess, acquired in the countryside, stood him in good stead. He quickly shone as a leader of men and as a capable and charismatic, if disrespectful and impertinent, young commander. He was appointed a sub-lieutenant after a year and returned, full of himself and as insufferable as ever, although with a newly acquired charm (his smile was said to light up his face), to gallant Caracas society.

There the cocky 15-year-old, heir to a considerable fortune, was warmly received by one of the noted beauties of the capital, a girl from the prominent Aristeguieta family. To the surprise of those who knew him, he fell madly in love, but the girl quickly tired of the vain and persistent youth. Humiliated, Simón became more disruptive than ever.

Chapter 2

MADRID

Simón Bolívar's exasperated uncle Feliciano hit on the solution of sending him to the care of a cousin in Madrid, Esteban Palacios. He warned, 'It is necessary to curtail him, as I have said, firstly because otherwise he will learn to spend money without rules or economy, and second because he is not as clever as he thinks . . . You must talk to him firmly or put him into a college if he does not behave with that judgment and application he should'. His uncle feared he had it in him to lose the huge fortune to which he was now heir. (This indeed happened, but in a manner Simon's guardians could not possibly have expected.)

The first great adventure of Bolívar's life was about to begin. Still only 15, on 18 January 1799 the teenager left aboard the ship *San Ildefonso* for the passage of several months across the Atlantic to stay with relations he had never met. An orphan, the despair of his guardians, he was now almost alone in the world, except for the promise of a fortune on attaining his majority in six years' time.

The ship's course was a roundabout one. To evade attack from British ships based in Havana, it tacked to Veracruz in what is now Mexico, where it was to join up with a convoy of Spanish warships. The boy was not entirely solitary. The captain of the *San Ildefonso*, José Borja, an old family friend of the Bolívars, invited him to his table and talked to him at length. He soon formed a surprisingly favourable opinion of Simón's intelligence and manners, and became convinced that he had a great future ahead. Bolívar, for his part, on the unfamiliar territory of a ship over which he had no control, for once managed to suppress his cockiness.

Three weeks later the ship docked at Veracruz and Bolívar obtained permission from the captain to travel to the capital of the Captain-Generalcy of New Spain, Mexico City. He was awed by the long journey in a carriage up from the coast, rising to the country's 9,000-foot plateau, travelling across deserts and past snow-capped volcanoes. It was a barren, harsh and exacting land – the biggest of Spain's possessions abroad.

In the capital he was put up by an old friend of his family, a counsellor to the Viceroy, Don Aguirre, who showed him Mexico City's sumptuous palaces and cathedrals. According to one account, he met the viceroy and expressed his liberal views, and was listened to indulgently. A week later he set off on the long journey back to his ship.

After an uneventful two-month crossing of the Atlantic, the *San Ildefonso* docked in the Spanish port of Santoña on 5 May 1799, some four-and-a-half months after it had departed Venezuela. With ancestral pride in his breast, Simón set off for the family domain of Bolívar, near Bilbao, from which his forebears had departed 300 years before. There he was dismayed to find, instead of the ruins of the great fortress of family legend, a miserable hamlet of some twenty houses and a half-ruined farmhouse beside which, Quixote-style, a windmill creaked wearily away. As the rain poured down on this desolate scene, the romantic youth felt betrayed. He returned to an uncomfortable inn to lodge for the night before setting off for Madrid, which he reached towards the end of June.

Simón was now in the majestic capital of one of the largest and most long-lasting empires the world has ever known – the authoritarian hub of a power whose cruel writ stretched for 6,000 miles from the north of Texas to the tip of the Magellan Straits. Madrid was a formidable and elegant city of imposing buildings huddled around the magnificent Puerta del Sol, Plaza Mayor and the lavish, baroque Royal Palace. The Spartan magnificence of the Escorial and the medieval town of Toledo peered across at the capital on Spain's central plain.

By a quirk of fate, at the time that the boy's carriage reached this great city his new guardian, Esteban Palacios, occupied a position close to the very heart of the Spanish court. Palacios's close friend and protector was Manuel Mallo, the current chief adviser and lover of Queen María Luisa de Parma, who dominated her ineffectual and capricious husband, King Charles IV.

Mallo, himself American-born, was a cheerful, good-looking man. On his arrival in Madrid he had quickly captivated the queen, an ageing nymphomaniac. The Russian ambassador in Madrid described her as 'completely worn out' by illness, excess and hereditary diseases. 'The yellow tint of her hair and her loss of teeth were mortal blows for her beauty,' he wrote. She was also increasingly fat; but as her attractions diminished her ardour increased, extending not just to Mallo but to her guardsmen and the clever and powerful prime minister, Manuel Godoy. The famous portrait by Francisco de Goya perfectly captures her fading charms and the vapidity of her insignificant husband.

Godoy, like Mallo, had risen to his eminence by satisfying the queen's carnal desires; but he seemed content to hand over the role for the time being to the South American adventurer. This proved to be a mistake. The queen developed an insatiable obsession for the good-looking gigolo, showered him with honours and gave him a large house close to the Royal Palace on the edge of the city.

Mallo was detested by the snooty Spanish courtiers and surrounded himself with fellow South American *arrivistes*, among them Palacios, whom he put up at his mansion. Palacios was appointed to the sinecure of minister of the court of the national treasury, which provided a comfortable living. Into this privileged household entered Bolívar, now 16, his intelligence and energy increasingly tempered by charm.

After the disappointment of his ancestral home, Bolívar's spirits must have soared to find himself elevated to the court of imperial Spain. In later life Bolívar told a famous story of how he played with the heir to the throne, Fernando, Prince of the Asturias, and lifted the cap off the boy's head with his lance, to the other's fury and the queen's amusement. The usually reliable Daniel O'Leary claimed that Bolívar was later to say: 'How was the prince to know then that I was also to strike from his head the fairest jewel of his crown with my sword?' There is no way of knowing whether this story is true.

The house in which Palacios and Bolívar were lodged was the scene of wild parties, which began with heavy drinking and ended as orgies, in many of which the queen indulged. It is not known whether Simón was invited to take part, but he was certainly presented to the queen by Mallo and moved in the highest court circles.

Bolívar was always short of money and became increasingly indebted as the British harassment of Spanish shipping crossing the Atlantic reduced the number of their convoys to just two a year. When his uncle Pedro from Caracas arrived, he was horrified by the atmosphere of decadence surrounding the boy. The two of them moved out of Mallo's unsuitable house. Soon after, Simón was set up in a modest establishment in Atocha Street in central Madrid. At the age of 17 he was now living by himself, independent both of his crotchety relations and the sleaze of the palace – although he continued to visit his high connections from time to time.

Instead, he came under the influence of a more serious figure at court, the Marqués de Ustariz, a wealthy nobleman from Caracas, the centre of a literary circle and, above all, a political liberal at a time when Spain was mired in reactionary decadence and decline. The Marqués became a kind of director of studies for Simón, sending him to eminent professors for tutoring in philosophy, history, literature and mathematics, and lending the boy his extensive library.

When Bolívar attended the Marqués's seminars, he heard defences of the French Revolution and other subversive liberal views. But he was no bookworm: he also enjoyed sightseeing around the streets of Madrid and visiting his friends and relations. Slowly, though, the youth's political views were beginning to take shape.

One day Simón returned to the common-room atmosphere of the Marqués's house to have an encounter that was to change his life. He was introduced to a tall, pale girl with deep, sad, dark eyes and a complexion of Madonna-like purity. Gentle and almost childishly enthusiastic by nature, she was shy, withdrawn and, to the eager young man, irresistibly beautiful. María Teresa Rodríguez y Alayza, whose mother had died in her infancy, had been brought up by her doting father to lead a sheltered, cloistered existence.

She had been kept away from the bustle of life in Madrid, and then out of the city altogether, being restricted to the grand, but oppressively dark, interior of a large country villa. Her health was delicate. She viewed the world outside, of which she had so little experience, with a joyous naivety and fascination which captivated the streetwise Bolívar, two years younger than her. He fell in love with her at first sight. It was noticed that while others in the Marqués's salon discussed politics, Simón and María Teresa had eyes only for each other as darkness fell and candles illuminated the room. Within a few days Bolívar went to her father, Don Bernardo, and asked for her hand in marriage.

The crusty old man, desperately protective, was shocked. Although from an excellent, if colonial, family, Bolívar was too young and was acting impulsively and with a speed he found offensive. Within days, ostensibly to flee the heat of a Madrid summer, Don Bernardo and his daughter were on their way to the cooler climes of Bilbao in the north – hundreds of miles from her young pursuer.

Distraught, Bolívar abandoned his bachelor apartment for Esteban Palacios's house – only to find that his fortunes had dipped alarmingly. The sex-besotted queen had tired of Mallo. As his influence waned, he unwisely sought to retain his hold on her by threatening to publish their love letters. Hysterically, María Luisa appealed to his rival, Godoy, who promptly ordered the arrest of Mallo and his friends. The former favourite escaped into hiding but Palacios was among those seized.

Bolívar himself, while out riding, was confronted one morning at Madrid's Toledo gate by a company of palace guards who demanded he stop. His horse reared. The young man drew his sword, shouting that common soldiers had no right to detain him. The officer of the guard replied that Bolívar was being arrested because he was violating a regulation prohibiting the wearing of jewellery in public – the Venezuelan was wearing diamond rings. The real reason was that he was suspected of being used as a courier to smuggle out Mallo's love letters. The youth angrily threatened the soldiers with his sword, and they gave way.

He rode to the Marqués de Ustariz for advice, and was told he must immediately leave the capital until the hue and cry had died down.

Taking the nobleman's counsel to go and join María Teresa and her father Bernardo in Bilbao – a course of action with instant appeal – he fled the next day and travelled north. The old man's reaction to Simón's arrival is not recorded, but he quickly decided that his holiday in Bilbao was at an end and that he must return urgently to the capital.

Bolívar and María Teresa, meanwhile, decided to wed. He wrote to his uncle Pedro in Madrid on 23 August 1801 that they intended to marry in the capital, after which the three of them (including Don Bernardo, who was ignorant of these plans) would embark on the next ship to North America. In practice, of course, Madrid was dangerous territory for him, and Bilbao was becoming so.

The lovesick young man lingered briefly in Bilbao before bolting across the border to France before he could marry, perhaps warned of impending arrest or perhaps because he hoped to try and strike a deal by which the Spanish authorities would release his cousin Esteban. Whatever the reason, Bolívar's next eight months in France are shrouded in obscurity. He made his way to Paris and, probably short of money, took modest lodgings. There he witnessed the great crowds and parades that marked the height of the glory he was later to emulate: the triumph of Napoleon Bonaparte. His subsequent writings show he was captivated by the mystique of the man who dominated all of western Europe and overturned its *ancien régime*.

Bolívar went back to Spain on 28 April 1802 when, to his own astonishment, he was given permission to return. With the haste of a man desperately in love, he rushed down to Madrid, where at last he secured Don Bernardo's assent to the match, and then obtained a marriage licence. On 26 May, in the church of San Sebastian, Bolívar, aged just 19, was married to María Teresa, aged 21.

The newlyweds left immediately from the port of La Coruña on a necessarily protracted maritime honeymoon across the Atlantic. Bolívar had secured the largest cabin, bedecked with congratulatory flowers. The two spent the journey closeted inside or walking the decks, arm in arm, or embracing. The change must have been daunting for the previously cloistered María Teresa, accustomed to Spanish interiors rather than bracing sea air.

Arriving in Caracas, Bolívar took his beautiful, shy bride immediately to his hacienda at San Mateo, where María Teresa busied herself promptly with ordering the household while he supervised the estate. It seemed that a life of rural tranquillity awaited him, with only a couple of years to wait before he came of age and inherited his substantial fortune. The intense young man had been tamed by love: the couple were devoted to each other. The tearaway had found an emotional haven.

It was not to be. A couple of months later, María Teresa contracted a fever; this always frail and protected slip of a girl weakened rapidly, while suffering a series of alarmingly high temperatures. She had succumbed to some deadly tropical malady. On 22 January 1803, just eight months after their marriage, she died.

Bolívar, always highly strung, went half-mad with grief. 'I looked upon my wife as an emanation of the Divine Being who gave her life. Heaven believed that she belonged there and tore her from me because she was not created for this earth.'

In María Teresa he had found an ideal of beauty, of perfection, of love that their two years' acquaintance had done nothing to dispel. Passionate love mostly turns to fondness or to boredom. Bolívar had no time to grow accustomed to María Teresa; for him the ideal never died. He was to make love to hundreds of women, but none with the romantic intensity he felt for María Teresa. His later passions, however ardent, were affairs by comparison. María Teresa was the love of his life, never dimmed by familiarity.

Furthermore, she had forever transformed this cynical young man of the world. His insolent, know-all attitude had been exposed as a facade. He was an idealist, a romantic, a man bent on achieving the impossible. In place of the search for perfect love was substituted the search for another impossibility: the liberation of a continent, the freeing of a whole people, perhaps even less attainable.

It is possible to trace through the tragedy of María Teresa an underlying motif in Bolívar's life: the search for love – the maternal and paternal love the orphan thought he had been denied. The idealized love of María Teresa was replaced by the abstract love of the multitudes (in addition to the remarkable affection he showed throughout his life to his two old nurses and one of his sisters).

Bolívar was later to confide to Louis Peru de Lacroix, 'See how things are: if I hadn't been widowed, perhaps my life would have been different. I would not be General Bolívar, not the Liberator, although I doubt my genius was fitted to be Mayor of San Mateo. The death of my wife placed me on the path of politics very early; it made me follow thereafter the carriage of Mars rather than the arrow of Cupid.'

In his grief, the 20-year-old widower promptly took a boat to Spain to give Don Bernardo some of María Teresa's personal belongings. The young man did not linger long in Madrid, with its painful personal memories. Instead, on the verge of being old enough to control the income from his personal estates, he set off for Paris, where he took a comfortable house in Rue Vivienne. There, surrounded by other exiles from South America, he indulged in a frenzied series of affairs, in furious gambling at the card tables and in the high society of his dissipated companions. Emanuel Roergas Serviez, a French colonel who played a part in the liberation of Latin America, later wrote, 'With an extreme passion for pleasure, and in particular sensual pleasure, it was truly exciting to hear the Liberator name all the beautiful girls he had known in France, with a precise recollection that does honour to his powers of memory.' Bolívar spent 150,000 francs on a first trip across the Channel to London, visiting clubs and revealing himself as a skilful fencer. It was plain that he was drowning his grief in a violent swing towards excess, but this was to leave him spent and unsatisfied.

In this state of physical excess and moral emptiness, Bolívar came to visit the celebrated salon in Paris of Fanny de Villars. This passionate, intelligent and attractive woman personified the radical spirit of the French Revolution, which believed that in place of the stuffiness of conventional society, people should be free to live and love as they chose.

Fanny's salon was fashionable among artists, intellectuals and professional people alike, who went there to enjoy affairs with the pretty girls that adorned it. The financial arrangements involved are not clear, but it may have been little more than an upper-class brothel. Fanny was of mixed race, exotic and beautiful, graceful and stylish. Her husband, in his fifties, was a distinguished botanist who turned a blind eye to her activities.

Bolívar was transfixed by the older and more experienced woman; he lavished money and attention upon her, and dressed with ludicrous extravagance. He may even have had his only illegitimate child by her. He once remarked, 'people should not think me sterile, for I have proof to the contrary'. Later Fanny wrote to him of his 'godson, Simoncito – I hope he is the only one you have in Europe'.

Years later one of Fanny's children described how Bolívar, walking in Fanny's garden, would 'destroy everything he found; the branches of trees, vines, flowers, fruits etc. My father, who cultivated his garden with such pride, would enter furiously on seeing him commit such follies. "Pick all the flowers and fruits you wish," he would say, "but by God don't pull out the plants for the sole pleasure of destroying them."'

It was in Fanny's salon that he had his celebrated encounter with Baron Von Humboldt, the famous explorer and scientist. Humboldt had visited Venezuela, tracking the Orinoco to its source, and then travelled across to Peru. He voyaged up the Pacific coast in the cold Antarctic current that was later to bear his name, then to Mexico, where he wrote his famous *Political Essay on the Kingdom of New Spain*, in which he argued that Mexico would become a greater power than the United States and, with rather more insight, that it was ripe for colonial revolt.

Bolívar joined the admiring throng around the baron. When his conversation touched on the sad fate of Spanish America, condemned to poverty and obscurity under the reactionary rule of Spain, Bolívar exclaimed that 'the destiny of the New World would be glittering if its people were freed of the yoke that oppresses them'. The baron contemptuously replied that 'although conditions in South America are favourable to such an enterprise, it lacks men capable of carrying it out' – one of history's most famous gaffes, as he was addressing the continent's future liberator. Humboldt, brilliant and conceited, disliked the verbose and arrogant young man. He later declared that he never believed Bolívar was 'fitted to be the head of the American crusade. His brilliant career shortly after we met astonished me.' It was hardly surprising the baron was deceived. Bolívar, a rich, self-confident wastrel, can hardly have made a favourable impression.

Yet it seems likely that the young man's sense of destiny and his lust for glory were formed at just this time by the luminous spectacle of Napoleon's coronation as emperor in Notre Dame de Paris amid pomp and popular acclaim. Bolívar was to maintain a profound admiration for Napoleon the warrior, politician and statesman. He confessed later to being 'a great admirer of the French hero as first captain of the world . . . philosopher and sage', although he was also careful to criticize him lest his enemies would wrongly assume that he sought domination over South America as Napoleon had over Europe. He observed:

> the crown that Napoleon put on his head I considered a miserable and gothic affectation. What was great was the universal acclamation and interest that his person aroused. This, I confess, made me think of my country's slavery and the glory in store for the man who would free her. But how far was I from imagining that such a fortune awaited me! Later, it is true, I began to flatter myself that one day I would be able to participate in her liberation but not that I would play the leading role in so great an event.

He told his later aide, Daniel O'Leary:

> I worshipped him as the hero of the republic, as the bright star of glory, the genius of liberty . . . He had himself made emperor, and from that day on, I looked upon him as a hypocritical tyrant, an insult to liberty and an obstacle to the progress of civilization . . . How dreadful were the feelings of indignation which this melancholy sight [the coronation] produced in my soul, possessed as it was of a fanatical love of liberty and of glory! From then on I was unable to reconcile myself with Napoleon; his very glory seemed to me a glow from Hell.

However, according to another adjutant, Louis Peru de Lacroix, Bolívar said:

> You may, no doubt, have noticed, that in my conversation with the persons of my household and others, I never praise Napoleon; on the contrary, when I speak of him or his deeds, I rather criticize than approve them; and more than once, I have called him a

tyrant, a despot, and have condemned some of his great political measures and of his military operations. All this has been and still is necessary, though my opinion is different; but I must hide and disguise it to prevent the view gaining ground that my policy is an imitation of that of Napoleon, that my ambitions and plans are similar to his, that I also want to become emperor or king and dominate South America as he has done Europe; all this would have been said had I made known my admiration and my enthusiasm for that great man.

My enemies would have gone further still: they would have accused me of wanting to set up a nobility and a military State similar to Napoleon's in power, prerogatives and honours. Do not doubt but that all this would have occurred had I shown myself, as I am, a keen admirer of the French hero; had I been heard praising his policy, speaking enthusiastically of his victories, commending him as the first captain of the world, as a statesman, as a philosopher and as a man of science.

These are my opinions on Napoleon, but I have taken the utmost care to hide them. The St Helena Diary, the campaigns of Napoleon and everything connected with him are for me the most agreeable reading and the most profitable; there it is that the arts of war, of politics and of government should be studied.

In fact, while Bolívar was to share the Emperor's vanity, he was never to abandon the ideal of liberty that first fired him. Bolívar could be capricious, arbitrary and in practice failed to promote liberty, but he was never corrupted by power in the way Napoleon was.

Indolent, spendthrift and sexually exhausted, Bolívar was also a young man in search of a cause on to which to hitch what he was convinced was his genius. He needed no prompting to hurry to Vienna, when he heard that his old tutor, Simón Rodríguez, was there. He found the moody intellectual far from welcoming. The master was disappointed in his star pupil: he told Bolívar that he was wasting his life. The old pedagogue, now obsessed by Rousseau's *The Social Contract*, had no sympathy to spare for the sense of emptiness from which Bolívar complained he suffered.

Rodríguez also revealed to Bolívar that he had inherited 4 million francs on his twenty-first birthday, and was now very wealthy indeed; but he chastised him bitterly before abruptly suggesting that they set off on a walking tour of Italy of the kind so common at the time, in an attempt to restore the young man's physical and mental stability. On 6 July 1805, this odd couple set out. It is not recorded how much of the journey was actually walked.

Bolívar, still obsessed with Napoleon, was keen to reach Milan as soon as possible to witness the coronation of his hero as King of Italy. Watching the ceremony, he:

> had eyes only for Napoleon, and among the great concentration of men gathered there could see only him. My curiosity was insatiable, and I assure you I was a long way from predicting that one day I too would be a centre of attention or, if you prefer, curiosity for an entire continent and, one can say, the whole world. What a huge and glistening general staff Napoleon had and how simple was his own clothing. All of his officers were covered with gold and rich linings, and he only wore his trousers, a hat with decorations and a tunic without any medals. I like this, and in these countries [America] I assure you I would have adopted this usage myself if I had not been frightened that they would say I had done so to imitate Napoleon, and they would have added that it was my intention to imitate him in all things.

After this display of power and military might that so impressed the two companions, they visited Venice, Verona, Bologna, Florence and Rome.

On 15 August 1805, as Britain girded its loins against a possible Napoleonic armada from across the Channel while Austria, Prussia and Russia quivered in anticipation of a great land invasion from France, a bizarre, even ridiculous scene was being enacted on top of the Aventine Hill in Rome, the Monte Sacro, where Silenius had once led the revolt of the ordinary people against their patrician rulers. It was one of Rome's most important feast days, the Assumption of the Blessed Virgin Mary – Ferragosto, the centrepiece of the overpowering Italian summer.

A smallish, thin, wiry young man with a furrowed brow, penetrating, feverish eyes, pursed, determined lips and jutting chin knelt alongside an older, slightly dishevelled, disturbed-looking man and a suave, beautifully dressed aristocrat, Francisco, the Marqués del Toro. The young man stretched out his hands in supplication over the city as though blessing the multitudes in biblical style. Any passer-by would have been startled, or burst into guffaws. The eccentric-looking one, the young man's former tutor, Simón Rodríguez, claimed that the 22-year-old's eyes were 'wet, his breathing heavy, his face red, and with an almost fevered manner he told me: "I swear before you, I swear by the God of my fathers, I swear by my fathers, I swear by my honour, I swear by my country that I will not rest body or soul until I have broken the chains with which Spanish power oppresses us."' Later he told Rodríguez that this scene was the turning point in his life. 'Do you remember how we went together to the Monte Sacro in Rome, to vow upon that holy ground to the freedom of our country? You cannot have forgotten that day of eternal glory for us, a day when we swore a prophetic oath to a hope beyond our expectations?'

Bolívar's gaucheness and arrogance earned him the scorn of the very proper Spanish community in Rome – but he was descended from one of the most aristocratic families in Venezuela and with the country's foremost patrician, the Marqués del Toro, as one of his closest kinsmen he could hardly be disowned or denounced. He further scandalized the Spanish community in Rome when he refused to prostrate himself and kiss the cross on the shoes of the Pope, as was then customary, to the Spanish ambassador's consternation. Instead Bolívar respectfully kissed the Pope's ring. Later Bolívar commented: 'The Pope must have little respect for the sign of the Christian religion if he wears it on his sandals, whereas the proudest sovereigns of Christendom place it upon their crowns.'

The youth's presumption in declaring war upon Spain, then the strongest and most extensive military empire on earth, dominating an entire continent and defended by some 80,000 troops and sailors, drew only sniggers and ridicule.

Chapter 3

THE LONGEST EMPIRE

Few major political movements can have had less auspicious beginnings than the struggle for Latin American independence from imperial Spain. The image of Cervantes's Don Quixote is ingrained on the Spanish psyche: the ridiculous, posturing *hidalgo* – gentleman or knight – dreaming of honour, caste, his own genealogy, great deeds, splendid victories and beautiful, virtuous women, but who is, in reality, just a man with a broken lance riding an old nag, with a faithful, exasperated but practically minded retainer: the image has echoed down the ages to *The Diary of a Nobody*, Jeeves and Wooster, and *Billy Liar*.

Bolívar was seeking, with little or no evidence of support among the 21 million people he sought to liberate, to wrest an entire continent of more than 7.7 million square miles, stretching 7,000 miles from a latitude of 30 degrees north of the equator to 50 degrees south, out of the grip of a 300-year-old empire, the longest-lasting European one since Rome. He faced the world's biggest overseas military machine, which had 36,000 troops in Latin America, as well as 44,000 sailors and marines. This was not a question of tilting at windmills, but at active volcanoes. It must have seemed madness at the time. Yet in his intuitive, farsighted way, Bolívar, absent for a few years, had come to understand the Spanish empire better than his continent-based counterparts. It is to that remarkable entity, so often described as a barbaric, religiously obscurantist behemoth, that we must now turn.

Empires have tended in history to divide into two types: those that begin as trading enterprises, usually dotted along coastal regions, which eventually turn into military and administrative empires as it becomes necessary to discipline the rapaciousness of the traders and to protect these outposts from predatory powers: such were the Portuguese, Dutch and British empires, which are sometimes termed 'accidental' empires. The others are those which are created primarily by conquest and quickly become political, economic, ideological, administrative and military empires: such as the Roman, Chinese, Aztec, Inca, Moorish, Spanish and French empires, and the brief Belgian, German, Italian and Japanese ones.

The enduring nature of the Spanish empire in South America under Habsburg rule arose partly from its autonomy, and relaxed, sleepy, live-and-let-live outlook (underpinned, though, by a vicious treatment of political opponents); and partly from a variety of phenomena which were present at its inception. Spain, uniquely, had been forged as a military-theocratic power; it was occupying a continent with a large indigenous population unevenly distributed around one of the most dramatically diverse geographies in the world; and it was an El Dorado of gold, silver and precious minerals.

The first phenomenon arose from the protracted Moorish occupation of Spain. In order to reconquer the country from the Moors, it had been necessary to create a strong military tradition to do the fighting, supported by a Christian ideology, which surfaced as the strongest expression of the militant Catholicism of the time. Catholic Spain became the most serious prosecutor of the Inquisition (although its extent has been much exaggerated), which was notably less tolerant than the somewhat relaxed Islamism espoused by the Moors. Long before most countries, Spain developed a genuine sense of unity (while Britain was still only just emerging from dynastic wars), symbolized by the marriage of Ferdinand of Castile and Isabella of Aragon, unifying what was in fact a very disparate nation before the Moors. Without this sense of nationhood, the centuries-old struggle would never have been won. The Moorish occupation was rolled back province by province throughout Spain.

The expulsion of the Jews in 1492 – the same year that Columbus, funded by the Spanish crown, reached the New World – marked the apotheosis of this military-theocratic-nationalistic ideological triumvirate: for the Jews represented commerce and scholarship rather than militarism, a different religion and a deeply suspect quasi-universalism. From that moment on the Spanish state glorified military prowess, religious purity and subordination to the crown above commerce, industry and material gain.

With the discovery of Latin America, the opportunity arose to channel Spain's military and nationalist energies into conquest. The era of the conquistadors was the result, spearheaded by the figures of Hernán Cortés, a cultivated if ruthless man and brilliant general, and Francisco Pizarro, uncouth, brutal but hugely effective militarily. The contrast with the British penetration of eastern North America could not have been more striking. Essentially the British colonies were trading outposts with a relatively small military presence until they required protection from the French and Spanish, and to a lesser extent from native Americans.

Following hard on the heels of the conquistadors was the Church, abhorrent to some in its hostility towards the Indian cultures, but also civilizing and seeking to counter the excesses of the warriors; and then the crown administrators of the Spanish nation. The lure of South America was its fabulous mineral wealth and plenty was found, in particular in Peru and Mexico. There was enough to provide Spain itself with a glitteringly prosperous court and central administration, even though little of it filtered beyond its European empire through to the more backward provinces. This river of gold and silver across from Latin America further confirmed the Spanish state in its prejudice against commerce: for did it not show that a country became extremely rich by military conquest rather than trade? Hidalgos were vaunted, merchants despised.

A second distinguishing feature of the Spanish empire was its conquest of other peoples. In this it contrasted sharply with the position in North America where the British colonial settlements were for 200 years restricted to the western coast and where there were relatively few native Americans (although a good many more than initially admitted). The Spanish conquered and colonized the habitable parts of their new continent with determination, bravery and often savagery. The achievement was all the more remarkable in view of the immense distances and geographical obstacles the continent presented. Only the inhospitable interior of Portuguese Brazil went unconquered and unsettled, with its continent-sized Amazon basin and extensive highland Mato Grosso plateau largely ignored by the Portuguese coastal settlers.

The Spanish empire acquired differing characteristics, despite the common language and culture and the superficial unity epitomized by almost identical, beautiful grid-patterned one-storey colonial cities and towns, originating from the simple Moorish style, grouped around their Plaza de Armas of cathedral, bishops' palace and municipality. There were areas almost entirely populated by white settlers, in particular what is now southern Argentina, Chile and, in the north, southern California, New Mexico, Texas and Florida. By contrast, indigenous peoples abounded in Mexico, Central America and the northern Andes, particularly modern Peru, Bolivia, Ecuador and parts of southern Colombia. These were the prosperous highlands, with temperate climates, away from the sultry and uninhabitable areas near the Equator, but not as high as the southern Andes, where the mountains form a narrow range and the lowlands are temperate and habitable (Paraguay was a special case with a large indigenous population and a quasi-tropical but survivable climate). By contrast, Caribbean Latin America and Brazil, as the slave trade expanded, became a magnet for blacks, both slaves and freemen.

A further feature that distinguished the experiences of South and North America was the absence of a racialist prohibition on intermarriage and interbreeding, which prevailed particularly in the slave states of the southern British colonies. In part this was because very few white women travelled across from Spain to Latin America; and in part because the Spanish did not suffer from the same type of racism and puritanism as northern European Protestantism. In large areas of South America there were just as many slaves as the north but no such furious social segregation and stigma: the hues of brown, black and white, indigenous and Caucasian features were as varied as the colours of the rainbow.

That is not to say that race did not matter. It did, immensely: a person's social standing could often be judged by the colour of his skin: the paler, the more upper class he was likely to be; the more indigenous or black, the lower down the scale. But racialism was not written into law; the races were not forbidden to interbreed on pain of criminal sanction or social ostracism and there was a real measure of toleration.

The evolution of these three categories of Latin American countries – pure white, those white with a massive indigenous underclass but also many people of mixed blood (mostly urban middle class), and those white with a black slave underclass and, again, many of mixed blood – created three distinct cultures behind the apparent unity of Spanish America, with its common heritage. Argentina and Chile, lacking a racial underclass and workforce, and also enjoying temperate climates, were reasonably well run by industrious whites (except in the north where there were indigenous peoples working plantations). Mexico, Guatemala, Peru, Bolivia and Ecuador were slave societies except in name: the indigenous peoples lived in great privation and formed a brutally ill-treated workforce for the powerhouse of the Spanish empire, its silver and gold mines, as well as the big estates producing tobacco and cacao (although it should be acknowledged that these formed a minority in the indigenous Indian economy and the people working there were actually better off than those living in pre-Inca sharecropping backwardness on the remote mountains). Gran Colombia, with its prosperous middle class and miscegenation in its fertile and temperate uplands, was a kind of lost world of prosperity plunging down to the coast, where there were large black slave plantations, as well as plenty of free blacks.

In addition, the Spanish empire enjoyed a great degree of autonomy, as long as the silver and gold flowed. So often caricatured as a despotic, centralized and backward entity, the empire survived much longer than other ones due to some of its regionalized characteristics. The white-populated south had few tensions, while the white-dominated northern Andes with their overwhelmingly Indian populations had only a minority working the mines, and a few more on the ranches and plantations; the same was true of Mexico and central America. The racial tensions there, although immense, were containable.

In the Caribbean area of northern Spanish America, black resentment, while significant, was not so prevalent or angry as in the West Indies and the southern states of North America, and it was much leavened by interbreeding. The Spanish crown was skilful at playing upon the fears of the white minority, both in the largely Indian northern Andes and in the Caribbean littoral with its large black population, arguing that without its military protection, uprisings and racial bloodbaths would ensue.

Another pillar of Spanish domination, apart from that of being able to protect the whites against racial upheaval, was moral: as in Spain, religious influence was pervasive, although often in conflict with the political authorities. The intolerance applied in the campaigns against the Moors was extended to Latin America and in particular to indigenous religions, which were extinguished or absorbed at an often terrible cultural loss. But the Church also brought humanity and enlightenment to offset the militarist drive of the Spanish empire. Between 1520 and 1830 the Inquisition in Spanish America judged just 6,000 cases – an average of fewer than 20 a year, and only 100 were burnt at the stake in 300 years, although others died of torture in prison. Most were pardoned and released.

The Church became the defender of the indigenous people. As Gerhard Masur, in his magisterial biography of Bolívar, writes of this military-theocratic system:

> In any considered understanding of the Spanish method of governing the colonies, we must not forget that Spain was the mediaeval country of modern Europe, the land without a Renaissance, and the politics of Spain during the sixteenth century carried the inevitable stamp of absolutism – for the reason that the country had been in the front line of the war against the Moors. Administratively, Spanish rule seemed absolute: in 1511 the Council of the Indies had been set up in Madrid, directly responsible to the crown, both to administer government and justice: an elaborate structure of viceroys and councils ruled their administrative districts, which were adapted to meet each region's special needs – for example the viceroyalties of Peru and Mexico followed the examples of Naples and Sicily, while Bogotá and Quito were modelled on the systems in Granada and Valladolid, while Venezuela and the regions around the River Plate – modern Argentina and Uruguay – were under military rule.

Latin America, at the time of the continent's first great uprising against Spanish rule in 1781, was divided into five viceroyalties: that of New Spain, embracing the Audiencia of Mexico and the Audiencia of Santo Domingo, as well as the Captaincies-General of Guatemala and Cuba; the Viceroyalty of New Granada, including the Presidency of Quito (roughly equivalent to modern Ecuador), the Audiencia of Santa Fé de Bogotá (modern Colombia), and the Captaincy-General of Caracas (modern Venezuela); the Viceroyalty of Brazil, under the Portuguese crown; the Viceroyalty of La Plata, which was subdivided into the Audiencia of Buenos Aires (Argentina), the Presidency of Asunción (Paraguay), the Presidency of Charcas (Bolivia) and the Banda Oriental (Uruguay); and the richest, the Viceroyalty of Peru, embracing the Audiencia of Cuzco and the Captaincy-General of Santiago de Chile.

Of these subdivisions, Mexico was extremely rich, powerful and productive, but its southern zone was impoverished, wild bandit country and its northern reaches, which extended into modern California, New Mexico, Texas and Florida, were sparsely populated, much of it desert. The uplands around Quito and Santa Fé de Bogotá were remote but prosperous, while Caracas was wealthy too, and temperate, in stark contrast to the torrid wilderness of much of the rest of Venezuela. Colonial Brazil was in reality just a string of settlements on its long coastline. Buenos Aires was a commercial centre stimulated by a thriving contraband trade with Europe that distant Spain had difficulty in policing. In the north, La Plata, Tucuman and Chuquisaca were prosperous colonial cities, while Chile was a remote settlement of about half-a-million people cut off by the Andes in the east, by Araucanian Indians and virgin forests in the south, to the west by the Pacific, and to the north by the Atacama Desert.

The vibrant yet decadent heart of the whole system in South America (Mexico dominated the centre) was the Viceroyalty of Peru where silver mines had created a glittering city, Lima, of idle rich living alongside a teeming and wretched Indian underclass, and provided the wealth needed to keep the parasitic and crumbling Spanish economy afloat.

So powerful was Peru in this system that it sought to ban Buenos Aires from trading and, ludicrously, all commerce with Spain was required to take place through the ports on the Pacific coast, brought there either by sea and land across the isthmus of Panama, or by sea alone around Cape Horn in twice-yearly crossings by convoys accompanied by Spanish warships. Goods for Buenos Aires had to be carried overland from Lima across the Andes and down from Potosí, a journey of 3,000 miles, which took three months. Only the ports of Cádiz and Seville in Spain were permitted to trade with Spanish America, even by this route. Merchandise was sold for five or six times its original costs of production. Trade with other countries was strictly forbidden.

In practice, contraband flourished, in particular in the River Plate estuary and the Orinoco basin. A contemporary British officer and traveller, Captain Basil Hall, sums up the system:

> The sole purpose for which the Americas existed was held to be that of collecting together the precious metals for the Spaniards; and if the wild horses and cattle which overrun the country could have been trained to perform this office the inhabitants might have been altogether dispensed with, and the colonial system would then have been perfect.
>
> Unfortunately, however, for that system, the South Americans . . . finding that the Spaniards neither could nor would furnish them with an adequate supply of European products, invited the assistance of other nations. To this call the other nations were not slow to listen, and in process of time there was established one of the most extraordinary systems of organised smuggling which the world ever saw . . . conducted by the Dutch, Portuguese, French, English, and latterly by the North Americans . . . Along with the goods no small portion of knowledge found entrance, in spite of the increased exertions of the Inquisition . . . Many foreigners, too, by means of bribes and other arts, succeeded in getting into the country, so that the progress of intelligence was encouraged, to the utter despair of the Spaniards, who knew no other method of governing the colonies but that of brute force.

This centralization, and the growth of a powerful upper class of whites in Latin America, was counterbalanced by municipal councils elected on a very restricted suffrage based on property, which represented the interests of townspeople. These councils were to be in the vanguard of the drive towards independence. In 1680 a codification of the Laws for the Indies was drawn up, which was relatively liberal and lenient for the time. The Spanish crown also declared that the indigenous population were free men – at least in theory.

With the motherland several weeks' sailing away, the reality on the ground was very different. As the great friar Bartolomé de las Casas wrote in his *History of the Indies* the Indians were reduced to the status of slave labour by repressive laws both in the mines and the fields. A great number sought refuge in the remote mountains and jungles where they could not be got at, living desperately poor, short lives and rapidly diminishing in number. Masur describes the indigenous peoples pithily as a 'people servile but resentful, talkative but dishonest, complacent but lacking in confidence, vigorous and vengeful' and quotes the poet Chocano: 'Oh ancient and mysterious race / With your impenetrable gaze / Who without enjoyment sees happiness / and without suffering sees pain.'

The Church pressed in particular for laws to protect the Indians, although in the early years of the empire it had been blamed for ruthlessly suppressing much of the religious culture, some of it extremely cruel, of the indigenous populations. The Laws of Burgos of 1512, for example, provided for Indian self-government in Church lands. In 1537, Pope Paul III declared that the Indians were 'truly men', and should be converted to Christianity. This was a radical document for the colonizers, who regarded the Indians as subhuman to the extent that, for instance, they believed there was no sin involved in seducing indigenous women (Cortés had an Indian mistress). The resulting children, the 'mestizos' (half-castes), were treated as a subcaste. De las Casas staunchly upheld their cause in Europe, but except in the areas it controlled, the Church failed to make much impression on the Spanish system of punishment, repression, forced labour, extortionate taxation and virtual slavery.

Under the *mita* system Indians were forced to work in the mines, where they earned half the meagre wages of agricultural labourers. They were not allowed to wear certain clothes; and those among them who obtained an education found they could study only the humanities, not science. The Spaniards argued that the Indians were better and less cruelly treated than they had been under their ruthless ancient empires, such as the Maya, Aztec and Inca. This may have been true, but it was an ugly system nevertheless.

For a long time the Church managed to preserve a number of model communities, theocracies, in which the Indians were treated with a measure of human dignity. In Chile the Capuchins established stable settlements even among the primitive, nomadic and often murderous Araucanians. In New Granada and, more successfully, in the Orinoco basin, they set up a series of exemplary mission settlements. The most celebrated of the Church's 'states within a state' was the system of Jesuit 'reductions' in an area sprawling over the borders of present-day Paraguay, Uruguay and Argentina. Some 100,000 people lived in these 48 settlements, which were economically viable and humanely run. Soon they attracted the attention of the slave-bosses of Brazil, the *bandeirantes*, who captured more than half the Indians in raids before the Jesuits led them out of reach, below the Iguazu Falls, in a mass migration between 1627 and 1631. The Jesuit reductions continued to attract controversy, both for the way they suborned the colonial caste system and because they represented a challenge to the political power of the state. In 1768, following the expulsion of the Jesuits from Spain, the reductions were also dissolved, and a major experiment in enlightened rule in Spanish America ended.

The royal administration soon degenerated into an immense bureaucracy based on jobbery, favours and corruption. Land in the colonies was theoretically owned by the crown, but was parcelled out to its followers as vast *encomiendas* (labour systems), which in turn became private haciendas, worked by the indigenous people in a new form of feudalism. When the Spaniards arrived there were at least 13 million indigenous people. Within a century the number fell to 3 million, and then returned by 1800 to around 8 million 'indios', compared to 4 million whites ('criollos'), 3 million blacks ('negros'), 5 million of mixed white and indigenous descent ('mestizos'), 0.5 million of mixed white and black blood ('mulattos') and a few hundred thousand of mixed Indian and black blood ('zambos').

A major feature of the first 250 years of the Spanish empire was its deliberate and enforced isolation from the rest of the world. Spain viewed Latin America as its treasury of precious minerals, and as a captive market for its own goods, but was not interested in developing its industries. The locals were not only forbidden to trade with other countries, but between themselves, with goods being shipped to Spain and then re-exported back across the Atlantic to other parts of the empire. In practice Spain's own underdeveloped industries failed to meet the demand from the colonies and, as mentioned, contraband trade with other countries flourished. One of Bolívar's most famous and bitter passages was his description of Latin America as exploited by Spain, 'to cultivate fields of indigo, grain, coffee, sugar cane, cacao, and cotton; to raise cattle on the empty plains; to hunt wild beasts in the wilderness; to mine the earth for gold to satisfy the insatiable greed of Spain'. Culturally, too, Latin America was straitjacketed by the mother country. The Laws of the Indies contained no fewer than 15 laws strictly regulating the flow of books into Spanish America.

Isolated politically, commercially and culturally, run by a corrupt if often locally recruited bureaucracy, an enormously wealthy class of landowners and a military presence, with the Catholic church acting as its protector and conscience, the Spanish empire lasted for a full quarter millennium without serious disaffection. It was sleepy and sometimes cruel and obscurantist, but also reasonably contented, well-ordered, and tolerant, with different races rubbing shoulders together: such was Habsburg Spanish rule.

In the mid-eighteenth century there began the process that would unravel the bonds that held the colonies captive. With the replacement of Habsburg by Bourbon rule in Spain coinciding with the European Enlightenment, colonial rule was revolutionized from the largely self-governing benevolent autocracy that had kept the colonies steeped in backwardness and poverty for a quarter millennium. The Bourbons at that time considered themselves children of the Enlightenment, as in France, but they were also fiercely dirigiste, desiring state control of both economic and social matters. Philip IV and Ferdinand III began the process by ending tax-farming, appointing French-style intendants to run the regions and slashing both the privileges and the numbers of provincial noblemen in a centralization of authority in Spain.

Charles III, a clever, shrewd man whose sharp, foxy face and eyes peer amusedly out of Goya's portrait, came to power in 1759 and appointed the Marqués de Sonora, an able administrator, to carry out reforms in the colonies. Sonora was a mirror image of George Grenville, Britain's incorruptible and administratively brilliant prime minister who imposed the eminently rational Stamp Act on Britain's North American colonies without regard for local sensibilities.

Tobacco taxes were increased and sales taxes raised. Goods from Spain flooded in, while exports were stifled. Mexico's textile industry was ruined by imports, and only its silver mines flourished. Controversially, Sonora initiated the expulsion of 700 Jesuits from Mexico, leaving the many thousands who attended their missions leaderless and causing an insurrection which he brutally put down. But he was also responsible for the seizure of New Orleans from the French, and the colonization of California as far north as San Francisco. His successor, Antonio María de Bucareli, introduced popular social reforms. Educated criollos became infected by modern concepts regarding administration, commerce, agriculture, industry, science and even political rights. They found it increasingly difficult to understand why they should be ruled by low-born peninsular officials, or why their economies should be so brazenly exploited. By the late eighteenth century, such seditious ideas, challenging authority, were commonplace in schools, universities and in upper-class salons, but they were still a long way from active revolt.

Under Charles III a big effort was made to boost the wealth coming from the Indies, with the emphasis on agricultural products now that mineral revenue was declining. A policy of freer trade was introduced instead of the annual rigorously controlled bullion convoys – although this was monopolized by a great Basque enterprise from Guipúzcoa, upsetting colonial merchants. In the space of a decade, non-mineral trade between Spain and the colonies, also for other reasons, jumped from 148 million to 1.1 billion reales. In 1784 the monopoly of the Caracas company was withdrawn and imperial free trade was extended to Venezuela five years later. Between 1784 and 1789 trade doubled in value. But the Spanish still controlled imports and exports and administered 'the spirit of monopoly under which this province groans'. The goal was to increase the wealth the crown enjoyed from the colonies but there were positive outcomes of the liberalization of trade. Restrictions on books were also lifted and the works of Adam Smith – the apostle of free trade – Descartes and Newton, but above all Rousseau, were disseminated in the Americas.

The consequence was an unprecedented era of prosperity in Latin America as a whole, and in particular in Venezuela, hitherto a sleepy tropical backwater compared to the great mineral-producing vice-royalties of Mexico and Peru, even though it was the closest province to the motherland and Europe. This is how Mariano Picón Salas, the Venezuelan historian, portrays it, if a trifle rosily:

> The second half of the eighteenth century in Venezuela was a period of prosperity and happiness. With agriculture booming, cities and villages were developed in even the furthest corners of the country, and the criollo class, which loved luxury and refine-ment, asserted its power. There was a spiritual development, which, if lacking the magnificence of the great vice-regal capitals, attracted European travellers like Segur and after him Humboldt for its amiable modernity. Caracas was the Latin American city in which Humboldt found the greatest interest in European politics, in its laughing streets and its charming lively people. [Venezuela was more Bourbon than the still largely Habsburg-inspired Spanish colonies.] The closeness of the British and Dutch colonies, which were nests of contraband, allowed some of the surge of criticism and subversion and the propaganda of the capitalist nations of Europe to penetrate the colonial monopoly of the state.

More controversially, Picón Salas argues that the fear of the white minority of a vengeful uprising among the indigenous population that existed in Peru and Mexico was largely absent in Venezuela. The black minority had been 'assuaged by 200 years of Catholicism and loved singing and fiestas, in spite of their oppression; their imagina-tion was more docile than that of the resentful and reserved Indians of the uplands'. The blacks, he argues, were more integrated with the whites than the slaves of the nearby British colonies, although they were forbidden by law, bizarrely, from carrying walking sticks, sunhats or umbrellas. We shall see later how correct Picón Salas was in this analysis, for race was to play a key part in Bolívar's revolution.

John Lynch, in his magisterial study of Bolívar, sees racial tension as underpinning many aspects of Venezuelan life. Mestizos in Caracas were more commonly called 'pardos', of whom there were some 400,000 out of a total population of only 800,000; there were also some 200,000 poor whites of descent from the Canary Islands, virtually treated as 'men of colour', 120,000 Indians and 70,000 blacks. Dominating these were some 2,500 creoles or 'Mantuans', the wealthy landowning upper class, and around 1,500 'peninsulares' (Spanish-born administrators).

The uncrowned king of Venezuelan criollo society was the Marqués del Toro, Bolívar's companion on the Monte Sacro in Rome, along with 13 other families, including those of the Conde de Tovar (from whom Venezuela's greatest painter, Tovar y Tovar derived), the Conde de la Granja, the Conde de San Xavier, the Moreno family, the Marqués de Casa León, Marcos Ribas and Juan Vicente Bolívar, father of Simon. Bolívar's father was worth some 350,000 pesos, compared to around 500,000 owned by the Marqués del Toro. Bolívar senior owned four houses in Caracas, three cattle ranches, and an indigo plantation, a sugar plantation and two cacao plantations, as well as a copper mine.

Along with the trade liberalization and enlightenment of Bourbon rule came a centralization of political authority: Charles III's ministers concluded that the criollo aristocracy was a reactionary and exclusive caste likely to resist Spanish reforms. So it appointed peninsulares to administrative posts previously occupied by American-born criollos to carry out the reforms. As the Jesuit Juan Pablo Viscardo y Guzman wrote bitterly, Spaniards were appointed 'to the permanent exclusion of those who alone knew their country, whose individual interest is closely bound to it, and have a sublime and unique right to guard its welfare'. Fatefully, Venezuela was taken out of the Viceroyalty of New Granada in 1776 and was placed under the economic control of a Spanish intendant, and in the following year under the political control of a captain-general directly responsible to Madrid. In 1786 a supreme court – audiencia – was set up in Caracas, and not a single one of its 14 members between then and 1810 was American-born. A consuldor – trading guild – was also set up in 1793 responsible to Spain, as was the Caracas Company, which monopolized trade.

Alongside this surge in prosperity and centralization came a far-reaching measure, the expulsion of the Jesuits in 1767, decreed by the minister Carlos Aranda, which was intended to crush a main rival for power of the Spanish crown, as well as to eliminate the theocratic and, to an eighteenth-century follower of the Enlightenment, obscurantist element of Spanish rule there. It was a disastrous move. At a stroke 2,500 of the cleverest and most educated men in Latin America, founders of the great universities in Mexico City and Lima, as well as countless educational institutions, were torn away from their schools and congregations and left to roam in poverty in Europe and abroad. They became inveterate enemies of the Spanish crown, fomenting and plotting for the freedom of its American subjects and, not least, stirring dissent among the Indians whose protectors they had been for so long. In the swirl of secret societies and Masonic lodges that incubated the South American revolution, the expelled Jesuits played no small part.

At around the same time another Spanish hammer-blow struck at the sleepy hierarchy of Venezuelan society: the mixed-race pardos were given the right in 1760 to join the militia and become officers. In 1795 they were allowed to buy certificates of whiteness which permitted them to be educated, marry whites, hold public office and become priests. The white criollos were furious: these measures, they said, were 'a calamity stemming from ignorance on the part of European officials, who come here already prejudiced against the American-born whites and falsely informed concerning the real situation of the country'. For 'the whites of this province to admit into their class a mulatto descended from their own slaves' was abhorrent. 'The establishment of militias led by officers of their own class has handed the pardos a power which will be the ruin of America, giving them an organization, leaders, and arms, the more easily to prepare a revolution.' It was wrong to grant them, 'by dispensation, from their low status, the education which they have hitherto lacked and ought to continue to lack in the future'. In 1789 the Spanish issued a slave law which sought to codify and improve the conditions in which slaves were held: after furious protests from the criollos, this was suspended in 1794, triggering off a slave revolt.

Chapter 4

TREMORS

The first really big tremor to hit the wider Spanish empire was that of the self-styled Tupac Amaru II, a supposed descendant of the last Inca emperor, Tupac Amaru I, in highland Cuzco in Peru.

A devout, educated half-Indian, José Gabriel Condorcanqui, had been recognized by the Spaniards as Marqués de Oropesa, a title acknowledging descent from the old Inca ruling family of Peru. In 1780 he suddenly styled himself the second Tupac Amaru, the Gifted One, after the most famous of the last native emperors, also known as Manco Inca, who was put to death in 1574 as leader of an uprising. The new rebel had seized a *corregidor* (Spanish governor) and had him killed.

Dressed in a blue velvet suit bordered with gold, an embroidered surplice, a red velvet cloak and a three-cornered hat, and wearing an image of the sun around his neck, this self-styled reincarnation of the Inca Sun-King then led an uprising of several hundred thousand Qechua, Aymara and Araucanian Indians in a lynch war against the whites. He laid siege to Cuzco, in a restaging of the ten-month investment of that city by 160,000 Indians in 1537. But Spanish cavalry, with the help of 60,000 militia, eventually crushed the uprising and Condorcanqui was betrayed.

In the spring of 1781, on the upland plains outside the Inca capital of Cuzco, Condorcanqui watched as his wife, small children and closest friends were hacked to death. Then it was his turn. His tongue was cut out, and each of his arms and legs were tied to a horse. When the signal was given they were loosed, bolted, and pulled his body apart. Condorcanqui was executed by the emissary of the crown, the

Visitador José de Areche, for leading the most dangerous insurrection against the rule of the Spanish Empire in 230 years. The brutal suppression of the revolt suggested that Spanish rule was as solidly entrenched as ever.

The next uprising occurred the same year in upland Bogotá in New Granada, under the leadership of José Antonio Galán and Juan Francisco Berbeo, who also wanted to restore an indigenous throne, although some of their followers merely wanted American-born whites to be given administrative jobs and new taxes to be abolished. The viceroy fled to the coast and the government promised to meet some of their demands, after which they laid down arms. Galán was promptly seized and hanged, then quartered, with his body parts being displayed around the city. Berbeo managed to escape.

Around the same time in Bogotá the scholar Antonio Nariño formed part of a clandestine literary circle which discussed the possibility of independence, but he was arrested along with ten others and sentenced to a decade in prison and the confiscation of his estates. He was transported to the notoriously impregnable Cádiz jail, but astonishingly managed to escape and became an itinerant preacher of rebellion in Madrid, Paris and London, finally travelling to Venezuela disguised as a priest. However reformist the Bourbons aspired to be, they were merciless against any political threat to the empire.

In 1795 José Chirino led a revolt against Spain in the prosperous Curimagua Valley in Venezuela. He and his fellow rebel, José González, were free blacks stirred by the example of the successful rebellion in nearby Haiti and the French Revolution; their slogan was, 'The Law of the French, the republic, the freedom of slaves, and the suppression of the alcabala [sales tax] and other taxes'. Their slave army of 300 went on the rampage, killing landowners and occupying ranches, as well as briefly occupying the town of Coro. The revolt was easily crushed and, as discussed, the 12-year-old Simón Bolívar was taken to see Chirino's execution; his tutor Simón Rodríguez was implicated and had to flee the country.

Two years later Manuel Gual and José María España, white criollos this time, led a revolt inspired by Rousseau's writings in the port of La Guaira, calling for liberty, equality and the rights of man under a republican government, promoting the cause of the Indians as well as demanding the abolition of slavery. The uprising was easily suppressed and España was executed in the usual grisly way.

Beneath the untroubled crust, the magma was bubbling. The Bourbon reforms had put into a place a lethal combination – an economic boom which had benefited the American-born white upper classes, while at the same time stripping them of what few rights to rule they had previously enjoyed. The criollos were subjected to modernizing ideas now coming from Europe to Latin America for the first time, while the Jesuit-educated class had been dispossessed. Greater racial emancipation had been imposed on the whites against their will, which also encouraged the beginnings of slave revolts. All that was needed was a catalyst, a spark in this volatile mixture.

The spark came from abroad. South America was no longer insulated from events in the mother country, still less from its sister, the North American landmass.

In 1761 the Spanish under Charles III joined the French in the Seven Years' War against the British. This proved to be a disaster: Spain lost both Manila in the Philippines and Havana, while the British occupied the Mosquito Coast in Honduras, Campeche in the Yucatan Peninsula and Jamaica. Through the Peace of Paris of 1763 Spain regained Manila, but had to accede to Britain's insistence that Spain give up Florida to regain Havana. France ceded half of Louisiana to Spain in compensation for its help in the war.

Following the Seven Years' War, the global scene was dramatically transformed by the uprising of the North American colonies against Britain. To Charles III and the Spanish it seemed a godsend, a setback to predatory Britain, although Spain's chief minister, the enlightened and capable Conde de Aranda, a man whom Voltaire described as a close friend, feared that independence in the north would set a dangerous precedent for Spain's own restless colonists. In the event the intervention of France and Spain behind the North American colonists proved decisive, with the Spanish fleet harassing the British navy and her army conquering Florida.

In 1783, at the Peace of Versailles, Florida, Honduras and Minorca were ceded to Spain, and the threat from Britain seemed over. The cost of the war to France brought on the French Revolution six years later, however; and the example of independence gained by North America in 1776 was, as Aranda had feared, carefully noted in the south. Moreover, Britain, licking her wounds, was determined to wreak revenge on the Spanish empire, believed in London to be ripe for insurrection.

In 1788 Charles III died and his son, the amiable Charles IV, ascended the Spanish throne. He lacked the political shrewdness of his father and was under the influence of his terrifying wife, María Luisa of Parma, who, as we have seen, was a strong-willed nympho-maniac, her lusts all too often directing Spanish policy. At this time her favourite lover was a young soldier from Badajoz, promoted to field marshal, Duque de Alcudia and, by 1792, at the age of 25, first minister. Good-looking, shallow, but adroit politically, Manuel Godoy was to dominate a Spanish court now mired in decadence and incompetence.

To this transformation of the global landscape as perceived from South America – the weakening of Britain, the independence of the United States and the decline of the previously enlightened Spanish court – was added the French Revolution of 1789. Initially this further undermined the legitimacy of Spanish absolutism, but as it veered from its early moderate course into revolutionary frenzy, it temporar-ily boosted Spain's monarchy in her colonies, whose people wanted nothing to do with regicides and *sans-culottes*. They shuddered when civil war broke out between the French-descended upper class and the mulattos of Haiti, soon overtaken by an uprising of the 50,000 black slaves in the colony and the massacre of both French and mulat-tos. Order was restored under the moderate and statesmanlike leader-ship of Toussaint Louverture, a freed slave.

Meanwhile, Charles IV made a botched attempt to rescue the French King, Louis XVI, and his reward was a declaration of war by France, whose forces crossed into Spain at each end of the Pyrenees and set up revolutionary governments in the towns they took. The war against France was as popular in the Spanish colonies as in Spain, however, and the empire seemed as strong as ever. The British, now allies of the Spanish, no longer intrigued against them or threatened them overseas.

Godoy, fearful of French incursions across the frontier and heartened by the re-emergence of moderate elements after the fall of Maximilien Robespierre in France, sued for peace in 1795 – a catastrophically inept move which undermined every diplomatic gain of the first four years of his ascendancy. As well as ceding to France Santo Domingo (the western half of the island of Hispaniola, of which Haiti was the eastern half), Godoy sought to appease the French further by introducing some of their reforms into Spain; these included an attack on the Inquisition and on clerical privileges, the threat of land redistribution and permitting the circulation of revolutionary texts. At a stroke, he alienated Spanish sympathizers and the still dominant Spanish colonial classes, who viewed France's ambitions in the Caribbean with deep suspicion; facilitated the spread of revolutionary ideas; and, not least, reinvigorated the old enmity between Spain and a Britain dismayed by Spain's pro-French tilt.

The British moved to disrupt Spanish trade with the Americas, and the colonists made up their shortfall by trading illicitly with Britain and the United States. British landings were staged in Puerto Rico and Central America, and Trinidad was occupied. A Spanish fleet was mauled off Cape St Vincent in 1797, bringing Horatio Nelson to full prominence for the first time. In the space of just three years, Spanish Americans acquired a withering contempt for the weakness of the mother country to add to the sense of grievance and injustice they had long borne against Spain for her commercial monopoly and the dismal quality of the administrators and traders sent to lord it over them. Meanwhile, Godoy, supposedly dismissed in 1800, continued to act as the court's chief adviser, pursuing his policy of appeasement towards France.

A dramatic new turn ensued with the accession to power in France of Napoleon Bonaparte. His policy towards Spain was to bully her; towards the Americas, to establish a French empire there. He insisted that Spain and Portugal close their ports to the British; this the Spaniards did promptly, while the Portuguese put up only a show of resistance. The criollo upper class was horrified afresh by these signs of Spanish cravenness, and by the arrival on their doorstep in 1802 of a French force of 20,000 men under the command of Napoleon's incredibly brutal brother-in-law, General Leclerc, Pauline Bonaparte's first husband, despatched to Hispaniola as the vanguard of a new French presence in the Caribbean. Toussaint was seized by the French and sent captive to France, where he died. Leclerc's attempt to reintroduce slavery into Haiti was met by a fresh black revolt, ending with the expulsion of the French into Santo Domingo and, in 1804, the assertion of Haitian self-government – the first declaration of independence in Latin America. Leclerc, along with thousands of his men, died from yellow fever.

Napoleon meanwhile treacherously seized the previously ceded half of Louisiana from the Spanish, then forced Spain to declare war on Britain, in order to attach the Spanish navy to his own for his projected invasion across the Channel. The combined fleets were destroyed by Nelson at Trafalgar, and Spain thus lost almost its entire navy at a stroke. This drastically affected its capacity to put down insurrections in its empire – a point which did not go unnoticed there. Resentment against the political and economic impositions of the Spanish was at its height. Spain was involved in an unpopular alliance with France, and the British were again bent on subverting its empire, desperate for commercial outlets now that Napoleon had closed the European continent to them, and aware of tempting opportunities. The seriousness of Britain's long-term desire to add the suppurating Spanish empire to its dominions – thereby making good the losses in North America – should not be underestimated.

On 27 June 1806 the Spanish Viceroy of La Plata, Rafael, Marqués de Sobremonte, was at the theatre in Buenos Aires when he was informed that a British army of 1,600 men had landed outside the capital. The first-ever overthrow of a Spanish colonial administration in South America had begun – under British auspices. British soldiers commanded by General William Carr Beresford and naval forces under Commodore Sir Home Popham had sailed from Cape Town, having retaken it in the name of the British crown following the breakdown of the Peace of Amiens and Nelson's victory at Trafalgar.

Although the British government almost certainly had no direct hand in the Popham-Beresford expedition, which it was swift to disown, the roots of it ran deep. The head of the government, William Pitt the Younger, had long coveted South America as a potential market for the products of Britain's growing industrialization, and other eminent men of the time also interested in its possibilities included Lord Melville, First Lord of the Admiralty between 1802 and 1806; Nicholas Vansittart, a young Tory politician who later became Chancellor of the Exchequer; and the prominent trading house of Turnbull and Sons. As we shall see, the focus of the plotting was Francisco de Miranda, the flamboyant would-be liberator of Venezuela. Popham later recorded that in 1805:

> I had a long conversation with [Pitt] on the original project of the expedition to South America; in the course of which Mr Pitt informed me, that from the then state of Europe, and the confederation in part formed, and forming against France, there was a great anxiety to endeavour, by friendly negotiation, to detach Spain from her connection with that power; and, until the result of such an attempt should be known, it was desirable to suspend all hostile operations in South America; but, in case of failure in this object, it was his intention to enter on the original project.

Pitt died towards the end of January 1806, less than a week after the capitulation of Cape Town; and Popham sailed – without orders – for Buenos Aires. William, Lord Grenville, Pitt's brilliant cousin, formed the 'Ministry of all the Talents', so named for its dazzling array of senior political figures from all parties and its engaging liberalism. It featured such luminaries as Charles James Fox, Foreign Secretary until his death in September 1806, a dissolute figure in his youth who had become a politician of notable calibre and Pitt's perennial opponent; Lord Howick, who later as Earl Grey steered Britain to peaceful political reform in 1832; and, as Secretary for War, William Windham, an enthusiast for a British role in South America.

The British forces occupied Buenos Aires with the loss of only a single man and 12 wounded, while Sobremonte fled inland to Córdoba (in modern-day Argentina) with the treasury. Beresford proclaimed himself governor on behalf of King George III, but promised that private property and the Catholic faith would be respected

by the British crown, and announced the establishment of free trade
– a display of breathtaking arrogance. As Popham later noted, 'The
object of this expedition was considered by the natives to apply prin-
cipally to their independence; by the blacks, to their total liberation;
and if General Beresford had felt himself authorised, or justified, in
confirming either of these propositions, no exertions whatever would
have been made to dispossess him of his conquest.'

But 'exertions' were made: a French-born officer, Santiago de
Liniers, assembled a force of irregular soldiers outside Buenos Aires
while inside the city Juan Martín de Pueyrredón, an able criollo aristocrat, organized opposition in the form of passive resistance and a
general strike. Six weeks later the two forces joined up; the British
were surrounded, Popham was taken prisoner and, with impressive magnanimity, the whole expedition was placed aboard ship
and despatched ignominiously to London. Liniers was treated as a
hero while Sobremonte, now regarded as a coward, was informed
he would be shot if he returned to Buenos Aires. It was unprecedented for a Spanish viceroy to be so humiliated; he took refuge in
Montevideo, capital of the Banda Oriental across the Plate estuary,
and Buenos Aires' traditional rival.

When news of Beresford's and Popham's initial success in Buenos
Aires had reached London, the City had gone wild – crowds
had thronged the streets, singing 'God Save the King' and 'Rule,
Britannia!' Britain's trade with South America was already running
at £1 million a year, and it seemed as though her next great colonial adventure was beckoning, a sense reinforced by the news of
Napoleon's victory at Jena and Davout's at Auerstadt in October
1806, which Grenville thought spelt the end of British influence in
Europe. Windham bristled with ideas: Cape Horn would be navi-
gated and the port of Valparaiso in Chile seized, then an expedition
eastwards across the Andes would establish a chain of forts before
conquering the whole Audiencia of Buenos Aires, thus securing the
southern half of the continent. Sir Arthur Wellesley (the future Duke
of Wellington), recently returned from his successes in India, would
be appointed to replace Beresford. Grenville himself favoured the
seizure of Montevideo, and the despatch of troops from India to take
Manila from the Spanish and then sail on across the Pacific to land

on the west coast of New Spain (Mexico), while his elder brother, the 1st Marquess of Buckingham, urged attacks on Peru and Panama.

The news of Beresford's subsequent surrender of Buenos Aires in August 1806 did not reach London until 25 January 1807; when it did, all these dreams crashed to earth with the realization that here were no ill-used children grateful to exchange the harsh paternalism of the Spanish crown for the comparative benevolence of the British, but people mature and sophisticated enough to be determined upon securing their independence.

The affront to British arms could not be tolerated. All other plans were to be shelved until Buenos Aires was regained, and an expedition under General Samuel Auchmuty and Lieutenant-General John Whitelocke was despatched to this end. The unfortunate Sobremonte was still in Montevideo when news reached him that 12,000 British had landed on the east bank of the Plate estuary. The inhabitants of Buenos Aires, across the water, unilaterally deposed him as Viceroy, proclaiming Liniers their chief.

Whitelocke's instructions repeated the error made by Beresford: he was 'not to introduce into the government any other change than that which must necessarily arise from the substitution of His Majesty's authority for that of the King of Spain'. But Whitelocke and Auchmuty soon understood the reality on the ground. Auchmuty announced that the royal court of the Audiencia had been abolished and the Spanish king's authority set aside, and that the Spanish flag should no longer be hoisted. As he wrote later:

> These reports were circulated with avidity, and I soon found that they were acceptable to the principal part of the inhabitants. The persons who before appeared hostile and inveterate, now pressed me to advance a corps to Buenos Aires; and assured me, if I would acknowledge their independence, and promise them the protection of the English government, the place would submit to me . . . The party now in power are mostly natives of Spain . . . It has been their policy to inflame the minds of the lower orders against the English, by every species of exaggeration and falsehood, and to lead them to such acts of atrocity as may preclude the possibility of any communication with us. The second party consists of natives

of the country, with some Spaniards that are settled in it . . . They aim at following the steps of the North Americans and erecting an independent state.

If we would promise them independence, they would instantly revolt against the government, and join us with the great mass of the inhabitants. But though nothing less than independence will perfectly satisfy them, they would prefer our government, either to their present anarchy or to the Spanish yoke, provided we would promise not to give up the country to Spain. But until such a promise is made, we must expect to find them open or secret enemies.

However, the British government favoured establishing its own foothold on the Plate, and in the summer Whitelocke's forces were ferried across the estuary to march on Buenos Aires. After crossing the swamps of Quilmes, Whitelocke drove back a force of 6,000 under Liniers. But as they entered Buenos Aires, calamity ensued: 'The British troops,' as General Bartolomé Mitre wrote later, 'worthy of a better general, marched resolutely to their sacrifice, advancing as fearlessly as on parade along those avenues of death, enfiladed at right angles every 150 yards: Whitelocke remaining with the reserve at the Miserere, entirely cut off from the rest of his army. The result of such tactics could not but prove disastrous.' By nightfall 2,200 Britons had been killed, wounded or taken prisoner, and Whitelocke had promised to evacuate the Plate region within two months.

Complimented on their good behaviour in defeat, the British sailed away from Montevideo after this latest debacle. A former protégé of Liniers, Francisco Xavier de Elio, was installed as governor of the city, and Liniers was recognized by the Spanish government itself as acting viceroy. The two immediately quarrelled, however, it being alleged that Liniers was a Bonapartist stooge, and the Spanish took advantage of this to send out their own viceroy, Baltasar Hidalgo de Cisneros. Neither Montevideo nor Buenos Aires was happy with this imposition. In 1808, in the wake of an incendiary pamphlet on the subject of free trade written by Mariano Moreno, a brilliant local economist, Cisneros was obliged to offer to open Buenos Aires as a free port. Twice now the city had cocked a snook at the Spanish government – first in appointing Liniers, now in breaking the Spanish trade monopoly. The British intervention had, unwittingly, sparked off local defiance.

Britain's extraordinary escapade in Buenos Aires was no more than a side-show for a Spanish government preoccupied with Napoleon. The Spanish court had now divided into two factions: those who supported Charles IV, the Queen and Godoy; and those who looked to Prince Ferdinand, Charles's heir, to rescue them from distasteful appeasement of France.

In 1806, as Napoleon soared to new heights with his victories over the Austrians and Russians at Austerlitz and the Prussians at Jena, Godoy, with consummate ineptness, appeared to switch sides against France. The Emperor determined to punish him. An opportunity arose when Godoy too trustingly invited Napoleon into Spain to enable him to conquer Portugal, the last piece of Europe outside his control. The plan was that Charles IV should become Emperor of the Americas and Godoy himself ruler of a southern portion of Portugal, while the French got the Portuguese fleet.

In 1807 a substantial French army under General Jean-Andoche Junot marched across Spain. The mad Queen of Portugal, María I, her son João, the Prince Regent, and the royal court embarked in an armada of Portuguese ships – the entire Portuguese navy – and were escorted by the British down the Tagus estuary, bound for Brazil. It was the first link in the chain of events which was to lead to the independence of Brazil in the 1820s. The French may not have got the ships they wanted, but they occupied Lisbon and then, to the dismay of Charles IV and Godoy, proceeded to reinforce their army to 100,000 men, annexing a corridor across northern Spain between France and Portugal. With mounting horror Charles realized that Napoleon intended to swallow Portugal, and was threatening Spain. The court moved from Madrid to Aranjuez in order to get away from the French and as a preliminary, perhaps, to escaping to South America like the Portuguese royal family. But the French intervention on top of decades of misgovernment now combined to provoke even the sullen, disunited Spanish to revolt. In March 1808 there occurred the Tumult of Aranjuez – effectively a military coup with mob support – which forced Godoy to resign at last and then, three days later, Charles IV to abdicate in favour of his son. The young king, Ferdinand VII, managed to get his parents to France, for their safety.

Napoleon then ordered both the deposed monarch and his successor to attend on him at Bayonne, just inside the French border. Ferdinand agreed, despite the entreaties of his court and of the ordinary people, who unhitched his horses several times on the journey north. Thus the fly put himself into the spider's web. At Bayonne, father and son argued furiously, and Napoleon was able to induce both to sign abdication instruments. Charles IV, María Luisa and Godoy were despatched to Rome, where they later died, and Ferdinand was temporarily immured in a château on the Loire. Napoleon's older brother, Joseph, was appointed King of Spain, and a new liberal constitution was introduced.

In Madrid, popular anger against the French exploded, to the astonishment of Napoleon, who had assumed that his new government would be warmly welcomed. Hundreds of Spaniards were killed by French troops in the famous massacre of the 'Dos de Mayo' in 1808. Guerrilla bands and civil resistance groups were formed. Local notables led committees against the French. Everywhere French soldiers were ambushed and killed. Joseph Bonaparte, arriving to take his throne, was at first forced out of Madrid but later returned, to be derided as 'Pepe Botellas' (Joe Bottles). In September 1808, the main anti-French resistance organization was established in Seville in the form of a junta which claimed to rule in the name of Ferdinand VII.

In Spain's colonies these events had the effect, at first, of stimulating patriotic support for the young King Ferdinand. In September 1808 the independent-minded Viceroy of New Spain, José de Iturrigaray, who had begun to take action against the Spanish clergy and merchant houses, and was widely supported by the Mexican criollo aristocracy, was arrested and deported to Spain, but it was the following year that the first tremors of real revolt were felt in Spanish America. In May in Upper Peru (modern Bolivia), at Chuquisaca (now Sucre), seat of the Presidency, the students and professors suddenly rose in fury, not against the French but against the authority of the Seville junta; their allegiance, they insisted, was to the Spanish crown, not to Spain as a nation. The president and the archbishop were deposed.

Nearby, in La Paz, another student revolt broke out. In August 1808 in Quito a group of liberal criollos, headed by the Marqués de Selva Alegre, set up an assembly loyal to Ferdinand VII but opposed to the Seville junta – a pretext, in fact, for expelling Spanish officials and governing themselves. In Santa Fé de Bogotá the same thing happened. In Valladolid, near Mexico City, criollos set up an independent junta.

The Spanish authorities reacted with speed and firmness. The Viceroy in Lima sent a force to crush the uprising in La Paz. An army from Buenos Aires suppressed the rebellion at Chuquisaca. Another force from Lima restored order in Quito. The Santa Fé de Bogotá and Valladolid rebellions were quickly snuffed out. This left only Venezuela still in the hunt for liberty.

Chapter 5

MIRANDA: POSEUR, SEDUCER, GENIUS

The early career of Simón Bolívar is inextricably linked with that of Francisco de Miranda, 'the father and mother of Venezuelan independence' as one of its historians has called them. The two men are more often described in almost religious terms as that of the 'Precursor' (modelled on St John the Baptist) and the 'Liberator'. So it is to the first exotic figure that we now turn.

On 28 March 1750 a boy had been born into a sleepy, temperate city of red-roofed houses with whitewashed walls in the lower northeastern Andes cordillera. Sebastián Francisco de Miranda was the son of a first-generation immigrant (also called Sebastián) from Spain, a merchant from the Canary Isles of distinguished family but looked upon with scorn by the old Caracas aristocracy; he was denounced as a mulatto, performing 'an occupation unsuitable for white people'. When appointed captain of the Sixth Company of Fusiliers, he was prevented the use of the uniform and baton of the new battalion, under threat of two months' imprisonment. His wife, however, was of good Caracas stock.

The Captaincy-General Audiencia of Caracas was permeated by a sense of hierarchy and discrimination. The white overclass was uncomfortably aware that it was sitting on a volcano. Yet the whites themselves were sharply divided. The backbone of the country comprised the old settlers, the criollos, the most elevated of whom traced their descent from the conquerors of the continent 300 years before. They regarded themselves as of (usually exaggerated) noble Spanish descent, but foremost as American citizens; and many bore traces of racial intermarriage. They looked with hatred upon the swaggering officials from Spain or the Canary Isles, and with contempt upon Spaniards newly arrived to make their fortunes. In many ways, this colonial aristocracy was not attractive: the contemporary historian Miguel José Sanz describes them as ill-educated (Spain deliberately discouraged education in the colonies), vain, proud and prone to 'abusing the prerogatives of their birth because they were ignorant of what these were for'.

Miranda, known as Francisco rather than Sebastián, nonetheless had an idyllic childhood, the eldest of two brothers and three sisters, playing with neighbouring children, eating perfumed chocolates and sipping cold drinks in the heat. Instructed by private tutors, he then attended the Academy of Santa Rosa, followed by the Royal University. However, he was envied for his wealth and snubbed for his Spanish blood. He was a soldier by calling but in his teens he was refused entry to the 'White Battalion', the elite junior army cadet corps, and threatened with prison when he challenged his exclusion. The Spanish government took his side and he was forcibly admitted, which hardly increased his popularity. The criollo nobility did, however, manage to keep him out of the prestigious senior corps, the Royal Corps of Cadets. Conceited and overbearing, apparently unconcerned about making enemies, Miranda was delighted to be invited subsequently to serve in Spain.

In January 1771, not yet 21, he embarked on the two-month journey across the Atlantic to Cádiz. The wealthy young man set off on a month-long tour of Spain, ending in Madrid. There he found lodgings, studied mathematics, and collected the first volumes of what was to become an impressive library. From the beginning Miranda was a howling snob: from the official college of arms he obtained copies of his family arms and tree, showing his descent from the Dukes of Miranda, one of Spain's oldest and most distinguished families.

In December 1772, he finally joined the Spanish army, as an infantry captain. From the first his superiors disapproved of his haughtiness and his independence of mind that verged on insubordination. He cut a strong and unusual figure, tall and well-built, always immaculately and expensively dressed, with a prominent nose, which detracted from otherwise refined features, a small, pursed mouth with a disdainful expression and strong, penetrating, determined, intelligent eyes. His chin jutted confidently, and his hair fell forward insouciantly on to a large brow. His looks made him irresistible to women, and as vain as a peacock.

He was despatched to serve in Spain's African colonies. In 1775, Abdul Hamid, the Moroccan Pasha, launched a war to expel the Spaniards from his country, and Miranda found himself caught up in the siege of the fortress of Melilla. He distinguished himself by leading 230 men in a night attack that succeeded in spiking Hamid's main battery of cannon. The Moroccan way of war – slitting soldiers' throats, executing one of their own generals for failing to break the Spanish resistance – impressed Miranda at an early stage with a horror of unnecessary bloodshed. He himself narrowly avoided death – or worse – when three bullets, passing between his legs, tore his trousers.

In Spain, Miranda's abilities were recognized, but he continued to be prickly towards his superiors, feeling he was treated as a second-class soldier because of his American origins – which was probably true. In his mid-twenties he was twice briefly imprisoned in Cádiz for disobedience. Then a new commanding officer accused him of withholding funds he had been given to pay a merchant who supplied his regiment, and of stripping and beating two of his soldiers, wounding one with his sword. Miranda denied the charges, claiming that an adjutant was responsible for the embezzlement and a soldier for the beatings. In truth, such deeds seem out of character: although a disciplinarian as a commander, Miranda was neither impetuous nor cruel; nor was he financially dishonest.

However, the case was brought to the attention of the inspector-general of the army, Conde Alejandro O'Reilly, who like most of his superiors intensely disliked the bumptious Miranda, and eventually reached the ears of the King himself. Miranda found himself confined to routine duties. He subsequently visited Gibraltar, where he was invited to the British Governor's New Year ball: it was the beginning of a lifelong passion for all things British, and it may be that he was even recruited by the British secret service. With his military career in the doldrums, nursing a grudge over his shabby treatment by the Spaniards he had so passionately admired a decade earlier, and alive to the intriguing rife in Cádiz, a hotbed of Latin American grumbling against Spanish excesses, it was probably about this time that Miranda first began to nurture his revolutionary views.

The American War of Independence broke out in 1775; under the Franco-Spanish alliance of 1779 Spain was obliged to help the fight against the British, and Miranda, appointed aide to General Juan Manuel Cajigal, the new Spanish commander in Cuba, distinguished himself in the two-month siege of the British stronghold of Pensacola in the spring of 1781. Promoted to lieutenant-colonel, he helped a French fleet to reach Chesapeake Bay and assist George Washington at the battle of Yorktown in the autumn of that year. At about this time, Miranda's detractors accused him of having permitted a British officer to inspect the defences of Havana – which if true would have amounted to treason. Cajigal, however, demonstrated his confidence in his aide by letting him supervise an exchange of prisoners between Spain and Britain in Jamaica. In 1782 Cajigal and Miranda were sent to the Bahamas to accept the surrender by the British of the capital, New Providence.

By the age of 32, Miranda had a reputation as an able and prominent officer. But if once he had resented the snubs of the criollo aristocracy of Caracas, he now much more deeply disliked the arrogant Spaniards he had served for more than 10 years. The American War of Independence led him to conclude that the liberation of the Spanish colonies could not be long delayed; it was unnatural for such vast and far-flung territories to be ruled by a country so many thousands of miles away.

Friends and relations in Venezuela bombarded him with letters complaining of the brutality of Spanish rule under the new Captain-General, Bernardo de Gálvez – 'a new Nero and Philip II rolled into one!' According to Miranda's correspondents, Gálvez had 'just sent an order to all governors that no American gentleman may travel abroad without the King's permission'. They begged Miranda, Venezuela's 'eldest son', to save them:

> The least sign from you will find us ready to follow you as our
> leader to the end, and to shed the last drop of our blood for causes
> that are great and honourable . . . We do not want to take a single

step except on your advice, and we shall not do so; for we have placed all our hopes in your good judgment . . . We send you . . . the information which we think necessary so that in our name and that of our entire province you may make compacts or contracts with our full power and consent. Also, if you judge it convenient, you may negotiate with foreign powers in order to release us from this accursed captivity.

Returning to Havana, Miranda was suddenly arrested, on Gálvez's orders, accused of engaging in contraband – clearly a trumped-up charge – and sentenced to ten years in jail. Cajigal, standing as his guarantor, had him released, and Miranda spent several months under a cloud, sometimes in hiding. He had reached a turning-point. He was fearful of re-arrest, although he was still protected by Cajigal, beset by enemies, and suspected of spying and intrigue. He planned, although it was tantamount to desertion, to travel back to Europe, via North America, in order to prove his innocence to the King of Spain in person. In June 1783 he set off, very bitter about the way he had been treated.

He left in style, with a piano, a sofa and his growing library. He disembarked in North Carolina, where he confided to his diary his astonishment at the sexual liberty afforded single women there, while married ones were forced to live like recluses in their homes. In Philadelphia he was greeted by senior government officials, and in December at last met George Washington. Impressed by the American leader's entry into the city, 'like the redeemer entering Jerusalem', he found him moderate and urbane but curiously lacking in intelligence, and rather taciturn. In New York Miranda met Alexander Hamilton and Thomas Paine, and visited the principal battle-sites of the War of Independence: Saratoga, Albany, Newhaven and Boston (where he met the Marquis de Lafayette – who impressed him not at all: 'a mediocrity accompanied by activity and perpetual motion').

He was appalled by the low level of debate in Congress and by the representatives' obsession with trade:

Why, in a democracy whose basis is Virtue, is there no place assigned to it? On the contrary all the dignity and powers are given to Property, which is the blight of such a democracy. Another point is the contradiction I noticed between admitting as one of the rights of mankind that of worshipping a Supreme Being in the manner and form in which it may please one, yet afterwards excluding a man from office if he did not profess Christianity.

Miranda's visit to America hardened his conviction that his own continent could and must secure its freedom. He became suspicious that the United States' intentions were expansionist when Thomas Jefferson argued that the Confederacy should be thought of as the heart 'from which all America, north and south, should be peopled' and suggested that Spain's colonies could be gained 'piece by piece'.

England, however, held an intellectual fascination for him, and after a year-and-a-half in the United States Miranda arrived in London early in 1785. He lodged at the Royal Hotel and there penned a vigorous defence of his actions to the King of Spain, resigning his commission and seeking a formal exculpation. Even at this stage, it seems, he regarded himself as a loyal Spanish subject bent on having his good name restored. The Spanish Embassy in London received him courteously, but there was no reply from Madrid to his letters.

His blend of charm and self-importance proved as seductive in London as it had in the United States. A poseur of a characteristic Latin American kind, Miranda soon numbered among his friends – although the closeness of the relationship may have been more obvious to him than to them – Jeremy Bentham, Lord Howe, Lord Sydney, Lord Shelburne, Lord Fitzherbert and General Rainsford. Snubbed by Madrid, he decided the time was ripe for public advocacy of independence for Spain's colonies. The *Political Herald & Review* recorded that:

In London, we are well assured, there is at this moment a Spanish American of great consequence and possessed of the confidence of his fellow-citizens, who aspires to the glory of being the deliverer of his country . . . This gentleman, having visited every province in North America, came to England, which he regards as the mother country of liberty, and the school for political knowledge . . . He is a man of sublime vision and penetrating genius gifted in modern

tongues, learned and worldly-wise. He has spent many years studying politics ... He looks on England as the mother-country of
freedom and the school of political knowledge. We admire his
talents, we admire his virtues and for the least wish well to the
most noble aspiration that can occupy the mind of any mortal, that
of giving the benefits of freedom to millions of his fellow citizens.

This glorious tribute signalled to the Spaniards that Miranda was not
only beyond redemption, but dangerous as well.

In the summer of 1785 an American friend, Colonel William Smith,
came to England, and he and Miranda decided to tour Europe
together. Miranda's motive was to gather diplomatic and financial
support for the cause of Latin American independence. Renegade
colonel that he was, Miranda particularly wished to observe the
military manoeuvres of Frederick the Great of Prussia. Bernardo del
Campo, the wily Spanish ambassador in London, who frequently
invited him to dine, obligingly presented Miranda with a letter of
introduction to the Spanish minister in Prussia, but secretly sent word
to the Spanish legation in Berlin to watch his movements carefully,
with a view to having him extradited once he crossed into Prussia.

In August, with a party which included the Duke of Portland,
Miranda and Smith left for Rotterdam, The Hague, Leyden, Haarlem,
Amsterdam and Potsdam. Apparently unaware of the Spanish plot
to apprehend him (which may have been aborted due to Portland's
presence), Miranda and his party travelled to Berlin, where they saw
the disciplined ranks of Prussian infantry wheel in formation under
the command of General Wichard von Möllendorf. Treated like an
exiled head of state, Miranda was invited to dine by Frederick and
toured the libraries and museums of the Prussian capital. His 'royal'
progress continued, to Prague, Vienna – where he was lodged in the
impressive Schönbrunn – and Hungary. There he met Haydn and
visited the famous Esterhazy Palace as a guest of the prince, before
returning to Vienna in a coach drawn by huge Transylvanian horses.

He turned south to Venice, then on to Verona, Modena, Florence,
Lucca, Pisa and Siena. In Rome he visited the papal apartments, saw
every conceivable church and palazzo, visited each of the Seven Hills,

the Lateran Palaces, the Terme of Agrippa, Castel Sant'Angelo, the Sistine Chapel and St Peter's, where he attended a Papal Mass.

He was also an indefatigable sexual tourist. Everywhere he went, he gallanted the ladies. Among other amorous escapades, he met an 18-year-old girl who punctured his vanity by refusing to sleep with him because she had a son by the King of Sweden, to whom she was devoted. Miranda confided to his diary that it took all his powers of persuasion to get this young, high-class courtesan to change her mind. In Viterbo he encountered, so he said, the most beautiful women in the world.

From Italy he travelled to Greece, where in Athens he befriended a French academic, Monsieur Villoison, who had scandalized the city by declaring that 'to put one's hands on the breasts of women [at parties] was not indecent, because that was what was happening in Paris'. When Miranda crossed to Turkey, he complained that the lack of pretty girls there at first caused him severe headaches and that he was spat upon in the street, having been mistaken for a Frenchman. He visited the celebrated cultural salons of Madame Michel and Madame Heidenstan, falling briefly in love with the beautiful Greek Eufrosina Phrossini. He witnessed Turkish orgies, and also managed a trip to the celebrated library of Rahib Pasha. On the way back to Greece he sipped chocolate with Countess Ludolf and, surrounded by beautiful Greek girls, heard the Orthodox Mass sung.

Crossing the Black Sea in a storm, Miranda became one of the first South Americans to visit Russia. As usual he made an impression; he was taken up by the Russian nobility and met Prince Grigory Potemkin, chief minister and former lover of Catherine the Great, who over tea laced with vodka took an instant liking to him. So began Miranda's relations with the Russian court. He soon became Potemkin's favourite, went on outings and hunting parties with him, and stayed at his Crimean estate. In front of Potemkin he had a blazing row with the French Prince of Nassau, who had claimed that Spanish women were all dirty whores who smelt of garlic. Miranda retorted sarcastically that the French were of course the best judges of cleanliness.

In February 1787, in Kiev, Miranda was formally presented by Potemkin to the Empress. So began one of the most curious love affairs in history, between a Latin American poseur and Russia's notoriously lascivious but most civilized and intelligent ruler. Her first question was, 'How low is the temperature in your country, when it gets cooler?' – a thoughtful question for a man who suffered intensely from the bitter Russian cold and gloried in the warmth of the palaces. From the head of the table at a banquet, Catherine sent him choice morsels to eat. Afterwards when the court settled down to cards she asked Miranda if the Inquisition still existed in Spain; he replied that regrettably it did. The Empress said, 'In Russia there are still some Dominican monks that work for the tribunal [of the Inquisition]. But when I see them, I say under my breath, "God help me!"' Discreet laughter coursed around the room and she left to bows and curtseys.

A few days later both Catherine and Miranda attended a party at Prince Vranitsky's house. After a conversation with him, Catherine was heard to remark that Miranda was 'truthful and learned'. At another party they discussed literature. Shortly afterwards Potemkin suggested that unless Miranda left soon, the rivers would be too swollen to navigate. It seems that the prince was fuming: not only was Miranda apparently abusing his introduction to the Empress to ingratiate himself in Potemkin's place, but Potemkin himself missed his protégé's company. Miranda got the message, and prepared to leave. Coldly, Potemkin asked him whether he intended to say goodbye to Catherine before he went. When they next met, Miranda ostentatiously failed to rise as Potemkin entered the room.

The following day Potemkin told Miranda that the Empress herself insisted he should not travel because crossing the rivers had become too dangerous. At a party that evening she chided him: 'Did you want to drown? I would never have permitted it.' At the same party, Potemkin was seen to greet his former friend, now his rival, with all his old warmth. Clearly Catherine had been annoyed by the news of Miranda's imminent departure, and blamed Potemkin, who now had to make amends. From then on, the Empress conversed with Miranda at every reception, while courtiers alternately fawned upon and grumbled about the new favourite. Even the Prince of Nassau became deferential, while the Spanish ambassador seethed. In March, at another party, Miranda was seen to compliment the Empress on her

exquisite silk dress, and even to touch it. Catherine smilingly asked
what was ailing him. His sexual liaison with Catherine is believed to
have begun the same night.

Shortly after this, Potemkin thought he had found another way
of ridding the court of Miranda: he ordered him to welcome the
King of Poland, Stanislaus (like Potemkin, a former lover of the
Empress), on Catherine's behalf, at the start of his visit to Russia.
Again Miranda's educated, graceful conversation made a favourable
impression. He soon returned, not just to the bed of the plump,
middle-aged Empress, but also to that of his own court passion, the
beautiful Countess Pototka. The Empress was now so infatuated that
she pressed a close friend both of Miranda and Potemkin, Marshal
Mamonoff, to lend him a palace in St Petersburg so he could live
there, saying it would be a tragedy if impoverishment consumed such
a man. This was a serious proposal and Catherine was intending to
establish him as her recognized lover and favourite. Mamonoff refused,
arguing that Miranda must return to his mission in life, the fight for
South America's independence. Almost certainly Potemkin and the
other courtiers had now united to oppose Miranda's influence.

Faced with this rebuff, Miranda decided to leave. Catherine replied
sadly that she appreciated his way of thinking, 'but I will always give
you my imperial protection, wherever you are'.

As the day of his departure approached, Miranda bade farewell to
his latest, now tearful, conquests, Madame Tarnowska and Princess
Lubomircka. On the evening of the celebration of Catherine's saint's
day, a spectacular fireworks display was staged. Miranda appeared
with the Empress on the balcony of the imperial palace, where he
took his public leave, kissing her hand as the sky blazed with light
over the canals and palaces.

In a luxurious coach Miranda travelled across the Russian landscape towards Moscow, where he was put up in the palace of Marshal
Roumaintzoff. Once again he entered the social whirl, visiting the
opera, libraries and museums, and the Russian bath houses, where
men and women took the hot waters naked – but, he observed
regretfully, none of the women resembled the Venus of the Medici.
Then a summons came from the Empress to return to St Petersburg.
Prince Orloff invited him to stay at the Hermitage Palace there. A

courtier told him how Peter the Great, whose palace it had been, once cut open the stomach of a man who had died in a drunken stupor in order to observe the condition of the liquid inside him.

Catherine received him once more. The Spanish chargé d'affaires, meanwhile, asked him for proof that he was a count and an officer of the King of Spain – neither of which Miranda could provide. It seemed he was certain to be exposed as a charlatan, until the Empress intervened to say she supported him as a person, no matter what his official position. She scolded her courtiers for requiring that he kiss her hand on being presented to her, on the grounds that she already knew him, and invited him into her private apartment. He was offered the uniform of a Russian colonel, and Catherine gave him 10,000 roubles and 500 ducats of gold. But now he refused to stay. He despatched crates of papers and books to London, then embarked himself. It is impossible to say whether his decision to leave was prompted by the certainty that the Empress' infatuation could not last and that his Russian enemies would sooner or later trip him up; whether he felt the tug of destiny and his American ambitions; or whether he simply could not bear the prospect of years of cold Russian winters.

The ship took Miranda across the Baltic to Stockholm, where he was housed in the Russian Embassy. Fearing an attempt to kidnap him to Spain he went incognito at first, meeting only trusted contacts. Sweden's celebrated beauties and coal mines were alike objects of his interest: he descended 600 feet down a mine, meeting the women and children who worked there, and was impressed by their cheerfulness in adversity. He also witnessed his first aurora borealis, admired Sweden's canals and criticized Stockholm's hospitals and prisons.

Soon King Gustav III learnt of his presence and ordered that all official doors should be opened to him, as a favourite of the Empress of Russia. During his Swedish sojourn Miranda took as his principal lover the passionate Cristina Strandez. After making love to her he would relax with a Swedish friend, Count Rousamousky, who regaled him with court gossip, in particular the story of how the impotent King discovered that his wife was pregnant and behaved as though the prospective infant was his own until its birth, when its colour made it obvious that it was the offspring of a black page. Gustav then arranged for a Swedish page to sleep with the Queen, and the union provided a child that he was able to call his own.

Miranda travelled on to Norway, wondering at the clarity of the night sky as his carriage was pulled across high mountains to the city of Kristiansand; there he was received ceremonially by the authorities, and Count Rantzau placed a 17-year-old girl at his disposal to warm his nights, as well as providing a list of available women. After a dangerous journey across broken roads to the town of Uddevalla, during which he fractured his arm, Miranda cuckolded his British host, Mr Holt. Miranda and Catherine Holt visited the Holts' country estate, where their love-making urges were frustrated by the presence of another guest. On the way back they copulated passionately in the carriage, but it overturned, and they narrowly avoided being discovered in flagrante.

In Denmark, Miranda was unimpressed by Copenhagen and its 'degenerate' royal family, and found the girls unattractive. He did the usual rounds of theatres, art galleries, museums and churches. He considered the Danes a backward, barbarous people; he told a government minister that the law which permitted a father to immure his daughter if she had sex outside marriage must be repealed, and interceded to save the life of a demented girl sentenced to death for infanticide. He also pressed for prison reform – in particular the separation of the sexes in jail and of young offenders from hardened criminals, and for one prisoner to a bed in hospital, instead of two sharing.

Back in Germany, in Kiel, he had a fling with one of the three beautiful Von Bulow sisters. He was prevented from seducing his pretty 15-year-old guide on the top of a church tower, and so fulfilling his fantasy of 'sacrificing to Venus at the highest point in the city' by the attention of other tourists, 'but slept with a beautiful Englishwoman the same night instead'. He also visited 'the Parthenon', a bordello run by Madame Poppe, and boasted of despatching 'two towers and two fine girls' in a single day. In Haarlem Miranda attended musical hideaways 'where staid citizens procure girls cheaply and make love watched by other equally respectable types smoking pipes to the sound of a violin'. In Strasbourg he bought a complete edition of the works of Voltaire as well as Virgil's *Georgics*. He was impressed by

Hans Holbein and read Virgil under a tree by a lake under the Black Mountains. In Switzerland he visited the scene of the martyrdom of Jan Hus. Observing that Protestant countries were better off than Catholic ones, he wondered whether Catholicism was opposed to material wealth, a theme he discussed with Catholic friends.

He crossed into Italy again before returning to Switzerland and then to France, passing through Lyons and Avignon and down to Toulon, where he inspected French ships. He visited Cannes and Nice, where an actress and a Venetian girl spent successive nights with him. He embarked for Genoa and thence to Turin, where he attended masked balls and slept with ballerinas before returning to Marseilles and then up to the Gironde to taste the region's great wines. From there he went to Brest and on to Paris which, towards the end of May 1789, he found in turmoil, on the brink of revolution – though this failed to distract him from his round of pleasure, before his return to London. There he attended a banquet at which William Pitt was present; and, methodically and admiringly, noted that in a single day in London, 40,000 lobsters were sold.

Miranda's later apologists argue that the motives behind this fantastic peregrination were always high-minded: the assimilation of culture and information, of political and military ideas, combined with the need to press the cause of Spanish American independence and to secure allies. Russia and Germany were certainly potential counterweights to France and Spain, often in alliance. Historians of South America view the whole four-year odyssey as the subtle manoeuvrings of a master diplomat, of a New World Talleyrand, Metternich or Lafayette preparing European opinion for the revolutionary idea of Spanish American independence. However, reading his meticulously kept diaries – which have to be considered accurate, even allowing for an element of sexual exaggeration – it is hard to conclude that he was on nothing more than a prolonged joy-ride, during which he displayed an astonishing variety of sexual and intellectual appetites, in that order. He posed as statesman, aristocrat and military hero, his charm and sheer bravura carrying him from one European court to another, much of the time living lavishly at other people's expense.

Yet Miranda represented nothing. He had resigned his commission under a cloud; he was arguably a traitor and deserter; and he could not establish his credentials as a count. He was a chancer, and he took everyone in, to an awe-inspiring degree. In later times he might have made a great journalist. He observed everything, visited everyone who mattered, inspected everything – warships, copper and iron mines, hospitals and prisons – displaying genuinely liberal and enlightened sentiments with indefatigable self-confidence and authority, and he always wrote everything down. On top of that his appetite for culture was limitless – music, painting, museums, antiquities, the theatre, local colour, the customs of ordinary people, conversation and, above all, books, which he vacuumed up as he crossed Europe, despatching them back to England to join his ever-swelling collection.

What no one found credible was that Miranda, now nearly 40, was a political figure, or leader of his people. Hardly anyone in Venezuela, except his family and the most rarefied of intellectual circles, had heard of him. He had been away from his homeland for nearly two decades. His sole political significance was that it suited the British and, to a lesser extent, the Russians (for very different reasons) to take him seriously. To the Germans, Scandinavians, French, Italians, Austrians, Greeks, Turks and Americans he was merely a social phenomenon. Only the Spanish, his old employers, paid him the compliment of regarding him as a potential danger and shadowing him across the European continent.

In London, in 1789, Miranda continued to dabble, albeit with a little more method. He found lodgings in Jermyn Street and from there he toured the country, visiting Oxford, Cambridge, Southampton, Winchester and Norwich, shooting hares and pheasants with an English friend. He attended Lady Sheffield's drawing-rooms and fell for the young and beautiful Lady Webster, later to become the formidable Whig hostess, Lady Holland. In 1790 Thomas Pownall, former Governor of Massachusetts, who believed that in exchange for British assistance to the Spanish colonies in shaking off rule from Madrid, both Britain and the United States should be given unfettered access to trade with them, succeeded in arranging a discreet meeting between Miranda and Britain's first minister, William Pitt. This was the most important event in Miranda's life to date: Catherine of

Russia could merely provide peripheral support to the cause of South American independence, but the helmsman of the world's biggest colonial power apart from Spain was a different matter. The meeting was a sign he was being taken seriously at last.

Miranda prepared himself feverishly, drawing up an ambitious and unrealistic plan for liberation. He gave a careful estimate of the colonies' resources, and of Spanish strength there. There were 21 million people, he claimed, in 'the Spanish Indies', half of them Spaniards, criollos, whites and of mixed blood, the rest Indians and blacks. The colonies produced annually around 55 million pesos in gold, silver, sugar, cacao, hides, tobacco, indigo and cochineal, and imported roughly 22 million pesos' worth of goods from Spain, and a similar amount in contraband. Spain had around 36,000 troops in the colonies, of whom some 20,000 were locally raised militia, with the rest being regular soldiers; it also had a navy of 123 ships and 44,000 sailors.

Miranda subtly underlined South America's potential by suggesting – with remarkable foresight – that a canal could be cut through the isthmus of Panama to facilitate trade to the Far East for Britain and North America. He argued that although Spanish America, more populous than Spain, should be able to stage its own revolt, its communities were cut off from one another by distance and communications. With control of the seas, the Spanish could send reinforcements wherever they liked: a crucial insight. Britain, he insisted, as a maritime power, could cut the Spanish lines of communication.

He argued that Britain was a natural ally for South America, ending on a flattering note:

> In view of the similarity that exists in the character of these two nations, and the effects that must naturally flow from liberty and the fact that a good government can instruct the general mass of men, progressively doing away with the religious prejudices that cloud its people's minds . . . these being otherwise honest, hospitable, and generous – we must expect soon to see a respectable and illustrious nation emerging worthy of being the ally of the wisest and most famed power on earth.

His grandiose blueprint was for a kind of united states of Spanish America, stretching from the Pacific to the Atlantic, excluding only Brazil and Guyana but including the land east of the Mississippi and south of the source of the river, below Parallel 45. The constitution of this great new state would be an extraordinary hybrid of the monarchical and republican systems: a descendant of the Incas would sit on the throne – this to give the monarchy an authentic pre-Columbine flavour – but he would be accountable, British-style, to a two-chamber congress, with an upper house elected for life and a lower one by regular popular (if restricted) vote. A two-thirds majority would be needed to amend the constitution, as well as a three-quarters majority of a council composed of the Inca emperor sitting with the highest judges of the land. The clergy would retain many of their privileges, but the Inquisition would be done away with. The Spanish monopoly on trade would be ended, and the new state would be open to commercial treaties with Britain and other countries. On seeing this blueprint later, President Adams of the United States is said to have remarked that he didn't know whether to laugh or to cry. The son of the Bostonian James Lloyd, however, wrote to Adams describing Miranda as 'the most extraordinary and marvellously energetic man I have ever met'.

In May 1790, equipped with this fantastic plan, Miranda met the cold, analytical young man dominating British politics. He asserted to Pitt that the South American people would rise in revolt as soon as a British fleet appeared; but he was in no position to give this assurance, having not set foot in South America for 20 years and being in contact with only a handful of wealthy criollo dissidents. He had not the slightest idea of the real opinion of the educated classes there, much less that of the populace. Pitt made it clear that he would help only in the event of a war between Britain and Spain. This in fact looked to be imminent, which was why Pitt's officials had set up the encounter in the first place: Spain was claiming as its own the Nootka Sound, high up on the Pacific coast of North America, then in Britain's possession. Miranda no doubt left the meeting with a spring in his step.

Five months later, however, the Nootka Sound dispute was settled and the project was off. Miranda, given financial support by the British government as long as his potential nuisance value to the Spaniards was useful, now found this source of funds drying up, and was upset that he had revealed his plan to Pitt. Pownall tried to get them back around the table, unsuccessfully.

Miranda had by now founded the Gran Réunion Americana, a society for Spanish-American dissidents. Its members, now or at a later date, included Bernardo O'Higgins, future liberator of Chile, to whom Miranda taught mathematics; Antonio Nariño, later founder of New Granada's independence movement; Carlos María de Alvear, friend and rival of Argentina's General José de San Martín and, briefly, ruler of the country; Francisco Montufar, later aide to Colombia's General Antonio José de Sucre; and a future Mexican liberator, Vicente Rocafuerte. But Miranda felt harassed by the continuing efforts of the Spanish Ambassador, Bernardo del Campo, to spy on him and by Spanish attempts to get the British to arrest him for debt. The years of touring the courts of Europe in grand style were past; he was running out of money.

In 1792, Miranda moved to more modest quarters at 33 Great Pulteney Street in Soho. After three years in London, he felt betrayed by the British government, and depressed that all his talk of leading South America to revolution had come to nothing. He switched his attention to the revolutionary ferment in France: a group of monarchists there had tried to get him to join a counter-revolutionary mercenary army of Russians, Swedes, Germans and Frenchmen partly backed by Catherine, who had suggested Miranda's name. But for all his aristocratic pretensions, Miranda's intellectual sympathies lay with the revolutionaries.

He made a good impression on a prominent Girondin who visited London, J.P. Brissot: between them they developed the idea that the revolution in France could spread both to mainland Spain and to Spanish America. The Girondins were idealistic middle-class revolutionaries, and moderates compared to the Jacobins who replaced them in 1793. Brissot had been lobbying the commander of forces in northern France, General Charles-François Dumouriez, to appoint Miranda as head of an invasion force of 12,000 French infantry and 10,000 mulattos then garrisoned in Santo Domingo in the Caribbean who, with the assistance of the French navy, might be expected to topple Spain's hold on her colonies, something France wanted almost as much as Britain.

Crossing to Paris, Miranda found little enthusiasm for the plan there, however, and was considering a return to London when Austrian and Prussian armies invaded France from the east. In August 1792, as the country reeled at the prospect of defeat, Miranda, who had perhaps sold his military credentials a little too successfully, found himself offered the rank of marshal in the French army and the title of baron, as well as a fat stipend: very attractive to a man now hard-pressed for the money to live in the grand style to which he had become accustomed. At the age of 42 he was at last a real nobleman and real general – both in the service of revolutionary France. His Russian supporters, who loathed the French revolutionaries, were appalled at the transformation, but did not sever their links with him altogether.

Chapter 6

REVOLUTIONARY GENERAL

To Miranda's own surprise, in his first engagement as a French marshal, along the border between Belgium and Holland, his force of 2,000 men succeeded after seven hours of fighting in putting to flight some 6,000 Prussians led by Count von Kalckreuth, a capable commander. It was the first French success of the war. With uncharacteristic modesty, Miranda spoke of his 'beginner's luck in the French army'. He was promptly appointed to command a division in the front-line, under Dumouriez's overall command. En route to Vaux, the 10,000-strong division commanded by General Chazot suddenly encountered 1,500 Prussian hussars. The French panicked and fled; a rout seemed imminent, until the retreating forces reached Miranda's position at Wargemoulin. There, sword in hand, he stopped their flight, and reorganized the two forces into three columns to march on Valmy.

Dumouriez boldly attacked, believing that he faced a Prussian army of 50,000 men and a major battle. Instead, he was met only by covering fire; the Prussians had retreated after the French rally. Miranda's reputation soared. The decadent voluptuary was proving himself to be an outstanding soldier in the field. However, he viewed with distaste the rise of the revolutionary party in France, in particular the Jacobin faction led by Robespierre and Jean-Paul Marat; as he wrote to Alexander Hamilton: 'The only danger which I foresee is the introduction of extremist principles which would poison freedom in its cradle and destroy it for us.'

Miranda moved up to join Dumouriez as second-in-command of the French army in Belgium. He went to the relief of Dumouriez's army at Anderlecht, and was appointed to take over General La Bourdonnais' command of the Northern Army. As the grip of winter intensified Miranda's forces reached the outskirts of Amberes, where he personally supervised the digging of the trenches, encouraging his men while maintaining rigid discipline. Amberes was heavily fortified by the Austrians; on 26 November 1792 the French guns opened up and were answered from within, but not a single besieger was killed. By five in the afternoon, as plumes of smoke from the burning city curled into the sky, the Austrians were seeking terms. These took four days to negotiate and amounted to unconditional surrender, at the cost of just 30 casualties to Miranda's army. It was another major and morale-boosting victory for the hard-pressed French under their inspired new general, who immediately set about reinforcing the city's defences. He arrested some of its leading citizens to exact tribute to pay for provisioning his troops, and dissolved the convents and monasteries, stripping prelates, abbots and monks of their titles. The 22,000 men under his command were soon joined by thousands belonging to the Army of the Ardennes, swelling his command to 70,000 men.

In February 1793, against his own advice, Miranda was ordered to send out 12,000 of his men to besiege the city of Maastricht. As he expected, the 30,000 or so enemy forces proved too well entrenched. They fired some 32,000 cannon-shot in six days, but failed to inflict many casualties upon the smaller French force. Miranda decided to withdraw, lest he lose his guns to an Austrian sortie. He was bitterly criticized for what was clearly a sensible tactical move; he was also hated by many of his own men for his draconian punishments for looting and raping.

Another much more dangerous threat now loomed. Early in March 1793, Miranda's commander-in-chief, Dumouriez, asked his staff officers what they thought of the growing Jacobin outrages towards the French army. King Louis XVI had been executed in January, the revolutionary Terror was gathering pace, and the radicals mistrusted nothing so much as the army, even though they depended upon it for the Revolution's survival against external enemies. Miranda primly replied that he disapproved of seeking the opinions of soldiers on such issues. Soon afterwards two disgraced generals, La Nove and Stengel, were arrested on grounds of conspiring against the Revolution. Dumouriez demanded to know what Miranda would do if the order came to arrest him, Dumouriez. Miranda said that he would have no option but to obey, adding that General Valence, as the senior general in the French army, would however be responsible for executing it. Dumouriez angrily retorted that the army would refuse to carry out such an order. A few days later Dumouriez announced that he intended to march on Paris to restore freedom; the counter-revolution was under way. To his astonishment Miranda, despite his own disapproval of the increasingly radical turn taken by the Revolution, told Dumouriez the soldiers would not obey him and that he, Miranda, might also oppose him. It was a moment of truth: from then on, Dumouriez no longer trusted his subordinate.

Miranda's action is inexplicable, except in terms of self-preservation – he believed Dumouriez could not succeed. Miranda had little romantic commitment to the French Revolution and was privately critical of the direction it was taking. His enemies believed his ambition was to replace his superior: already the Girondin leaders had identified him as the best candidate for Dumouriez's post, should anything happen to the commander-in-chief.

Dumouriez then decided on a high-risk tactic, one which Miranda's partisans have always believed was an act of deliberate treachery designed to discredit their hero and lead to his downfall. Holding good defensive positions, though vastly outnumbered and outgunned, Dumouriez determined to risk the whole French flank in an offensive against the Austrian-led forces. His motive may have been to give himself enough prestige, through victory, to march on Paris and take over the reins of power. On 15 March Miranda had successfully repulsed an attack on Tirlemont, but with General Champmorin's forces, was ordered to attack the right flank of the enemy at Neerwinden. It was suicidal, since Miranda's 10,000 men were opposed by Austrian-led forces around 18,000-strong, well entrenched in a defensible position. The French were mown down without pity. Although he was in the thick of the fight, Miranda survived; after nightfall, he had no alternative but to sound the retreat, leaving 2,000 of his men dead. The retreat was orderly, and he handled it with great coolness.

It soon emerged that Dumouriez had known the enemy was strongest on their right flank and weakest on their left, where his own forces were superior: the weakest part of the French force, under Miranda, had thus been ordered to attack where the enemy were strongest. From the start, Miranda had opposed the plan, which he later described as 'against the rules of the art of warfare. I am astonished that Dumouriez was capable of such an error'. The suspicion must be that Dumouriez wanted Miranda to do badly by comparison with the other commanders, in a bid to discredit him and remove him before the coup attempt. But he had miscalculated in believing that the centre would hold, and the whole French army was thrown back as a result of this disastrously conceived attack.

On 21 March the Austrians attacked at Pallemberg. Miranda held his positions for a day, despite severe losses, then staged another orderly retreat at night. Four days later Dumouriez and Miranda met, and exchanged furious words. Dumouriez railed against the Jacobins, while Miranda criticized his commander's military ineptness.

The Jacobins at last came to learn of Dumouriez's plotting, and of his criticisms of his second-in-command. Dumouriez was arrested; Miranda was summoned to Paris. Arriving at the end of the month, he was immediately interrogated by Citizen Petiot, a Girondin sympathizer, who arranged for him to appear before the Committee of War and Security. At a hearing on 8 April 1793 questions were put to him as to the conduct of the war. The questioning was barely polite. Miranda knew that his life was on the line, not just his command. He impressed his interrogators with his eloquent replies, and it appeared that he would be exonerated.

On 19 April, the much feared chief prosecutor of the Revolution, Antoine Fouquier-Tinville, ordered Miranda's arrest on charges of conspiring with Pitt and the British government as well as with the Russians and the North Americans, and of aiding Dumouriez in his counter-revolutionary attempt to reinstate the monarchy. It seemed all too likely that this dissipated, haughty, good-looking man who had cut a swathe through the beauties and courts of all of Europe, who had led his men with brilliance, even perhaps turning the tables

in the war, and who had acted with impeccable correctness in spurning Dumouriez's overtures, would be guillotined, a long way from
his native Caracas, on trumped-up charges.

On 20 April he was taken before a Revolutionary Tribunal
presided over by Jacques-Bernard-Marie Montane, with Fouquier-
Tinville prosecuting. Miranda surprised those present by his calm
demeanour and his eloquent and natural way of defending himself.
He was also vigorously defended by the respected lawyer Claude
François Chauveau-Lagarde (who later attempted unsuccessfully to
save Queen Marie Antoinette from the tumbrils): 'An irreproach-
able republican', he argued, 'never fears death but cannot bear the
suspicion of crime, and for a month Miranda has been suspected.'
Fouquier-Tinville rose, and in the precise, reedy voice which had
condemned so many to the blade, accused Miranda of negligence in
the war, and of being Dumouriez's chief co-conspirator. Meanwhile
Marat's rabid newspaper, *L'Ami du Peuple*, had charged Miranda with
looting Amberes after its capture. A procession of hostile witnesses
was led by General La Hove and General Eustace. It was alleged
that Miranda had a son and a brother-in-law in Maastricht, hence
his discontinuance of the siege. A sergeant testified that the Dutch
considered him 'better than a Dutchman'. The national gendarmerie,
whose excesses he had tried to contain at Amberes, accused him of a
succession of crimes.

Summing up, Chauveau-Lagarde claimed that no defence
was necessary, because Miranda had already defended himself so
eloquently; he should be 'listened to with all the dignity that became
true republicans and with the full confidence the court deserves'.
As the judges withdrew and the prisoners were led away, sobbing
could be heard. When the judges filed back, generals d'Hangest,
Dumouriez and Valance were pronounced guilty; Miranda was
declared innocent. The court erupted in applause, in which even
Fouquier-Tinville joined. Miranda rose to declare that 'this brilliant
act of justice must restore the respect of my fellow citizens for me,
whose loss would have been more painful for me even than death'.
On 16 May he was released and carried through crowds in the streets.
He was one of the very few to stare the Terror in the face, to come
under the shadow of the guillotine, and yet to escape.

Now common sense deserted him. Believing himself immune from further persecution, he withdrew to a large and luxurious château in Menilmontant to rest and to defend his reputation against the unceasing vituperation of Marat's newspaper. Attacks were still raining down upon him as 'an intriguer, a creator of faction' who, it was alleged, had bribed the jurors to let him go. His wisest course of action would have been to leave at once for England.

On 9 July he was arrested again and conducted to the prison of La Force, from which very few had ever emerged free. Robespierre himself demanded the guillotine for Miranda's alleged connivance in a royalist plot. On 13 July he was brought before the Convention and again made a stirring defence, accusing his jailers of violating the constitution 'because the body politic is oppressed when any citizen is oppressed'. He complained that he had been accused of seeking to flee the country, when he had neither horses nor a carriage and could not move two leagues out of Paris without permission from the government. He accused the dreaded Public Safety Committee of tyranny, in disregarding his previous acquittal.

Miranda had asked his doctor to prepare a dose of poison so that he could cheat the guillotine, undoubtedly a wise precaution. Whereas there was a single major prison in Paris before the Revolution, the Bastille, there were now 20, containing some 40,000 people; 7,000 had already been guillotined. Paris was in the grip of fear.

There was a club-like atmosphere in La Force. Miranda beautifully caught the mood when he wrote that it was as though he were 'making a long journey by boat, during which it was necessary to fill the tiresome emptiness of time with the search for useful knowledge without knowing if the journey would end in death at sea or would arrive happily in port'. The Marquise du Châtelet became an inseparable companion; the two men talked at length of art, literature and travel; they played cards with packs from which, to their amusement, the court cards had been removed, and read Tacitus and Cicero. One day du Châtelet decided to swallow poison, leaving his few goods to Miranda and the other prisoners. The months continued to drift slowly by, and Miranda made new friends in jail, including the celebrated antiquarian and savant Antoine-Chrysostome Quatremère de Quincy.

In December 1794 Miranda loosed a formidable broadside against the Convention, denouncing Robespierre's 'execrable maxim that the individual's interest must be sacrificed to the public interest', an 'infernal' idea that had given tyrants from Tiberius to Philip II the justification for their misrule. His letter ended, with courageous dignity, 'I do not ask for mercy from the Convention. I demand the most rigorous justice for myself and for those who have dared . . . to compromise the dignity of the French people and poison the national image'. For a man under the shadow of revolutionary terror and in jail for more than a year, Miranda showed a robust and indomitable spirit.

On 26 January 1795 Miranda was finally released from La Force, and promptly installed himself in a splendid apartment at Rue St Florentin costing £1,400 a year – a staggering sum for those days. He was determined to make up for the deprivations of the past year-and-a-half, of which sex – although he seems to have had access to some women in prison – was probably the most terrible. Women, the theatre and elegant parties were resumed with renewed vigour. In prison he had met 'Delfina', the beautiful Marchioness of Custine, whose husband was also in jail. Miranda embarked on a torrid affair with her – until he discovered she had also satisfied the lusts of François-René de Chateaubriand, Joseph Fouché, Alexandre de Beauharnais, M. de Grouchy, Comte Luis de Segur, Boissy d'Anglais and Dr Koreff. Passionate and intelligent, but undoubtedly a nymphomaniac, Delfina failed to win him back to her bed, but they continued to quarrel with the intensity of lovers. Supposedly an illegitimate daughter of Louis XV, Delfina was the greatest French coquette of her time and, according to a contemporary wit, 'loved everyone, even her husband'. She showered Miranda with letters, saw him frequently and was his last companion when he left France.

Two months after his release Miranda met the young Napoleon Bonaparte for the first time in the salon of Julia Segur, then gave him dinner. Napoleon's judgment is worth setting down:

I dined yesterday in the house of man who is really extraordinary.
I consider him a spy both of the Spanish court and of Britain.

He lives on a third floor, and his furniture is that of a satrap. He
complains of his misery in the middle of all this luxury . . . I am
used to very important people, and he is one of those I most want
to see again, a Don Quixote with the difference that he is not
mad . . . General Miranda has the sacred fire burning in his soul.

After several further meetings, Napoleon concluded less flatteringly
that Miranda was a 'demagogue. He is not a republican.' Miranda
himself observed that his guest 'had a surprised air at the luxury which
I liked to surround myself with'. Another visitor spoke of Miranda's
apartment as 'absolutely beautiful . . . unhappy with the way things
are going here [politically], he consoled himself with art and science;
he has the most exquisite little library and an apartment with a taste
I have never seen bettered. I thought myself in Athens, in the house
of Pericles.'

Miranda seems to have been sucked into an alliance between the
moderates and the royalists as one of two possible leaders of a military
coup. A prominent royalist remarked contemptuously that it would
be astonishing if the King of France should be replaced 'by a Spanish
Creole, the lieutenant of a provincial regiment of her Catholic
Majesty's, and a total stranger in France where he has lived only a
few years and where he has only been known since the Revolution'.

As the showdown between royalists and republicans approached, it
is unclear whether Miranda sat on the fence or took part. When the
government sent 1,500 troops to close down a radical 'electoral body'
gathered in a French theatre at two in the morning, 4 October 1795,
revolutionary newspapers reported Miranda to have been in charge of
the illicit proceedings. Napoleon fought hard to crush the insurgents.
Miranda went underground, was accused of being one of the principal conspirators, and then emerged to declare that he had taken no
part in the 'parliament'. Arrested and ordered out of the country, he
secured a stay of execution of the order and continued to live in his
usual style, but always followed by a gendarme. He managed to give
him the slip one night and went into hiding, whence he bombarded
the press with letters defending himself and attacking his enemies.
He was eventually given official permission to stay, and continued
to survive through the aftershocks of revolutionary France, always

active in half-plots, always preaching his own brand of liberal anti-monarchism and anti-extremism.

In September 1797, another alleged monarchist conspiracy was suppressed by the government, and again Miranda was named as one of the plotters. Once more he went underground, once more the police were ordered to hold the 'Peruvian' general if he had not, as was widely believed, escaped to Athens. In fact, at last wholly disillusioned with the French Revolution, fearing another long spell in prison and especially angry that France had formed an alliance with the Spain he so hated, he had resolved to go to Britain.

After passionately kissing Delfina goodbye, Miranda, wearing a wig and green spectacles and passing as a minor businessman, took the coach to Calais, then a Danish boat, arriving in Dover in January 1798. A customs inspection there found that his case had a false bottom, filled with papers. After discussion, documents were furnished for him to travel to London. Flatteringly, he was at once summoned to William Pitt's country home at Holwood in Kent, where he reported on the situation in France and, indefatigably, pressed for support for Latin American independence. After that first dizzying interview Miranda returned to London, where he set about organizing his network of contacts and friends in South America and in Europe.

His experiences in France had changed him: there he had been taken seriously, performed spectacularly as a general and twice nearly lost his life. The dilettante had become a man of action, of stature, of determination. To his surprise, he was informed that his old mentor, Juan Manuel de Cajigal, had been acquitted of the charges against him, and that he himself was no longer regarded with suspicion by the Spanish authorities – he could return to his homeland. Miranda immediately assumed this to be a trick to lure him back and arrest him, now that (as he saw it) he had become a tangible threat. He redoubled his efforts to persuade the British to mount an expedition to invade Venezuela, but Pitt continued to prevaricate.

Miranda was furious that only £500 of what he thought was a promise by the British government of an annual stipend of £1,500 was paid: he considered he had been treated as a minor player. He wrote to Pitt, 'After this, I cannot but insist that you send me back the papers, plans and memoirs I entrusted to you. An honest person would consider it sacred to return such an archive when asked.' Miranda, while respectful, was intensely wary of the 'colonial' detachment of Pitt. The latter's opinion of this flamboyant adventurer was not confined to paper. At every stage, Miranda feared that Pitt was trying to outwit him, that he was insincere in his protestations of sympathy for his cause and that cold calculations of the British national interest were at his heart. Yet it remains amazing how much time the leader of what was then the world's superpower devoted to what must have seemed a florid man of high intelligence, an advocate of a far-fetched cause.

At 50 Miranda was a figure both sublime and ridiculous. The striking features showed signs of age, the piercing eyes were duller, the curly hair beginning to grey and recede. He was a man without country, job or title. His Russian partners had cut him off, the French had expelled him and the Spaniards hoped to lure him into imprisonment. The British were civil, but did nothing to help. His last hope seemed to be the Americans, for whom he had in the past shown such contempt. Yet he was at last a figure of real political and military stature.

Miranda was soon in contact with the intensely educated, resentful and exiled Jesuits of the Spanish empire. Jesús Clarijeros' *Ancient History of Mexico* was almost a call of arms against the Spaniards. Father Alegre pressed for directly elected democracy. The Jesuit Father Tomás greeted Miranda in Russia. The Peruvian Jesuit Juan Pablo Viscardo y Guzman was a plotter and polemicist who wrote the first genuinely pro-independence tract, 'A letter to Spanish Americans'.

Miranda made his home at 27 Grafton Way, a modestly comfortable mid-Georgian townhouse in Bloomsbury, which became a Mecca for South American exiles. The young Bernardo O'Higgins from Chile, the most distant part of the Spanish Empire, studied mathematics, politics and the humanities; the brilliant young Venezuelan Andrés Bello studied Greek; and other promising patriots were also taught there, men such as Antonio Nariño from Santa Fé de Bogotá.

Miranda's obsession was to launch a formal expedition to Venezuela, which he believed was ripe for revolution. Pitt had been replaced in 1801 by the more modest Henry Addington, whose chief adviser was Nicholas Vansittart, an enthusiast for Miranda's ideas. Miranda struck up a close friendship with, of all people, the Earl of St Vincent, as hard-headed and peppery a personality as has ever run the British navy. In August 1801, St Vincent agreed that a liberating army should leave from Portsmouth for the Caribbean, where it would be reinforced, then land near Coro and march on Valencia, while a second naval force would ravage the eastern coast between the Orinoco, Barcelona and La Guaira, throwing the Spanish off balance. After this the army would march across to New Granada, via Barinos in the southern foothills of the mountains, gaining access to the world's biggest and best tobacco plantations, yielding some 5 million pesos a year. Miranda's further fantastic plan was to hope that the British fleet in India would cross the Pacific to liberate Mexico and Peru.

However, Miranda became suspicious that the British wanted to colonize Latin America for themselves, in particular the orderly colony of Chile and the less orderly ones of the Plate (modern Argentina, Uruguay and Paraguay). In 1802 the Peace of Amiens between Britain, France, Spain and Holland once again dashed any hopes that Britain might help. The lull lasted only a year, however. Miranda warned the British that the French might launch their own invasion of Latin America – as they had intended to do, with Miranda as commander when he was serving France.

To Vansittart, Lord St Vincent, the first Lord of the Admiralty, and Admiral Home Popham he proposed a new blueprint for an independent South America: patriotic governments were to be set up, consisting of two executives in charge of justice and the police in each 'liberated' district advised by eight councillors. Eventually, when enough territory had been liberated, a federal government would be established headed by two 'Incas' – responsible citizens over 40 – one based in the capital, one who would tour the vast outback. They would be responsible to the 'Colombian Council', which would be elected on a franchise without racial bias but with a property qualification. A capital of the new state, to be called Christopher Columbus, would be built on the isthmus of Panama.

To this pipedream constitution was added an even more ambitious plan. An expeditionary force would be assembled on the island of Curaçao, off the Venezuelan coast, then landed in Coro: it would march upon San Felipe, Valencia and the Aragua Valley. Meanwhile, the British fleet based in Grenada and Trinidad would bombard Cumana and La Guaira. After taking Tenerife and Cartagena, further west, an attack would be made on the Viceroyalty of Santa Fé de Bogotá (modern Colombia), while another fleet would sail to Peru and Chile to seize those countries. It was to be an invasion of the whole Spanish Empire, based, with good reason, on sea power, which the British could provide. He brandished long lists of prominent citizens who, he said, would join the 'patriot' forces.

The British said a contingent of their soldiers would be necessary to accompany the insurgents on their march to Caracas, which alarmed Miranda; he had no wish to replace one colonial empire with another. The sizeable sum of £20,000 would have to be spent on the project, and Miranda was to be granted a handsome allowance of £500 a year to maintain himself.

It soon emerged that Addington, ever-cautious, was turning against the project. Desperately, Miranda came up with another, much more modest, proposal: in exchange for British military support and the use of 600 soldiers, plus transport ships, arms and ammunition, he promised 4,000 head of cattle and 1,000 mules in payment – to be obtained after a successful landing. He was working himself into a fever of expectation: reports came daily to the exiles that Caracas was ripe for insurrection. He believed also that he had the support of some prominent backers in the City of London. The Americans seemed about to go to war with France, and Miranda hoped also for their support.

At the beginning of 1804, however, the British government dropped a bombshell: there would be no strike against Spain's colonies as long as the two countries were at peace, since Britain's interest now lay in securing Spain's support against Napoleonic France. Miranda's rage exploded in a letter he wrote to Vansittart in March 1804; he threatened to leave the country – and, by implication, to join forces with Napoleon. By December fortune had begun to favour him once more, however: war was declared between Britain and Spain. He informed Pitt, now restored to office, that he was leaving for Trinidad. Pitt was cordial, but reminded him that he would have to submit himself to the authority of the British governor there, and then in January 1805 advised him to be patient 'because political affairs in Europe are not mature enough to begin the enterprise'. Miranda was incandescent with rage: for three years now his grand design had been stalled by the British government. Now that the British were at war with Spain, what were they waiting for?

It seems clear that the Foreign Office regarded Miranda as a card with which to threaten the Spanish, but to be played only *in extremis*. There was no official confidence that Miranda's invasion would succeed; and a botched land assault would endanger Britain's colonial possessions in the Caribbean. Moreover, Britain's local resources were limited. The priority had to be resisting the Spanish – and possibly the French as well – in European waters.

A new side to Miranda was revealed about this time. He made a trip to Scotland with a pretty English girl, Sarah Andrews; she returned pregnant, and was installed in Grafton Way as his 'housekeeper'. They lived as a couple and many thought them married, but Miranda insisted they were not; two children were born, Leandro and Francisco. The audacious lover had become a family man at last. As he prepared for his great adventure, Miranda drew up a will; his possessions in Venezuela were left to his family by Sarah, his voluminous papers to the city of Caracas, his possessions in London for the upkeep of his children, and his house to Sarah. His executors were his lifelong business friend, John Turnbull, and Nicholas Vansittart.

Chapter 7

THE 'INVASION' OF VENEZUELA

On 31 August 1805 Miranda set off, determined to secure American support for his expedition in place of Albion's perfidy. The autumn of 1805 witnessed some of the fiercest storms ever experienced in the North Atlantic, including the one which nearly wrecked the British fleet on its way back after the battle of Trafalgar. Miranda, crossing into the full force of the westerlies, described it in an understatement as a 'dog's journey' and 'the most unpleasing I ever experienced in my life'. His ship, the *Polly*, reached New York in November after a rough voyage of 67 days. Miranda's old friends Rufus King and Colonel Smith were on hand to meet him, and he was introduced to a businessman, Samuel Ogden, who expressed enthusiasm for the venture.

Miranda was received cordially enough by the Secretary of State, James Madison, and on 1 December he travelled to Washington D.C. to meet the President, Thomas Jefferson. America's policy was laid down at this meeting: he would be given no official help, but private individuals would be permitted to back him. Madison hinted that the prohibition on arms sales to the enemies of neutral states like Spain would not apply in Miranda's case. However, Jefferson and Madison's political opponents in the United States were quick to seize on this tacit support for Miranda's expedition as a pretext to attack the government, and the President prudently muted, but did not abandon, his support. Miranda took this as American approval. He was invited to a lunch in his honour as a guest of the President a week later. Shortly after Christmas he returned to New York, where Ogden had prepared the *Leander*, a brig of 190 tons named after Miranda's son, along with two smaller ships.

Miranda had received £2,000 from his London friends for the expedition, and had put up his 6,000 books as surety. With this money about 200 young men were recruited from the streets of New York with the offer of good pay and the prospect of making their fortunes in lands abundant with gold and silver. On a bright, breezy day, 2 February 1806, the little expedition set sail on choppy seas.

It was foolhardy to suppose that one ill-armed brig and two defenceless troop transports carrying 200 men from the streets of New York would make any impression on the military might of the Spanish empire when Miranda's own calculations suggested that the Spanish deployed about 35,000 trained and heavily armed men in New Granada alone. Miranda had no grounds for his belief that the empire was so rotten within that it would need only a small push for it to collapse. He had not set foot in Venezuela for three decades; his hopes were fed only by the feverish stories of exiles – he had no hard, first-hand evidence. Even more culpable were the Americans who gave the enterprise a tacit nod and a wink, and may indeed have subsidized the expedition.

The Spanish ambassador had precise information about Miranda's exploit, and protested angrily to the American government. The French also complained. Diplomatic relations between the United States and Spain were almost severed. Jefferson denied helping the venture, while the American press, on the whole, supported what they saw as a romantic expedition.

After the cold of New York the Caribbean was blissful – until the little convoy spied a British warship, which called upon it to heave to. Its commander saw that Miranda's papers were in order, however, and he was allowed to continue. The 200 recruits were divided into engineers, artillerymen, dragoons and infantrymen, given officers and uniforms, and taught, in the confines of their ships, how to handle weapons. On 12 March, Miranda hoisted his flag – white, red and yellow: in fact, it was an old Russian flag, some of whose white had been soiled to yellow by time. To the roll of drums the American hands learnt to chant, in Spanish, 'Death to tyranny! Long live liberty!'

Aboard the 'invasion' force was a motley assortment of exiles from Caracas, a few Americans such as Colonel Kirkland and Commander Powell, a French aristocrat, the Comte de Rouvray, a couple of

Englishmen and a few Austrians and Poles. Most of the crew and prospective invaders were jobless American flotsam recruited from the New York waterfront, but the expedition had aboard its own butcher, one John Fink, carving fine Virginia hams, and its own baker.

The strangest figure was the expedition's 56-year-old leader, Francisco de Miranda, in a magnificent Ruritanian self-designed uniform, a man of almost overwhelming pomp, haughtiness and superciliousness, his fine head, brow and powdered hair turned upwards like those of a king gazing down upon his subjects. One of those aboard described him:

He is about five feet ten inches high. His limbs are well proportioned; his whole frame is stout and active. His complexion is dark, florid and healthy. His eyes are hazel coloured, but not of the darkest hue. They are piercing, quick and intelligent, expressing more of the severe than the mild feelings. He has good teeth, which he takes much care to keep clean. His nose is large and handsome, rather of the English than Roman cast.

His chest is square and prominent. His hair is grey and he wears it tied long behind with powder. He has strong grey whiskers growing on the outer edges of his ears, as large as most Spaniards have on their cheeks. In the contour of his visage you plainly perceive an expression of pertinaciousness and suspicion. Upon the whole without saying he is an elegant, we may pronounce him a handsome man.

He has a constant habit of picking his teeth. When sitting he is never perfectly still; his foot or hand must be moving to keep time with his mind which is always in exercise. He always sleeps a few moments after dinner, and then walks till bed time, which with him is about midnight. He is an eminent example of temperance. A scanty or bad meal is never regarded by him as a subject of complaint. He uses no ardent spirits; seldom any wine. Sweetened water is his common beverage.

He is a courtier and gentleman in his manners. Dignity and grace preside in his movements. Unless when angry, he has a great command of his feelings; and can assume what looks and tones he pleases. In general his demeanour is marked by hauteur and distance. When he is angry he loses discretion. He is impatient of contradiction. In discourse he is logical in the management of his thoughts. He appears conversant on all subjects. His iron memory prevents his ever being at a loss for names, dates and authorities . . . He appeared the master of languages, of science and literature . . . Modern history and geography afforded him abundant topics. He impressed an opinion of his comprehensive views, his inexhaustible fund of learning; his probity, his generosity and patriotism. Yet this man of renown, I fear, must be considered as having more learning than wisdom; more theoretical knowledge than practical talent; too sanguine and too opinionated to distinguish between the vigour of enterprise and the hardiness of infatuation.

Miranda would wear a fine red bathrobe as he went to bathe in a humble barrel on board ship every morning, for all the world as though still frequenting the salons of London and Paris. Another passenger described the day-to-day scene on the nearly three-month journey:

One side of the quarter deck is occupied by a printing press, at which several young men of that profession are busy in striking off the general's proclamations to the people of South America, and setting the types for printing our commissions. The other side is taken up with two groups of Mars's youngest sons, employed with military books; some studying, some reading, and others looking at the pictures.

　His excellency is at the head of one of these parties, philosophising on various subjects, and passing from one to another with his peculiar volubility. At this moment he is painting the dangers of a military life . . . I am sorry to find he loves dearly to talk of himself; I believe that vanity and egotism, which are qualities destitute of any recommendation whatever, are generally associated with other traits that have no claim to approbation. I must confess too, that he appears not a little tinctured with pedantry . . .

　Next is seen the armourer's bench, with all his apparatus for repairing old muskets, pointless bayonets and rusty swords. This

tinker has his hands full, as our arms are none of the best, and seem
to have been already condemned in some other service. Whoever
purchased them for the expedition was either no judge of arms,
or he has been kinder to himself than his employer . . . A few feet
from the place where I am now writing is a noisy set of animals
called volunteers, going through manual exercise under the direction of a drill sergeant, who looks as bold as a lion, and roars nearly
as loud.

The voyage had been beset by the usual delays and petty quarrels
of cramped shipboard life. The captain, an American named Tom
Lewis (and his hot-tempered younger brother James, who had set off
in advance aboard another ship, the *Emperor*), detested the equally
hot-tempered Colonel William Armstrong, who was in day-to-day
charge of the 'troops' – raw recruits being given rudimentary drill-
ing as engineers, artillerymen, cavalrymen and infantry. Each man
aboard had to swear a pantomime oath: 'I swear to be faithful to the
free South American people, independent of Spain, to serve them
honestly and rally against their enemies and opponents and observe
and obey the supreme government of this country as legally constituted and the orders of the general [Miranda] and my superb officers.'

They harboured in Haiti, the liberated 'slave republic' which had
now degenerated into civil war between feuding warlords including,
among others, the Duke of Marmalade and Duke of Lemonade. Just
ahead of them was James Lewis in the *Emperor*, which he then refused
to allow to join the expedition, having prepared no supplies. Miranda
had to acquire two frail, sluggish troop transports, the *Bacchus* and the
Bee.

Miranda, a veteran general, tried to impose military discipline
upon his crew in the disease-ridden port of Jacmel, through flog-
ging and putting men in irons in the hold, which aroused mutterings
as to what kind of liberator he was and caused some to desert into
the arms of the waiting women of the port. The expedition wasted
five precious weeks in the harbour re-equipping – which permitted
Spanish spies to make a dash for the coast of South America and alert
the authorities as to this imminent, pathetic 'invasion'.

*   *   *

On 28 March 1806 three ships of the flotilla – the *Leander, Bacchus* and *Bee* – left Haiti for the island of Bonaire towards the entrance of the Gulf of Venezuela, but got lost and ended up on the tiny islet of Aruba, where fresh water was taken aboard. They made for Ocumare, near Puerto Cabello, and attempted a landing at night, but were intercepted by two Spanish coastguard gunboats, the *Argos* and *Celoso*, which opened fire and attempted to drive the little flotilla within range of the guns of Puerto Cabello. The *Leander* became separated from the *Bacchus* and the *Bee*, and although it returned fire, it was unable to come to the rescue of the two smaller boats. Captain Tom Lewis later attracted abuse for his 'cowardice' in steering the *Leander* back out to sea. The two little boats surrendered and their crews were captured before they were sunk.

The vengeance of the Spanish empire was implacable. Ten of those captured, including four British, three Americans, a Portuguese and a Pole, were publicly hanged in the main square of Puerto Cabello; the rest, including the butcher Fink, were left to rot in wretched prison cells. A torrent of propaganda was unleashed against Miranda on the mainland: he was denounced as an atheist, the new Beelzebub, a rebel against his king, a servant of the devil, a traitor working for the British and a convert to Lutheranism. In fact this outpouring had the effect of vastly magnifying his importance in a skirmish off the Venezuelan coast that would have barely been noticed otherwise.

In a fit of hysteria, immediately after the debacle, the celebrated revolutionary general threatened to throw himself off the ship. Captain Lewis had him arrested and taken below for his safety. The *Leander* spent the next six days dodging Spanish ships, and Miranda's supporters feared Lewis was plotting to hand him over to the Spaniards. But the first ship to encounter this sorry boatload of desperadoes was English, the *Lily*, and it seems she was just in time to forestall a mutiny by the furious young soldiers and sailors of fortune whose friends had been so cruelly abandoned to their fates. Her captain, Donald Campbell, was able to inform Miranda that William Pitt, who had become first minister again in 1804, had died, to be succeeded by his first cousin, Lord Grenville. An old friend of Miranda's, Nicholas Vansittart, had become Chancellor of the Exchequer in Grenville's Ministry of All the Talents.

The *Lily* escorted the *Leander* to Grenada, then to Barbados, where Miranda met Admiral Sir Alexander Cochrane (uncle of the future commander of the Chilean navy). It was a stroke of luck for Miranda, defeated and suicidal as he felt, to encounter a Briton reasonably sympathetic to his cause. The old charmer persuaded Cochrane that he needed help, and that the British would reap huge commercial rewards by overthrowing the Spanish. Cochrane promptly wrote to London demanding 5,000 men, while Miranda wrote to Vansittart begging for help. Much heartened, Miranda's flotilla proceeded to Trinidad, accompanied by two British vessels, the *Express* and the *Trimmer*, and there he was welcomed warmly by the British governor, Thomas Hislop.

Miranda was far from unknown: a disciple of his, Pedro José Caro, had been sent out in 1797 to scout the island and the Caribbean. The then governor, Thomas Picton (later one of Wellington's most outstanding generals, killed at Waterloo), had immediately put Caro in jail, although he did occasionally have him to dinner. Caro soon came to understand that Venezuela was far from promising as a breeding-ground for revolt: 'The Venezuelans have no concentrated plan. They do not work with foresight. They are better prepared to change their masters than to become free. They believe that it is the same to acclaim independence as to be independent, and that independence will be accomplished simply by rejecting the yoke of Spain and placing themselves under the protection of some other nation.'

Picton was unimpressed, either by Caro or by what he heard of his master Miranda. Yet Trinidad itself, so close to Venezuela, was under constant threat of attack from Spain, and Picton seems to have thought it useful to keep alive the threat of retaliation. A brutal but able administrator, described by Wellington as 'as rough, foul-mouthed a fellow as ever lived', he kept a constant watch on events in Venezuela from his offshore base; he had been widely condemned in 1799 for offering to help José de España, the Venezuelan plantation owner who staged an uprising with 5,000 men, and then failing to do so. Eventually Picton had Caro expelled from the island. Manuel Gual, an old friend of Miranda's, lingered on there as his agent until he was mysteriously poisoned, possibly by Spanish agents, possibly by Picton himself.

*   *   *

Governor Hislop, a more moderate man who had succeeded the controversial Picton, lodged Miranda in Government House, grandly named but in poor repair. Under Cochrane's prompting Hislop became genuinely intrigued by the extraordinary personality of Miranda, offering him 500 local recruits to help him in his cause. On 1 August 1806, the invasion was set for a second time, far more plausibly, with 15 small boats and those 500 volunteers. The Comte de Rouvray and two British officers, Colonel Downie and Lieutenant Bedingfield, were seconded as Miranda's commanders.

Miranda's target this time was Coro, a town on the Venezuelan mainland further to the west, and its port of La Vela, which he supposed was ready to join his revolution. He arrived at the height of the rainy season, with thick clouds enveloping the mountain range just inland, rendering the trails across them almost impassable. The fleet arrived in the middle of a raging storm: it took three days before they could anchor opposite the enormous sand dunes along that stretch of coast. But this much more formidable force alarmed the local inhabitants, and the site was well away from Spanish military strongholds.

They landed on the Venezuelan coast at three in the morning. Pounding surf on the beach delayed the landing but they had the advantage of surprise, and fell upon a contingent of Spanish troops, spiking their guns. Soon the Spanish were forced out of the port of Coro and Miranda's troops were pursuing them up the streets of the main town; by the time their leader arrived, the Spaniards had abandoned it. Miranda proclaimed the territory liberated and had his flag hoisted: he had conquered a corner of Spanish America.

The garrison had fled to the neighbouring hills, but the invaders found few sympathizers in the town and no provisions. One of Miranda's aides was shot beside him. After a few days he withdrew to the more easily defended port. He issued proclamations and appeals to Venezuelans to join him, set up a provisional government, and declared that all those between the ages of 16 and 44 must join up. His 'Colombian' citizens were instructed to wear French revolutionary-style cockades in their hats. But few rallied to his cause: so long away in Europe, he could not have known that Coro was a stronghold of royalist sentiment.

The British sent no more help – Grenville's government in fact disapproved of the pact between Miranda, Cochrane and Hislop. Meanwhile, the Spanish were assembling a formidable force of 1,500 opposite the town. Another 4,000 were said to be approaching. Captain Johnson, who had replaced Lewis at the helm of the *Leander*, and six of his sailors were taken prisoner in an ambush. The position began to look desperate.

On 13 August the decision was taken to re-embark, in another raging storm, and the expedition took refuge on the offshore island of Aruba, ready for yet another attempt. There they stayed until Cochrane told them to return to Trinidad, threatening to withdraw all British aid unless they did so. On 22 September Miranda, perverse and indignant as ever, sailed instead for Grenada, his men hungry and mutinous, and then on to Barbados. Only when British support was indeed withdrawn did Miranda finally abandon hope and return as instructed to Trinidad. He despatched de Rouvray to London to argue the case for continued aid, but in vain. His only real success had been in alarming the Spanish, who denounced him as a thug and a traitor, claiming that he intended to free the slaves in Venezuela and that he was a foreign agent. This had the reverse effect, immensely boosting the prestige on the mainland of this largely unknown revolutionary. The Spanish authorities in Venezuela sought reinforcements from Spain.

In fading hope Miranda lingered on in Trinidad for a year, hard-pressed by the creditors who had financed his expedition, which appeared to have been a complete failure. His faithful British friend John Turnbull told him that his house in Grafton Way, London, might have to be sold and his mistress, Sarah, and their two children turned out. She wrote him pathetic letters: 'My dear Leander has been scribbling this hour to his papa, and telling him he will not tease brother so much, that he will learn his book, but he fonder of his hoop and his top, we have had a fair in the road, he has bough[t] a gun, a sword and drum, so that you can hardly hear one another speak, these are his happiest days my dear Sir.' Miranda wrote to the British requesting 4,000 troops for an invasion; they refused. It was not until November 1807 that he gave in and set sail for Portsmouth to argue his case personally.

The second setback had been much worse than the first, for it suggested that the cause of independence from Spain had virtually no popular support. Just two runaway slaves and an accused criminal – a woman accused of murder – joined Miranda's tiny army in Coro. Moreover, Miranda had shown a seemingly remarkable lack of courage – he would have called it realism – in failing to march inland from the abandoned city in order to try to rally support, perhaps fearing he would simply be picked off by the royal forces being hastily assembled, and that the mountain trails were impassable in the rain (but this equally would hamper the royalists). He may have feared he would lose face by acquiring no support. This time he had had arms, men and proper boats as well as the barely covert backing of a superpower. Yet no popular uprising had occurred or even begun to do so. The spark of revolution had failed to ignite the sodden countryside.

Miranda returned to London in 1808 to a surprisingly warm welcome for a man who had presided over a fiasco and then a failure. The political theorist Edmund Burke had published a tract in 1807, *South American Independence and Achievable Reasons for our Increasingly Emancipating Latin America*, arguing that the continent had in effect become a vassal of Napoleon – whom he hated – and that it could provide a major source of commerce to bypass French naval blockades in imports of sugar and tobacco to besieged Britain. Miranda became flavour of the month once again, being received by the Prince of Wales' brothers, the Dukes of Gloucester and Clarence. The foreign secretary, George Canning, received him; the prime minister, Lord Castlereagh met him in Downing Street the following day. His adoring mistress and two small children had to compete for his attention.

Indeed, he was something of a popular hero. *The Times*, while faintly deriding his objectives, suggested that Miranda had won the confidence of the South American people and the British government. Miranda had, it seems, turned his reverses into what today would be called a public relations triumph. In Venezuela he had been puffed up by the authorities into a greater danger then he actually represented; in London his quixotic tilting against the Spanish empire had captured the popular imagination.

To Miranda's excitement, Sir Arthur Wellesley, the general to watch among Britain's senior military establishment, invited him to call. In preparation for this visit, he came up with his most ambitious plan yet for the liberation of Latin America: this time at least 10,000 men would be needed, based on the islands of Granada and Tortuga, to land at La Guaira itself. The British fleet, meanwhile, would take the fortified harbour of Puerto Cabello. Miranda's fevered calculations called for 6,000 infantry, 2,000 cavalry, 2,000 black soldiers, 300 artillerymen, 30,000 muskets, 2,000 pairs of pistols, 50,000 lances and 4,000 swords. Wellesley was surprisingly sympathetic to these extravagant demands.

To Miranda it seemed that at last the British really had decided to back him. A military expedition began to be assembled at Cork, in southern Ireland. Miranda's only serious fear was that the British might be intending to replace the Spanish empire with their own: the unauthorized invasion of Buenos Aires by Popham and Whitelocke's disastrous expedition suggested this. But the British had disassociated themselves from Popham's actions and court-martialled Whitelocke; now they only wanted access to South American markets, or so they said. At last, Miranda's lifelong dream seemed on the verge of being realized. He could not know that Wellesley, having initially fallen in with the idea of a landing in Venezuela, had since concluded that Veracruz in Mexico would provide a better bridgehead for attacking the Spanish empire.

But then developments in the Iberian Peninsula changed everything. The Tumult of Aranjuez and the events of the Dos de Mayo resulted in Wellesley's invasion army being diverted from the Spanish colonies to Portugal to help the forces resisting Napoleon. The war between Britain and Spain was deemed at an end: now they were allies against the French. Miranda was to be offered a senior post in Wellesley's Iberian expedition, by way of compensation.

Given the task of informing Miranda of this turn of events, Wellesley decided to take the irascible Venezuelan for a walk. As anticipated, Miranda exploded in fury and stood shouting at him in the street. Sir Arthur chose to distance himself, so as not to draw the attention of passers-by. Once Miranda's fury had subsided a little, he caught up with Wellesley. 'You go to Spain,' he told him. 'You will lose. No-one will save you. That's your problem. What maddens me is that no better opportunity ever presented itself.'

Miranda refused to serve in the expeditionary force; his enmity towards Spain as regards her colonies was unalterable, and in any case he did not want to fight former French comrades-in-arms. That same month he wrote to his old friend the Marqués del Toro: 'civil war rages in Spain and there is no solution. France and Britain are fighting over the peninsula which, probably, will be captured by the first. We must avoid getting involved in this conflict and permitting the Colombian continent [South America] being sucked into the calamities of war. Let us not take part in the quarrel, but take advantage of it to free ourselves from foreigners.'

Miranda's supporter Edmund Burke fired off an angry broadside:

> The expedition actually preparing to co-operate in the emancipation of South America has its destination changed; and is now to be sent with all speed to the shores of Old Spain. I should be exceedingly sorry to find we thus risked certain and important advantages, for what are extremely dubious gains; and that we hazarded by delay the present opportunity – rendered so peculiarly favourable, by the events taking place in Spain, for successfully offering emancipation to Spanish America – events which, it is not improbable, the people of that country will seize for asserting their independence themselves.

At first Miranda's and Burke's pessimism seemed justified. Wellesley arrived in Portugal in July 1808; Napoleon entered Madrid in triumph in December. Meanwhile, as discussed in the next chapter, Napoleon's envoys had arrived in Caracas to take formal control of the colony and supplant the governor, Juan de las Casas. In a public café they were insulted openly and aggressively. De las Casas warned that he could not guarantee their safety. When a mob rioted, the French envoys slipped away just in time – on a British ship. Englishmen in Caracas were cheered for opposing Napoleon. All Venezuelans – royalists and independence agitators alike – were united in their hatred of the French. As Miranda had argued, in spite of his disappointment at the cancellation of Wellesley's expedition, events were beginning to play into the patriots' hands: Venezuelans, in casting off the hand of the French government in Madrid, established the precedent of self-rule – even though most remained loyal to the Spanish crown.

Spain, Britain's new ally, deemed Miranda 'a revolutionary who has become famous only for betraying his king and country' and demanded that he be extradited. A junior foreign office official was despatched to instruct Miranda to stop communicating with sympathizers in Venezuela, on pain of being expelled from Britain. Miranda ignored this and kept up a steady correspondence with his adherents, not just in Venezuela but elsewhere in southern South America. The visitors to Grafton Way became less frequent, more circumspect. As the Spanish continued to press for his extradition, Castlereagh and Vansittart came to Miranda's defence. Back from Portugal, Wellesley had a long conversation with him and promised that once the war in Spain was over, liberation of the colonies would be next – yet another British promise to be cruelly broken.

Chapter 8

¡ INDEPENDENCIA!

We left Simón Bolívar an immensely wealthy, discontented young widower tending his estates in Venezuela. When Napoleon Bonaparte deposed the Spanish monarchy in 1808, in the blink of an eye it became patriotic and pro-Spanish to reject the dictates of the new foreign masters in Madrid, now under enemy occupation. On 15 January 1808, an emissary from the Spanish Council of the Indies – the body that administered the colonies on Spain's behalf, which now reflected the dictates of the French – arrived in Caracas. This official pompously demanded recognition of Joseph Bonaparte as King of Spain and Prince Murat as lieutenant-general of the kingdom.

The once peaceful and sleepy city in its mountain bowl erupted: mobs roamed the streets swearing allegiance to Ferdinand VII of Spain. Priests denounced Napoleon's 'heretical proclamations'. The American-born leaders seized the initiative and decided to create a supreme council (junta) of Caracas representing the dominant classes to replace the discarded French-controlled colonial authority. Juan de las Casas, the Captain-General of Venezuela, and its ruler until then, saw that he had no choice but to accept.

Within a day news reached Venezuela that the Spanish king's former loyalists had set up a provisional government in the Spanish city of Seville; de las Casas, regaining confidence, promptly announced the dissolution of the Caracas junta and announced the setting up of an inquisition against 'traitors to Spain and the monarchy'. He at least understood that the goal of some people was nothing less than full independence. In particular, leaflets had been distributed from Miranda to his followers announcing the setting up of a 'representative municipal governments which would send envoys to London to establish the security and future of the new world'. The uprising was for the time being over: de las Casas knew that the creation of such an assembly was the forerunner for independence for the homeland, however much its protagonists protested their loyalty to the king and opposition to the French.

Bolívar formed a driving group, with a small group of aristocratic Venezuelans – his brother Juan Vicente, the Marqués del Toro and his family, his uncle Felix Ribas (not so much older than Bolívar because his mother had married at a young age), and Tomás and Mariano Montilla, as well as his old tutor Andrés Bello, who at the time was the right-hand-man of the governor of Venezuela. Bolívar's group would meet in the evening at El Palmito, one of his properties on the banks of the River Guaire.

When the conciliatory Field Marshal Vicente de Emparán arrived from Spain to become the country's governor, Bolívar grew bolder and at a banquet attended by the new governor toasted the freedom of Spain and all America.

The authorities tried gently to persuade Bolívar to moderate his opinions, but the angry young man said he had declared war on Spain and would not go back. Bolívar's brother-in-law, Fernando, Marqués del Toro, was appointed inspector general of the militia, and the conspirators were able to learn from him the government's military intentions. The conspirators planned to raid the Aragua barracks on 19 April 1810, but Emparan learnt of the plot and exiled them, including Bolívar, to their country estates.

On 17 April 1810, word reached Caracas that Seville and most of Andalusia had been occupied; in addition the provisional government had been overthrown by the French. Caracas exploded into mutiny once again: the leaders of the American-born party gathered at the home of José Angel Alamo, and planned a mass uprising.

Two days after the arrival of the news, on the morning of 19 April, the new Captain-General, Emparán, went to meet the existing Spanish-appointed council, where he was met by angry demonstrations in the streets. Retreating with as much dignity as he could muster, he resolved he was not opposed to the establishment of a native-run council, as long as it gained the approval of the Council of Regency, which had been set up by the short-lived provisional government in Seville. He then suspended the sitting and set off for Caracas cathedral to take part in the ceremonies for the Thursday before Easter.

However, he was seized by Francisco Salinas, one of the conspirators, and ordered back to the council chamber. The chief of the Spanish commander's bodyguard did nothing to stop this outrage to the established order and the discomfited captain-general returned to the building, where other prominent citizens had gathered. They proposed restoring the junta of criollo councillors and giving its titular leadership to Emparán as representative of the Spanish crown.

But not everyone was in accord: one of the most radical criollo leaders, Canon José Cortés de Madariaga, a rabid preacher and friend of Miranda, rose and accused Emparán of perfidy, intrigue and deceit, and pronounced him stripped of all authority. Emparan, reddening with anger, declared that he would resign if he was not welcome, and strode out on the balcony of the city hall to ask the crowd outside if it supported him. Cortés de Madariaga had his supporters well-placed in the throng and orchestrated a cry of 'No! No! No!' The official promptly resigned, and Spanish authority in Venezuela was at an end. A revolution had occurred.

The new council promptly went into session. It was decided that Emparan should be sent back to Spain; export tariffs were removed; non-Spanish goods were no longer to be punitively taxed on entry to Spain; primary produce and food were exempted from taxes; Indians were absolved from paying tribute and slavery was prohibited.

The Venezuelan revolt was quickly followed by an uprising in Buenos Aires on 25 May, and a revolt against the Viceroy of Bogotá, capital of New Granada on 20 July. Chile and Mexico soon followed. The revolutionaries, far from being the poor and dispossessed, were the old colonial aristocracy. It was a patrician, not a popular, revolt.

It was also decided that envoys should be despatched to seek support from Britain and the United States. Simón Bolívar, young, impetuous and disliked for his recklessness, extravagance and womanizing, offered to pay for the costs of the delegation to London and was appointed its nominal leader alongside two other men, Luis López

Méndez and Andrés Bello. The mission arrived in Portsmouth on 10 July 1810. Bolívar and his party were met by foreign office officials who accompanied them to Martin's Hotel the same day. A week later the three Venezuelans were offered a meeting with the foreign secretary, Lord Wellesley, elder brother of Arthur, who was making his name in the Peninsular campaigns.

However, the meeting was not to take place in the Foreign Office, but in his private residence, Apsley House, an elegant mansion on the corner of Hyde Park. Bolívar was furious as he understood the significance of the snub: the British were hedging their bets. An invitation to the Foreign Office would have conferred a mark of recognition on the new Venezuelan government. The British, while welcoming the Venezuelan revolution as a setback for the French, were anxious not to upset their allies in the Spanish government of resistance. It was also clear that Lord Wellesley harboured doubts about how long the rebellion could last.

As the young Bolívar ascended the steps of Apsley House in his unaccustomed new official role to meet one of the most experienced statesmen of one of the world's greatest powers, he was nervous and insecure. Ushered upstairs into Wellesley's private office, he was greeted by an imperturbable figure with a courteous smile. On being invited to state his case, he described what had happened in Caracas and stated that he and his government were all still loyal to the Spanish cause. Bello added that the circumstances in Caracas were extraordinary, and the uprising there was 'purely provincial and calculated to preserve the province's liberty from any external threat . . . one of the primary aims of the revolution in Caracas was to retain the territorial integrity of Venezuela for the monarch and protect them from the intrigues and seductions of the French'. Wellesley argued hard that they must display their loyalty to the Spanish crown through concrete action. Bolívar argued that the Spanish colonies should exercise self-government.

Wellesley dryly retorted that Venezuela's declaration of independence was an act without precedent in the annals of Spain and its colonies. Bolívar angrily shot back that the American people should not be deprived of the right to defend their essential interests, that a 'new order' was required and that no one could understand better than Wellesley the vices of Spanish colonial administration. In effect, though, he was conceding Wellesley's point that independence, rather than obedience to Spain, was Venezuela's ultimate aim. The British foreign secretary smiled, and congratulated Bolívar for the passion with which he was defending his country's cause. Bolívar sarcastically congratulated the Englishman for defending Spain's interests so vigorously, whereupon Wellesley went on the defensive, saying that the British had tried to recognize the claims of Spain's colonies to their nationhood. He ended the interview, and agreed to see them again two days later.

On this second occasion he greeted the Venezuelans with the demand that they should end their dispute with the Spanish crown, in view of the close relations Britain enjoyed with the exiled monarchy. In exchange he would offer them some military aid against France, and would try to urge the Spanish crown not to take action against Venezuela.

However, the British would not offer recognition to the Venezuelan junta, for fear that if Spain's other colonies revolted, the Spanish crown would have to re-route resources necessary for the continued struggle against the French. Bolívar emerged deeply cynical about the British attitude. In January 1810, Britain had offered to help Spain militarily provided that its colonies were opened up to British commerce. Now the threat of helping the rebellious Venezuelans would be used to ensure that the Spaniards stuck to their agreement.

Bolívar nevertheless continued to pursue his case with vehemence, but also with good humour. And it was soon Spain's turn to over-play its hand. The Spanish ambassador in London protested at the British government's cordial reception of the 'Venezuelan separatists'. Wellesley invited the Venezuelans and Spaniards to meet to resolve their differences and unite against Napoleon. The Spanish ambassador at the last moment refused to attend, and the Venezuelans promptly followed suit.

Bolívar and his companions had overstayed their official welcome and had lodged on camp beds in Miranda's London house. On 30 August they decided to leave, having failed to secure British backing. Bolívar's conduct of the mission had however won him new respect among his countrymen when he arrived in Caracas in November

1810. Yet as Bolívar planned his journey back, he was determined to persuade Miranda to return – but on another ship, for fear of associating the celebrated revolutionary too closely with the new Venezuelan government.

Bolívar knew that he needed to persuade his colleagues that the 'dangerous' Miranda should be readmitted. Setting up the 'Sociedad Patriótica' – Patrotic Society of Agriculture and Economy – he used this as a kind of platform for the more radical views espoused by younger criollos like himself. Whipping up a popular demand for Miranda to be admitted, Bolívar succeeded in persuading the moderate junta not to refuse him entry when he arrived a month later. His return on 11 December 1810 was tumultuous. Years after leaving his homeland, its most controversial son was back – aloof, imperious, greying, well-built, a revolutionary become elder statesman. As the ship docked in the tropical port of La Guaira, Simón Bolívar was there to greet his hero: thousands were present at the dockside.

Miranda believed he had returned to his homeland to take up the reins of an independent country. One of his companions observed on the tortuous journey by carriage up from the port into the central highlands that Miranda spoke 'ill of the United States and in the crossing of the Venta river and many other places suggested they needed improvements or repairs and said he would carry them out as if he had the tiller of the new Republic of Venezuela in his hands'. Miranda's long years in London, at the heart of an increasingly out-of-touch Venezuelan community, had gone to his head. Yet his welcome was fulsome: his carriage was surrounded and pulled by an enormous crowd as it reached Caracas. Huge banquets were held in his favour and he received the toasts in his honour without a word in reply, without raising his glass, but simply smiling benevolently, like a king with his subjects. He soon gained jealous rebukes: 'He behaved as though all were inferior to his merit. The expressions which usually suggest good education, modesty and decency never came out of his mouth.'

It was soon made clear that neither he nor his young henchman, Bolívar, were in charge yet. Miranda was venomously opposed by many vested interests and only just secured a seat in the assembly as a representative for Pao, a tiny constituency in the llanos. In February he was appointed a lieutenant-general by the government of Caracas. When the country's new Congress met during the following month, Miranda was dismayed when it chose its 'executive power'; he himself polled insufficient votes, which dented his vanity and caused him to declare, with an edge, 'I am happy that there are more convenient people than myself to exercise supreme power'. The majority of delegates from the criollo upper classes feared Miranda's alleged radicalism and possible Spanish retaliation if he was chosen. The assembly immediately divided down the middle on the issue of whether to proceed to full independence.

Bolívar was no more than a minor member of Congress and represented the Patriotic Society, which pressed with vigour for outright independence. When, angrily, Congress denounced the society for trying to set itself up as an alternative assembly, Bolívar seized his chance to deliver a powerful and extremist speech:

It is not that there are two congresses . . . They say in congress that there must be a confederation. As if we were not all confederated against an external tyranny! What does it matter if Spain sells Bonaparte its slaves, or keeps them, if we are resolved to be free? These deals are the sad effects of old chains. It is said that great enterprises must be prepared calmly. Are not 300 years of calm enough? Do we need another 300 years?

To shouts of approval, Bolívar went on, 'the Patriotic Society respects, as it must, the nation's congress; but congress must listen to the Patriotic Society, centre of light and of all revolutionary interests. Let us lay down the cornerstones of South America's freedom. To vacillate is to yield!' On 5 July 1811, pressured from below by Bolívar's young radicals, congress passed the act of Venezuelan independence.

From the moment it was formed, the new state degenerated into chaos and confrontation. A bitter row broke out over whether it should be federal – decentralized to the scattering of cities and rural communities that made up Venezuela – or unitary – a single government run from Caracas. With each little town demanding virtual self-government, Miranda and the Patriotic Society pressed furiously in Congress for a centralized state. The two were bitterly attacked, Miranda as a 'foreigner' in the pay of Britain and Bolívar as a 'Caracan'. They were defeated. In December 1811, the new constitution advocated internal self-government to each city.

There was further danger when an insurrection broke out in the city of Valencia, some 60 miles from the capital, against the new government; local Spaniards allied to 'black followers' declared themselves for Ferdinand VII. The counter-revolution was under way and the royalists mustered their troops. A government force sent out from Caracas was defeated, and Congress started to panic. Eventually they turned in desperation to Miranda, the only competent and experienced general among the rebels, who was nominated generalissimo to subdue the rebels.

Gripped by a strange mixture of pessimism and vainglory, Miranda assembled an army of 4,000 poorly trained and badly armed peasants all marching out of step. He disdainfully asked his aides where were the armies which a general of his prestige 'could bring to the battle without compromising my dignity'. At this stage an extraordinary thing happened: Miranda, who had been persuaded to return and set himself up as the revolution's leading figure by Bolívar, suddenly turned on his young ally, who sought to serve under his command, denouncing him as a 'dangerous and uncontrolled young man'.

Bolívar was furious, and in turn denounced his hero as 'a tired-out old soldier who did not know Venezuela as a nation nor a social entity. He is a pretentious person, of insatiable vanity. Dangerous youth, indeed! He calls me that because I dare to oppose his erroneous policies!'

Miranda's sudden change may have been the result of pressure from congressional conservatives, a price paid for his being given supreme command of the army. Bolívar instead secured a post in the service of the Marqués del Toro, Miranda's second-in-command and an old aristocratic ally, and at the late age of 29 the wordy hothead at last saw military action – something his enemies believed would break him.

When the Venezuelan forces reached the hills of El Morro outside Valencia, they were ambushed. Royalist troops opened fire from behind rocks on one side and from boats hidden in the tall reeds of the huge Lake Valencia on the other. The troops at the front fell back in confusion. Bolívar spurred them forward, yelling and waving his sword in one hand and pistol in the other. On his first engagement he showed bravery and ferocity.

After a furious fight, the royalists withdrew to the city, and Miranda ordered his troops forward to take it. Once again the rebels were ambushed, and he and Bolívar were forced to retreat amidst horrendous carnage: 800 of the patriot soldiers had been killed and 1,500 wounded. Bolívar's friend, Fernando del Toro, the marqués' son, lost his leg in the fighting. Miranda then drew up cannon to lay siege to the city.

In August, outnumbered, outgunned and likely to be starved, the royalist garrison in Valencia finally surrendered. It had been the first major battle of the Latin American wars of independence, and won by the patriots only through superior numbers and cannon. But it was heartening all the same.

A curious episode followed: Miranda publicly berated Bolívar for indiscipline at a parade after the battle. There could be little doubt that the older man was intensely jealous of the younger – although their cause was the same. Again, Miranda may have been trying to reassure his new conservative allies. For his part, Bolívar suffered the slights in silence; he still partly believed in the legend of Miranda. The general, however, failed to follow up on his victory, returning to Caracas rather than marching to support the embattled patriots in the towns of Coro and Maracaibo to the east.

When the new constitution was promulgated in December 1811, it enshrined federalism, liberty, equality, abolished all distinctions between races and guaranteed property and freedom of the press. It also stripped the clergy of many of its privileges, even though the liberal clergy had been instrumental in bringing about Venezuelan independence. The constitution reflected a compromise between the self-interest of the criollo upper class, which wanted to govern itself, and the genuine liberals, who sought equality between the races. But Miranda was unimpressed by the impossibility of a constitution which dispersed power to the provinces: 'It is not adapted to the population, habits and customs of the states, and may result, not in uniting us in one consolidated group or social body, but in dividing us, jeopardizing our common security and our independence. I enter these observations in fulfilment of my duty.'

The new country shakily entered the year 1812, under blockade from the Spaniards, its economy in ruins with large areas going uncultivated, its trade badly damaged, and a government at odds with itself and no longer in control of a large part of the country.

On 26 March 1812, the Thursday before Easter – the same feast-day on which Captain-General Emparán had been deposed two years before – providence joined forces with the royalists to deliver the cruellest blow of all. At four in the afternoon of a peaceful and pleasant early spring day, a terrifying roar shattered the calm. Houses shook as an earthquake thundered beneath them and Caracas, Mérida, Maracaibo, Barquisimeto, Trujillo and San Carlos were left in ruins.

Bolívar was awoken from his siesta:

certain that I would find no more than a sad pile of ruins ... I immediately set about trying to save the victims, kneeling and working towards those places where groans and cries of help were coming from. I was engaged upon this task when I saw the pro-Spanish José Domingo Diaz, who looked at me and commented with his usual scorn, 'How goes it, Bolívar? It seems that Nature has put itself on the side of the Spaniards.' 'If Nature is against us, we will fight it and make it obey us,' I replied furiously.

Some 10,000 had been killed in Caracas alone, where the mud houses had fallen in upon themselves. A whole regiment of 1,500 patriots had fallen into a fissure at Barquisimeto and were killed. San Felipe, along with its 600-strong patriot garrison, was completely wiped out. Fuelling superstitious minds, royalist strongholds such as Valencia, Coro, Maracaibo and Guayana, as well as all the royalist army, were untouched. On Easter Sunday itself, further violent tremors shook the country. Some 20,000 altogether were killed in the two earthquakes.

Royalist priests preached that this was divine retribution against the deposition of the anointed king's representatives two years before. The Archbishop of Caracas, Narciso Coll y Pratt, thundered that the vices of Venezuela were being punished and invoked the story of Sodom and Gomorrah. The earthquake shattered the dwindling morale of the patriot forces, while thousands of ordinary Venezuelans now swung over to the royalists.

A new and fearsomely more effective royalist commander had also emerged. Domingo de Monteverde, a former Spanish naval captain, was an energetic, brave and able commander, besides being abundantly possessed of the cruelty traditionally associated with Spanish imperial commanders. The Captain-General of the Spanish forces in Venezuela, Fernando Miyares, based in Coro, and General Antonio Cortabarria in Puerto Rico ordered Monteverde to move forward to Carora, where the patriots were butchered and the town sacked. With the patriots retreating to the garrison town of San Carlos, most of the country in between was abandoned to the royalists. Valencia went over to them after mass desertions from the patriot ranks.

Monteverde had ordered forward his most brutal commander, Captain Eusebio Antoñanzas, on to the plains of Calabozo. On 23 March, just before the earthquakes, he had taken the town of San Juan de los Morros. According to the contemporary historians Baralt and Diaz, 'neither women nor children could find mercy. Captain Antoñanzas enjoyed perpetrating the crimes with his own hands, being the first to set fire to the houses and cutting down the unfortunates who fled the flames'. In Los Guayos, half the garrison defected to the royalist onslaught; the Indian leader of Sequisiqui also went over to the king.

Faced by setbacks on all fronts, the Venezuelan leaders discarded the Marqués del Toro as their commander-in-chief and appointed Miranda absolute dictator. The powdered, greying dandy of the salons of Europe, the sweet talker of old ladies and diplomats was, at the age of 62, at last the leader of his people – in their darkest hour. He was a deeply inappropriate choice, although almost certainly no one else could have saved the situation. He moved his headquarters to Maracay to try to defend the approach to the capital, but his prognosis was gloomy: 'They have approached me to preside over Venezuela's funeral, but I cannot deny my services to my country in the calamitous circumstances in which man and nature have placed it.' It was hardly the rallying cry of a leader of his people.

He devised a defensive strategy, while also fearing further desertions. He again despaired of the wretched guerrillas he commanded, in contrast to the disciplined French ranks he had led in Europe. Yet his only hope would have been to seek to rally the desperate Venezuelans through bold, even suicidal, leadership. The prospect of assistance from abroad was remote. He despatched emissaries to the British and French governments, and to his friends Lord Wellesley, Jeremy Bentham and Lord Castlereagh, but Britain had decided to stay on the sidelines, fearing the worst for the new republic.

Miranda's forces secured a few minor victories against Monteverde, but in La Victoria and Guacara heavy fighting resulted in a stand-off. Meanwhile, there were setbacks within the patriot troops. The former commander in chief, the Marqués del Toro, refused to serve under Miranda. In San Juan de Los Morros and Guanaré, whole garrisons passed over to the royalists, while news of a slave uprising in Barcovento further dented morale. It seemed the country was slipping into anarchy.

Miranda's only hope seemed to lie in a vigorous offensive which he refused to embark upon, for fear of overextending himself, and also of upsetting the British, who were suspicious of his 'revolutionary' intentions. He feared that aggressive tactics might alienate them, giving rise to the belief that he was embarking upon a new 'republican terror'; even in Britain there were still those who were suspicious of Miranda's old French revolutionary links. The patriot cause was paralysed by the old man's indecisiveness and reluctance to shed blood. When the Spaniards seized the Heights of Cabrera, overlooking Miranda's forces at Maracay, the Venezuelan commander retreated to La Victoria, whose garrison was threatened by Monteverde from San Mateo.

Chapter 9

THE AVENGER

Events now moved towards their climax with the intensity of a Greek tragedy, throwing together the two principal protagonists of Latin American independence in a terrible tale of deception, disillusion and filial betrayal that was destined to destroy one of them. Having been publicly rebuked by the very hero he had helped to power, Simón Bolívar had undergone a partial reinstatement to favour as a result of his undoubted courage and ability (he had also inherited another large estate on the death of his brother, Juan Vicente, in a storm off Bermuda). He had been sent as a colonel to command the garrison town of Puerto Cabello, which dominated the approach from the west to La Guaira, gateway to the sea for Caracas and strategically crucial.

The garrison at Puerto Cabello was on a small island connected by a bridge to a peninsula jutting out to sea. The island was defended by two batteries of cannon. Across the bridge was the castle of San Felipe, which overlooked the fortifications, as well as housing both the arms and ammunition of the garrison, and the local jail. There were three little warships in port under Bolívar's control. The jail contained a number of royalists taken prisoner at Valencia. The town itself was full of Spanish sympathizers, who managed to smuggle letters to the prisoners.

On 30 June 1812 Bolívar was playing cards with his officers when shooting broke out. Rushing outside he learnt that the prisoners had seized control of the fortress with the help of a group of 120 men led by one Captain Camejo, who had changed sides and also seized one of the boats. Bolívar, who shortly before had narrowly escaped assassination when invited to address the town council, realized he was in extreme danger. A few days before he had asked Miranda to send forces to the town to resist the besieging royalist forces. None had come, in spite of Miranda's later claim that Puerto Cabello was of the utmost strategic significance.

Now the royalists had established a stranglehold within Bolívar's own garrison and could fire down upon his forces at will, having taken control of most of his arms and munitions. The patriot commander, in this desperate situation, held on for several days, first attempting to storm the impregnable fort, and then merely exchanging fire, with his own side progressively weakened by desertions and lack of supplies.

He sent a frantic plea to Miranda:

> I repeat, as an officer unworthy to be one, with the garrison under the prisoners' control, there has been an uprising in San Felipe and fire has rained down on us from one o'clock in the afternoon on this garrison. Almost all the munitions and supplies are in the castle, and we have only 16,000 rounds outside. The boats are beneath the fire, and only the Celoso is safe, but damaged badly. I will soon be attacked by Monteverde [stationed outside the port], who has heard the shooting; if you do not attack and defeat him immediately, I don't know how this garrison can be saved; because when this letter arrives, he will already be attacking me.

The letter went unanswered – possibly because Miranda did not receive it in time. A few days later Bolívar, his officers and a handful of loyal soldiers escaped the murderous fire from above in the remaining boat. For Bolívar, it had been only his second major military engagement and his first command: he had failed calamitously. He appears to have been on the verge of the total breakdown that seemed always to be near the surface of his brittle personality.

Landing safely after the short boat journey to La Guaira, he travelled up to Caracas where he locked himself into his house, refusing to see anyone. He wrote letters to Miranda that reflected his wretched state of mind:

My general.

After having exhausted all my material and spiritual resources, only with whatever courage remains could I dare to take up the pen to write to you, having lost Puerto Cabello at my own hands . . . My general, my spirit is so defeated that I do not feel strong enough to command a single soldier. My presumptuousness made me believe that my desire to achieve and my ardent zeal for the fatherland would supply the talents I lacked to command . . .

Thus I ask you to make me obey the lowest official, or give me some days to calm myself and recover the serenity which I lost on losing Puerto Cabello. To this can be added my physical state of health which after three nights of insomnia and grave warnings, finds me in a sort of mortal torpor. I am immediately beginning my report on the operations of the troops that I commanded and the disgraces which ruined the city of Puerto Cabello, to defend in the eyes of public opinion your choice of me as well as my own honour.

I did my duty, my general, and if the soldiers had remained on my side, I would have had strength to fight the enemy. If they abandoned me, it was not my fault. Nothing remained for me to do to contain the enemy and . . . save the fatherland. But, alas! This was lost in my hands.

Simón Bolívar.

It was a plaintive, rambling note of self-justification, desperately seeking approbation and forgiveness from Miranda for a failure, which if only tangentially Bolívar's fault, nevertheless seemed irrevocably to besmirch his reputation. Whining in tone, hysterical and shrill, it accorded with most of Bolívar's career to the age of 29: a spoilt, highly-strung, egocentric show-off, who was more concerned with his own reputation than the setback for his cause.

He had been on the field of battle only once before and displayed valour. Now he showed he had no special skills and poor management in the treatment of prisoners, failing to appreciate the danger they posed. In hindsight he should have let them go rather than keep them as a pistol pointed at the very heart of his garrison. In addition, he had abandoned his post, although there was nothing else he could have done. Miranda, who deserved his own share of the blame for classifying Puerto Cabello as a major strategic objective and then doing nothing to reinforce Bolívar, was disgusted. His response to Bolívar's letter was eloquent: there was none at all. His young admirer and supporter, pleading for his mentor's forgiveness, was brushed aside with disdain.

Indeed, when news had reached Miranda of the defeat he turned to his soldiers and said in French, 'Tenez: Venezuela est blessé au coeur' (Venezuela is wounded to the heart). He went on:

> You see, gentlemen, how the affairs of this world are going. A little while ago all was safe; today all is uncertain and ominous. Yesterday Monteverde had no powder, lead or muskets; today he can count on 40,000 pounds of powder, lead in abundance and 3,000 muskets [from the arsenal at Puerto Cabello]. Bolívar tells me the royalists are attacking, but on this day they are already in possession of everything.

Bolívar, whom Miranda had found increasingly insupportable, became the scapegoat for defeat, the loss of Puerto Cabello a decisive blow. The young upstart had failed him, disastrously and hysterically.

A second, shorter, even more imploring letter arrived with Bolívar's report as the dictator of the foundering country pondered the future.

> My general, full of a sort of shame I summon the confidence to send you this enclosure [the account of the battle] which is only a shadow of what really happened. My head, my heart, they are good for nothing. I beg you to permit me an interval of a few days to see if my mind can be returned to its ordinary state. After having lost the best fortress in the land, how can I not be insane, my general? Please do not oblige me to see you face to face. I am not to blame, but I am dispirited and it is enough.

These pathetic pleas fell on deaf ears. The experienced general had seen it all before. Bolívar, shell-shocked by defeat, had gone to pieces. Again, the dictator did not deign to answer. He had no idea, however, that by doing so he was signing his own death warrant.

Salvador de Madariaga wrote a fine passage seeking to unravel the complexity of Bolívar's mind:

When on the top of the Sacred Mount Simón Bolívar swore to free his country from the tyranny of Spain, he was swearing to rescue Simón Bolívar from insanity and death. For Bolívar, a life of glory was the only alternative to a miserable life as a mental wreck such as his nephew (most like him) lived. But when, at twenty-two, he saw himself ascending the peak of glory, Bolívar did not yet possess the inner force which alone could hold together his many and discordant parts. His youthful petulance and vanity were not of the fibre which his unruly self needed. They had first to be crushed by the hammer of adversity.

The generalissimo, the lord of the flies of crumbling Venezuela, had more important things to think about. The war was over and it remained only to secure the best terms possible.

How justified was Miranda in this decision? The capture of La Guaira would have cut the main supply route to Caracas. The slave uprising in Barcovento, under the cry of 'Viva el Rey!', had deeply alarmed the whites, as slaves massacred householders and burnt plantations. Meanwhile, the treasury was all but exhausted, the currency being issued by the patriots was worthless and Monteverde's forces were advancing, gathering support and butchering those who failed to join them as they went.

Miranda was old and tired, luxury-loving and inclined to pessimism. The two insurrections he had launched had ended in abject failure; and now a realist, he did not want to sacrifice thousands of lives in a futile cause. A more vigorous, younger man, without his inhibitions, might have waged a more dynamic war from the beginning; but energy and savagery were on the enemy's side, in the person of Monteverde. When Miranda learnt that his British friends, while disposed to mediate between him and the Spanish crown, would not intervene on his side, he decided to secure the best terms possible while he still had a few cards left. Although his earlier defensiveness was unjustified, his decision now was probably not at fault.

Nor did he impose his will like an autocrat. He summoned the senior members of his government – Francisco Espejo and Juan Germán Roscio; the secretary of war, José de Sata y Bussy; his finance director, the Marqués de Casa León; and Francisco Antonio Pall, minister of justice. They met on the night of 17 July 1812 in the barracks of La Victoria. All concurred that Miranda must sue for peace.

Envoys were despatched to the brutal, efficient Monteverde who refused Miranda's requests that his forces stop advancing and that the island of Margarita, off the coast, become a place of refuge for the patriot forces. Miranda sent back more modest demands that the persons and property of people in the lands about to be surrendered should be respected, that no one should be imprisoned for their opinions, that passports should be guaranteed to those who wanted to leave the country and that prisoners should be exchanged on both sides.

On 25 July these terms were agreed. Miranda accepted the negotiated surrender, but kept the details secret from his people. It is not known whether Bolívar was still in the capital at the time of the capitulation, but he soon joined the huge throng of refugees clambering down the narrow trail from Caracas to La Guaira some 3,000 feet below, in a lather of confusion and fear of Spanish reprisals. By 28 July he was staying in the residence of Manuel Las Casas, military governor of the port.

In Caracas insurrections broke out in several barracks when news of Miranda's 'betrayal' came through. The cry went up that 'we were sold to Monteverde'. It was rumoured that a secret protocol had been attached to the deal – whose terms were anyway not publicly known – under which the minister of finance, the Marqués de Casa León, had granted 1,000 ounces of gold to Miranda as well as an order for 22,000 pesos to be transferred to Miranda's agent in Curaçao, George Robertson.

There is some evidence for the latter accusation: it is conceivable – and indeed would not have been surprising – if Miranda had not tried to rescue some of the national treasury from the hands of the advancing Spanish in order to finance a future attempt at independence. The generalissimo, vainglorious and full of hauteur as he was, had sacrificed a life of comfort and pleasure in London to back the revolution in harrowing and unpleasant conditions, but he had no need of personal wealth on that scale. He enjoyed the good life, certainly, but he would have been unlikely to betray the cause he had fought for purely out of greed.

Miranda assembled his huge collection of papers for safe evacuation to a British ship, the *Sapphire*, off La Guaira. It was Miranda's intention to go east, to the now independent Audiencia of Sante Fé de Bogotá, to seek to continue the revolt. He told his aide, Pedro Gual, that he intended to join up with its leader, Antonio Nariño, to launch a new attack on Venezuela once the defeatism induced by the earthquake and the royalist excesses was past.

On 26 July Miranda left his headquarters in La Victoria for Caracas. With some 5,000 troops now marching disconsolately back to barracks, complaining that they had been stabbed in the back, the capital was a hotbed of intrigue, described vividly to Miranda by one of his aides: 'My general, the people are not in good faith; they are absorbed by intrigue; they know nothing else; they are cowards and at the same time daring . . . Yesterday and the day before various crowds called out, "Viva Ferdinand VII" . . . You are being conducted towards the precipice . . . You, your friends and your fatherland have never been in such danger as now.'

Miranda was being denounced from the pulpit by Archbishop Coll y Pratt and by his rival the Marqués del Toro – who was also Bolívar's patron. On 30 July, the dandified, powdered figure of the generalissimo set off amid the refugees down the mountain trail for La Guaira, arriving there at last at eight in the evening, exhausted and despairing of the treachery that surrounded him, greeted by a large crowd. The baggage of Venezuela's first independence leader was put on board the *Sapphire*.

Miranda had been forced to agree, as part of the terms of the surrender, to respect the Spanish blockade of the port, but Captain Haynes of the *Sapphire* urged him to ignore this and come aboard. Tired and in no hurry to show his people that he was fleeing the country, Miranda refused; sailing had anyway been postponed until the following morning. Miranda went to the house of the military governor, Manuel Las Casas, where Bolívar had also been staying, and retired to bed.

Miranda was indeed surrounded by the intrigues of desperate men. Las Casas himself disliked the foppish general intensely, having heavily criticized him for ordering him earlier to send 'absolutely naked men, some without even a shirt, their arms in the worst possible state and many without guns or bayonets, to do battle for the port'. Las Casas also believed that under the terms of the surrender he would be held responsible by the fearsome Monteverde for ensuring no one left the port and that, if Miranda escaped, he would be severely punished. The civil governor of the port, Miguel Peña, who himself disliked Las Casas, had tried to flee, offering to spirit out Miranda for 4,000 pesos; Miranda refused to pay the lawyer more than 800 pesos. But Peña was also treacherously in touch with the Spanish commander, Monteverde.

After Miranda had retired for the night, Las Casas, Peña, Bolívar and several other officers met in a room. By all accounts Bolívar led the discussion, accusing Miranda of vacillation at Maracay and La Victoria, and denouncing his surrender to inferior Spanish forces. Fevered, his black eyes blazing beneath his huge forehead, Bolívar denounced Miranda for seeking to escape and leaving them all to their fates. The captain, he argued, was the first to leave the sinking ship; worse, he was fleeing having plundered the treasury.

The radical hothead persuaded the others with his eloquence and ferocity. Las Casas and Peña supported him; but their motives were less fanatical, more self-interested. They argued that Miranda must be turned over to the Spanish authorities or the latter would exact vengeance if he was allowed to escape. In reality, they were already in touch with Monteverde and hoped to secure their own safe conduct or, at the least, favourable treatment. Bolívar furiously argued in favour of executing the 'traitor' by firing squad; in the event, this might have been the more merciful course of action. However, Las Casas and Peña were determined to ingratiate themselves with the Spanish authorities by handing Miranda over to them.

At three in the morning, as rival bands of supporters and opponents of Miranda and the monarchy roamed the streets of the chaotic, refugee-swollen port, Bolívar led two captains and a detachment of soldiers to the captain-general's residence. Miranda was awoken in his nightshirt by Carlos Soublette, his secretary, believing he was being readied to embark. But he soon heard the voices of the conspirators and knew he was betrayed.

Bolívar stepped forward and announced that Miranda was under arrest. The swords of the party he led were drawn, flashing in the light of the lantern carried by Soublette. The weary, haughty old man peered out at the intense dark eyes staring into his and declared languidly, 'Bochinche, bochinche, these people are capable of nothing except bochinche' meaning, politely, hubbub or, less so, cock-ups or mischief.

With disdain he asked to be allowed to dress. Then he was roughly seized and insulted, and marched off to prison. Peña took off on horseback for the hills to inform Monteverde, who was now occupying Caracas, what had happened. The former governor of the port was rewarded by being asked to become the Spanish commander's aide.

One of Monteverde's commanders descended from the sierra to take control of La Guaira from Las Casas, who was sent under escort to Caracas where he was freed for his part in apprehending the fallen leader. Meanwhile, Bolívar and the other young republicans, who believed they would be allowed to escape the port, had been prevented from doing so by the treacherous Las Casas.

In due course, Miranda was shipped to Cádiz in Spain and incarcerated in the Arsenal de la Carracca. He died in prison in 1816 and his body was buried in a mass grave.

Bolívar's actions cannot be excused: denouncing Miranda for having betrayed the patriotic cause to the Spanish, he nevertheless betrayed him into the hands of their Spanish enemy, rather than carrying out his own summary justice. He thereby had become the oppressors' accomplice – 'perfidy' as Andrés Bello called it. Bolívar sought to justify himself by calling Miranda a 'coward' and only later was to recognize him as 'illustrious' – the highest possible compliment.

It had been one of history's epic betrayals, a tragedy of Shakespearean dimensions, where errors and bitter inevitability had conspired to bring about the clash between these two seminal men in the making of a continent. Blame, although certainly present, was secondary.

Two years before, the young playboy had arrived to meet his hero in London and persuade him, in spite of his doubts, to return to Venezuela. The two most famous protagonists of Venezuelan freedom, they had at first been kept on the margins by the local oligarchy, who then had to place their faith, in the face of despair, in the old soldier and revolutionary.

At first showing little regard for his young disciple, Miranda had at last placed him in a major command – at which Bolívar had failed spectacularly, although through little fault of his own. On the edge of a breakdown, apparently spurned and blamed by the figure he had worshipped and been instrumental in bringing to power, he had undergone a terrible transformation in attitude: hero worship had mutated into hatred. His own sense of guilt and culpability was reinforced, refined and cleansed into a deadly desire for vengeance.

Guilt is perhaps the most powerful human emotion. Bolívar could save his own reason only by transposing his overwhelming sense of shame to the man who had failed to come to his aid, who had made him the scapegoat for his surrender, who had fought an unnecessarily defensive war and who was now fleeing the country with part of the treasury: Miranda.

Subconsciously, there may have been a modicum of envy as well: a wish to supplant Miranda as the standard bearer of independence. Throughout Bolívar's career a streak of psychopathic ruthlessness would appear to spear any real rival, a trait which failed him only at the end. There were no obvious ideological differences between Miranda and Bolívar; indeed, the latter was largely to carry forward the projects of the former without acknowledging his debt until much later. The betrayal was personal and psychological, the son turning on the father. The assassination of his hero was as brutal as that of Brutus against Caesar, or in contemporary terms, Robespierre against Georges Danton in the French Revolution. Bolívar's action would have turned him into one of the most despicable figures in history – but for his subsequent career.

Certainly Miranda, the father figure, bore his share of the blame: he was vain, effete, snobbish, a serial whorer, contemptuous of his supporters and overcautious. Worse, he was regally disdainful towards the young man whose hero-worship had brought him at last to the power and fulfilment that had eluded him all his life, as leader of a free country and, albeit briefly, to his dream of steering Venezuela to independence. The old man largely dug his own grave. The truth may have been simpler: with the exception of two battles in France, Miranda was simply not a very good general, but a highly cautious professional soldier – a point Bolívar instinctively grasped. Ironically, the old soldier was far better as an ideologue, while Bolívar, not a professional soldier at all, was to prove much the better fighter.

Bolívar's revenge had been biblical, his manner of reprisal murderous. The figure who was to be immortalized in history as Latin America's Libertador had slain the one to be immortalized as El Precursor as savagely as if by his own hand, and certainly more slowly, squalidly and painfully (although in his defence Bolívar had sought an immediate execution). To this day Latin American historians, who venerate both men, find it difficult to come to terms with the fact that their greatest hero slew their second greatest. The two are still portrayed in popular iconography as the greatest of friends.

After the arrest of Miranda, Simón Bolívar himself remained in considerable danger. Under the armistice, he was still free, and he rode up the trail of so much misery in the opposite direction from La Guaira to Caracas, where he went to the house of a family friend, Francisco Iturbe. This worthy was close to the Marqués de Casa León, the minister of finance in the Venezuelan republic, and allegedly a co-conspirator in Miranda's plot to embezzle its funds, but he was a man of high standing.

Iturbe and Casa León now intervened with the Spanish conqueror, Domingo de Monteverde, to suggest that Bolívar be given safe conduct in gratitude for his role in securing Miranda's arrest. Iturbe and Bolívar were summoned before the ruthless Monteverde, an impressive-looking man with a commanding gaze and a self-confident, sardonic smile. The Spanish commander and new ruler of Venezuela chatted amiably with Iturbe, paying little attention to the small and sullen young man before him. 'I will concede you a passage for your service to the King in surrendering Miranda,' he said at length.

Bolívar replied with his customary suicidal foolishness, 'I arrested Miranda because he was a traitor to his country', which could be read either way. Monteverde was visibly irritated, Iturbe apologized and Bolívar was dismissed from the room. He was a man of no importance to the Spaniards. But Monteverde had previously written: 'I cannot forget the interesting service of Casas, Bolívar and Peña, owing to which the persons of all three have been respected, and passports for foreign countries given only to the second, since his influence and connections might be dangerous in the circumstances.'

Without realizing it the ruthless Spanish commander had gazed into the eyes of the man who was to destroy him and Spanish rule in Latin America. If he had ordered Bolívar's execution then and there, history would have been very different. Iturbe advised Bolívar to leave as soon as possible, before the Spaniards changed their minds, and on 12 August 1812, in the sailing ship *Jesus, Mary and Joseph*, Bolívar and a few companions left La Guaira for the island of Curaçao.

There his life was one of penury, and he received the news that he and his brother had been stripped of their estates under a law confiscating the possessions of revolutionaries. At the age of 29, he had been dealt a terrible hand by fate: the pampered, wealthy, multimillionaire aristocrat had lost everything he had; his self-respect had been lacerated by the brainstorm he had suffered following the fall of Puerto Cabello; he had betrayed his mentor and hero; and his properties were in the hands of a heartless conqueror.

The terms of Miranda's armistice were hardly dry on the page before they were ignored by the marauding bands of freed slaves and Monteverde's militia. In Guatire a savage massacre of criollos took place, and while a few escaped to the hills, those fleeing such villages as Calabozo and San Juan de Los Morros were butchered.

Some 1,500 patriot leaders were rounded up and tied to the backs of mules to be dragged to prison. Juan Germán Roscio, one of the founders of independence, was put in the stocks before being shipped off to Cádiz prison in Spain. Miranda wrote bitterly from his own confinement about Monteverde's violation of the Treaty of San Mateo:

> I have seen old age, youth, rich and poor, the laborer and the priest,
> in chains, breathing air so foul that it extinguishes a flame, poisons
> the blood and brings inevitable death. I have seen distinguished

citizens, sacrificed to this cruelty, expire in these dungeons, deprived of bodily necessities, of the consolation of their families and of the spiritual rites of our religion – men who would have preferred to die a thousand deaths with the weapons, which they so generously surrendered, in their hands.

He had every reason to feel remorse. His only justification for surrendering had been to secure terms and avert unnecessary bloodshed. Instead, his detractors had been proved right: the people of Venezuela might have suffered less if they had fought to the end. There were no compromises to be had with the evil empire.

Bolívar, once one of the wealthiest men in Venezuela, was now destitute, brutally buffeted by misfortune.

I was detestably received [in Curaçao], for hardly had I landed when my baggage was embargoed for two very odd reasons: because my belongings were in the same house as Miranda's and because the brig *Celoso* had contracted debts in Puerto Cabello which I was now to pay because I was commandant of the harbour when the debts had been contracted . . . I am therefore without means to feed my life, which I am beginning to look upon with too much loathing and horror.

He was a man transformed. Almost simultaneously he displayed three traits that those who had known him up to that point would never have suspected were in him. He resolved to display ruthlessness of the kind that had proved so effective to the enemy. The once easygoing dilettante also began to show extraordinary reserves of strength and energy. And, added to the verbal proficiency that had emerged in the ranks of the Patriotic Society, he displayed a command of language and writing that was to inspire a continent.

Chapter 10

UP RIVER, ACROSS MOUNTAINS

During a couple of months of poverty in the sun-baked tropical island of Curaçao, Bolívar and his friends yearned to strike back. He declared that 'by the same methods as the oppressors of Caracas managed to subdue the confederation, with those same methods and with more certainty than them, I will try and redeem my fatherland'. They took a boat to Cartagena, the last major city on the northern coast holding out against the Spanish government. It was situated in a sweltering, low-lying natural harbour in blue and calm Caribbean waters, dominated by one of the most formidable maritime fortresses in the world.

When the Venezuelan boat arrived in Cartagena, Bolívar and his young companions offered themselves for military service to the governor, Manuel Rodríguez Torices. They were greeted warmly, and Bolívar, their leader, was immediately appointed a colonel. The governor was desperately in need of good fighting men, and previously had resorted to employing mercenaries. One of them, a former French pirate, General Pedro Labatut, an old friend of Miranda, had become virtual dictator of the city and Torices undoubtedly saw in Bolívar a possible means of ridding himself of Labatut's tyranny. The port was cut off from the capital, Santa Fé de Bogotá, 400 miles inland and upland, which had also declared its independence under a different administration. Cartagena, which swore fealty to the city of Tunja in the mountains, was being blockaded by the Spaniards and running short of supplies.

Labatut, who had heard from Miranda how difficult Bolívar was, and now learnt to his horror of his old friend's fate at the hands of the

young man, decided to send him as far away as possible, to the small
sleepy town of Barrancas on the huge swirling Magdalena river, one
of the world's greatest torrents which trundles down mountains and
across jungles 9,000 feet from Bogotá to the sea. In that backwater
by the big river, Bolívar settled down to compose his first famous call
to arms, the Cartagena Manifesto. He criticized the divisions which
had brought down the Venezuelan Republic: 'The laws were framed
by certain well-meaning visionaries who, building republics in the
air, have tried to reach political perfection on the assumption that
humanity is perfect. So we have had philosophers instead of leaders,
philanthropy instead of legislation, dialectic instead of tactics, and
sophists instead of soldiers.'

Then he turned to the federalists:

What weakened the Venezuelan government most was the federal
form it adopted in keeping with the exaggerated precepts of the
rights of man; this form by authorizing self-government, disrupts
social contracts and reduces nations to anarchy. Such was the true
state of the Confederation. Each province governed itself inde-
pendently; and, following this example, each city demanded like
powers, based on the practice of the provinces and on the theory
that all men and all peoples are entitled to establish arbitrarily the
form of government that pleases them.

Federalism — though it may be the most perfect and the most
capable of bringing happiness to human society, is nevertheless the
most detrimental to the interests of our infant countries . . .

Popular elections by country rustics and intriguing city-dwellers
are one more obstacle to the practice of federation among us; because
the former are so ignorant that they cast their votes mechanically,
and the latter so ambitious that they convert everything into factions;
therefore in Venezuela there has never been a free and just vote,
and the government has been placed in the hands of men who have
either betrayed the cause or were inept or immoral. It is our lack of
unity, not Spanish arms, that has returned us to slavery.

Bolívar thus established himself as an unashamed advocate of
strong government. He went on to argue that the Viceroyalty of

New Granada and the independence of Venezuela were inextricably linked – indeed that freedom for Venezuela was necessary to secure Santa Fé de Bogotá as part of a single entity, which he called Gran Colombia. This was needed to justify the plan forming in his mind: to use troops from Santa Fé to cross back and liberate Venezuela. This was Miranda's own avowed intention after the armistice, which can hardly have been what the people of Bogotá and Cartagena wanted to hear, several hundreds of miles away and largely indifferent to the fate of Venezuela.

Bolívar ended with a ringing declaration: 'Let us hasten to break the chains of those victims who groan in their dungeons, awaiting salvation at your hands! Do not abuse their confidence! Do not turn a deaf ear to the lamentations of your brothers! Let us fly quickly to avenge the dead, to give life to the dying, freedom to the oppressed and liberty to all!'

It is not hard to see how the rich, educated young Bolívar acquired his burning ardour to expel the Spanish from Latin America and to rule in their stead. Yet for the moment Bolívar was not concerned to fight for the rights of everyone. He placed a priority on the criollo upper classes so affected by Spanish Bourbon reforms – a restoration of the old colonial class system, not its overthrow. Bolívar was declaring a reactionary rather than revolutionary goal which would benefit himself and his own aristocratic friends; in due course his attitudes would change.

Bolívar was just 29 years old when he wrote the first of his manifestos, the Cartagena letter, a polemic of great passion, high intelligence and idealism. But it still lacked maturity or wisdom and remains the least substantial of his great tracts: much of it was aimed against the stupidity of the government of the first republic. Nonetheless, the manifesto was warmly endorsed by Torices and by Camilo Torres, the president of the Congress in Tunja, the independent statelet to which Cartagena adhered.

At that time Bolívar was but one of many fluttering fireflies in the demi-monde of Spanish American rebellion. His record so far had been unimpressive and inspired derision among at least some of his revolutionary rivals and contemporaries. This almost certainly explains the fanaticism with which he sought to seize control of the reins of the revolutionary cause: at this early stage he seemed possessed of a kind of demonic energy that bordered on madness and psychopathic cruelty. Bolívar's reputation as a soldier was very limited, which further propelled him to risk his own life and those of his men in seemingly insane ventures – unlike Miranda, the defensive military professional. Bolívar's reputation was that of a spoilt young patrician, more to be feared in bed than on the battlefield, although an inspiring orator and propagandist. Now he intended to prove himself as a military commander, uninhibited by conventional tactics. Like Robert Clive before him and Giuseppe Garibaldi after, he had not been conventionally trained in an individual branch of warfare, and thus like Clive he was to be, in William Pitt the Elder's phrase, a 'heaven born general'.

Bolívar did not while away all his time composing manifestos and once he arrived at Barrancas he found a shambles of ill-trained, ill-dressed, ill-equipped, grumbling layabouts rather than meek troops. With grim determination he set about moulding them into a fighting force. In this tiny, tranquil town of mud-roofed huts in the jungle by the lower reaches of the wide, sluggish river, men were soon to be seen marching and wheeling about as on a parade ground.

In December 1812, Bolívar requested Torices' approval to go up the Magdalena river to liberate it from the Spaniards. Without waiting for a reply he set out towards Tenerife, a royalist stronghold, and on the way reached the sleepy hamlet of Salamina, home to Anita Lenoit, a beautiful blonde girl who spoke a strange language and would talk to no one.

He rode out to the well-to-do little villa on the outskirts, finding her in the garden. She was indeed fair-haired, blue-eyed and extraordinarily beautiful: she had a dimpled chin, a pretty sensual mouth and pink cheeks in contrast to the sun-baked skin of many Venezuelans. She was confused by his penetrating gaze, and he spoke to her gently in French.

They spent the rest of the evening talking on the patio of the house, reminiscing about Paris, and he told her that he would shortly have to leave on his military expedition. He left her in the evening, as good manners dictated, and returned only the following day, when her father was back. They spent the rest of the day together, as though old and fond lovers: and on this occasion, he stayed the night as well. It was easy to see what this lonely French girl so far from home in the Colombian outback saw in the colonel. Bolívar himself seems to have fallen genuinely and hopelessly in love for the first time since he had left Fanny de Villiers in Paris and his love resembled his passion for that other lonely innocent, María Teresa, his wife.

The following day, Bolívar was authorized to march on Tenerife by Torices, and he set off up the river in a convoy of small rafts, which moved slowly along the edge of the Magdalena beneath the tree canopy, sometimes going aground, as he sought to avoid the strong downstream currents. They would stop for rests in primitive river villages before pressing on to Tenerife on 23 December, where his small force silently surrounded the town. The sleeping Spanish garrison was astonished when a delegation arrived under a white flag and asked them to surrender, offering safe conduct. The local commander refused, and a withering fire broke out from all around the settlement. After the guns had blazed away at each other for some time, the Spaniards, not knowing the exact strength of the enemy surrounding them and fearing that they were in a trap, hurriedly evacuated the town, leaving behind their artillery and small gunboats in the river harbour.

There is a famous story, perhaps apocryphal, that Bolívar was resting after the skirmish when Anita Lenoit, who had followed him upriver, reappeared and they spent a joyous night together; if so, it was the last time she saw him alive. But the brief dalliance made a profound impact on him, for he frequently spoke of her afterwards – the ultimate romantic liaison, a girl he had loved for barely a few days.

Moving upstream, Bolívar's force reached the town of Mompox, which had already been abandoned by the Spaniards on his approach. He was received enthusiastically, in the first of what were to become his trademark triumphal entrances: 'I was born in Caracas,' he declared grandly. 'My glory in Mompox.' It was over the top for the little settlement; but it didn't matter and earned him hundreds of recruits.

With his strengthened force he marched on the villages of Guamol and El Banco, where small garrisons were quickly put to flight, before he decided to engage the main Spanish force which had moved inland to Chiriguaná. His oarsmen pulled the rafts forward vigorously down a branch off the Magdalena, the César, and fell upon the Spaniards in a surprise attack on New Year's Day, 1813. After a few hours the royalists were routed, and Bolívar returned to the main river, where he easily subjected the town of Tamalameque and, after another bloody skirmish, that of Puerto Nacional.

A more glittering prize beckoned: the important city of Ocaña, in the mountains to the east of the river. Leaving most of his force on the river, he set off with a detachment to reconnoitre. No sooner had news of his approach reached the city than the small Spanish garrison there was put to flight by an uprising among the townspeople and Bolívar, without a fight, found himself marching triumphantly into the town in a second victorious entrance.

He was delighted on two accounts. Firstly, he had freed a large swathe of the royalist-controlled Magdalena. When news came that Labatut had captured the key port of Santa Marta, the whole province of Cartagena was rid of the Spaniards. Secondly, Ocaña lay on the way to the Venezuelan border; and Bolívar was far more interested in liberating his homeland and exacting his revenge on Monteverde than ascending further into the interior of New Granada. Bolívar promptly set up his headquarters in the city and sent word to Tunja: 'I have succeeded in opening the navigation of the Magdalena, in reconquering all the territory held by the enemy, completely destroying its troops and taking one hundred prisoners, many officers, ammunition and provisions . . . All these operations have been executed within two weeks' time.'

However, on 23 January 1813 news reached the rebel government in Tunja that a large force of Spaniards under Colonel Ramón Correa was approaching the town of Pamplona, on the New Granadan side of the border. Bolívar's political masters urged him to take action to defend his flank and he was delighted to comply: here was the excuse he needed to move towards the Venezuelan border.

Bolívar's first real military campaign established a pattern: his river-raft army, pushing up the rapids and currents of the Magdalena, had shown itself to be a master of a new type of guerrilla warfare – the movement of small forces across large distances to inflict surprise attacks on sleepy outposts where they were least expected. In this type of war, Bolívar understood that speed, movement and manoeuvrability were all-important. Most jungle fighting up to then had consisted of desultory exchanges between outposts controlled by one or other side – a small attack, a small victory or a small repulse. By using highly trained irregulars, impervious to the discomfort of covering large distances, he commanded the element of surprise and he could secure one victory after another.

For the moment Bolívar was a nuisance on the New Granadan side of the border, and one that the large royalist forces on the Venezuelan side were gathering to deal with. Ramón Correa, the royalist commander, had 1,000 well-armed men at Cucúta, while on the New Granadan side the rebel commander Colonel Manuel Castillo had 1,300 at Pamplona, at the base of the soaring Andean peaks to the south.

Between Cucúta and Bolívar's forces lay an appalling piece of territory, the Alta de la Aguada, one of the fingers of the Andes which descend nearly to touch the Caribbean, a mixture of dense jungle interspersed by soaring, barren plateaux before plunging down vertiginous slopes to the valley floor. Correa assumed the barrier to be impenetrable, which gave him the chance to destroy Castillo's rebel forces at will. Castillo himself was a vain, unimaginative commander who had no better plan than to entrench himself in a defensive, hedgehog position and wait for the attack.

The two men reckoned without Simón Bolívar. Departing on 24 January, Bolívar divided his little army into two columns, setting off across the uninhabited badlands. For the first time the full extent of his vigour and energy manifested itself. Cajoling and goading his men on, pushing animals and helping to pick up exhausted men himself, he forced his troops through the dense jungle, ferocious thorn brush lowlands, and then up rocky passes that clung to crumbling ledges that sometimes gave way, sending men and animals plunging to their deaths. At night fires kept out the bitter cold of the plateau, while freezing rain and sleet paralysed them in their camps.

Three days later he had at last reached the summit of the pass, the

Alto de la Aguada, where 100 Spaniards waited in the freezing cold. The Spanish general, Correa, had rapidly brought a small force there on learning of Bolívar's approach by that impassable route. The rebel commander, who realized that to assault this redoubt from below would be fatal, arranged for a runner to be captured by Correa's men suggesting that Castillo's forces were approaching from the rear to seal the Spaniards in a trap.

The half frozen Spaniards on the pass fell for the ruse and started to move back down towards Pamplona. Bolívar promptly ordered his 500 men forward, across the top of the pass and downwards, where they fell upon Correa's fleeing force and dispersed them. He descended rapidly towards Pamplona, where he liaised with Castillo's forces and his exhausted troops rested. He then continued along the Zulia river valley, encountering minor resistance from Spanish positions. Within days he was on the commanding heights overlooking the great valley of San José de Cucúta: there, on his horse, he observed the frenzied manoeuvrings of the main body of Correa's army. The Spanish commander had tried to head him off at the pass, and failed; then at the river; now he was making a stand outside the town of Cucúta.

Bolívar's army was still drained by the march across a supposedly impassable mountain range, but he recognized that to retain the advantage he must not let up; the enemy must not have time to dig in. On 28 February he sent forward his advance troops, holding the bulk of his forces in reserve. The Spaniards decided that Bolívar's force was small and vulnerable enough to be attacked on the valley floor and surged out of the city in strength to surround them.

Bolívar awaited until they had emerged, then ordered his main force out of the hills nearby. Correa realized that he was now in danger of being surrounded and cut off from the town, and in a desperate move ordered his men to seize the rocky hills to the left of the rebel forces. It proved a brilliant countermove: Bolívar's forces were caught in the open under a withering fire, and casualties among the rebels multiplied.

Desperately, Bolívar ordered Colonel José Félix Ribas, a distant relative, to lead a bayonet charge up the hills – seemingly a suicidal assault. But somehow the attack succeeded. The royalist lines broke into a panic-stricken retreat through the town and across the Táchira river into Venezuela where Bolívar, who lacked authorization to cross the frontier, broke off the pursuit.

Bolívar addressed his exhausted troops in the town square, calling them the heroes of Cucúta and they were despatched to well-earned rest. He sent a message with news of his triumph to his masters in Tunja, claiming credit for having 'freed a large part of New Granada from the tyrants who oppressed it', reminding his superiors that, 'Now all that remains is to defeat the opponents of Venezuela, who I hope will soon be exterminated, as those of Santa Marta and Pamplona have been.'

He had won his first major, and decisive, victory. Although the battle of Cucúta had been a close-run thing against a superior enemy, it was a remarkable achievement. Crossing the Andes had been a feat of speed and endurance, and had dealt a punishing blow. It was the first of a series of feats of generalship and leadership in perhaps the most geographically varied, taxing and savage continent on earth. He had turned the topography to his advantage.

In the pleasantly temperate city in the valley he prepared his next offensive: a march into Venezuela, his homeland, at the head of New Granadan troops. He dared not do so without authorization: otherwise he risked arrest from his own commanders. So he requested authority to pursue and destroy Correa's army across the border.

Castillo, the commander of the forces in Pamplona, bitterly resented the upstart commander from across the mountains and opposed any crossing of the border, as did his more formidable second-in-command, Francisco de Paula Santander, a good-looking, politically astute and devious young man whom Bolívar now met for the first time. Back in Cartagena, Labatut also detested the young Venezuelan. As the dispute became more intense, Bolívar threatened to resign, but the Congress in Tunja refused to accept his withdrawal and appointed him a brigadier-general as well as a citizen of New Granada.

Bolívar did not waste his time quarrelling with resentful and mediocre local commanders. He sent a mission to Santa Fé de Bogotá, in the highlands, to secure backing and reinforcements; and he vigorously recruited and drilled his army into a more effective fighting force. Ribas was despatched up the cordillera to the oldest and most beautiful of the Spanish colonial capitals in the north, in its huge saucer in the mountains.

There the Republic of Cundinamarca, confusingly separated from the Congress of Tunja which Bolívar now served, was headed by Antonio Nariño, a brilliant intellectual who had been tutored by Miranda and imprisoned in Cádiz for attempting to circulate a copy of Thomas Paine's *The Rights of Man* in Santa Fé de Bogotá. After escaping from Cádiz he had been imprisoned again in the upland capital, but released in the 1810 uprising and set up as president.

Nariño's sole interest was an independent Santa Fé de Bogotá: he had no wider ambitions for Latin America. Nevertheless, he despatched 150 soldiers under Ribas to help Bolívar. They were followed by men like Anastasio Girardot, Antonio Ricaurte, Rafael Urdaneta and Pedro Briceño Méndez who were young aristocratic criollos imbued with Bolívar's romantic military ardour, some of whom, like him, had lost all their possessions. Most of his supporters came from well-to-do families. Bolívar recruited among the inhabitants of the Cucúta valley, and during the two months of peace in that tranquil region ceaselessly drilled his men into a more effective fighting force. Even so, his army totalled only around 700, although it was well supplied with guns and ammunition from the captured garrison there, as well as 1 million pesos from the treasury.

By contrast the Spanish army was almost entirely recruited from among blacks, mestizos and impoverished peasants, many nursing grievances against the landowning aristocracy, but most joining for the pay and prospects of plunder.

While in Cucúta, Bolívar considered his next daring move.

Chapter 11

INTO VENEZUELA

At last, on 7 May 1813, Bolívar received the order to march on Venezuela – but only to liberate the border provinces of Mérida and Trujillo. That was good enough for him – although it sparked off a furious row with the local commanders, Castillo and Santander, the latter flatly refusing to march. Bolívar threatened to have him shot for disobeying orders, and he grudgingly gave way, although he bore that first slight throughout his life. In exchange, Bolívar had to pledge solemnly in front of the city council to obey the orders of the Congress, so as to dispel fears that he was invading Venezuela. He set off towards the small town of San Antonio.

Facing the rebel troops were some 6,000 royalists, spread in a fan set back from the border: in the north, based in Trujillo, Barquisimeto and Coro, around 2,400 Spaniards were under the control of Captains Cañas and Oviedo. In the south, near Guasdualito, there were 900 men under Captain José Yañez; in Barinas there were 1,500 men under Captain Antonio Tizcar and, in San Carlos, 1,200 soldiers under Captain Izquierdo. It was a formidable force, and many feared that Bolívar was walking into a trap. However, the opposition was scattered and Bolívar had already evolved his guerrilla strategy of picking off enemy garrisons one by one, using his speed and manoeuvrability to prevent them joining forces. Advancing on San Antonio, Bolívar gave the order for Castillo to advance on the town of La Grita, where Yañez and Tizcar had just joined forces under Correa's overall command.

With ill grace, Castillo proceeded and, in the steep hills near the town, thanks largely to Santander's skilful and brave leadership,

Correa's forward troops were driven back. Castillo then reckoned it to be madness to continue the advance into Venezuela and resigned his command. This now fell to Santander, a 21-year-old sergeant-major brought up in New Granada. He was highly educated, with a brilliant mind, and he was a formidable tactician, but also pedantic, devious and over-cautious. Santander advised Bolívar that it was folly to proceed across the border and predicted mass desertions. Bolívar contemptuously left him in charge of the frontier garrisons at the rear and appointed four young lieutenants to command the vanguard. His forces then rode out across the green foothills under the easternmost spur of the Andes, the mountains of the Cordillera de Mérida towering above them.

At first, Bolívar's judgment seemed amply vindicated: the royalists appeared to have melted away and San Cristobal fell without a fight. After an easy ride of a fortnight through magnificent rolling country, by 23 May he reached the city of Mérida. He was now 100 miles into his homeland of Venezuela, a fifth of the way to Caracas from which he had been expelled just nine months before.

In the mountain air and the steep narrow streets of that delightful colonial city beneath nearly 70 peaks with an average height of 13,000 feet, the Liberator's thoughts must have been heady indeed. There had been no opposition: the whole town had turned out to greet his army. Bolívar's entry was triumphal, his speech in the plaza a promise of freedom almost incomprehensible to people who had grown to accept that the natural order of things was oppression and serfdom. In addition a volunteer force under a Spaniard, Major Vicente Campo Elías, joined Bolívar. Elías pledged to kill every Spaniard he encountered, and then himself and his own family, so that no more of that accursed race would remain alive. With two columns of 560 men in front and 883 in the rear, Bolívar's army was now beginning to attain a respectable size – and its training and discipline were formidable.

His run of luck continued to hold. He despatched a force to engage Correa's remaining army at Escuque; this was defeated in a minor battle and Correa, always retreating, withdrew into the fetid, dismal lowlands around the huge inland sea of Lake Maracaibo, one of the hottest and most desolate places on earth. An advance guard was sent forward to the city of Trujillo, and Bolívar himself, after marching along the ancient trail of the conquistadors with the bulk of the army, arrived there on 14 June.

He was halfway to Caracas, having completed the task set him by the council at Tunja and at the limits of the territory he was authorized to capture in a so far wholly successful campaign to clear the royalists out of the border provinces. The only unsettling aspect of the campaign – which had become a triumphal march – was the way the Spaniards had fallen back without a fight, hardly ever opposing Bolívar's army.

To the rebel commander it was evident that Correa was trying to lure him into overextending his lines of communication – now stretched to 200 miles – with the intention of encircling him in a trap; or, at the very least, by not fighting Bolívar, he was waiting for the invaders to turn about, leaving the Spanish army intact and in a position to reassert its authority when they had gone. Bolívar seemed to have walked into the jaws of danger: there were major Spanish forces to north and south of him, as well as in front of him to the east. He appeared to have no choice but to retreat, or at least, stop in accordance with his instructions and seek to consolidate the territory gained. That, evidently, was what the Spaniards expected. Instead, he took everyone – the Spaniards and his own side – by surprise. With sudden animal-like ferocity, he flung himself at the enemy in an apparently suicidal onslaught that was to deliver his greatest triumph to date.

The night of 14 June 1813 marked Bolívar's Rubicon. By advancing, he would be breaking with the limits of constitutional legality empowered him by the Congress of Tunja. He would be using New Granadan troops to promote his own personal cause: the liberation of his homeland, Venezuela. This he could justify in his mind because he was a pan-American: he believed in the liberation of all Latin America, not just New Granada, and he had already underlined his belief that as long as Venezuela remained in Spanish hands, New Granada was under threat. But he was now taking the law into his own hands and directly defying his political masters: he had become a buccaneer who now appointed himself not just above the law but as the law. Worse, he was endangering the lives of his own men in an apparently hopeless quest.

The contrast with the man he had destroyed, Miranda, could hardly have been greater: that punctilious general had nothing but contempt for irregular Latin American guerrillas, and refused to shed blood when the odds suggested he would lose. Bolívar regarded his toughened, hardy fighters as capable of winning any fight and was prepared to take on overwhelming odds. To take the offensive, he believed, was to win. He could certainly not retreat after his fateful decision to move forward that June: the penalty for insubordination and failure would have been death. He was burning his boats.

Yet the outlook could hardly have been less auspicious. Overstretched and surrounded on all sides by superior forces, he also faced the cruel reality that he was in hostile territory. Unlike the people of Mérida and the mountains who had welcomed him, the people of Trujillo had fled in the face of the rebel advance. The peasants were in hiding, their animals driven away.

The fetid lowlands around Lake Maracaibo were teeming with passive resistance. Here the great population of slaves and mestizo labourers bristled at the proud criollo landowner class typified by Bolívar. The Spaniards had cleverly instituted a ferocious class war of the lower, exploited orders against upper-class Americans. Ordinary people looked to Spain and king to preserve them from the depredations of their local-born masters – and were ignorant of the fact that the Spanish economic system was the most exploitative of all. Bolívar could look for little support among such people.

Another factor kept them hostile to his cause: fear. Monteverde and his legions, recruited from the lowest ranks in society, had violated Miranda's armistice without compunction and instilled a climate of terror across the land: the people were more frightened of Spanish retribution than of Bolívar, who had not been exaggerating when he had written:

> The revolution of blacks, both freemen and slaves, provoked,
> helped and supported by the agents of Monteverde, these inhu-
> man and atrocious peoples, steeped in the blood and the goods
> of the patriots . . . marching upon the neighbourhood of Caracas,
> committed in those villages and in particular in the town of Guatire
> the most horrible murders, thefts, violence and devastation . . .

Those who had surrendered, peaceful workers, men of the highest esteem, were killed with pistol shots and swords or were barbarically beheaded even after the armistice was published. Blood showed everywhere and bodies decorated the squares and streets of Guatire, Calabozo, San Juan de los Morros and other towns occupied by peaceful, hard-working people who, for having taken up arms, or on the approach of the troops having fled to the mountains were dragged, bound, to have their lives taken without further formality, hearing or judgement. Any official was authorized to hand out death sentences to those they considered patriots or who they wished to rob.

Bolívar had already encountered Monteverde's terror. When his forces had advanced from the west, the rebel leader had heard of a small but ferocious anti-Spanish uprising in the hills led by an old neighbour of his, Antonio Nicolás Briceño, a distinguished and cultivated lawyer of 'gentle and peaceful disposition'. Briceño had been so appalled by the Spanish atrocities that his character had undergone a complete transformation. Instituting his own mini-insurrection, he offered to promote soldiers on the basis of the number of Spanish heads they took: 30 heads would earn the post of lieutenant; 50 that of captain. Bolívar, appalled, ordered Briceño's arrest, but received a gift of two heads by way of reply.

Before Bolívar could act, the Spaniards captured Briceño and his men, court-martialling them and shooting the avenging lawyer and seven of his men at Barinas. The Spanish commander, Antonio Tizcar, did not however go so far as to massacre all the insurgents. The death of Briceño, although justified by any standards, deeply offended Bolívar, although nothing can excuse what he did next.

In Trujillo Bolívar issued a solemn proclamation:

The Spaniards have served us with rapine and death. They have violated the sacred rights of human beings, violated capitulations and the most solemn treaties; committed, in fact, every crime. They have reduced the Republic of Venezuela to the most frightful desolation. Thus, then, justice demands vengeance and necessity obliges us to take it . . .

   Every Spaniard who does not conspire with the most active and effective means possible against the tyranny in favour of our just cause will be held as an enemy and a traitor to the fatherland; and in consequence will be inexorably put to the knife. On the other hand, an absolute and general indulgence will be granted to those who pass to our army with or without their arms . . . Spaniards who render conspicuous service to the State will be treated as Americans . . .

Moved by your misfortunes, we have been unable to look indifferently upon the afflictions the savage Spaniards have caused you to suffer, exterminating you by plunder and destroying you with death; violating the sacred rights of men; breaking the most solemn agreements and treaties; and, in short, committing every kind of crime, reducing the Republic of Venezuela to the most dreadful desolation. Therefore justice demands vengeance, and necessity compels us to exact it. May the monsters that infest our land and have covered it with blood vanish forever from Colombian soil. Let their punishment be equal to the enormity of their betrayal, in order thus to wash out the stain of our disgrace and to show the nations of the world that the sons of America cannot be offended with impunity.

He concluded with this ringing and Solomonic declaration: 'Spaniards and men of the Canary Islands, if you are lukewarm and do not work actively for America's freedom, you may be certain of death. Americans, even if you have done wrong, you may be certain of life.'

   There can have been few more terrible pronouncements from a major figure in modern history. While atrocities are, of course, inevitable – even the norm – in warfare, only in the French Revolution two decades before were they expressly authorized by the constituted legal authority, and even then to a much more limited extent. Usually the authorities on either side are at pains to stick to legal propriety, whatever the truth on the ground. Monteverde's own decision to sign the armistice a year earlier, which his soldiers promptly flouted, was a typical example.

Bolívar's proclamation instead explicitly authorized the use of atrocity and terror by launching what became immediately known as the 'war to the death'. Bolívar's secretary was to sign his letters, 'third (year) of independence and first of war to the death' to underline the point.

The purpose was clear: to instil in the populace the same terror of his own forces as Monteverde had through his own atrocities. In a land ruled by fear of the Spaniards, fear of Bolívar's forces was henceforth to be as potent a weapon. The people of Trujillo would not join him; therefore they must learn to fear him.

Bolívar's South American hagiographers have sprung to the defence of the death proclamation. The most curious feature of this extraordinary and, at first glance, crude document was that it was very carefully crafted – and, as such, Bolívar's apologists argue, was actually rather merciful. It was nothing less than an amnesty for his American-born opponents – 'even if you have done wrong, you may be certain of life' – because their state of subjugation did not make them responsible for their actions.

The purpose was to secure the allegiance of the ill-educated majority who were serving in the Spanish forces, even though these had been responsible for the worst atrocities. For Spaniards and those born in that country, there would be no quarter unless they actively joined Bolívar's ranks. Those that were not with him were against him. Bolívar wished to sow among low-caste Americans the same kind of racial and class hatred of Spaniards as the latter had effectively utilized against the criollo rebels; and to secure whatever conversions were possible among the ranks of privileged Spaniards. The confusion of the last days of Miranda's republic were uppermost in Bolívar's mind, when nominal adherents of the new regime crossed over without a qualm to Monteverde's side in an effort to be spared his vengeance.

Now they had no such easy choice. Unless they openly backed Bolívar, they would be killed – even the peaceful civilians among them. Yet the very selectiveness of Bolívar's policy of legitimized slaughter is particularly chilling: this was not some proclamation issued by a young hothead in the thick of the fighting, or the ranting of a murderous local warlord. It was the calculated authorizing of racial murder even of the innocent, to secure the greater advantage for his own side: its very selectiveness made it all the more coldly inhuman.

Bolívar has been excused as acting against a truly barbaric enemy. The American politician, Henry Clay, was to defend him five years later in a famous speech in Congress:

> The gentleman from Georgia cannot see any parallel between our revolution and that of the South American provinces and contends that their revolution was stained by scenes which had not occurred in ours. If so, it was because execrable outrages had been committed upon them by the troops of the mother country which were not upon us. Can it be believed, if the slaves had been let loose upon us in the South as they have been let loose in Venezuela, if quarter had been refused, capitulations violated, that George Washington would not have resorted to retribution? Retaliation is sometimes mercy, mercy to both parties. The only means by which the coward's soul that indulges in such enormities can be reached is to show him that he will be visited by severe but just retribution.

The Spanish were certainly fiendishly inhuman in their cruelty: they would rape women, then tie them in their hammocks and set fires under them, literally cooking them to death. They peeled prisoners' feet and made them walk across hot coals; ears were trophies of war; and so on. Yet the flaw in Clay's argument is evident: Bolívar was not threatening 'severe but just retribution', he was threatening unjust retribution, indiscriminately targeted against Spaniards because of their place of birth, whether they were guilty or innocent. Moreover, he was putting behind it the full sanction of his law. He was setting himself up as Liberator, a quasi-legal authority, and preaching as part of his new jurisdiction the barbarity of the pirate or the vengeful warlord. Retribution can only be merciful if it helps to shorten a war or to instil respect for the law. It is impossible to argue in favour of Bolívar's proclamation on grounds of realpolitik. Bolívar was lapsing into tyrannical mode – itself a feature of romantic thinking.

A figure of historical immensity such as Bolívar has to be judged not just by his generalship, statesmanship and leadership, all of which were outstanding, or by his compassion and humanity, which in certain circumstances can even be rated as defects, but by his sense of justice and observance of the law, even in a state which has none, where he himself makes the law. The 'war to the death', while it may have made eminent military sense, flouted every standard of decency, fairness and the legal perception that men can only be culpable for crimes they have themselves committed, that a class or a race cannot be held collectively responsible for the atrocities committed by some of them, and that the state has no business punishing wrongdoing by taking reprisals against the innocent. Bolívar's statesmanship was irreparably harmed by this cold proclamation of inhumanity.

Worse, it is possible to trace in that decision the ancestry of many of the terrible excesses that were later to befall the Latin American continent under a succession of tyrants: the notions that he who is not with us is against us, that atrocity must be met with atrocity, that the many can be punished for the acts of the few, that there is no such thing as moderation or a middle way in war are ones that have reverberated all the way down to the military dictators and murderous juntas of Latin America until as recently as a couple of decades ago. The bestial cruelties of the Spaniards were to leave their mark in the retaliatory cruelty of Bolívar, who could instead have represented a break with these practices, as his idealistic politics did.

In his defence, it must be said that he was not usually a cruel man, and his sudden acts of vengeance tended to occur in times of extreme difficulty. The 'war to the death' proclamation may have been no more than a natural response to what seemed a desperate situation of encirclement, just as Miranda's arrest may have seemed the only way of salvaging his own reputation at the time.

It is impossible to judge to what extent these were considered and premeditated actions, or the consequence of the snapping of the nerve of a man who was always deeply sensitive, replacing his usual humanity with the ferocity of a trapped animal. The key to Bolívar is that his extraordinary statesmanship could suddenly, subject to the colossal pressures his highly strung mind laboured under, lapse into

almost insane single-mindedness, paying no attention to the conse-
quences of his actions on other people – often including his own
men.

While Bolívar's proclamation was fatally to detract from his
historical stature, it was to reveal more closely than ever before one
facet of the man which was to be perhaps his most effective facet as
a commander: his fanatical adherence to the cause of victory. He
would not retreat in the face of overwhelming odds. He would give
no quarter in hostile territory. He knew only how to advance. This
demonic ferocity played a huge part in his success, and in the fear he
induced in his opponents. In adversity, he displayed the energy and
ferocity of a trapped wolf; not for him to go to the slaughter meekly
like a lamb.

Bolívar now gave a virtuoso performance as a commander. Like a
swordsman he thrust and parried with such speed that his enemies were
left dazed and confused. To the south, Tizcar commanded an army of
1,500 men at Barinas, on the slopes of the Andes where the mountains reach the famous Venezuelan outback, the llanos (plains); to the
north lay some 2,000 Spaniards in Coro and Maracaibo. The bulk of
Monteverde's army was ahead of Bolívar. The danger was that Tizcar
would wheel behind Bolívar and cut him off from the frontier.

In a masterstroke, Bolívar decided to turn the tables: he led a smallish force in a rapid surprise march up and over the steep cordillera,
tumbling down the other side of the mountains to seize Guanaré,
behind Spanish lines, cutting off Tizcar's army from Caracas. Behind
him, his two trusted lieutenants, Girardot and Ribas, marched to
protect his flank. A force of some 400 men under Ribas met a royalist
force twice as large at Las Mesitas. A ferocious battle was resolved at
last by a successful bayonet charge led by Ribas.

Bolívar meanwhile force-marched on Tizcar at Barinas – only to
find that the Spanish army had fled on hearing of his approach, leaving behind 13 cannon and all of its stores. The patriot commander
pursued them down into the vast remoteness of the llanos without
catching them. He turned about and marched his men 100 miles
along the edge of the llanos to Araure, towards the town of San
Carlos.

The young general then ordered Ribas to march on the Spanish forces still dispersed between Barquisimeto and El Tocuyo. But Ribas failed to prevent the Spanish forces in the two towns from joining up, and his force of 500 was outnumbered by 1,500 supported by four cannon. This rather engagingly simple, extraordinarily brave man, sporting a trademark French revolutionary tricolour hat, attacked the Spaniards on 22 July, but was twice repulsed before launching an assault on their weaker flank and capturing their artillery. This he turned on the Spanish forces, who broke into a headlong rout.

Triumphantly, he occupied Barquisimeto and then marched on San Carlos to liaise with Bolívar. The Spaniards in that town fell back in order to meet up with the bulk of Monteverde's force now marching from Caracas to make a stand at Valencia. These brilliant parallel manoeuvres had thrown the Spaniards so much on the defensive that they were forced to make a stand in Venezuela's second city, having effectively yielded control of the western third of the country. It was the Spanish reoccupation of the year before in reverse, with them now defending the central highlands and major cities against the advancing rebels.

Bolívar permitted his united army of 2,500 men only a few days' rest before spurring them on to catch up with the retreating Spanish force from San Carlos before it could join up with Monteverde. It was a race against time. Soon they sighted the Spanish force on a mountain spur at Tinaquillo. Marksmen had been left there to delay Bolívar's forces as the main army retreated.

Bolívar ordered his cavalry forward on the rocky terrain to the right of the retreating forces in an attempt to harry them and block them before they could reach the shelter of the mountains near Valencia. With the last plain before the mountains ahead, he improvised desperate, brilliant measures, sending a hundred cavalrymen forward, with an infantryman also mounted on each horse, to get ahead of the Spaniards. These troops scrambled through the scree and bush on the right, under heavy fire, to burst out on to the plain just ahead of the retreating royalists and turning around, commenced firing. Bolívar and his main army meanwhile attacked the Spaniards from behind and, caught between two fires, their forces were destroyed. Most were shot or taken prisoner.

The Spanish captain-general, Domingo de Monteverde, had reached Valencia with his main army of 3,000 men less than a year after defeating Miranda and so cynically violating the armistice between the two, but he was a chastened man. In the eastern end of Venezuela he had been dealt a bloody nose by a much smaller insurgency led by Santiago Mariño, a rich and charming young landowner of Irish extraction, 'tall and athletic and with a very open countenance', from the island of Margarita, and José Bermúdez, a huge musclebound giant of a man, who had fled to Trinidad a year earlier. Other young insurgents there included Manuel Piar, a tough, brilliant young fighter, and the dashing and brave Antonio José de Sucre.

After repeated snubs from the British authorities on Trinidad, who were anxious not to antagonize the Spanish, some 45 of these exiles had landed on the desolate easternmost tip of Venezuela, the Güiria Peninsulas. Commanded by Mariño, they reached a small army supply fort, defeated the ferocious local Spanish commander, Captain Eusebio Antoñanzas, and seized the provincial capital of Cumana, as well as the town of Barcelona on the road to the capital. Monteverde had been humiliatingly rebuffed in an attempt to dislodge them at Maturín.

Faced by the much more alarming challenge of Bolívar's larger forces to the west, the Spanish commander left Manuel del Fierro as acting captain-general in Caracas, while he moved to Valencia. On the way he was discouraged by stories of Bolívar's successes and did an astonishing thing: the terror of Venezuela decided to avoid open battle and slipped away with his army intact to the royalist stronghold of Puerto Cabello.

Del Fierro, unprotected in the capital, had no alternative but to sue for peace and sent the Marqués of Casa León and Francisco Iturbe as his emissaries, the very men whose intercession before Monteverde had saved the life of Bolívar the year before. Bolívar met them in the town of La Victoria, where he embraced his old friend Iturbe with warmth and emotion. It was a poignant and wonderful moment: the enemy had melted away before him, demoralized by his rapid advance and brilliant, unpredictable guerrilla strikes.

*   *   *

On 7 August 1813, just eleven months after the fall of the first republic and Bolívar's escape in ignominy by boat, he re-entered Caracas in triumph to establish the Second Republic. It had been a staggering achievement and one of the most brilliantly executed campaigns in military history. In three months, a man just turned 30 with very little previous experience of battle and none at all of generalship had waged a punishing push up-river in enemy-held territory, taken his army across a supposedly impassable mountain barrier, won six battles, routed five separate armies, built up a force of 2,000 men virtually from scratch and covered 750 miles, returning in triumph to his homeland as liberator. The rich, spoilt, vainglorious, hyperactive young loudmouth, who had so excited Miranda's contempt and failed spectacularly in his first command, had shown powers of leadership, organization, tactical skill and ferocious energy that had enabled him to succeed where the Precursor, languishing in jail in Cádiz, had failed.

Small, tough and wiry, anchored to the saddle of his favourite mule, his once soft, pampered, even feminine face, previously so pale and refined, was now hardened by endurance, his cheeks hollowed out by privation, his eyes burning more brightly than ever before, his curly black hair retreating across the domed forehead, his thick quizzical eyebrows, long aquiline nose and pursed lips drawn in the mask of command and decision.

He made a formidable impression upon Iturbe, who had last seen the demoralized youth in the depths of depression and defeat. The terms of the armistice displayed a magnanimity at odds with the 'war to the death'. No vengeance was to be taken and property was to be respected. That did not stop some 6,000 refugee royalists, fearing reprisals after Monteverde's atrocities, fleeing down the mountain to the port of La Guaira.

On Bolívar's triumphal entry into Caracas on 7 August, his dirty uniform was replaced by a new one of white and blue, with gold buttons, braid and epaulettes. He rode a white Arab stallion at the head of his exhausted, filthy and tired army. It was a display of the theatricality that Bolívar both enjoyed and believed to be necessary to enthuse the masses.

Describing a scene both moving and absurd, one cynical observer, the French officer and mercenary named Henri Ducoudray-Holstein, takes up the story:

The women came to crown the Liberator and covered the streets where he would pass with heaps of flowers and branches of laurel and olive. The greetings of thousands of people mixed with the thunder of artillery, the ringing of church bells and the blare of martial music.

The prisons were opened and the unfortunate victims there, with their pale and thin faces, looked like ghosts risen from their graves. Before Bolívar's arrival a regal and triumphal cart had been prepared, similar to those which Roman consuls had on their return from a glorious campaign . . . Bolívar went on foot to the cart, his head uncovered, dressed in a general's uniform, carrying a baton as the symbol of command.

The cart was drawn by a silken rope carried by 12 beautiful girls and it was decorated by gilded angels. The triumphal procession was showered by flowers and thousands cheered its passage to the municipality. Even Archbishop Coll y Pratt, who had behaved so badly during the revolution, was there to make his peace with the Liberator. The festivities lasted all night, with Bolívar attending a great ball.

He returned at length to his old family home in the city, where he was repeatedly drawn to the window by the crowds. His sisters, María Antonia and Juana, fussed over him; his old black nurse, Hipolita, wept as she embraced him. Simón, the dissolute young wastrel who had lost a colossal fortune amid defeat the year before, had regained his honour and established himself as a man at last. It was a wonderful homecoming, the apparent dawn of a new era for independent Venezuela.

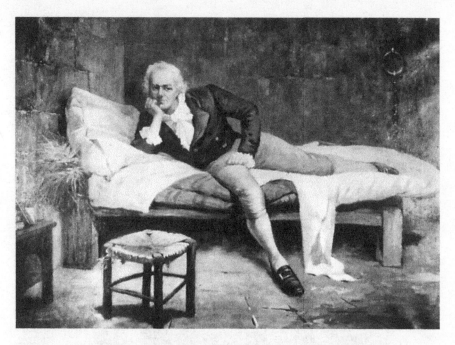

(above) The precursor: Francisco de Miranda in prison.

(below) Bourbon opulence and decadence: Charles IV, María Luisa and family by Goya.

The Liberator, Simón Bolívar, in his prime.

(above) Caribbean stronghold: Cartagena.

GENERAL PAEZ, OF VENEZUELA.—[FROM A PHOTOGRAPH BY BRADY.]

(left) Llanero chieftain: José Antonio Páez.

(above) Bolívar and his men cross the mighty Orinoco.

(below) Hit and run tactics: the Battle of Araure.

(above) Soaring mountains, plunging abysses: crossing the Andes.

(below) The Battle of Boyacá: a lightning strike on the Bogatá Antiplano.

(right) Bolívar's triumph: victory march in Caracas.

(below) Bolívar and his generals, including Santander (second from right) and Sucre (seated on left).

(above) Manuela Sáenz: the fiery, leather-clad beauty, a match worthy of Bolívar.

(below left) José de San Martín: Bolívar saw off his rival.

(below right) Tragic protégé: Antonio José de Sucre.

(above) Bolívar liberates Peru's slaves: an imaginative representation.

(below) Bolívar on his deathbed: ploughing the sea.

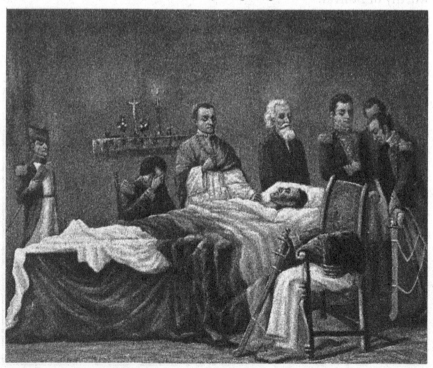

Chapter 12

HELL'S LEGIONNAIRES

For the moment there was also time for flirtation. Among the 12 maidens who had drawn his chariot was one who had eyed him with coquettish intensity, Josefina Machado, of medium height, dark-haired, with a broad thick-lipped mouth and striking, lively eyes. Her body was full, and she moved alluringly. She was quick-witted, with a frequent, infectious laugh. Yet her face was too plump and coarse to be described as pretty. She made up in sexiness what she lacked in looks. Not of noble birth, she had been excluded from high society, which had left her both resentful and deeply ambitious. Her detractors were to call her hot-tempered and aggressive. Her dislike of the vaunted social status of royalists in Caracas made her a natural revolutionary and she formed a hero-worship for Bolívar, managing to get herself appointed to his guard of honour and seeking his attentions as much out of political fervour as of attraction.

Bolívar was a relatively easy prospect for a woman seeking to bed him: usually, he sought only momentary relief. The difficulty was hooking him for any length of time, which Josefina, surprisingly for a girl with such ordinary looks, did with determination and perseverance, becoming his regular mistress and accompanying him, along with her sister and mother, in times both of success and danger. She was to become known as Señorita Pepa among his men. The acerbic French observer, Ducoudray-Holstein, comments of her:

> Bolívar paid tribute to the national temperament and, like most of
> his fellow countrymen spent much precious time in the boudoirs
> of his numerous mistresses; he was accused of spending even whole

days in his hammock in the midst of a crowd of female admirers. The most important business was in the hands of his admirers, especially Josefina, his known mistress, an intriguing and vengeful woman. I have seen this siren more than a hundred times and I confess that I don't understand the predilection of the dictator for her.

She was reputed to have a major influence upon affairs of state, was outspoken, had a sharp tongue, and was hated by many of his friends and associates for pursuing the interests of her own friends. She was not unusual, in a continent that was much later to venerate Evita Perón. She was, however, an unusually forceful and homely looking woman for Bolívar, who liked pliable and pretty girls. Her very ambition and tenacity, in catering to a wholly unfaithful man whose desires for history and his country were always uppermost, were necessary to ensure she retained her place alongside him.

Bolívar, by superb generalship, had conquered his capital. However, his role and those of the Spaniards were reversed once again. He was left holding the vulnerable centre, while they were left in possession of large swathes of the countryside, and of their intact armies. The humiliation suffered by the Spanish cause at his hands was immense. The onus of vengeance had shifted back to them.

None of this was obvious in the first heady days of power while Bolívar behaved with modesty and discretion. He set up a government under the authority of the long-suffering Congress of Tunja, in whose name he had marched to Caracas, more than 1,000 miles away. He sent detailed reports of his actions, dictating to his secretary at three in the morning, pacing up and down alone. He pledged constitutional government for Venezuela: 'Nothing shall turn me, Venezuelans, from my first and only intentions – your glory and liberty. An assembly of notable, wise and virtuous men must be solemnly convoked to discuss and approve the nature of the government and the functions it shall exercise in the critical and extraordinary circumstances that surround the republic.'

He refused to fall into the federalist trap and retained supreme executive and legislative powers. He appointed as his two chief ministers his old tutor, Miguel José Sanz, and Ustariz, who had drawn up the declaration of independence a year before. His understudy was a civilian governor, Cristobal Mendoza. The young playboy turned natural soldier now seemed a born statesman, but perhaps appeared to be too good to be true. Faithful to his promises, he took no reprisals against his royalist opponents. The man who had promised a 'war to the death' had partially redeemed himself.

His intention was to establish a self-governing state based on constitutional government, the rule of law and the exercise of firm power from the centre. In an age of cruelty and tyranny, he was behaving with restraint and clemency. Bolívar amicably accepted Santiago Mariño's authority in the east of the country, where he had styled himself Supreme Chief and Director. But he argued earnestly against dividing the nation in two:

> Can I answer you with the military frankness which I must use with you? I don't think it's right to delay the establishment of a centre of power for all Venezuela's provinces . . . If we create two independent powers, one in the east, one in the west, we will have two distinct nations, which from their inability to support themselves and to count among others, will look ridiculous. Venezuela even united with New Granada [Colombia] hardly makes a nation which inspires respect among others. Can we divide it into two?

Bolívar recognized he still faced two military challenges: the bulk of the royalist army remained intact in the strongly fortified Puerto Cabello; and, in addition, substantial royalist forces were based at Coro further up the coast. At this stage, the Liberator was unaware that he faced a far deadlier foe as well – from the llanos to the south. However, Bolívar had no reason to believe that, unless Spain sent massive reinforcements, the liberation of Venezuela had not been definitively achieved on the second try.

The general despatched his aides, Urdaneta and Girardot, to the outskirts of Puerto Cabello, where a series of unsatisfactory skirmishes had taken place with no major battle being fought. Bolívar had no fleet, so he could not blockade the port. Supplies were ferried in by the Spaniards and, after three months, a large army of 1,200 men under Colonel José Miguel Salomon was shipped in from Puerto Rico. To intimidate the Spanish garrison, Bolívar had a Spanish war criminal hanged in full view of the garrison – the man had stitched prisoners together back to back, so that every movement was agony, and had made a collection of rebel ears which he carried on his hat.

In a skirmish on the hills of Barbula outside the town, young Girardot was killed. Bolívar, who was particularly close to him, created a massive propaganda set piece in honour of the dead hero, whose heart was placed in a gilded urn and borne before Bolívar by a large armed force to the cathedral in Caracas. Bolívar replaced him with his boyhood companion, Fausto d'Elhuyar.

Bolívar was formally appointed Liberator of Venezuela, a title that he regarded as 'more glorious and satisfactory than all the empires on earth'. Meanwhile, Monteverde attempted a major sally, but had been defeated at Las Trincheras and driven back to Puerto Cabello. The cruel Spanish commander was badly wounded in the action and replaced by Salomon. The republic seemed more capable of resisting its enemies than ever. But, just in case, Bolívar appointed Rafael Urdaneta, his most experienced, loyal and cautious commander, as his chief of staff. Having bottled up Salomon in Puerto Cabello, his main concern was to contain the two other armies converging upon the west, some 1,300 loyalists under José Ceballos based at Coro and some 2,500 under José Yañez on the plains of Apure.

There at Barquisimeto, Bolívar unexpectedly suffered his first defeat in this campaign, through a retreat being mistakenly ordered just as victory beckoned. It was a salutary lesson, but it only increased Bolívar's determination. His forces regrouped to try and prevent the armies of Yañez and Ceballos joining up. He failed, and the two almost evenly matched armies met on 5 December 1813 – some 4,800 patriots against some 5,200 royalists, each disposing of infantry, cavalry and artillery, on the plains of Apure.

Bolívar this time was no longer the intrepid guerrilla leader, but a general in the field, directing his forces from a low hill, as he had seen Napoleon doing in manoeuvres. It was a set-piece battle lasting all day, until at last the royalist lines broke, leaving behind 1,000 dead, 700 prisoners and all their artillery and supplies. It was by far Bolívar's biggest victory to date: once again the little general had proved his military prowess. Ceballos' men returned licking their wounds to Coro, and Yañez retreated to the shelter of the cordillera.

Bolívar returned to the plaudits of his countrymen, and disclaimed all ambition for political power:

> The possession of supreme authority, so gratifying to the despots of other countries, has been for me, lover of liberty, painful and depressing . . . Return, therefore, Venezuela, to happiness under the protecting laws decreed by your representatives and under magistrates named by legal and popular election . . .
>
> I repeat what I have always declared; that I will retain no part of my authority unless the people themselves confer it upon me. To fight for my country is my sole ambition: and it will be satisfied with whatever position is assigned me in the army that wages war against the enemy.

Instead, he was appointed 'dictator' by acclamation. The word then implied the exercise of absolute authority, but was not a word of opprobrium. It was to be his last real moment of glory. For in spite of the triumph at Apure, the royalists were far from defeated and Yañez's forces were regrouping. His army met Urdaneta's at Uspino, where they were defeated again, and the Spanish commander killed, his body dismembered and its parts sent as trophies to nearby villages. However, the relatively disciplined royalist forces against which Bolívar was fighting so energetically and which he might have defeated in due course were no longer the main danger.

The same fickle, brutal fate that had deposited him in a boat as a half-demented, muttering disgrace a year before was to cast its fearsome spell again. Within 12 months he would again be an outcast in a boat; the nation he had conquered would be prey to one of the most virulent and terrible orgies of savagery in human history, far eclipsing that of Monteverde; his dream would once again be in ruins, his name excoriated and despised, his estates once again stripped from him.

Behind the great sub-Andean cordillera that bisects Venezuela from west to east, the mountains descend to forest and then to a vast area that comprises half the land mass of the country known as the llanos, which in turn drain away to the great basin of the River Orinoco and its tributaries, the Apure and the Arauca. They are known as the plains, the llanos, but in reality they are one huge flatland, a kind of green desert of tall, wild grass, resembling the steppes of central Asia except that they are much wilder and more hostile to human habitation. They resemble a great green sea, immobile, desolate, endless.

These lowlands have a fiercely inhospitable climate. In the rainy season, the vast territory floods because their hard, shallow soil fails to absorb the water. In the dry season the water subsides, the grass becomes yellow, and a ferocious heat descends whose harshness is accentuated by the desert storms that swirl across its vastness.

Before the arrival of the Spaniards, these inhospitable lands were almost deserted, with only a handful of fierce tribesmen struggling to live on them. After the opening up of the new world, and the introduction of horses and cattle by the Spaniards, there gradually grew up in these badlands vast herds of both, roaming wild, offering the prospect of a living for desperate, poor men, many of them slaves of the absentee owners.

The llaneros were extremely tough, as they had to be, and very primitive, denied even the rudiments of civilization. Glued to their saddles, they were the cowboys or gauchos of Venezuela, but there was nothing either romantic or organized about them. Mostly black, Indian or mestizo, they rode about naked except for rough trousers and broad-brimmed hats to protect them from the sun. Their diet consisted of the brackish water of the llanos and raw beef, tied to their saddles in strips and salted by the sweat of their horses. They roamed the vast interior, herding their cattle on to dry land in the rainy season and to oases in time of drought. Theoretically subject to slave overseers, the hated *hatos*, their toughness ensured they were subject to no one – except their own local leaders.

Initially, they traded their cattle up the cordillera, across on to the central highlands, and then down to Venezuela's Caribbean ports. However, with the opening up of the navigable Orinoco river basin to the east, a huge contraband trade began to flourish beyond the control of Caracas. In effect, Venezuela became two virtually separate countries above and below the Andes.

A year before Simón Bolívar's birth in 1783, a boy was born to a rough, lower middle-class family in the Spanish city of Oviedo. The child studied at the naval academy there and, at the age of 15, was sent off as a pilot to Puerto Cabello in Venezuela. Crafty, rough-hewn, a born leader with a vein of psychopathic cruelty, the youth soon became a smuggler; he was caught and sentenced to 18 years in prison.

Through the intercession of friends, this tough-minded Spaniard secured his release and departed into exile in the town of Calabozo on the llanos. He was soon smuggling again from the Orinoco region to the town of Barinas on the edge of the llanos. He established himself as a natural leader of the primitive herdsmen. His name was José Tomás Rodríguez Boves.

Small, with a hugely muscular torso and a barrel chest, he had an unusually large head, surmounted by red hair, grey eyes, a prominent nose and a small, cruel mouth with a meagre red beard. The writer and adventurer Robert Cunninghame Graham described him as: 'active, bold, fearless, impetuous, rash, astute, hungry for power, cruel and bloody', while Daniel O'Leary, who was to become Bolívar's closest personal aide, wrote:

No trace was visible in his countenance of the demonic ferocity which marked his character. Light hair, large grey eyes, and a fair complexion stamped upon it rather an air of humanity. He was active, brave and capable of undergoing extraordinary fatigue . . . I have heard related that when [Bolívar] evacuated Caracas in 1814, followed by an immense emigration, the camp was often disturbed at night by the people terrified at the noise made by . . . the toads in the woods which resembled, in the sound, Bo-vez. The name used [to] be re-echoed in a moment by the terrified families.

Boves was a kind of land pirate. When Venezuela's first revolution began in Caracas, Boves immediately understood that it was doomed by its internal contradictions, and said as much. He was arrested as a traitor and held in the grim little dungeon at Calabozo. There the insane hatreds of this psychopathic fiend were nurtured by injustice until the famously vicious Spanish commander, Eusebio Antoñanzas, attacked and freed the town, appointing Boves and other convicts as his officers.

He rose quickly through the ranks and, in August 1813, he was appointed by the new Spanish commander on the llanos, Cajigal, to go and raise troops in the Orinoco basin itself. Boves proved an inspired leader of men. He instantly understood that to secure the allegiance of the savage llaneros he must urge a racial and class war against the white men who were their nominal masters. 'White lands to the blacks' was his rallying cry – ignoring the fact that, as a Spaniard, he was white. Blacks were preferred for positions of responsibility in his army. He was known by his men as 'Taita': 'Uncle'. He designated the 4,000 horsemen he drilled 'the Legion of Hell' (*legion infernal*), with a black flag he called his 'pennant of death'. For weapons they carried bamboo lances. Bolívar was to say of him: 'He was not nurtured with the delicate milk of a woman but with the blood of tigers and the furies of hell . . . He was the wrath of heaven which hurled its lightning against the patria . . . a demon in human flesh which drowned Venezuela in blood.'

When Boves judged his new army sufficiently trained, he led them on his huge black horse, Antinoo, forward across the llanos to meet a patriot force under Colonel Carlos Padrón, which had been sent to deal with this nuisance. In Santa Catalina Canyon, near Calabozo, these troops were speared to the last man by the lances of the llaneros. Reaching Calabozo itself, where he had been imprisoned, Boves gave the order to spare no one, including women and children. The few prisoners taken were tied to stakes with their heads shaved to die in the heat of the sun.

When news of the massacres reached Bolívar, he despatched his most ferocious general, the Spanish-born Vicente Campo Elías, with 1,000 men to deal with the brigand. Reaching a village called Mosquiteros near Calabozo, this column was attacked by the 4,000 soldiers from the Legion of Hell. The wild horsemen flung themselves against Campo Elías' left flank, routing it and massacring the soldiers there.

But the patriot centre held, and Campo Elías counter-attacked in disciplined ranks, creating havoc among the demon horsemen. Campo Elías gave the order that no mercy should be extended to these savages, and thousands were butchered. Only a few hundred escaped with Boves, who had been wounded by a lance. It seemed that Bolívar had decisively rid himself of this nuisance.

Yet, after his triumph in the field of Araure, Bolívar returned to Caracas only to hear that in the space of a few weeks Boves had assembled a still bigger force of some 6,000 horsemen which, attracted by the prospect of destruction, murder and plunder, was engaged in an orgy of destruction across the remote settlements of the llanos. At San Marcos, on 8 December 1813, they fell upon the garrison left by Campo Elías, killing the soldiers there without quarter. The way was now open for the barbarian hordes to ascend to the uplands.

They were indeed barbarians. O'Leary tells a story of Boves himself:

One day an old and emaciated man was brought before him, the only inhabitant of the town from which the rest had fled on learning of his approach. After some questions to which the old man responded gently and truthfully, he was ordered to be decapitated. At that moment a youth of about 15 years came forward and, kneeling in front of the horse of the barbarian, told him, 'I beg you sir, on the blessed Virgin, that you pardon this man who is my father. Save him, and I will be your slave.' 'Good,' said the monster, smiling on hearing the fervent supplication of the young man. 'To save your father's life you will have to allow your nose and ears to be cut off without crying out.' 'Yes, yes,' replied the unhappy boy. 'I give you my life to save my father.' The boy suffered the horrible test with admirable calm. Seeing which, Boves ordered that the boy be killed alongside his father for being too brave and for fear that he too would become an enemy.

The fiend's army had soon swollen to around 8,000 men. To the west, Yañez remained a threat and in December had recaptured Barinas, burning down the town of 10,000 inhabitants and executing the 80-strong garrison. To the north, Ceballos and Salomon, although beaten back, still had some 4,000 men in Coro and Puerto Cabello. To the east Cajigal commanded his own force of 3,000.

Nearby, a new threat raised its head under the command of another bloodthirsty Spanish general, Francisco Rosete, at the head of 1,000 men in the valley of the Tuy. He occupied Ocumbre, close to Caracas, killing all the inhabitants. Rosete ordered his soldiers to force their way into a church and behead the entire congregation. A sadist in the Boves mould, he would skin men alive, disembowel women and gouge out the eyes of children, cutting off their heads afterwards.

Bolívar's army fought magnificently against this sudden profusion of challenges, tearing up and down the central highlands and valleys of the country, fending off one attack after another. At Carabobo, he personally defeated the Spaniards and chased them back once again into Puerto Cabello. But from their strongholds in the coastal lowlands, where they were kept well supplied and reinforced by Spanish ships, from the baked badlands of the llanos and from the humid lowlands of the east, the challenges were proving remorseless. The defenders of the highlands were increasingly hard-pressed and exhausted.

Nor was there significant help from abroad. The British, Miranda's great hope, watched cynically, anxious not to antagonize the Spanish empire. The United States gave nothing. Bolívar, who had more or less ignored the need for foreign assistance and could have done with Miranda's diplomatic skills, was fighting almost entirely from his own resources against an enemy constantly reinforced and resupplied from the coast.

The empire, with a cynicism almost unparalleled in the annals of European history, had incited the black mulatto and Indian populations against their white overlords in a ferocious class and racial war in a country where the 200,000 whites were vastly outnumbered by 500,000 blacks and 200,000 Indians. The result was near-genocide. The Spaniards could always find recruits motivated by plunder and hatred, while the criollo aristocracy found that their visions of liberal constitutional rule appealed to few ordinary Venezuelans except the more resilient mountain people of the west.

The Spaniards also dominated the war of terror. For ordinary people, the fear of being killed was always the primary consideration; and although Bolívar had preached a 'war to the death', only two of his commanders actually pursued it wholeheartedly. In contrast the murderous strategy of men like Boves, his even more bloodthirsty lieutenant Tomás Morales, a Canary Islander, and Rosete needed no enunciation. Those not engaged in the fighting were terrified not of Bolívar and the patriots but of the royalists and their allies.

Bolívar nevertheless still believed he could win, but his hope became desperate when Boves decisively defeated Campo Elías at La Puerta, the strategic gateway to the capital. Bolívar had three last throws: he ordered his valiant, straightforward subordinate Ribas to take the offensive to 'save Caracas at any cost'. He hurried his own forces from Valencia and entrenched himself in his boyhood family estate at San Mateo. And he continued desperately to beseech the strutting Mariño, his rival patriot ruler of eastern Venezuela who had no wish to add to Bolívar's glory, for help.

Ribas rose to the exigencies of the moment. He recruited from among the young college graduates of the capital and with an army of 17- and 18-year-olds he charged the lances of the Legion from Hell time and time again. Those murderous backwoodsmen, unaccustomed to fighting on the highlands and to being vigorously resisted, finally fled when Campo Elías arrived with the remains of his army to reinforce Ribas. The courage of the youths was astounding. One dying boy asked to be remembered to Ribas for 'never having taken a backward step'. Three horses were killed under Ribas himself. The capital had won a respite. Ribas ignored a paranoid order from Bolívar to 'shoot all Europeans and Canarians in the city'.

It was Bolívar's turn to face the barbarian cowboys from the llanos. But first, as his dream of an independent Venezuela was being slowly hacked away in a series of gruesome bloodbaths, and his pedestal of just two months earlier seemed about to be toppled, he allowed his own high ideals again to be reduced to those of his opponents. As when he betrayed Miranda in his own moment of disgrace in January 1812, as when he issued the order to fight 'war to the death' in July 1813, now he showed that he too could be merely vengeful in the face of unrelenting savagery. On 8 February 1814 he ordered all the royalist prisoners held in Caracas and La Guaira to be executed. There were more than 500 in the former and 800 in the latter. The dreadful headcount began:

A report comes from Palacio: 'In obedience to the order of the Most Excellent General Liberator for decapitation of all the Spanish and Canary Island prisoners held in his port, the executions have commenced this night with 100 of them.' On February 14th: 'Yesterday afternoon 150 men of the Spanish prisoners were decapitated and between today and tomorrow the rest will be executed.' On February 15th: 'Yesterday afternoon 247 Spanish and Canary Island prisoners were decapitated.' On February 16th: 'Today all the Spaniards and Canary Islanders who were sick in the hospital were decapitated, constituting the last of all those included in the order of Your Excellency.'

It was to be the most repulsive action of Bolívar's life. But he was to defend himself by pointing out that the governor of Caracas prison had warned him of unrest there. Bolívar bitterly remembered the revolt at Puerto Cabello that had so nearly cut short his military career before it began. If the prisoners had succeeded in breaking out of their jails, another 1,300 would have been added to the ranks of the royalists. As Bolívar put it: 'One less of such monsters in existence is one less who has slaughtered or would slaughter hundreds of victims.'

To many Latin Americans today his act is not only understandable but admirable, evidence that he was a leader capable of the terrible decisions necessary to safeguard the lives of his own men. But nothing, in truth, can excuse this appalling conduct, the worst of Bolívar's career. As prisoners of war, even in the early nineteenth century, they had earned the right to be treated with respect by their jailers, but they were helpless and disarmed. The slaughter was on a huge scale, a barbaric atrocity against humanity, an instance of the worst of the Latin American despotism that was to follow, born of Bolívar's despair when he was at his lowest ebb.

Feverish now, and suffering from perpetual piles as a result of riding from one front to another, Bolívar believed in spite of all the odds that he could still win. The sullen, debased Liberator, depressed, angry and tired, had ridden to his beloved ranch at San Mateo to face the demon cavalry from the llanos. He withdrew his army from Valencia. All-powerful just two months before, he assumed it was his last stand, and was uncharacteristically savage in mood. His army consisted of 1,500 infantry, 600 cavalry and five or six cannon.

A witness, Francisco Rivas Vicuña, sketches the scene of Bolívar's intended stand: 'The chosen site was a fairly narrow valley crowned on the north side by a chain of mountains whose highest peak was known as Calvary and on another of which was the Liberator's house. To the south were the highest peaks of the range.'

Bolívar had chosen the narrow valley with the greatest skill – although he may also have been influenced by psychological reasons: having been stripped of his magnificent estate once by defeat, and plunged into destitution, he seemed to be making a stand as much for his inheritance and fortune as for his country at San Mateo, where once as a boy he roamed free with his tutor, Simón Rodríguez.

When Boves' advance horsemen attacked the entrenched positions at the head of the valley, they were easily beaten back. Boves, the victor of countless engagements in the flatlands below, was out of his element. He withdrew, and the following morning sent his cavalry up the slopes of the southern mountains in an effort to turn the left of the patriot line and reach the Calvary mountain behind them.

As Boves personally spurred his men on, his beloved giant black charger Antinoo was shot out from under him. Boves fell to the ground and hugged his beloved steed, first sobbing like a baby, then swearing furious vengeance on the horse's killers. But his lancers, although much more numerous, were no match for the firearms of the patriots. In a flash of tactical inspiration he sent a force to seize the patriots' arms and munitions depot, based in a sugar mill overlooking the valley.

The depot was defended by Antonio Ricaurte, one of Bolívar's most attractive aristocratic lieutenants. At the approach of the enemy, he knew that his small detachment would be overwhelmed. He despatched his men to safety and, in a famous act of heroism, blew up the powder keg and himself along with it, just as the enemy reached the door of the depot.

Meanwhile, Bolívar's forces continued successfully to hold back wave after wave of attacks by the frenzied horsemen. Suddenly, it seemed that relief was at hand for Bolívar: the news came that Mariño had at last decided to rise to his fellow liberator's aid. At the head of a force of 3,500 men he had defeated the sadistic Rosete at Los Pilones and was now on his way to Vila de Cura to meet up with Bolívar's forces.

Boves reacted quickly, abandoning the siege of San Mateo to the relief of Bolívar and his hard-pressed men, and hurrying his horsemen to intercept Mariño at Bolachica. There the eastern patriot leader managed to beat him off. Meanwhile Bolívar, no longer under pressure, moved back to Valencia, forcing Yañez and Ceballos to raise the siege of the city. He rode, hope renewed, to La Victoria, to meet Mariño. The two prima donnas met at last and reached an agreement, by which Mariño was permitted to retain the command of his own forces. Bolívar then departed to help the siege of Puerto Cabello.

It seemed as though the tide was turning. However, Mariño, impetuous and self-confident, decided to engage the Spanish forces led by Cajigal at Arao, and suffered a bloody nose. Learning nothing from this setback, the arrogant Mariño decided to set out on his own against Boves, refusing to wait for Bolívar's forces to reinforce him, and came upon the fiend's army camped near La Puerta. Horrified, Bolívar hurried his men up from Puerto Cabello to reinforce Mariño, but Boves had been engaged on his preferred terrain and battle had begun.

On 15 June 1814, the second and more terrible battle of La Puerta took place. Thousands of Boves' horsemen poured out from side valleys to ambush the armies of Mariño and Bolívar. By nightfall, 1,000 had been killed and a further 300 captured and put to death. Campo Elías was among the dead, as was Bolívar's chief civilian adviser, Antonio Muñoz Tébar. General Freitas killed himself to avoid being captured and tortured by the subhumans. Bolívar himself, Mariño and the faithful and brave Ribas escaped and galloped back to Valencia, to arrange the defences of the last major city blocking the road to Caracas.

At last, Bolívar had understood that the Second Republic, like the first, was doomed. The hopes of a year before, the victorious entry into Caracas, were a mockery beside the reality of thousands slaughtered and imminent defeat. It was no consolation that Mariño, his rival liberator, had been primarily responsible for the rashness that had led to the disaster. The empire had struck back, devastatingly, for a second time.

The Spanish commander, Cajigal, ordered Boves to put his troops under his command. The commander of the Legion from Hell, retorted, insolently, that he had recovered 'the arms, munitions and honour of the flags which your excellency lost in Carabobo'. At the head of 6,000 horsemen, the stocky, red-headed fiend rode forward through the highlands in triumph, black pennants flying, towards Valencia. For ten days the patriots there resisted Boves' siege, as food and ammunition ran low. Then Boves offered terms – surrender in exchange for sparing the soldiers and civilians. As the brigand rode into the city, he was received with rejoicing and a Mass in the Cathedral, at which he swore on the Bible that no blood would be spilt.

By nightfall, the civil governor had been shot. A girl in the household of the former patriot commander of the city was tied in her hammock and gang-raped by several soldiers, after which her tongue was torn out, her breasts cut off and a fire lit under her until she was cooked in her bed. The other women were forced to attend a huge fiesta:

Meanwhile the men had all been taken into custody, led to the outskirts of the city and put to the lance like bulls, without spiritual consolation . . . The women at the dance drank their tears and trembled to hear the hoofbeats of the cavalry outside, fearing what was taking place, while Boves, whip in hand, made them dance the piquirico and other country dances, to which he was greatly addicted . . . The killings continued for several nights more.

Bolívar had ridden back to Caracas, his country and dream shattered. Less than a year before he had arrived in triumph, treated as a Roman conqueror, dragged through the streets by pretty girls, feted in his own house of birth. Now he was a fugitive once more, his people facing untold suffering at the hands of the barbarian hordes of a psychopathic killer.

The tough, short, thin man with the cavernous cheeks and the

blazing black eyes rode back into town wrapped in his cape, humiliated. There he asked for the churches of Caracas to provide him with
their silver vessels to help his cause, and emerged with 24 cases of
silver containing 28,000 ounces of the metal. The word soon got out
that he and the remnants of his forces had decided to evacuate the
capital in the face of the searing atrocities being carried out by Boves
in Valencia, and panic spread through the city.

There followed one of the most pathetic exoduses in history. The
sufferings of the Venezuelan people during the last two years of
strife had been awesome. Around 30,000 had been killed in the
two wars, and about two-thirds as many in the earthquake two
years before. Now 20,000 terrified old people, women and children left in a wretched column behind Bolívar and the few that
remained loyal to him. Bolívar has been criticized for ordering the
people out, but their fate at the hands of Boves would have been
terrible. It is also suggested that he should have marched west, and
joined with the small army of General Urdaneta, instead of east;
but the east offered the only chance of reaching the coast and of
evacuation.

Caracas was abandoned to Boves and his vultures. This miserable
exodus, which included Bolívar's sisters and the ever-faithful Señorita
Pepa, all of whom could expect to be slaughtered when Boves
arrived, consisted largely of old and genteel people who had never
experienced discomfort – the upper classes and their servants. As they
tramped down from the uplands of Caracas towards the lowlands,
hundreds died and many became insane at the discomfort.

The bedraggled high society of Caracas were led across 200 miles
of disease-ridden swamps, fleeing from the class vengeance of Boves'
savage and illiterate hordes, abandoning their beautiful houses and
possessions. After three weeks the survivors of this wretched column
reached the town of Barcelona. Bolívar himself was in a pitiable
state, unwilling to assert his authority over men who believed he was
responsible for the holocaust. None of this would have happened if
he had not raised the standard of revolt against the Spaniards a second
time.

Boves would not let even these wretches escape: he sent a force of 8,000 men under the still crueller Morales in pursuit, and they reached Aragua, south of Barcelona. Bolívar's few soldiers liaised with what was left of Mariño's army in the east as well as José Bermúdez, and pulled together a force of around 3,000 men. Bolívar's plan was to turn and face the approaching enemy along the River Aragua, but Bermúdez insisted it would be better to fight on the streets of the town of Barcelona itself.

Morales' forces crossed the river virtually unopposed, and proved Bermúdez wrong: the town became a slaughterhouse. The Spanish historian Mariano Torrente wrote, 'Everything perished in that day of blood and horror. Because they were the battleground, the streets, houses and even churches were all steeped in blood.' Hundreds were killed. Some 3,500 of the genteel civilians took refuge in the cathedral, where Boves' hordes slaughtered them to the last one, in by far the biggest massacre of this cruellest of wars. Bolívar escaped with his depleted refugee column, now only 10,000 strong, the rest having perished through disease, famine, fatigue and war, to the port of Cumana, along with his sister, María Antonia, the ever-faithful Josefina and the Soublette family. This miserable trek was in stark contrast to his triumphalism of the year before. The suffering of his own criollo aristocracy was beyond belief.

At Cumana, they met up with the small fleet which had fled the port of La Guaira with the silver and gold of Caracas under the command of Captain Bianchi, an Italian adventurer who had not been paid for his services. On the arrival of Bolívar's bedraggled horde, Bianchi raised anchor and left, along with the treasure. Bolívar and Mariño furiously commandeered a sailboat and went in pursuit. They caught up with Bianchi on the beautiful but sun-baked tropical island of Margarita, where they negotiated the return of two-thirds of the silver and gold.

They set off in two ships back to the Venezuelan coast. There, at Carúpano, they were met by an angry mob on the beach. The remaining commanders, the usually faithful Ribas and the devious Piar, believed they had themselves absconded with the treasure. The Liberator and the El Supremo of the east were seized and taken to a dirty prison. The mood, after all these terrible events, was bitter. Bolívar was judged not just to have placed his country in peril, but to have attempted to flee with what was left of its wealth – whereas the reverse was true: he had been trying to save it. He was now accused of the very crimes he had pinned on Miranda two years before.

In his cell at Carúpano, the irony and injustice of it all must have struck him forcibly. In the space of just two years, he had been blamed for defeat, fled to exile and returned to reconquer his homeland in a spectacular military campaign whose ferocity had caused untold suffering among his people. Now, blamed for this and regarded as a failure, just like Miranda, his own people had turned against him as a traitor and plunderer. Miranda, imprisoned up in Cádiz, would have laughed contemptuously if he had known.

Leading Spain's colonies to freedom was much less easy than had originally seemed to the hot-headed Bolívar. But he proved to be luckier than the Precursor. Soon after his arrest, Bianchi's fleet put in; grateful for having been paid at last, the Italian threatened to bombard the little port unless Bolívar and Mariño were freed. The two were released on condition that they leave Venezuela immediately. Ribas appointed himself to continue leading the forces of resistance in western Venezuela, and Piar in the east. Bolívar's career seemed at an end.

Bolívar, stripped of his titles, authority, estates and territory, prepared to say goodbye to Josefina who, with her family, was departing for the island of Santo Tomás to start a new, more peaceful life. The embittered, wretched, yet still dreamy Bolívar sat down to write an extraordinarily eloquent testament of the terrible events that had just occurred:

> If inconstant destiny made victory alternate between ourselves and the enemy, it was only in favour of the American people, who under an inconceivable madness took up arms to destroy their liberties and restore their tyrants. Heaven, for the sake of our humiliation and glory, decided that our conquerors should be brothers, and that our brothers should triumph over us. The liberating army encountered the enemy arms, defeated them and was careless of them, despising the people we fought in hundreds of engagements . . .

Your own brothers, and *not* the Spaniards, have ripped open your breast, shed your blood, burnt your homes and condemned you to exile . . . I am very far from having the moral presumption to consider myself blameless for the catastrophe of my fatherland, and indeed suffer from believing myself the unhappy instrument of its frightening miseries, but I am innocent before my conscience because I have never held malice . . . I promise you, beloved compatriots, that this august title [Liberator] which your gratitude bestowed upon me when I broke your chains will not be vain, I promise you that, as Liberator or in death, I will always deserve the honour that you gave me: no human power on earth will hold me back from the course which I have elected to follow, to return for the second time to free you along the trail of the west, stained by so much blood and adorned by so many heads.

Bolívar went on to excuse those Venezuelans who preferred to suffer enslavement to freedom. This astonishing document continued:

Be noble in your grief, as the cause that produces it is noble . . . The destruction of a government . . . the overthrow of established principles, the changing way of life, the remoulding of opinion, and, in a word, the establishment of freedom in a land of slaves is a task beyond all human capacity to carry out quickly. So our excuse for not having achieved what we hoped is inherent in our cause; since even as justice justifies the boldness of having taken it upon us, so does the impossibility of achieving it reflect the inadequacy of the means.

It is praiseworthy, it is noble and sublime, to avenge Nature when it has been outraged by tyranny. Nothing can compare with the greatness of such action, and even if desolation and death are the reward of such a glorious endeavour, there is no reason to condemn it, for it is not the easily attainable that should be undertaken, but that which justice demands that we do . . .

It is fatally stupid to attribute to public men the changes of fortune which the unfolding of events produces in states, for it is not within the sphere of influence of a general or a magistrate, in a moment of unrest, of clashes, and of divergent views, to stem the torrent of human passions. Agitated by revolutionary movements, these grow in proportion to the force that resists them. And even though serious mistakes or violent passions in the leaders cause frequent harm to the Republic, these very setbacks ought nevertheless to be fairly assessed and their roots sought for in the primary causes of all misfortunes: that is, the frailty of our species and the hazardous nature of all events.

Man is the weak toy of fortune, which he may often predict quite well but can never be sure of; for our situation has no contact with it, it being of a much higher order than ours. To imagine that politics and war will proceed according to our plans, unfolding blindly by the mere strength of our desires and encouraged by the limited means at our disposal, is to wish by human means to emulate divine power.

His testament is lucid and surprisingly reflective for that of a man who had just gone through defeat, victory, and again defeat. It is also vain, self-exculpatory and imbued with an optimism that seems, in the circumstances, mere hysteria. Bolívar's cause had been crushed as comprehensively as was imaginable. His dream had ended in the butchery of thousands – at least 10,000 during and after the march from Caracas – yet he finished defiantly and proudly: 'Do not compare your physical strength with the enemy's, for spirit is not to be compared with matter. You are men, they are beasts, you are free, they are slaves. Fight and you shall win. God grants victory to the steadfast.'

With that, on 7 September 1814, Bolívar, his sister María Antonia and Mariño boarded the appropriately named *El Arrogante*, bound for Curaçao and his second exile in 18 months. Thousands of other refugees set sail for the Antilles.

As Bolívar departed, Boves advanced at the head of his horsemen to occupy Cumana, where he had another 'fiesta' and slaughtered a thousand civilians: the men were taken off to be executed by night, while the women were forced to perform for his men, then raped and killed – as were the musicians. He had a pregnant woman killed and then ripped open, so that he could laugh uproariously at the convulsions of the foetus.

The pitiable but courageous remnant of the patriot army was defeated first at the hamlet of Sabana de El Salad and then at Urica – where a patriot lance cut open Boves' own stomach. He at last perished, but so too did Miguel José Sanz, Bolívar's old family lawyer, and Ustariz, father of Venezuelan independence and drafter of the first constitution. Piar fled to Jamaica and Bermúdez to Margarita. Only Ribas stayed behind on the mainland, and made for the llanos. There he was captured. His head was cut off and preserved in oil in a jar sent to Caracas, its jaunty cap with the French revolution tricolour rosette still perched on it, as an example to the people. The cruel Morales killed seven of his brother officers to become the new commander of the Legion of Hell.

Chapter 13

DOWN AND OUT IN JAMAICA

On 20 September 1814, as Simón Bolívar returned to Cartagena, Colonel Manuel Castillo, his old enemy, was ready to accuse him of treason, while Brigadier Joaquín Ricaurte sought to have him censured by Congress: 'The barbaric and unwise project of the "war to the death", which converted whole towns and provinces into enemies, not only made the army hated but also what it stood for, and the very same people who were supposed to receive us with olive and laurel in hand to unite their efforts to ours to throw the Spaniards off the territory, seeing our bloody behaviour, became our enemies.'

As well as being accused of having waged a campaign of terror, Bolívar was alleged to be plotting to impose the rule of Venezuela upon New Granada. As Bolívar rode into the highlands of eastern New Granada to the capital, Tunja, he must have felt alone and abandoned. But for once luck was with him: he encountered at Ocaña a division under his most loyal lieutenant, Rafael Urdaneta, who had fought furiously in the west and struggled back into New Granada. The exhausted men fell joyfully upon their leader, breaking ranks to embrace and cheer him. He chided them for their indiscipline, but was alive to the fact that he suddenly had a small and effective army at his back, battle-hardened men whom the peaceful people of New Granada were unlikely to want to anger. Bolívar and his column were feted by hundreds as they passed along the mountain trail to Tunja, where he delivered to the Congress an account of his successes and failures: 'All of America is steeped in American blood. It was necessary to wash out so ingrained a stain. It is the first time this unhappy continent, always a land of desolation but not of freedom, dresses in

honour . . . for freedom, I say the earth has been sown with arms –
that earth which only a little time ago suffered slavery'.

Bolívar had by now become a powerful orator, which was even
acknowledged by his enemies, and at the end of his speech the president of the assembly, Camilo Torres, invited him to take a seat on
the dais beside him: 'General, while your sword exists, your country
has not died; with it you will return to rescue it from the realm of its
oppressor. The Congress of Granada will give you this judgment on
your rebellion. You have been an unfortunate soldier, but you are a
great man.'

There was another reason why Congress speedily embraced
Bolívar: they needed him as a mercenary. The independent province around Santa Fé de Bogotá, which co-existed with the Tunja
republic, had been betrayed while its leader Antonio Nariño was sent
back in chains to Cádiz in Spain. One Manuel Alvarez had since set
himself up as dictator and declared his opposition to Tunja, if not
outright support for the royalists. Congress hoped that Bolívar and his
desperadoes were the men to bring Bogotá to heel. The general was
unhappy about attacking what he called 'fellow-citizens of America',
but fell in with the plan. On 12 December 1814, he arrived on the
outskirts of Bogotá to find that the Spaniards had come to the aid of
Alvarez. Nonetheless, he was able to crush the upstart in three days of
hand-to-hand fighting across barricades, through windows and over
rooftops. It was a much-needed triumph.

Bolívar entered Bogotá – one of the most beautiful colonial cities
in Latin America – as Liberator. In time the Congress of Tunja
moved to Santa Fé de Bogotá as the new capital, unifying the former
Viceroyalty of New Granada under a single government. The victory
helped Bolívar regain a little of his old confidence and prestige. For
a man who had led his country into a disastrous civil war, his powers
of recovery and optimism were remarkable. Many were struck by his
maturity and sense of proportion. He was lucid, calm and rational,
rather than emotional, a man of destiny not to be distracted from his
cause by a setback, however great. In time his resolve was to prove
his greatest strength as well as his worst failing; especially when he
believed that he was the only man capable of doing the job. Awarded
the new title of Pacificador – the Peacekeeper – and nominal

command of all of the forces, he was despatched down to Cartagena to take control of the army there and attack Santa Marta, the last royalist outpost in New Granada. He was given about 2,000 largely unarmed men, who were to receive their weapons in Cartagena.

As his army was transported down the Magdalena river, he was confronted by Castillo, the commander in the north who abandoned his siege of the royalist army in Santa Marta and returned to Cartagena, where he persecuted Bolívar's supporters and placed his sister María Antonia under house arrest. Bolívar appealed to Torres, now president of the united republic, who reaffirmed that the Liberator had been appointed to act as commander of the forces in Cartagena. Bolívar was resolved not to fight his own supposed allies – and with too few arms and men he was in no position to do so. He promoted Castillo to brigadier-general as a conciliatory gesture, and even offered his own resignation as commander.

However, Castillo would not let him into Cartagena. When Bolívar occupied the hills of La Popa above the city, his forces were fired upon and found that the water supply had been poisoned. The port was defended by massive walls and forts, originally erected as a defence against English buccaneers. An attack by Bolívar's forces stood no chance, and both commanders knew it. In addition his men were now dying from disease. The sympathetic insurrection he had expected would occur in Cartagena when he occupied La Popa never materialized. The alternative was to move his forces to the front against the Spanish and leave Castillo to his own devices – something he said 14 years later he wished he had done.

But news reached New Granada of a far more terrible threat to its existence than this squabbling between supposed allies: the Spanish empire was at last striking back in force. Following the defeat of the French in Spain, the blatantly reactionary Ferdinand VII – whom Bolívar had allegedly played with in adolescence – had returned to the Spanish throne. Fifteen thousand men, many of them veterans of the fighting in Spain, had been despatched in 42 troop transport ships escorted by 18 men-of-war to subdue Spain's rebellious colonies.

Bolívar's reaction was realistic and decisive. Recognizing at once that the chances of prevailing against such an army were small, particularly if New Granada's forces were divided, he resigned his command and announced his immediate intention to depart into exile. 'If I remain here, New Granada will divide into parts and domestic war will be eternal. By withdrawing, there will be only the fatherland's party which, being united, will be better.' He had no desire to preside over another catastrophe. He had learnt from his mistakes and his decision, if hardly courageous, was sensible. After five months of a fruitless stand-off with Castillo, he set sail into exile on 9 March 1815 on an English boat bound for Jamaica.

The cruelties of the Spanish in Venezuela were attested to not only by their patriot enemies – themselves guilty of many atrocities. José Ambrosio Llamosa, the chaplain of the Spanish army, sent a memorial of Boves' merciless brutalities to Ferdinand, also highlighting the racial element: 'He [Boves] always repeated that the goods of the whites were for the blacks. In his military calculations and in his type of government this system formed the principal part.' One result of Llamosa's revelations was a change in the tactics to be employed by the formidable army now bound for Venezuela, away from the exacerbation of racially based resentments.

The commander of the royalist forces that now headed towards New Granada was Pablo Morillo. Of humble birth, from Fuentesecas de León in Spain, he had fought his way up the ranks until, after a particularly distinguished role in the Battle of Vitoria, he had been promoted to field marshal, and fought alongside Wellington. He was of medium height and toughly built; dark and black-eyed, with prominent black eyebrows, he had a hard expression, a steely voice and an abrupt manner. Now aged 37, he was five years older than Bolívar.

Arriving at Carúpano, he took an instant dislike to the brigand Morales, new commander of the Legion from Hell, 5,000 of whose horsemen were drawn up to welcome him. Morillo was a man with a penchant for smart uniforms and high flown titles. Most of the Legion, naked to the waist, wore jaguar-skin caps atop their long, straggly hair. Striding up to them, Morillo declared that just one of his companies could wipe them out, then insisted that they be disciplined or disbanded; Morales warned him that they would prefer to join the insurgents.

Their first joint expedition was to the island of Margarita to snuff out a rebellion by Juan Bautista Arismendi. The rebel was once 'a moderate man of peaceful ways', but now, after his wife and children had been subjected to reprisals, he had changed into a patriot guerrilla leader famous for atrocities as appalling as those of the plainsmen. An English witness described Arismendi:

> his aspect exhibits a peculiar ferocity of expression, which his smile only increases. His laugh never fails to create a momentary shudder, and the dreadful distortion of the muscles of the face which it produces, can only be compared with that of the hyena when under similar excitement. His displeasure is always signified by this demonical grin, accompanied by a low lengthened exclamation resembling the suppressed roar of a tiger, his eyes at the same time flashing vengeance; and should the object of his rage be at these moments within its compass, death inevitably ensues. His general appearance might impress a superficial observer with a belief that he is so accustomed to scenes of horror and bloodshed, they afford him gratification rather than uneasiness.

In the face of overwhelmingly superior forces, Arismendi surrendered at once and Morillo was pleased to accept his obeisance. The contemporary Spanish historian Sevilla reports, however, that Morales' eyes blazed as he pointed to the kneeling guerrilla leader:

> General, don't do such a thing. This man you see on his knees is not repenting; he is tricking you miserably. This man grovelling before you like a reptile is not a man, but a fierce tiger of the wilds or from hell. The tears are crocodile ones, his protests are bogus and his promises lies. This miserable man has sent 500 peaceful Spanish traders from Caracas to Guaira to be burned alive. Those who escaped the inferno were killed with lances.

Morillo took no notice, and Morales blackly forecast the destruction of the entire expedition. Yet Morillo dismissed him contemptuously, and proceeded to Caracas, where he decreed a general amnesty and promised to what remained of the criollo upper class that their lands would be restored and the black uprising reversed. The savage men who had regained Venezuela for the crown of Spain were thus disowned.

To regain New Granada a two-pronged land offensive was ordered, one arm advancing through the mountains, the other, commanded by Morales, along the coast, with Morillo's forces being shipped by sea. The siege of Cartagena which followed was one of the most heroic and ghastly in history. It lasted 106 days, during which the Spanish ships' cannon pounded from the sea and the guns on land thundered from the hills outside the city. Manuel Castillo, inept and cowardly, was replaced by Bolívar's compatriot José Bermúdez. Yet some 6,000 died of starvation before, at length, on 6 December 1815, 2,000 survivors embarked in a small flotilla of fishing boats. Many were capsized by the swell, or picked up by Spanish ships waiting outside the harbour. The 300 that remained inside Cartagena, including Castillo, were executed.

Morillo's troops then set off up the Magdalena river towards Santa Fé de Bogotá, a journey of several months. On the way Morillo, hitherto forgiving wherever possible, heard that Arismendi had risen in revolt on Margarita, and slaughtered the small Spanish garrison there; he was incensed that he had been made to look a fool.

Although the leaders in Bogotá surrendered the city without a fight, Morillo set up a 'Pacification Tribunal' to purge the rebel leaders. On 30 May 1816, in desperation, the wives and daughters of the leading citizens went to him and begged mercy for their menfolk. The general pointed out that his pardons to the rebels on Margarita had been answered by the slaughter of the soldiers he had left there; those soldiers, he said, also had mothers, wives and daughters: 'If instead of forgiveness I had shot twenty people, I would not be troubled by remorse for these people today.' Some 600 were executed, among them Camilo Torres, president of the new republic and Bolívar's old supporter. It seemed that the flames of independence in Venezuela and New Granada had been extinguished.

In Kingston, the capital of Jamaica, the penniless Bolívar had found refuge in a run-down boarding house. He had also made a British friend, Maxwell Hyslop, a successful Scottish merchant who, with his brother, ran a varied import-export trade. Writing to Hyslop, Bolívar remarked perceptively that if Morillo were to act 'with speed and decisiveness, the restoration of Spanish government in South America seems inevitable'. Bolívar's main interest in Hyslop was as a source of financial support, which was doled out in small quantities, while also pleading desperately to the British for aid. However, the governor of the island, the Duke of Manchester, not only shunned his company but ignored his letters, as did the Marquess Wellesley. The British government had no wish to antagonize the renascent Spanish empire for the sake of what seemed a lost cause.

Bolívar, depressed, feverish and pathetic, begged Hyslop for support and threatened suicide:

> I don't have a penny now. I have sold the little silver I brought. I have no other hope than to seek your favour. Without it, desperation will force me to end my days in a violent manner, in order to avoid the cruel humiliation of begging for help from men harder than their gold. If you don't give me the support I need to sustain my sad life, I am resolved to seek help from nobody else, because it is impossible for me to offer any reward, having lost everything.

In need of a victorious army, Bolívar's days were spent idling in his hammock, playing chess or fencing with his exiled companions. He also faced assassination and at least three attempts on his life were instigated by the Spanish authorities. A servant of Bolívar, after several unsuccessful attempts to poison him, repeatedly stabbed what he thought was his master sleeping in his hammock one night; it turned out to be one of the Liberator's bodyguards, gone to sleep while Bolívar was out visiting. Consistently threatened with eviction by his hard-nosed landlady, his was a wretched existence.

Relief of a kind came when he met Julia Cobier, a creole lady from Dominica on the rebound from an unsatisfactory love affair. She had the added attraction for Bolívar of being wealthy, and beneath her ministrations his spirits revived, and he began writing what was to prove his most famous pronouncement, his 'Letter from Jamaica'. Addressed to an anonymous friend (in fact Maxwell Hyslop), it was to be published as a pamphlet and attracted worldwide interest.

Remarkable for its prescience, its idealism and its language, and for the curious mysticism that so often imbued Bolívar's pronouncements, it also showed the considerable evolution of his thought since his last exile. He proclaimed:

> This picture represents, on a military map, an area of 2,000 longitudinal and 900 latitudinal leagues at its greatest point, wherein 16,000,000 Americans either defend their rights or suffer repression at the hands of Spain, which, although once the world's greatest empire, is now too weak, with what little is left her, to rule the new hemisphere or even to maintain herself in the old. And shall Europe, the civilized, the merchant, the lover of liberty allow an aged serpent, bent only on satisfying its venomous rage, devour the fairest part of our globe? What! Is Europe deaf to the clamour of her own interests? Has she no eyes to see justice? Has she grown so hardened as to become insensible? The more I ponder these questions, the more I am confused. I am led to think that America's disappearance is desired; but this is impossible because all Europe is not Spain. What madness for our enemy to hope to reconquer America when she has no navy, no funds, and almost no soldiers! Those troops which she has are scarcely adequate to keep her own people in a state of forced obedience and to defend herself from her neighbours. On the other hand, can that nation carry on the exclusive commerce of one-half the world when it lacks manufactures, agricultural products, crafts and sciences, and even a policy? Assume that this mad venture were successful, and further assume that pacification ensued, would not the sons of the Americans of today, together with the sons of the European *reconquistadores* twenty years hence, conceive the same patriotic designs that are now being fought for?
>
> Americans today, and perhaps to a greater extent than ever before, who live within the Spanish system occupy a position in society no better than that of serfs destined for labour, or at best they have no more status than that of mere consumers. Yet even this status is surrounded with galling restrictions, such as being forbidden to grow European crops, or to store products which are royal monopolies, or to establish factories of a type the Peninsula

itself does not possess. To this add the exclusive trading privileges, even in articles of prime necessity, and the barriers between American provinces, designed to prevent all exchange of trade, traffic, and understanding. In short, do you wish to know what our future held? – simply the cultivation of the fields of indigo, grain, coffee, sugar cane, cacao, and cotton; cattle raising on the broad plains; hunting wild game in the jungles; digging in the earth to mine its gold – but even these limitations could never satisfy the greed of Spain.

So negative was our existence that I can find nothing comparable in any other civilized society, examine as I may the entire history of time and the politics of all nations. Is it not an outrage and a violation of human rights to expect a land so splendidly endowed, so vast, rich, and populous, to remain merely passive?

As I have just explained, we were cut off and, as it were, removed from the world in relation to the science of government and administration of the state. We were never viceroys or governors, save in the rarest of instances; seldom archbishops and bishops; diplomats never; as military men, only subordinates; as nobles, without royal privileges. In brief, we were neither magistrates nor financiers and seldom merchants – all in flagrant contradiction to our institutions.

He vigorously denounced the European allies who had failed to come to his help. It would even be in Spain's interests to lose her empire based on 'precarious trade and tributes exhorted from remote, powerful and enemy peoples', he argued.

Europe itself, by policy, should have prepared and carried out plans for South American independence; not only because it is necessary for the proper balance of the world, but because it is a legitimate and safe means for obtaining commercial bases on this side of the ocean. [I would] free half the world and place the universe in a state of equilibrium . . . The British can acquire (in return for aid) the provinces of Panama and Nicaragua, forming with these countries the centre of the world's commerce by means of canals, which, connecting the two great seas, would shorten the great distances and make England's control over world commerce permanent.

Although Bolívar now paid lip service to the idea of a single American republic with its capital in Mexico City, he forecast that the Spanish and Portuguese empires would be divided into 15 independent republics. In Mexico and Brazil, he believed that monarchies and despotisms would alternate in power – an uncannily accurate prediction; Chile, he said, would have largely stable governments, while Peru would suffer from continuing turbulence because 'she possesses two elements, enemies always of a just and liberal régime – gold and slaves. The first corrupts all; the second is corrupted by itself.' History would put its stamp of truth upon this gloomy prognostication.

He anticipated a single republic embracing Venezuela and New Granada, for which he favoured a government made from an executive elected by men of property, an hereditary senate and a similarly elected assembly. The views he set out were clearly republican and anti-monarchical; he argued that monarchs were inherently despotic and self-aggrandizing. Yet his concept of democracy was limited. Spanish Americans, he argued, were just not ready for it:

We were in the position of slaves – not in the sense of mistreatment so much as of ignorance. We had no part in our own affairs, no knowledge of the science of government and the administration of state. We were, in effect, slaves, suddenly risen, without knowledge or experience, to play a part in the world as administrators, diplomats, magistrates and legislators. If we had even managed our domestic affairs before, we should have known something about the nature and operation of state.

Pure representative government is not suitable to our character, customs and present conditions . . . So long as our compatriots do not develop the talents and political virtues which distinguish our brothers of the north [the United States] the entire popular system, far from being suitable to our conditions, may, I fear, be our ruin. Unfortunately, these qualities seemed not to be developed in us to the extent necessary; and, on the contrary, we are dominated by vices which, developed under the guidance of Spain, became weighted with ferocity, ambition, vengeance and cupidity.

He had clearly been influenced by his experience of the horrors of mob and popular rule as represented by the black and llanero uprisings in Venezuela, and this was also crucial in pushing his thinking towards the concept of benevolent autocracy – which was to have a marked effect on Latin American political systems for more than a century to come. For the same reasons, he rejected federalism in favour of centralization.

He touched on the idea of a kind of united nations of Latin America meeting at a congress in Panama. Then he turned mystical: he observed that Quetzalcoatl, the plumed servant of Mexican fable, 'the Hermes or Buddha of South America', had promised to return one day:

> Does not this tradition lead us to suppose that he will shortly reappear? Can you imagine the effect that would be produced if an individual were to turn up among the people having the characteristics of Quetzalcoatl, their Buddha of the forest . . . ? Is it not unity alone that is required to enable us to throw out the Spaniards, their troops, and the supporters of corrupt Spain, in order to establish in these lands a powerful empire with a free government and benevolent laws? . . . Is it not that very prophet or god of Anáhuac, Quetzalcoatl, who will be able to bring about the prodigious changes you suggest? This deity is scarcely known to the Mexican people, and even where he is known he is not greatly honoured: such is the fate of the defeated, even when they are gods.

This obscure disquisition in fact marked another major evolution in his thinking: the concept of the Man of Destiny, the personality who changes history and leads nations. He then went on to divide the world into a liberal and progressive alliance, represented by Britain and the United States; and a reactionary alliance of Spain, Austria, Prussia and – now, again – France, the Revolution having run its course.

But it was Bolívar's insights into the condition of his own people that provided the key to his next moves. In a separate and much less noticed letter to the editor of Jamaica's newspaper, he wrote:

> The Spaniards, after having experienced terrible and multiple reverses in Venezuela, succeeded, in the end, in regaining her. The army of General Morillo came to reinforce them, and completed the subjugation of the country. It seemed that the party of independence was desperate, as indeed it was; but, by a single occurrence, those same freed slaves and slaves who contributed so much, by force, to the triumph of the royalists, have changed to the party of independence which had not offered absolute freedom to the slaves as had the Spaniards. The present protagonists of independence are the partisans of Boves, until now against the white criollos, who never understood our noble cause.

When he wrote it, this was mere wishful thinking, but Bolívar was justified in believing he could convert Boves' desperadoes and thugs to his own cause. Morillo had brutally destroyed their hopes by reasserting the old social structure and property rights, and retaining slavery. Venezuela's bloody social and racial revolution, masquerading as the restoration of Spanish rule, had now been crushed by the empire herself. Bolívar proposed a brilliant strategy: nothing less than to take charge of the vicious, uncontrolled forces which had destroyed his independent state, to ride the very whirlwind which had unseated him.

Bolívar's exile in Jamaica, and his new manifesto, marked a turning point in his personality and thinking. He had blamed his first defeat and withdrawal from Venezuela on the incapacity of others, in particular Miranda, and he refused to accept responsibility for it. The second great setback was on his watch, and his responsibility alone: he had underestimated his opponents – Morillo, Boves and Morales, and their brilliance in harnessing the lower classes of Venezuela to the royalist cause. The Jamaica letter shows a much more mature determination to learn the lessons of his defeat – while never admitting his own failures – in particular to issue his own clarion call to the poor and dispossessed of Venezuela. Living for months on a largely black slave-populated island made him more aware of the problems of ordinary people: henceforth, never abandoning his love of ostentation, military parades, heroic welcomes, fiestas and above all dancing (although he was immune to avarice, money and corruption), he became a man of the people, not afraid to rub shoulders or exchange greetings with even the lowest in his armies.

The maturity of his views also affected his political programme, as he saw that liberation needed to include the guarantee of the same basic legal rights, even for the poorest, and pressed for a strong central state to act on their behalf, if necessary, against the exploiting urban middle class and the white criollo upper classes. Thus, he shifted his power base from the haves to the have-nots.

There was also a welcome transition from the war-to-the-death psychotic cruelty that he had displayed over the previous three years to a more humanitarian approach. Bolívar was not about to become sentimental – he had no qualms in executing his enemies or taking life in an almost casual way – but unlike Boves he had never enjoyed cruelty for its own sake, and he considered the policy of 'war to the death' at an end. It was acceptable to kill military opponents but not to indulge in atrocities against the civilian population.

The Jamaica period was also to mark the transition from commander of small armies to guerrilla leader. Bolívar was unafraid to take part in small operations to harass the enemy in the llanos and the jungle, as well as the lower cordillera, enduring the privations of his men, taking the same risks, living on his wits. He was no stuffy general on a white horse watching his troops from afar; operating as a partner with his new comrade, José Antonio Páez, he was happy to place himself on the front-line. This does much to explain the magnetic appeal he had for the simple, but hardened and sometimes murderous men he commanded in the Orinoco.

Early in December 1815 fate played one of its tricks again when Bolívar received a summons to defend Cartagena from the aforementioned siege by Morillo. Delighted, the man of destiny left Julia grieving and embarked once again for the mainland, dodging Spanish warships – only to learn as he was approaching the coast that Cartagena had already fallen, and its refugees were on their way to Haiti. He ordered his small boat to follow them. Arriving on the island of Hispaniola, of which Haiti formed the western half, his trek seemed to take a positive turn. At the port of Aux Cayes (now known as Les Cayes) he was warmly welcomed by the President of Haiti, Alexandre Pétion, whose liberated slaves had defied Napoleon and established an independent republic; Pétion had admired Bolívar's 'Letter from Jamaica'. He also met a wealthy Jewish merchant from Curaçao, Luis Brión, with whom he had corresponded and who espoused the cause of independence. Brión had a number of ships at his disposal, including a 24-gun corvette and a small frigate. For the first time Bolívar had the prospect of some naval forces and, with them, mobility at sea. A rich Englishman, Robert Southerland, also offered help.

A number of Bolívar's former officers had arrived with the refugees from Cartagena, including Carlos Soublette, once Miranda's aide, with his mother and two sisters, one of whom – Isabel, with her long red hair – became Bolívar's mistress. Old rivals of Bolívar landed, too, among them 'El Supremo' Santiago Mariño; Manuel Piar, good-looking and smooth-talking; José Bermúdez – 'an uncouth savage, and unlettered', as O'Leary described him; and Mariano Montilla, a former friend of Bolívar. Gregor MacGregor, a Scottish adventurer replete with kilt and bagpipes, was one of the number; as was Henri Ducoudray-Holstein, the puffed-up French mercenary and sardonic observer of the Liberator's triumphal entry into Caracas – but he left after two months of petty back-biting against Bolívar and later wrote venomously of their encounters.

When it was proposed that Bolívar become supreme commander of an expedition to reinvade Venezuela, many opposed him – until Brión insisted he would back only Bolívar: without Brión's ships, the planned invasion would get nowhere. Slowly, chaotically, arrangements were made for 300 men to sail in seven vessels with quantities of ammunition, several pieces of artillery and most of the officers' women. Bolívar aroused fury by delaying his departure for several days to wait for the loyal Josefina Machado, Señorita Pepa, and her mother to join him.

At last, in March 1816, the little expedition set out. In full dress uniform Bolívar harangued his troops, comparing them to the

300 Spartans of Leonidas. His chief opponents among the patriots, Montilla and Bermúdez, stayed behind; Montilla later sailed to the United States. Bolívar's small flotilla soon reached the island of Margarita, controlled by Arismendi for the patriots, and from there declared Venezuela independent once again before setting sail with a few more recruits for the mainland. Landing at Carúpano, he had seized the port in two hours, losing none of his men. Mariño and Piar were sent eastwards to rally support; they soon discovered that the local people were hostile and had withdrawn into the interior, and decided to go inland rather than return under Bolívar's command. Thus abandoned, Bolívar sailed for the little port of Ocumare, beyond La Guaira, hoping to strike behind the Spanish.

He despatched most of his men inland under Soublette and MacGregor, but they were cut off by the main Spanish army, which had reached Valencia. In panic his ships quietly put out to sea, leaving him stranded with a handful of men and all his remaining guns and ammunition; probably an *agent provocateur* named Alzuru had put it about that Bolívar had been defeated. At the last minute he was rescued by a small boat but encountered a Spanish coastguard cutter. When its captain came aboard to inspect its papers, Bolívar had him seized. On learning the name of his captor, the captain begged for mercy and Bolívar agreed, provided he conveyed Josefina and the other women to safety on a neutral island. Sailing eastwards after this series of fiascos, away from Morillo's armies, Bolívar's landed him at Güiria, where he intended to combine with Mariño, in August.

Soublette and MacGregor had managed to avoid being trapped by the Spanish, and had marched hundreds of miles to join Piar, who was recruiting dissident llanero guerrilla leaders in the east. In the course of the march MacGregor won victories against Morales in the Aragua, at Victoria, Sebastián de los Pleyes and Quebrada Henda, before combining with Piar at Barcelona; but they quarrelled after a victory at Juncal, and MacGregor left the country.

At Güiria, Bolívar learnt that Bermúdez had arrived from Haiti and had been stirring up Mariño against him. Bermúdez put it about that Bolívar was planning to abandon Güiria to the Spanish. A mob gathered, shouting 'Down with the dictator!' and 'Death to Bolívar!' His attempts to defend himself were met with a hail of stones, and he retreated with as much dignity as he could muster to the beach. Bermúdez pulled his sword on Bolívar, who fought back, then escaped in a boat. Enraged, Bermúdez was restrained from plunging into the water after him by his officers, while stones rained down from the mob.

It was Bolívar's fourth bitter send-off from the mainland, this time at the hands of his brother officers; the invasion had been a shambles from start to finish. 'The band of delinquents', commented Francisco Tomás Morales with contempt, 'believed themselves to be absolute possessors of Venezuela and, dispersed and disorganised, have disappeared like smoke.' Stoned and humiliated by his own patriot supporters, Bolívar seemed a man of straw, a figure of world vision and grandiose rhetoric who had put his expedition at risk so that his mistress could join him. He could not command respect among his own men, much less make an impression on the enemy. A lesser spirit would have been shattered.

He arrived back in Haiti anticipating the wrath of Pétion, but to his surprise he was received with honour and listened to with sympathy. Pétion and Southerland even offered to sponsor a new expedition, but Bolívar was reluctant to risk further humiliation. Brión, who now arrived with his small fleet, urged him to try again and Arismendi from Margarita begged him to do so. Most significantly of all, a group of local resistance leaders, appalled by the rivalry and insubordination of the commanders who had driven Bolívar from the mainland, sent an emissary, Francisco Zea, asking him to return. Zea also saw Pétion and told him: 'In Venezuela there still survives a remnant of good patriots. This country still lives in hopes; but the one superior man, capable of converting these hopes into reality, is no longer there. With this idea, the army and the cities have turned their eyes upon General Bolívar as the one chief in war.'

Chapter 14

THE ORINOCO

On 31 December 1816, Bolívar returned and on this occasion he could have no way of knowing that he was never to leave the mainland again. At the port of Barcelona, Bolívar proclaimed himself commander-in-chief and, liaising with a guerrilla force commanded by Pedro Zaraza further inland, marched along the coast in a bold bid to seize Caracas. He got as far as Clarines before furious cavalry attacks forced him back to Barcelona. He wrote desperately to his old rival, Manuel Piar, that Barcelona was in danger of being lost.

Piar had no intention of coming to his aid: he wanted Bolívar to be defeated and to take his place as Liberator. A contemporary account of this ambitious man describes him as 'young, of medium height and a martial air; brave, impetuous and of lightning speed in action; terse in his views, arrogant and impulsive almost to madness, he had a furious temper to the extent that he sometimes apologised to subordinates he had offended'. Many were convinced that Piar was the illegitimate son of an aristocratic criollo, who was the father of the unfortunate Manuel Ribas, Piar's close companion who had been decapitated two years before. Piar nursed bitter resentment against Bolívar for the debacle that led to the death. Others suggested he was the bastard son of Prince Carlos de Braganza of Brazil, while some hinted that he was the offspring of a prominent Venezuelan and a black slave. He was certainly an impressive, forceful and dashing personality.

The ambitious Piar decided to leave Bolívar to his fate as a huge army under Morillo was approaching Barcelona; at the same time a fleet was coming up from Puerto Cabello to cut off his escape by sea.

The Spaniards attacked as Bolívar's force retreated into the centre of Barcelona, which became a charnel house of hand-to-hand fighting. All seemed lost when a force under Bermúdez arrived, on Mariño's orders, to help. The fighting became even more bloody and intense, but it was the Spaniards now that were being pushed back street by street and were forced to pull out of the city.

In a famous and remarkable gesture, Bolívar rode to meet Bermúdez. Instead of castigating the subordinate who had mutinied and so humiliated him five months before, he declared, 'I embrace the liberator of the Liberator'. In spite of the momentary respite, Bolívar was still in dire peril. The Spanish army was several times bigger than his own and reinforcements were being brought. His way was blocked, and he was cut off from the sea. His only option seemed to be to join Piar in the mountains of Guayana, something he was deeply reluctant to do for fear of playing into his rival's hands. At length he took the plunge and set out from Barcelona for the Orinoco river, due south, accompanied by just 15 officers, leaving Brión's fleet to follow with his huge arsenal.

It was another bold and historic move – to escape the Spanish military machine advancing to crush him by heading towards the wildest and remotest part of Venezuela, rather than be forced back into Caribbean exile. He left behind a force of 400 under General Pedro María Freite to defend Barcelona. The Spanish juggernaut advanced on the town and Mariño's troops, camped just 30 miles away, refused to come to its help this time as the Spaniards secured an overwhelming victory. Morillo, once lenient, showed no pity. Some 1,000 people were killed, including women, children and hospital patients. He had issued the order to 'burn cities, behead their inhabitants, ravage the country; to respect neither sex nor age, to replace the peaceful farmer with a ferocious warrior, the instrument of the vengeance of an angry king'.

Mariño's lack of action so appalled his lieutenant Bermúdez that he decided to follow Bolívar. He found the general entrenched in the llanos, that vast badlands from which had come the murderous horde that had swept away his second republic. From distant Jamaica in his wretchedness, he had guessed correctly that the half-savage cowboys who had won the war for the Spaniards, only to be relegated again to their subhuman status in Venezuelan society, were now ripe to join the rebel cause – and Bolívar had promised an end to slavery.

The ground had to some extent been prepared – in the east by Piar and by another extraordinary figure from the region, José Antonio Páez, in the west. Piar was vain, hot-headed and overbearing; but he was a formidable commander, almost Bolívar's equal. Arriving from the north, he had threatened the city of Angostura, on the Orinoco, with only a handful of troops, and recruited an army of some 2,000 men in the Guayana region, an empty outback. Many of his soldiers were Indians, naked except for bows and arrows. With this primitive army he had advanced on the city of Guayana itself, lower down the Orinoco, while sending a force out to seize the food and supplies of the Capuchin mission on the Caruni river, as well as their Indian servants. All twenty-two monks of this famous outpost were slaughtered, possibly on the orders of Piar, who was as ruthless as the Spaniards themselves.

Just outside Angostura, on the open plain, Piar's forces at last engaged the experienced, well-trained Spaniards under General Miguel de La Torre. Piar's army of 2,000 outnumbered the 1,600 Spaniards, but the latter were all equipped with muskets. Piar's men had only 500 rifles, the rest being equipped with bamboo lances and bows and arrows. The battle was ferocious, but Piar's outstanding leadership prevailed, and 700 Spaniards were killed or taken prisoner, La Torre only just escaped back to the safety of Angostura. Piar had 300 prisoners executed. Piar, overconfident, laid siege to Guayana and Angostura. But his cavalry proved much less effective against dug-in Spanish positions.

On 4 April 1817, Bolívar caught up with Piar in a primitive hut outside Guayana and began to bargain for the future of the revolution. Piar had just won his greatest victory but not for the first or last time, Bolívar believed he held the winning hand. He had recently been reinforced by several hundred desertions from Mariño's forces, led by the capable Bermúdez. He had control of the main rebel arsenal, as well as the fleet that would be needed to supply the patriots down the Orinoco. He felt he could now act swiftly to assert his authority over Piar.

News had just arrived that the Spaniards had sent a colossal force

of soldiers on 36 transports up the Orinoco to raise the sieges of
Angostura and Guayana. Bolívar, although almost unaccompanied,
was nevertheless putting on a show of force before his rival. Piar's
only hope seemed to be to secure the Liberator's support to concentrate his forces at San Félix, midway between the two towns under
siege, the price being acceptance of Bolívar's leadership. The good-
looking, tempestuous young rebel saw he had no choice but to obey.
For good measure Bolívar, who had long abandoned the concept of
'war to the death', scolded Piar for executing his prisoners. Bolívar
then left to reclaim his arsenal, coming up behind.

The Orinoco river is one of the greatest in a continent of great rivers.
Not as wide or as long as the Amazon, it is still some 400 yards broad
even as far upstream as Angostura, which indeed derives its name
because it marks a narrowing. It wends its way over 1,500 miles
from its source in Venezuela's Roraima Plateau, around the country's
inland desert, the Grand Savannah, through the llanos to the tropical immensity of the Orinoco estuary. It is navigable for hundreds
of miles and sailing ships benefit from the easterly winds that blow
them upstream and from the currents that push them down. It was an
artery for a thriving contraband trade in hides, cattle and horses from
the llanos, and was virtually unpoliceable by the Caracas authorities.
    The town of Guayana, towards the mouth of the Orinoco, was
a run-down, dingy place, a disease-ridden jungle dive filled with
smugglers and layabouts. The city of Angostura, 250 miles away, by
contrast was an elegant Spanish town on the border of the llanos,
with a more tolerable climate and criss-crossed cobbled streets on
the familiar colonial grid pattern. It was to be the starting point for
Bolívar's greatest expedition.
    Piar, faithful to his orders once Bolívar had left, concentrated his
disparate forces around San Félix. This time the ragged and desperate
divisions of the dispossessed were on his side. Rough-hewn, leather-
faced llanero horsemen, stripped to their trousers under leopardskin
caps, served alongside wholly naked Indians, guerrillas from the
mountains and a few regular troops brought by Bermúdez. La Torre's
Spanish forces, by contrast, were well-disciplined, seasoned veterans,
many from the Peninsular War. But La Torre had no cavalry, as his

forces had come by boat, and he was fighting the irregulars on their own territory.

Bolívar, with his precious arsenal, moved further up the Orinoco. He was once again threatened from all sides. Mariño, in the north, had declared a United States of Venezuela in Cariaco, set up an assembly, and declared himself commander-in-chief. Piar, in spite of his promises to Bolívar, was conniving against him and retained his ambition of displacing the Liberator.

Mariño was to prove unlucky. On its return from New Granada the main Spanish army, headed by Morillo, had decided to proceed down the coast to liaise with an army of 3,000 men despatched from Spain – initially intended to subjugate a rebellion in Buenos Aires, but which the Spanish commander had ordered to alter course and come to his help. Mariño was forced to evacuate Cumana and then lost battles at Carúpano and Güiria. The whole of Venezuela's coastline, including the far east, was now in the hands of the royalists. Most of Mariño's young supporters, including the young Antonio José de Sucre, moved south to join Bolívar; Mariño himself begged to be allowed to rejoin Bolívar as his subordinate. The Liberator, sorely tried, decided to give his old rival one last chance.

Meanwhile, as commander-in-chief, he ordered Piar to divide his army into two, one under the latter's control to besiege Guayana, the other under the now faithful Bermúdez – who hated Piar, blaming him for the death of his brother – commanded to besiege Angostura. After a few weeks, astonishingly, Piar wrote to Bolívar resigning his command: the would-be rival liberator said he was going to the interior to raise support for the cause. In fact, he was off to raise the standard against Bolívar, claiming that Bolívar had dismissed him for being black.

One of the officers he tried to suborn reported that Piar had told him:

I became supreme general through my sword and my luck, but I am a mulatto and I must not govern the republic. However, I have penetrated the great mystery of the present administration and I have sworn my honour to restore freedom to so many innocents who are shedding their blood to shut themselves more and more in disgraceful slavery. I will go to Maturín and to the rest of the world, if necessary, to place myself at the head of those who have no support other than their own efforts.

This was open insurrection, and dangerous ground for Bolívar. Bolívar, at their meeting, had told him bluntly that 'never has my position been so strong. The supreme power is in my hands . . . Two thousand men obey me and are disposed to fulfil my commands. The ambitious ones and the intriguers must and will obey me.' The stakes were not just personal – as to who should control the revolutionary forces. Piar was attempting to set himself up as the new Boves, the leader of the blacks, and wage class and racial war upon the pure-blooded, 'Mantuan' criollo white, Bolívar.

The danger of igniting racial war again, and splitting the patriot forces, now provoked Bolívar into one of his occasional, though uncharacteristic, acts of savagery. The cause of independence had for two years been dogged by ferocious personal rivalries and strutting warlords contesting Bolívar's control. If victory was to be achieved, this could not be allowed to persist. Bolívar could not continue to act as no more than first among equals in a group of prima donnas who would not obey orders and chose to resign their commands when they felt like it.

Bolívar may also have genuinely feared Piar, the most impressive of his rivals and, because of his black blood, the most likely to attract the allegiance of the llaneros and the slaves he was courting. The Liberator decided to make an example of Piar and behave with cold-blooded ruthlessness. As with the declaration of the 'war to the death' and the execution of the prisoners in the dying days of the Second Republic, Bolívar decided to play executioner. Unlike on previous occasions, he was acting not in the heat of a desperate, hard-pressed campaign, but in cold and leisurely calculation.

His critics were to hold subsequent events against him but few military commanders would have gone to such lengths to accommodate a rebel as Bolívar had already. Bolívar sent forces after Piar to take him prisoner and issued a thundering denunciation to his troops:

General Piar, with his insensitive and abominable conspiracy has alone tried to stir up a war between brothers in which cruel murderers cut the throats of innocent children, of weak women, of tremulous old people, just because they were born of a more or less lighter colour ... General Piar has infringed the laws, has conspired against the republican system, has disobeyed the government, has resorted to force, has deserted the army and has fled like a coward. He has placed himself outside the law. His destruction is a duty and his destroyer a benefactor.

On 27 July 1817 Bolívar's pursuers caught up with the fugitive and persuaded his escort of loyal soldiers not to resist on his behalf. He was seized like a common criminal, bound across the back of a horse and charged with 'crimes of insurrection against the supreme authority, conspiring against order and public tranquillity, sedition and lastly for desertion'. He was sentenced to death by firing squad. Bolívar agreed to permit him to retain his military honours.

On 11 October Piar was taken to the main square in Angostura, under the shadow of the cathedral. Troops and soldiers lined up. Bolívar refused to attend the execution, but must have heard the shots from his residence and office in the stately municipality just opposite. In the words of an eyewitness:

Arriving at the place of execution, at the foot of the banner of the Battalion of Honour, [Piar] had greeted the sentence being read with an air of contempt, keeping his hand in his pocket, moving his right foot and looking in all directions. He didn't want them to blindfold him, and twice pulled off the blindfold they put on him. Blindfolded a third time, he opened his shirt, revealed his chest, and suffered the execution.

Defiant to the last, the cocky mulatto king who had aspired to Bolívar's position had been snuffed out by a newly grim and determined Liberator. It was a powerful demonstration of Bolívar's resolution and authority, with the intention of deterring other would-be pretenders to the crown. For the period and place, Bolívar was a remarkably restrained and humane leader but he did not shrink from ruthlessness when he judged it necessary. Too many tears have been shed by his detractors over the death of Piar, a man responsible for

executing hundreds of prisoners in cold blood and wiping out a peaceful and famous Indian mission. Bolívar later virtually admitted that Piar
had been shot as an example:

> The death of General Piar was a necessity at the time and saved
> the country: it upset and terrified the rebels, bowled aside Mariño
> and his Congress of Cariaco, placed everyone under my command,
> assured my authority, avoided civil war and the enslavement of the
> country . . . there was never a more useful, political and deserved
> death . . . Mariño deserved death like Piar for his disobedience, but
> his life did not present the same dangers.

While summary justice was dispensed on Piar, Bolívar and Bermúdez
continued the siege of the two river towns. After the execution,
Mariño was isolated and appointed commander in the east, while
Bermúdez was appointed military chief in impoverished Cumana.
It was a period of self-discovery for the Liberator, then aged 34, in
this remote tropical fastness. He had made the decision to harness the
very forces that had destroyed his Second Republic, and which had
been cheated of their promised spoils and freedom when the Spanish
empire reimposed itself on the colony. His method was to promise
to the lower castes of Venezuelans – the mulattos, blacks, Indians and
slaves – judicial equality.

   Hitherto the Spanish empire had been based on a system of rigorous apartheid-style caste differences based on exact degrees of racial
intermixture, the races involved and the shade of skin pigmentation.
Bolívar did not promise all people the wealth and property of the
white man, as Boves had, but instead he pledged equality before the
law and of opportunity – a much more limited ambition, but one he
could claim would be fulfilled.

   This was to stand the racial equation on its head, for the Spaniards
had hitherto enjoyed the support of the non-whites against the arrogant criollo aristocracy epitomized by Bolívar and the leading protagonists of independence. Now the Spaniards were restoring the caste
and racial system, and Bolívar was pledging to eradicate it. Bolívar's
position on this issue was both realistic and novel, although it would
have upset many of the old Venezuelan aristocracy – most of whom,

however, were dead or chased from their lands. Indeed, Piar had attempted a much more radical version of Bolívar's new line before being eliminated.

Bolívar's second objective was to project himself as the natural leader of the hard men of the llanos where a nervous, small, intense, fastidious, intellectual white man with his immaculate uniforms seemed at a disadvantage. He chose to achieve this through two methods: first, by not abandoning his own aristocratic and reserved personality; and, second, by seeking to excel in all the fields that the cowboys prided themselves upon. He shared in the privations of his men, sitting with them around campfires as they sang and played guitars, and sleeping in his hammock or on the ground. He would also feed and groom his own horse, a particular pride of the llanero horsemen. According to one description:

> He is in constant agitation. Watching him, you would take him for a crazy man. Walking the forest trails, he goes fast – runs, jumps, tries to leave his companions behind and offers to outjump them. In his hammock he swings violently, singing, talking rapidly, reciting verses in French. He is sometimes loud and sometimes profane. That is when he is among his friends. When a stranger arrives, he shuts up like a clam.

Two stories recounted by Bolívar himself give a vivid impression of his personality – vain, assertive and slightly ridiculous, yet aware that only through public relations, by impressing people, was he likely to secure the allegiance of the tough, sceptical cattle-drivers he needed to carry him to victory.

> One day, bathing in the Orinoco with all my high command, with many generals, one Colonel Martel, who was clerk in my headquarters, claimed to be able to swim better than anyone else. I said something which irritated him, and he replied that he also was a better swimmer than me. About 150 yards from where we were, there were two sunken gunboats; and I, also irritated, told Martel that with my hands tied I would be able to reach those boats quicker than he.

No one wanted such a test to be made. But, excited, I by now shed my clothes and with the braces of my trousers, which I gave to General Ibarra, I made him tie my hands from behind. I threw myself into the water and reached the gunboats with considerable effort. Martel followed me and of course I arrived first. General Ibarra, afraid that I would drown, had ordered two good swimmers into the river to help me. But it was not necessary. This episode proves the tenacity I had then and the willpower which no one could stop. Always forwards, never backwards; that was my maxim, and perhaps to that I owe my successes and anything extraordinary that I did.

Bolívar gave another example:

I remember that in 1817, when we were in Angostura, I gave one of my horses to my principal aide, General Ibarra, so that he could carry certain orders to the front at the gallop. The horse was big and very fast, and before saddling her Ibarra was jesting with some of the army commanders that he could tease the horse by mounting from the tail end and vaulting off the horse's head. He did it well, and I arrived at that very moment. I said he had done nothing special, and to prove it to those there, I took the necessary run and jumped, but landed on the neck of the horse, hurting myself where I had rather not talk about.

With my own horse, I did a second jump and fell on the ears, with a worse blow than before. This did not dishearten me. On the contrary I became more determined and on the third attempt vaulted the horse. I confess this was madness, but I didn't want anyone to say they were more agile than me, or to have someone say he could do what I could not. You must not believe that this is of no importance for a man who commands others. In everything, if possible, he must demonstrate his superiority to those who must obey. It's the method of establishing lasting prestige and indispensable for those who occupy the first rank in society and particularly for someone commanding an army.

These episodes demonstrate both his childish competitiveness and determination to excel, and his ability to understand how to inspire respect. In fact, his formidable skills as a horseman, his swimming achievements and his capacity to live rough impressed the rough-hewn llaneros all the more in that he was a well-dressed, dandified, meticulously bathed white man from the criollo aristocracy. He was to them an exotic species. And he could always go off to a more comfortable bed in his elegant residence in Angostura from time to time.

But life was not without its risks. According to O'Leary, on one occasion in 1817 Bolívar and his aides were surprised by a party of Spanish infantry and cavalry; they escaped by swimming across a large inlet of the Orinoco:

> Among those who dashed into the water was Arismendi, who walked on boldly till he got out of depth, when he sank. A servant saved him. On being brought to the side where [Bolívar] was, the latter asked him how he could have got into the water without knowing how to swim. 'If it had been boiling lead, I should have done the same rather than fall into the power of the Spaniards, dead or alive,' was his reply.
>
> Dionisio, his servant, was the last person that arrived at the safe bank. His delay was caused by a large knife which he persisted in bringing across with him, notwithstanding the repeated expostulations of those who witnessed his difficulty in effecting his purpose. On [Bolívar's] inquiring why he took such pains in saving the knife instead of something of more value, he told him that 'he meant to kill His Excellency with it rather than allow him to be taken by the Spaniards'.

After the patriots had sieged Guayana and Angostura for two months, Brión appeared at last with his small flotilla, and blocked off access up the Orinoco for supplies to the Spanish garrisons. When the men under La Torre had almost exhausted their meagre supplies, the commander made a bolt for it downriver with his troops and hundreds of civilians in flimsy boats, but he was intercepted by Brión's flotilla and around a third of those escaping were captured, along with most of the boats. Only a few reached the mouth of the Orinoco.

With the towns liberated Bolívar established his headquarters in Angostura and embarked on the next stage of the operation. He remained a tower of energy, issuing orders, visiting his men, pacing up and down his room as he dictated in the dead of night. He ordered Luis López Méndez, the rebel general's unofficial ambassador in London who lived at Miranda's old home in Grafton Street, to recruit Britons for the cause. Meanwhile, he sent out forces to crush the remaining royalist strongholds along the Orinoco.

He issued directives to the leaders of the five separate rebel forces now operating against the Spaniards – Urdaneta along the Orinoco, Bermúdez in Cumana in the centre, José Monagas (the future president of Venezuela) in Maturín in the north, Zaraza on the eastern llanos and Mariño in Cariaco. And he made contact with the name that was beginning to rival Bolívar's own as the terror of the Spanish forces now largely confined to the northern highlands of Venezuela: José Antonio Páez, the independent commander of the anti-government forces in the western llanos.

At his headquarters in Angostura, Bolívar began to lay the basis for a national army – as opposed to his current disparate collection of ragbag guerrilla forces controlled by autonomous warlords. This was resisted by the llanero guerrillas who remained completely outside the new martial structure, but it represented the beginning of the national armies that were to become so malevolently powerful in Latin America after independence. He established a general staff of the whole army and, emulating Napoleon, an individual staff for each division. Like the Emperor, he had already set up a guard of honour of 450 loyalists and had appointed the caudillos as generals. Bolívar wrote: 'All Venezuelans ought to have the same interest in defending the territory of the Republic where they have been born as their brothers, for Venezuela is no more than one single family composed of many individuals bound together by indissoluble ties and by identical interests.'

The recruitment of the British Legion was to be one of the most remarkable aspects of the whole war of independence. Ducoudray-Holstein, a troublesome but able former staff officer of Napoleon who had come to know Bolívar in Jamaica, had returned to Britain and with López Méndez in Grafton Street decided to set about implementing Bolívar's orders to recruit from abroad. Zea, Bolívar's chief civilian adviser, who had been a distinguished botanist in Madrid, was nominally in charge. Exceeding his authority, Zea raised a colossal loan of £2 million for the independence cause from greedy and eager speculators organized by the lending house of Herring, Graham and Powles. Bolívar was furious when he learned how Zea had abused his trust, cancelled the loan and ordered Zea to be recalled.

The three principal recruiters of men were Gregor MacGregor, the former hero at Ocumare and Juncal, who had married Bolívar's niece; John d'Evereux, an Irishman who had been in America; and a Colonel James England. These men were all too well aware that, with the end of the Napoleonic wars, London and Dublin were teeming with penniless, demobbed but battle-hardened soldiers who made perfect recruits. They were enticed by promises of generous pay, fine equipment and rapid promotion. Indeed, large quantities of military material and uniforms were available at low prices after the end of the conflict. These recruits were told by Méndez's press agent, William Walton, that Venezuela was a rich land, that the war there was all but won and that they would be granted extensive properties. The recruiters found that they could make handsome sums by selling commissions in the phantom army.

The half-insane MacGregor, besides making a sizeable profit, arranged a series of private expeditions to America on his own – including the siege of Fernandina on the coast of Florida, Portobello in Panama and Riohacha in Colombia – where he would dump his recruits and sail away with any available booty. Of the 2,200 recruits who went with him, including 100 women and 40 children, only two ever returned. The officers were shot while the soldiers were chain-ganged and employed in filling in a swamp.

D'Evereux, having been paid handsomely for his part in recruiting the British Legion, was eventually compelled to leave at the head of an Irish division of 1,000 men which landed on Margarita. When d'Evereux arrived to meet Arismendi in a splendid blue French officer's uniform, his horse spotted a pool. 'The animal, finding the element cool and comfortable, instantly plunged in up to the knees and, despite all the efforts of his rider to prevent it, laid himself down and rolled in it, splashing d'Evereaux with mud raked up from the bottom of the stagnant pool and leaving him to wade out at his pleasure.'

The thuggish Arismendi, who was in control there, was short of food and supplies for his own men, and refused to accept the new recruits. Nevertheless, the legionnaires landed anyway, without food, and a quarter of them died from typhus within a month. Urdaneta, who hated Arismendi, was sent by Bolívar to take charge of the Legion. According to a jaundiced British observer:

General Urdaneta, the commander of the land forces, selected be it remembered by Bolívar himself, was of diminutive stature, pale, effeminate, and a slave to indolence. He was a man so inert, and apparently mindless, that no cause could by possibility have been confided to a more incompetent leader. It was vain to look in him for one redeeming characteristic: not the remotest fitness for command could be discerned. A miserable sensualist, he took the field accompanied by two mistresses, and lounged from morning till night in a hammock, the slave to women and cigars.

Brión finally arrived with his flotilla to ship most of them to the Orinoco, while the remainder joined the forces in Colombia and helped free the Magdalena Valley from the Spaniards – but also burnt down the town of Riohacha in a mutiny.

In the five years after 1817, 8,000 volunteers left Britain and Ireland in 53 ships, including some Italians, Frenchmen and a disciplined battalion of Hanoverians. Many women and children went as well, to settle the lands their husbands had been promised. It was the story of El Dorado all over again.

The initial body of British Legion recruits were placed under the command of Lieutenant Gustavus Hippisley – promoted to colonel for the job – a snobbish but competent soldier who complained bitterly about the absence of a 'good table' in Venezuela, having to share quarters with ordinary soldiers, and the privations of life there. In December 1817, they sailed under Hippisley in five ships, one of which, the *India*, foundered in a gale off Ushant Rocks with the loss of all aboard. The motto of the Legion, or 'Albion Battalion' as it was known in Venezuela, was 'Die or Conquer'.

When the ships reached the West Indies, after a crossing of disorder, drunkenness and near mutiny thanks to the absence of proper authority, they found that there were no arrangements in place to meet them. They were greeted with indifference or outright hostility in Haiti, Trinidad and Granada and were told that Venezuela, far from being advanced and prosperous, was an untamed outback of jungle, cruelty, wild bears, naked Indians and disease. The Liberator, it was said, was a sadistic madman.

On the islands many of the units broke up through desertion, while scores died of smallpox, yellow fever, typhus, malaria and dysentery. A number left to become virtual beggars. In Haiti the First Rifle and Artillery Brigades effectively disintegrated, as did the military band. Another group, including the Hanoverians, reached the mainland of Venezuela and were assigned to Urdaneta's forces. They recaptured Barcelona from the Spaniards for him, then went on an orgy of drunkenness and looting. The Hanoverians remained disciplined, but their force was reduced from 1,000 to 233 through desertions and sickness. The legionnaires were appalled by the brutality expected of them. According to an anonymous naval officer:

> The Spaniards, who had behaved with great pusillanimity, had no sooner surrendered, than the natives, who had accompanied us, began their murderous work; and it was continued without intermission, until every individual of the entire 1300 was despatched. Myself and the whole of the British kept aloof from this spectacle as much as possible . . . I received a severe reprimand, as did my brother officers, and the seamen, for not having taken an active part in the slaughter; Admiral Brion, and subsequently General Urdaneta, both informed us, that as we had entered the service of Venezuela, we were expected to conform to its usages; and in future they insisted on our personal share of putting the prisoners to death. We made no reply; but I believe that all inwardly resolved never to obey any such order.

Urdaneta decided he would march them over the eastern mountains to Maturín.

All descriptions of the dreadful sufferings endured must fall far short of the reality. The streams were so swollen and currents rendered so strong and rapid by the falls of rain, that in fording them numbers of men, from their excessive debility, were unable to bear up against the force . . . The rush of waters bears down the body with the rapidity of a shot, dashing it in its course against stumps of trees, jutting rocks, and loose stones, until life is extinct, and the sweeping tide is stained with blood.

Climbing the mountains their shoes, from being constantly saturated with water, became so enlarged, that they were continually escaping from their feet; and to add to their misery, the surfaces of the mountains were chiefly composed of sharp-pointed stones, resembling in colour broken Scotch granite, but harder . . . Their feet were attacked by myriads of insects named chegoes . . . These tormenting creatures will penetrate the skin, even when it is unbroken, and breed under it to such an extent that unless they are speedily removed, the swarm becomes incalculable, and sometimes produces mortification. On the plains of Maturin the soldiers drank from puddles until several of them were found dead at the margin of these receptacles for small alligators and snakes of the most poisonous description. Others succumbed to a species of fish, called the raya, which oftentimes seized their thighs and calves of the legs, and tore large pieces from them, leaving those who survived altogether incapable of further service.

When they arrived they found 'irregular rows of mud-built hovels. The hospital was only two square plots of ground, enclosed with mud walls . . . Dirt, disease, and famine were the reward of the services of men who had left their country to embark in the desperate cause of those who now so ill requited them. Many were lodged in the worst hovels of the town, where they were left to perish.'

Urdaneta complained bitterly that 'six months with these men is worse than ten campaigns'; yet some went on to serve bravely under Mariño. After the novelty of life in the West Indies was over, groups of the deserters also began to make their way to the Orinoco. Eventually they arrived, and, grim though they found the conditions, they were to play a remarkable and key role in the campaign that followed. Many of their officers became Bolívar's most trusted and disciplined aides. Hope, despair, perseverance and eventual triumph were to be the lot of the survivors of the British Legion.

One of the first British legionnaires was Daniel Florence O'Leary from Cork, a 17-year-old who travelled aboard the *Prince* with the Red Hussars of Venezuela. He was shocked on first landing in Venezuela:

> Hitherto I had seen little to reconcile me to the service I had entered and on our arrival at Achaguas my prospects did not brighten. I was disgusted at the barbarous and unnecessary sacrifice of human lives. Prisoners were frequently brought in, for the most part Americans and that most probably had been compelled to serve with the Spaniards. Groups of ten and twelve were almost daily put to death. Though profuse of blood, the patriots were economic of gun powder, which was considered a more precious article, and the wretched [prisoners] were doomed to have their sufferings augmented and prolonged by the sword of the executioner. Officers were generally employed in this distinguished service and, to tell the truth, they displayed great dexterity. I have often seen the head severed from the trunk at the first blow. Whenever this occurred a loud laugh from the creole spectators expressed their satisfaction at the ability of the headsman.

He arrived in Angostura and was immediately appointed by General Carlos Soublette to the guard of honour of General José Anzoátegui. Soon promoted to captain, he joined the march across the Andes and, on Anzoátegui's death in 1819, was named aide-de-camp to Bolívar at the age of 19. He became one of his most trusted friends and married Soledad, one of Soublette's sisters. On Bolívar's death, O'Leary conceived of becoming his biographer, in the event only publishing his own extensive and fascinating memoirs. He was not merely a starry-eyed worshipper of the Liberator and his jottings are invaluable because of his lucid and reasonably detached assessments.

As the legionnaires drifted into Angostura, the welcoming Bolívar sent them up to San Fernando, where the local commanders held sway and needed reinforcements. The British officers and soldiers, dressed in the finest of discarded uniforms from the Peninsular Wars – green scarlet and gold for the First Venezuelan Hussars, light blue, gold and scarlet for the Second, with Wellington boots and plumed shakoes – arrived to find the most remarkable llanero commander of all, José Antonio Páez, sleeping under a tree. (The uniforms did not last long, soon degenerating into rags. One officer, Colonel James Rooke, invited to dinner by Bolívar, turned up in tails without shirt or collar.)

Hippisley recounts that Páez was exhausted and frothing at the mouth, having just killed 40 Spaniards with his lance in a skirmish at Ortiz. Nonetheless, he admired their splendid uniforms, in striking contrast to the half-naked llaneros, and promptly made a guard of honour of them. The British taught him a few words of English, and how to hold a knife and fork.

Chapter 15

PÁEZ

José Antonio Páez was, at first glance, no more than a second edition of the slaughtered fiend, Boves. He had been born in 1790 in the town of Curpa in Araure between the mountains and the llanos, the son of a white dirt farmer. As a boy he killed one of the hated over-seers – apparently in self-defence – and fled to the llanos proper to serve as a cattle rancher under a negro slave, who made the boy wash his feet. But his toughness and skill as a rancher soon established him as a farmer and leader in his own right, and he was a skilful vet.

In 1810, at the age of 20, he was pressed into service on the Spanish side in the civil war but, unusually for a llanero, deserted and joined the guerrilla bands in the western llanos. He led a squad of men and staged a raid on Barinas, where he freed 100 men from the jail. While Boves led the great majority of llaneros against the patriots, Páez at Achaguas formed an independent guerrilla group which gradually began to acquire a reputation.

He was famous for marching by night in order to avoid the heat of the day, guided by the stars in that vast sea of grass, and to make sure his movements were unobserved: the dust behind the horsemen of the llanos could be seen for miles, as could the buzzards that gathered if cattle were slaughtered for fodder. He knew the seemingly monotonous, empty terrain intimately, including the location of the dry spots during the rainy season and of waterholes during the dry. His men averaged 60 miles a day on horseback and could advance and retreat with astonishing rapidity when necessary.

Usually dressed in a coarse blue cloth, a cloak and a broad-brimmed hat, Páez, like Boves, was a short, tubby man with a barrel chest, powerful shoulders and a bull neck. Although darkened by the sun, his blue eyes and light brown hair attested to his white blood. His strong body was supported by spindly bow legs so adapted to riding that he had an awkward gait, like that of a seaman on land. Astute and intelligent, he was illiterate and had never been to a major city. He exuded leadership, shared the lives of his men and was endowed with two deep-seated Spanish characteristics – *hombria* (manliness), and *simpatia* (a feeling towards collective welfare and compassion).

He was a furious fighter, relishing the heat of combat, and was as adept with his machete as his lance. He was subject to epileptic fits at the height of battle, when he would have to be rescued as he toppled from his horse by his watchful men, including a colossal black called Pedro Camejo, who acted as his valet and chief bodyguard, and was armed with a large machete of his own. Camejo, known as 'El Negro Primero', would pick up his master as he fell and sling him across the back of his horse to carry him to safety. The simple cowboys looked upon epilepsy with religious awe.

Páez was a rough, brutal man, without any sentimental respect for human life. He recounted his experience with a Spanish officer he had badly wounded:

> I tried to remove a handsome cartridge belt which he wore about his waist and, as he broke out into a stream of blasphemy and ill-considered words not suited to the situation in which he found himself, I began to exhort him to make a Christian ending and recited the Creed to stimulate him to repeat it after me. Luckily, I looked down and saw that, instead of accompanying me in my prayers, he had half drawn a dagger from his belt. I confess my charity was completely chilled and, as my indignation did not allow me to waste more time on my adversary's future destiny, I freed him from the rage that was choking him more than the blood he was losing by a lance thrust.

His men were vicious and untamed, regarding plunder and women as theirs by right and showed no mercy to those that opposed them, although Páez did believe in taking prisoners. There was none of the demented cruelty, the sadism and lust for blood and suffering for its own sake that Boves, Morales and their henchmen displayed. Later, when he got to know Bolívar, he was described as: 'an innocent child, a primitive who looked on Bolívar as a god and at other times, when he was afar, as a devil. He was a child even unto his crimes, enamored of anything that shone.'

As his successes grew so did his army, becoming a formidable mobile force. By 1816, Páez commanded an army of 10,000 men, some of them naked Cunaviche Indians, as infantry. This force boasted around 1 million head of cattle and 500,000 horses, around 40,000 of which had been broken. Few commanders in history have had more absolute power over so vast an area. As Páez's reputation grew, the rebel forces over the border in New Granada, under the young Francisco de Paula Santander whom Bolívar had sparred with some four years before, sought to incorporate him on their side.

Santander and his men rode down to Páez's camp to order him to submit to their authority but soon became uneasily aware that they were surrounded by thousands of llanero cowboys incandescent at this display of hauteur towards their leader. Páez replied politely that his men would not let him obey Santander's orders but, on the contrary, that Santander must place himself under Páez's command if he was to get out alive.

Realizing the danger he was in, Santander agreed to resign his appointment in Páez's favour. The llaneros replied that the appointment had not been valid in the first place; Páez had always been the legitimate commander. There was a tense standoff, and for a while Santander looked in danger of being butchered, but Páez suddenly relented and agreed to this face-saver for the haughty criollo. Santander was humiliated, furious and not sure whether he had been the victim of an elaborate trick by Páez.

Páez had by now also attracted the attention of the Spanish commander, Morillo, who, in late 1816, greatly underestimating the strength and organization of the llanero troops, despatched a well-armed but inadequate force of 3,000 under La Torre to Mate de Miel near the Apure River. These were Spanish regulars equipped with artillery and their own cavalry.

Meanwhile, Páez was leading a column of 500 men and spotted the Spanish movements through the dust they sent up. They were unaware of his presence, as he did not move by day. Hoping to neutralize the cannon, he attacked at night, sending a detachment with 50 horses stampeding into the corral holding 3,000 Spanish horses, then charging in the confusion. The Spaniards fled in disarray, leaving their guns, horses and ammunition. Some 900 were killed or taken prisoner, the remainder regrouping in the wooded country along the banks of the Apure.

The illiterate and half-naked llaneros were delighted to have captured many of the uniforms of the sleeping Spaniards, and paraded about in them the following day. Badly bruised, La Torre waited for several months, until January 1817, before having another go. This time the Spaniards camped at Mucuritas, on the edge of the llanos. There were 1,500 Spanish cavalry and 3,000 infantry. At night, Páez's force of 1,100 moved upwind at the height of the dry season, when the dust would blow as a dense cloud towards the Spaniards. Then the llaneros were given their old battle order to attack repeatedly, regroup and then attack again at will. So well co-ordinated were the cowboys and their horses that no further orders were necessary. The wild horsemen descended in a series of frontal attacks along the entrenched Spanish position, routing the cavalry on their right flank.

After the initial surprise of the attack had passed and the choking dust had settled, the much larger Spanish hussar force held the line, while the infantry retreated to an easily defended wood and waterhole. To dislodge the hussars, Páez had the high, dry grass set on fire, and as the wind bore the flames down on to the Spaniards, the cowboys rode like demons behind. At this even the hussars fled before them. Morillo wrote to the King of Spain: 'Fourteen consecutive charges on my wearied battalions showed me that those men were not a scanty band of cowards as I had been informed, but organised troops, able to compete with the best in Your Majesty's service.' Bolívar decided that he must co-ordinate his actions with the ruler of the western llanos. This was tricky, as Páez had shown Santander that he took orders from no one.

The Liberator had been resting and training his men in Angostura. Tiring of Soublette's sister, Isabel, he had her married off to a merchant, who was delighted to be given, along with the girl, Bolívar's nuptial present of the only four-poster bed in town. Bolívar himself continued his addiction to night-time revelry, waltzing in the best houses in town or by the campfires outside, while his men joined in singing to the music of guitars. Dancing, he claimed, was good for thought: 'There are those who must be alone and away from all confusion in order to think and meditate. I can reflect and meditate in the midst of social gatherings, pleasures or the noise of battle. I am always alone in the midst of many people.'

One observer describes Bolívar at this time:

He wore a hat, a blue jacket with red epaulettes and three sets of gold buttons, blue trousers and, instead of shoes, leather sandals . . . The officers around him were almost all coloured. Few of them had jackets. Their clothing consisted of a shirt made up of different coloured patches, very wide and with huge sleeves; torn white trousers which came down to the knees; and hats of palm with feathers on top. Almost all were barefoot.

O'Leary describes Bolívar thus:

[His] forehead was very high but not unusually broad. It had many wrinkles. His eyebrows were thick, but well shaped; his eyes were dark and keen; his nose rather long and handsome. About the centre it had a small excrescence not perceivable until the year [18]20 when it gave him a little uneasiness, but this passed off as the wart did not grow. His cheek bones were salient, his cheeks sunken ever since I first knew him. His mouth was ugly, his lips being thick, the upper one long. His teeth were regular, white and beautiful. He took particular care of them. His jaw bones and chin were long. His ears were large. His hair, which he wore long, was extremely black and curly. His whiskers and mustachios [were] light coloured. He was of my own height. I don't know what this may be at present, something about 5'6 and 5'7, English measure. His chest was narrow and his whole figure thin, his legs particularly so. His skin was dark and rough, his hands and feet remarkably small and pretty.

His countenance at times was pleasing, when in good humour. When irritated, it was ferocious. The change was incredible. [He]

was a good eater and though [he] was as well able as anyone I knew
or know to live on any sort of diet, he was fond of a good dinner
when attainable and did it every justice. He was sober. The wines
he liked best were graves and champagne. When he drank most,
he never took at dinner a pint of the former or more than two
glasses of the latter. Whenever he filled his own glass, he helped
those who sat on his right and left.

[Bolívar] was always accustomed to take a great deal of exercise
and few men were able to endure more fatigue. He generally slept
six hours out of the four and twenty. He was a very bold, though
not a graceful, rider.

In the dispatch of civil business, which he never neglected, even
in campaign, he was quick. Sitting and swinging in his hammock,
he listened to his secretary read the thousand memorials which
never failed and in an instant dictated his decree, which was
generally irrevocable. He asked a question or two when he was
not cognizant of the demand or demandant, which very seldom
happened, as he knew almost every person in the country and was
gifted with a most extraordinary memory. His decrees were sometimes original . . . A curate, who was no great patriot, sought a
professional advancement. His decree was laconic, tho' not polite.
'Al culo mi padre' ['Up yours, Father'].

Yet even in this comparative tropical paradise, an oasis of peace
after the efforts of recent months, life was still punitive and hard for
ordinary troops and the foreign legion that was trickling in to join
them. In the hospital, according to Hippisley, men with amputated
limbs lay about, many bleeding to death, while others had half their
skulls blown off, exposing their brains.

When the Spanish army under La Torre descended the cordillera to the llanos on a major offensive to deal with these nuisances,
Bolívar was determined to fight back. After securing Páez's agreement to his command, he set out to join up with the llanero general
Zaraza in the middle of the country with 1,000 men. Zaraza had
been ordered to wait until his forces had been reinforced by Bolívar,
but rashly attacked the Spaniards at La Hogaza in December 1817.
La Torre inflicted a tremendous defeat on the patriots, killing 1,000

of Zaraza's men and securing all his stores and ammunition. Bolívar's nephew was killed in the fighting.

Bolívar, reeling from this defeat, retreated to Angostura and issued a general call-up, recruiting 5,000 men, most untrained, before setting out with his new force to join up with Páez. The army travelled at astonishing speed in long canoes, covering 560 miles in 20 days to reach Páez's headquarters at San Juan de Payara, near San Fernando de Apure.

On 31 January 1818, Bolívar and a small escort approached Páez's camp and the two most famous resistance leaders in Venezuela embraced warmly. Bolívar was deeply apprehensive about dealing with the wily little llanero leader, some seven years his junior. He feared that Páez would not obey him, or practise downright treachery, as Mariño and Piar had. Páez for his part was surprised to find Bolívar down-to-earth, energetic, and much less aristocratic and effete than he expected. But the cowboy leader's tough, well-trained horsemen easily outshone the mixture of trained troops and raw recruits Bolívar had brought with him.

The two men had a long and frank discussion. Bolívar was keen that this great and very mixed army should outflank the victorious Spanish army of La Torre, which had descended to the plains, by ascending the cordillera and marching straight on Caracas. Páez instead wanted Bolívar to join him in an assault on the capital of the western plains, San Fernando. Bolívar was always dogged by the problem that his powerful regional commanders were usually more interested in securing their immediate territories than in prosecuting the wider war. Páez wanted complete control of the western llanos, Zaraza the high plains just under the shadow of the cordillera, and Bermúdez the eastern territories and Cumana. Meanwhile, Santander, the patriot general in eastern New Granada, had joined them to urge help for his nation.

The decision was made for them: the Spanish offensive on the llanos had grown too big to be ignored and the patriots decided to march on Calabozo, the rapidly growing base of the Spanish army at the foot of the cordillera, which they came in sight of on 10 February 1818. Just before reaching it, they crossed the fast-flowing River Apure, where Bolívar was witness to a famous incident. With the river a quarter-of-a-mile wide, its current flowing at four miles an hour, and with no sign of Brión's flotilla to ferry the army across, they faced an indefinite delay. Páez pointed to a number of Spanish armed dugouts in midstream and proposed to seize them.

Bolívar watched incredulously as Páez, at the head of 50 men armed with lances, galloped into the water on white horses, forcing them to swim forward. The Spaniards were so astonished by the sight of the approaching horses and men through the water that they fired a few desultory shots before fleeing in canoes or plunging into the river, as the swimming cavalry fell upon them. This was probably the first time in history that cavalry had skirmished against armed boats.

Speeding forwards, the army of the two allies reached the enormous Spanish camp of Calabozo. Morillo, taken by surprise by the arrival of the enemy, immediately sent out forces to try and turn their wings. These were encircled by horsemen with lances who steadily cut them down to the last man '*culo a culo*', bottom to bottom, as Páez remarked. Morillo was now entirely surrounded by the patriot armies, and Bolívar issued a cheeky demand for his surrender, offering a pardon for the troops. The patriot forces then bivouacked for the night in the nearby town of El Rastro, while a detachment remained behind to watch for any sign of Spanish movement.

On the particularly dark night of 14 February, however, Morillo and all his forces slipped out from under the watchers' noses. By morning, when Bolívar was told, the Spanish had several hours' start and had escaped to defensive positions in the wooded country on the edge of the cordillera. Bolívar angrily wanted to go in pursuit but Páez was reluctant for his fighters to move out of their natural element on the plains into the mountains. Instead, he still sought to go south to seize San Fernando.

Reluctantly Bolívar agreed, on condition that once the city surrendered Páez would rejoin him. By this time Morillo himself had galloped back to his headquarters at Valencia across the cordillera, and ordered La Torre, his second-in-command, to bring more troops from Caracas to his aid. Francisco Tomás Morales and other commanders were also ordered to join him. The Spaniards had at last realized the size of the threat posed by the joint armies of Bolívar and Páez.

Frantically, Bolívar asked for Páez and Zaraza to rejoin him:

> The enemy is reinforcing its army by giving the impression that
> we have been beaten. Our suspension of operations [to allow Páez
> to settle scores down south] confirms what they say, and it is not
> surprising that people have been deceived by appearances. We
> must not lose a single moment. The speed of our movements and
> the convergence of our armies is the only hope of winning . . .
> Hesitation will produce ruin and destruction.

Zaraza's forces arrived, but not those of Páez.

In March 1818, Bolívar decided to gamble by taking the offensive
without Páez's support, in a bid to stop the royalist armies joining
up. His plan was bold: to climb the mountains and block the road
between Valencia and Caracas, and then to march on Caracas where
the weakest army was based, that of La Torre. To blockade Morales'
forces, he left an army behind under the command of Zaraza.

It was a daring concept: to seize the capital in one swoop and deal
a devastating psychological blow to the royalists. It was also foolhardy
to the point of craziness. Even if Bolívar had succeeded in taking
Caracas, he would have been surrounded by hostile armies in the
central highlands, as before, where Páez's forces would probably not
have been able to help him.

The ascending patriot army took the city of Maracay and Bolívar
was able briefly to visit his old estate at San Mateo, scene of his childhood joys and also his bitter defeat more than three years before. It
was in ruins, but he was recognized with joy by some of his old slaves.
The same evening, at Maracay, as his officers dined in a comfortable mansion, Bolívar learnt that Zaraza's forces had been surrounded
by those of Morales. Morillo, heavily reinforced, was riding upon
Bolívar.

The patriot army now risked being cut off from its retreat down
the cordillera to the llanos. Thanks to Bolívar's rashness, they were
nearly in a trap; he rushed back into the mess-hall and ordered a

retreat down the mountains by the most direct route possible, known as the 'Road of Death'. In a violent electrical night storm, Bolívar rode at the head of his troops down the rocky, precipitous pass in his cloak, while thunder and lightning rolled about him.

At a stream called El Semen, he decided to make a stand to cover the retreat: his rearguard put up quite a fight for six hours, and Morillo was halted. However, when La Torre's armies arrived to reinforce him, there was no choice but to withdraw to the already notorious La Puerta, where Boves had destroyed the armies of Bolívar's Second Republic. There the whole patriot army disintegrated into a head-long retreat amidst appalling bloodshed, leaving 1,000 dead, many of them officers. Urdaneta was wounded.

Bolívar himself only narrowly escaped to Calabozo, where the pitiful remnants of his army gathered. It was the most comprehensive military defeat he had ever suffered, and was almost entirely self-inflicted. It had been madness, tactically and strategically, to attempt, with an inferior force, a charge straight into the heart of enemy territory. His force had only just avoided being surrounded and cut down to the last man; instead he had been routed in a military disaster.

Páez, for one, viewed his own judgment in not joining Bolívar on his suicidal mission up the mountains as fully vindicated – although he failed to recognize the contribution he had made to the fiasco by failing to reinforce him at the right moment. As with Bolívar's pathetic efforts on Venezuela's northern coast, frontal attacks on the Spanish stranglehold on the high plateau seemed doomed and Bolívar was reduced once again to the state of a desperate man. In Calabozo he appeared exhausted, delirious and wretched; it was his worst mental crisis since the loss of Puerto Cabello. Hippisley saw him at the time:

> His appearance is uninteresting: at the age of 38 he appears 50. He is five foot six, dry, thin, restless and feverish. He seems to have borne immense weariness. His dark eyes, according to his friends, were piercing but now are opaque and heavy. He has dark hair tied back by a band, large moustaches, a black handkerchief around his collar, a great blue tunic and trousers of the same colour, boots and epaulettes. In the hammock where he rested wounded, while we talked, he didn't remain in the same position for more than two minutes.

He was a man close to the end of his tether, if not actually broken or insane. Over the next few months he led one small assault after another with a force of 200 or 300 men against the Spaniards in the foothills, sometimes losing, sometimes winning. Páez remarked caustically that 'Bolívar was overfond of fighting'. In fact, these seemed the obsessions of a man half-deranged by a string of failures.

In most respects Bolívar was now a pathetic figure, in charge of unimpressive forces, vastly reduced, alongside the huge hordes of horsemen from the plains. Bolívar was later to claim that there was method in his madness, that there was a game plan behind the repeated futile sallies into the mountains. First, to force the Spaniards into believing that this was his strategic objective, while a very different plan was forming in his mind; and, second, to keep the Spanish forces confined to the uplands, permitting him to assemble a new army at Angostura. Indeed, Morillo still took him seriously and remarked, 'Twelve consecutive pitched battles, in which his best troops and officers have been left killed on the field, have not been sufficient to break his self-confidence nor the tenacity with which he makes war against us'. But it is hard to believe anything so rational dominated the mind of this desperate man approaching middle age with no more to show for his dream of a free country than Miranda had, and a string of terrible defeats that had brought countless suffering to his supporters. To Morillo the real power in the resistance was Páez, and he was interested apparently only in becoming a local chieftain. The cause of independence had seldom looked more forlorn.

In his misery, Bolívar took foolhardy risks close to enemy lines, as though demonstrations of bravery would purge him of his incompetence as a general. On one occasion a group of enemy soldiers nearly surprised him when he was asleep, but he escaped when his restless horse awoke him. There were rumours that Santander, who hated him, had planned this as an assassination attempt. When Bolívar attempted to escape on a mule, he was thrown, spraining his ankle. It took him two more changes of horse to escape.

On another occasion, he and another soldier narrowly escaped discovery in the bush by a Spanish patrol. The soldier drew his knife and told Bolívar that he intended to kill his chief before the Spaniards could get him. Bolívar gave an odd laugh and went on to speak of how he intended to create a great union of South America. The guerrilla concluded that Bolívar really had gone insane. Another time a pretty girl in a farm offered to spend the night with him, having alerted the Spaniards nearby. Perhaps suspecting something, he declined.

Patriot commanders everywhere suffered setbacks. Páez was forced back from San Carlos and Barinas. Zaraza was pushed out of Calabozo by Morales. Bolívar received news of these setbacks, bathed in a sweat of fever at San Fernando, and decided to return downriver. The Spanish writer, Ciro Bayo, was to say of him: 'His career was a great vanity enlisted in the service of a noble cause'. As so often before, a setback was overcome in that complex mind by taking refuge in an even more impossible dream. The English commander of the foreign legionnaires, Colonel Hippisley, had arrived in Angostura with a bucketload of grievances. Bolívar decided to delay no longer and set off downstream in his long canoe, which had a kind of covered cabin in which he enjoyed his women on the long journey. Comically, Hippisley set off in pursuit, seeking an interview the whole way down, while Bolívar ignored him.

Only once he reached Angostura was he compelled to receive the insistent Hippisley, refusing to promote him to brigadier-general, which resulted in the latter's furious departure. At that last interview, as a jest, Bolívar offered to buy Hippisley's cocked hat; the Englishman sold it to him, and Bolívar wore it for a few days. On his return to Britain, Hippisley sued López Méndez for being misled as to his prospects in Venezuela, and even had him arrested. He was later to write a scathing book about Bolívar before, like MacGregor, being arrested himself for his involvement in a bogus scheme for colonizing South America.

Hippisley was by no means the only awkward ally. As soon as Bolívar departed for Angostura, one Colonel Henry Wilson of the British Legion started advising Páez that he should depose Bolívar as Liberator – which seemed not unreasonable in view of Bolívar's massive losses and Páez's preservation of his forces. O'Leary, accompanying Wilson, vividly described the occasion:

[Páez] reviewed our corps. He was dressed in a green ill-cut jacket with red cuffs and collar and small yellow buttons, white jean pantaloons, cotton stockings of the same colour and shoes with silver spurs. On his head he wore a large Spanish cocked hat with silver lace. His horse seemed good and was caparisoned with lots of silver ornaments.

A few days afterwards he dined with Colonel Wilson under a large shed in front of the colonel's house. Wilson flattered him in a most fulsome way. However, the general seemed not to dislike it, or rather accepted it as genuine praise which he was truly entitled to. That afternoon it was agreed that Wilson and the chiefs of Apure were to proclaim Paez captain-general of the army. Early in the next week a day was named for the purpose. The several chiefs of Apure who were at hand assembled, bringing with them as many llaneros as they could muster.

A motley group it was, to be sure. Some seven or eight hundred men on horseback, all badly clad and some almost in a perfect state of nudity, formed in anything but an orderly style in a plain to the east of the town. Our corps formed to the right of the whole – an honour meant to our splendid uniforms, I suppose. When the farce was ready to commence Paez, accompanied by some thirty or forty field officers and aid[e]s de camp, [presented himself]. The general was hailed by loud *vivas* and, as soon as these had ceased, an *acta* was read naming him Captain General. Another volley of *vivas* followed and then some of the most expert horsemen were ordered to show off. The field business over, the chiefs assembled to sign the *acta*. Thus commenced our career in favour of South American independence!!!

Paez, as was natural, was delighted with the new auxiliaries. However, the day had scarcely closed when some one whispered in his ear that he was doing wrong. On consideration, it was determined to send the *acta* to headquarters and require General Bolivar's permission for the acceptance of his new grade. In the meantime Wilson had made him splendid offers. A corps of several thousand English men were to be brought out. Wilson obtained leave to go to Angostura amid recommendations to General Bolivar to have his views attended to.

From Achaguas he set off, but, on his arrival at the capital, the castles he had been building in the air came to the ground. Wilson

was arrested, remitted to a fort in Guayana la Vieja until a vessel
was ready to sail for Europe, when he was embarked and dismissed
the service.

Bolívar had even more pressing things to worry about. He had
no money with which to pay the British mercenaries and claimed
– falsely – that they should have been paid by Méndez in London.
He did his best to find them food and accommodation, and even
considered sending them back to England. Their plight was, in truth,
pretty awful. Led to expect a land of wealth and incorporation into a
formidable army, they had braved the miseries of the West Indies to
arrive in a wretched tropical settlement.

Dr Robinson, an army surgeon, wrote of how on arrival he was
billeted in a huge old colonial house in Angostura, but thrown out
by its angry owner in the middle of the night. He found another
house, hung his hammock from hooks in the wall, and awoke to find
a decomposing pile of bodies outside. The hooks had been used to
hang Spaniards. His first encounter with Bolívar's soldiers was little
better. They were aged between 18 and 15; many were completely
naked while others sported a primitive loincloth. General Monagas,
their commander, had long, straggly dark hair, the ubiquitous jaguar-
skin cap, and a dirty white uniform.

The legionnaires themselves could not stand the raw dried beef
strips eaten by the ranks, and sold their belongings in order to get
proper food. Gradually, the quality of their own clothing declined
as they sold it off and they became emaciated by hunger. Robinson
wrote that they were 'shrunk and withered to mere walking skel-
etons . . . struggling patiently with a combination of disappointment
and disease . . . unparalleled in the history of the world'.

However, it soon became apparent that the British Legion, which
had indeed been shabbily treated and misled, contained many stoics
and idealists who were to become one of the bulwarks of Bolívar's
officer corps and army. The Liberator quickly adopted one, 'Colonel'
James Rooke, a former British army major, big, good-looking, with a
beautiful mulatta wife from St Kitts, as his aide-de-camp, and others
as guards of honour.

★   ★   ★

The longer Bolívar stayed along the Orinoco, the more fantastic and surreal the whole venture seemed to become. It wasn't just the city of Angostura, 'Queen of the Orinoco', with its picture-book Spanish colonial elegance set against a remote and inhospitable jungle; or the bizarre costumes of the soldiers and their extraordinary mixture of peoples and nationalities, from snobbish British ex-soldiers to naked Indians; or the spectacle of the Liberator waltzing late into the night around the campfire of his men. There was an inherent absurdity about the whole project. They were camped out in a remote river-jungle outback, hundreds of miles from anywhere of the slightest strategic importance, unable to make a dent in the Spanish control of the prosperous heart of their country, ineffectual and threatened.

In all this, their strutting leader now convoked, solemnly and even more fancifully, 'an elected congress of the whole nation'. In fact, it was attended by only 26 nominal 'representatives', including Mr Baptis Irvine, emissary from the United States, and Mr James Hamilton from England, as the rest of the country was not in Bolívar's hands. Nonetheless, Bolívar showed that even in the most adverse of circumstances, he was no slouch at pomp and grandeur.

His arrival was marked by a cannonade and a blast of trumpets, and he embarked on the third of his great declarations to the Spanish American people. For a man who controlled barely a fraction of Venezuela's territory – and the most remote and inhospitable fraction at that – the concept was breathtakingly grandiose and slightly ridiculous. It was, and remains, a masterpiece of literature and political philosophy – particularly in view of the surroundings.

His speech began with an uncharacteristically modest disclaimer of responsibility for the events which had plunged the patriot nation into its current predicament: 'I have been no more than a plaything in the revolutionary hurricane which blew me about like a feeble straw. I could do neither good nor bad: irresistible forces directed the march of our achievements: to attribute them to me would not be just and would give me an importance I do not deserve.' The tension between Bolívar the constitutional idealist, the protagonist of representative government and the aristocratic autocrat quickly emerged. On the other hand he rejected pure democracy and federalism:

We are not prepared for such blessings . . . Our weak citizens will have to strengthen their spirits greatly before they can take the salutary nourishment of liberty. Their limbs have been numbed by chains, their visions dimmed by the shadows of the dungeons . . . Can they march with firm steps toward that temple [of liberty], sustaining its splendid rays, breathing without oppression its pure air? . . .

It would be better for South America to adopt the Koran than the form of government of the United States, even though it be the best in the world . . . It is a marvel to me . . . that it [the United States] has continued to exist and prosper, that it has not been overthrown at the first sign of danger. In spite of the fact that this people is a singular model of political virtue and moral enlightenment, that liberty has been its cradle, that it has been reared in and fed upon pure liberty, it is a marvel that a system so weak and complicated as the federal has been able to endure . . . It has never even remotely entered my mind to consider a parallel between the positions and natures of two publics as distinct as the Anglo- and Hispano-American.

Bolívar admired the idealism of the United States, but was wary of its predatory intentions towards Latin America; his admiration of the British however seemed to know no bounds: 'Do not fear the Allies, for the ditch is large and the English fleet still larger . . . English power is on a rising curve, unhappy are those who oppose it, or even fail to ally themselves with her. The whole of America together is not equal to a British fleet; the entire Holy Alliance is powerless against her liberal principles combined with immense resources.'

Bolívar also deeply admired the British system of government: 'When I speak of the British government I refer only to its republican features; and indeed, can a political system be called a pure monarchy when it recognizes popular sovereignty, division and balance of powers, civil liberty, freedom of conscience and of the press, and all that is sublime in politics? Can there be greater freedom in any other form of republic? Can more be expected of any social order?'

His views of South America's heterogeneous racial mixture pushed him in an authoritarian direction: 'It is impossible to determine exactly to what human family we do belong. The greater part of indigenous blood has been wiped out; the European has mixed with the American and African and this has mixed with the Indian and European. Even though all of us were born from the bosom of the same mother, our fathers, differing in origin and blood, are foreigners; and all differ visibly in colouring.'

This determined the nature of local government: 'In republics the executive must be strongest because everything conspires against it, while in monarchies the legislature must be strongest, because everything conspires in favour of the monarch.'

He went on to argue that while the magnificence of the throne protected the king, there was no such protection for a republican leader who 'must be given more protection than a constitutional prince possesses . . . as no form of government is so weak as democracy its structures should be of the greatest solidity, and its institutions should be made for stability. If not . . . we will have a society that is loose, tumultuous and anarchic, with no social cohesion and in which happiness, peace and justice do not rule.' He then went on to argue, just as controversially, for the union of Venezuela and New Granada.

It is clear that he tipped towards the authoritarian view of government for the best of reasons and was both enlightened and informed for his age. However, his bias towards the need for firm government to keep Latin America in check was to be used for a century-and-a-half by the ruthless, tough-minded autocrats that were to terrorize the continent after him. Bolívar would be wheeled out as the prime rationalist of both the constitutionalists and the caudillos – and that, indeed, was a great flaw in his vision.

His argument for a republican leader stronger than a monarch leads naturally towards dictatorship: but the actual constitution he proposed, although impractical, was supposed to provide a check, offering civil liberty, freedom of religion and the abolition of slavery, as well as universal male suffrage with a property and income qualification. At Angostura Bolívar further developed his creed of equality among the races:

Under the Constitution, which interprets the laws of Nature, all citizens of Venezuela enjoy complete political equality. Although equality may not have been the political dogma of Athens, France, or North America, we must consecrate it here in order to correct the disparity that apparently exists. My opinion, legislators, is that the fundamental basis of our political system hinges directly and exclusively upon the establishment and practice of equality in Venezuela. Most wise men concede that men are born with equal rights to share the benefits of society, but it does not follow that all men are born equally gifted to attain every rank. All men should practise virtue, but not all do; all ought to be courageous, but not all are; all should possess talents, but not everyone does. Herein are the real distinctions which can be observed among individuals even in the most liberally constituted society. If the principle of political equality is generally recognized, so also must be the principle of physical and moral inequality. Nature makes men unequal in intelligence, temperament, strength, and character. Laws correct this disparity by so placing the individual within society that education, industry, arts, services, and virtues give him a fictitious equality that is properly termed political and social. The idea of a classless state, wherein diversity increases in proportion to the rise in population, was an eminently beneficial inspiration. By this step alone, cruel discord has been completely eliminated. How much jealousy, rivalry, and hate have thus been averted!

His denunciation of the institution of slavery was eloquent and unequivocal:

The dark mantle of barbarous and profane slavery covered the Venezuelan earth, and our sky was heavy with stormy clouds, which threatened to rain a deluge of fire. I implored the protection of the God of humanity, and redemption soon dispersed the tempests ... There will be no more slaves in Venezuela, except those who wish to remain so. All those who prefer liberty to repose will take up arms to defend their sacred rights and they will be citizens ... Nature, justice, and good policy demand the emancipation of the slaves: from now on there will be only one class of men in Venezuela, all will be citizens.

He failed to achieve some of these objectives – owing to the opposition of vested interests.

The president – in a reflection of Bolívar's authoritarian trait – was to be elected for life. This was an attempt to get rid of the worst aspect of monarchism, the hereditary principle which allowed fools to succeed, yet retain its authority. Bolívar had not completely understood that in England, which he so adored, power had already largely passed from the monarchy and the nobility.

The senate was to be hereditary – another aristocratic concept. The lower house was to be democratic. There was to be a five-man supreme court – an idea borrowed from the United States – and there was to be another chamber, the censors, a kind of supreme constitutional committee.

It was a kind of authoritarianism with checks and balances. Its basic ideas were sound – certainly much more so than in Miranda's projected constitutions – and its intentions were good. The ragged Congress of Angostura recognized its contradictions, throwing out the idea of an hereditary senate, a president for life (his term was sensibly restricted to four years) and the censors. It showed Bolívar to be a sometimes out-of-touch aristocrat in his political thinking; yet his concepts of freedom before the law were enlightened.

The British observer, James Hamilton, wrote that 'General Bolívar gave so brilliant a proof a moderation and patriotism as is not found in the annals of any country'. Bolívar was chosen as president of the republic, although in fact he controlled a fraction of Venezuela. It was a show for the foreign delegates.

Bolívar's third great manifesto – to the Congress of Angostura – was shot through with contradictions and ambiguities, championing of the rights of man and poor people while believing that they were too unsophisticated to choose their own governments.

But the Angostura manifesto was also designed to reconcile the interests of the dispossessed classes – his supporters in the Orinoco and the llanos – and those of the upper and middle classes in upland, temperate Venezuela. He also wanted to reassure both the bourgeois United States, Britain and the reactionary Holy Alliance powers in Europe – Austria, Prussia and Russia, with France trailing in their wake – that he was no Jacobin-style revolutionary. He ended the Angostura address with this stirring, oratorical address:

> As I contemplate the reunion of this territory, my soul ascends to the heights necessary to view the mighty panorama afforded by this astounding picture. My imagination, taking flight to the ages to come, is captured by the vision of future centuries, and when, from that vantage point, I observe with admiration and amazement the prosperity, the splendour, the fullness of life which will then flourish in this vast region, I am overwhelmed. I seem to behold my country as the very heart of the universe, its far-flung shores spreading between those oceans which nature kept apart but which our country will have joined by an imposing system of extensive canals. I can see her serving as the bond, the centre, and the emporium of the human race. I behold her shipping to all corners of the earth the treasures of silver and gold which lie hidden in her mountains. You can see her dispensing, by means of her divine plants, health and life to the ailing of the Old World. I can see her confiding her precious secrets to the learned men who do not know that her store of knowledge is superior to the wealth with which Nature has prodigally endowed her. I can see her crowned by glory, seated upon the throne of liberty with the sceptre of Justice in her hand, disclosing to the Old World the majesty of the New.

Bolívar had twice before shown his powers as a visionary, orator and propagandist: at Angostura he displayed consummate diplomacy and even high statesmanship – something amazing for a seemingly overdressed marionette leading a ragged army of down-and-outs in what must have seemed to the foreign observers present little more than a beggars' banquet. He was just about to add amazing strategic skills to his list of qualities.

Bolívar was determined to regain the offensive. Before marching with his men, Bolívar held a ball in honour of the American emissary, Baptis Irvine, whom he flattered at this rebels' coven by labelling ambassador. In a splendid uniform, he presided over a banquet, spoke with charismatic panache and force, then leapt upon the table.

'Thus', he cried, 'as I cross this table from one end to the other, I shall march from the Atlantic to the Pacific, from Panamá to Cape Horn, until the last Spaniard is expelled!' If it was hardly good manners it was certainly brilliant theatre.

Chapter 16

THE CROSSING OF THE ANDES

On 27 February 1819, Bolívar left on what seemed likely to be yet another doomed assault against the might of the empire. This time, the logic was that while Morillo was engaged on a furious campaign against Páez on the plains of Casanare in the west, Bolívar could team up with the forces in the east as well as some of Páez's men in the centre to stage yet another offensive against Caracas.

It appeared no more likely to succeed than his previous attempts against the entrenched Spanish positions in the highlands. From the first, the venture went awry. His forces marched along the southern shore of the Orinoco, through 280 miles of jungle and across hills, to liaise with Páez just 18 days later. When he met up with the llanero leader, the news was all bad. The Spaniards had driven him from Achaguas, his stronghold; Urdaneta reported that Mariño would not take part in the proposed offensive, and nor would Brión. Arismendi in Margarita had also decided not to let his troops take part.

Bolívar's latest proposed offensive seemed doomed from the start. However, he attacked the Spaniards with vigour, and Páez, taking new heart, descended on Morillo's forces outside Achaguas, killing 500. The rebels prodded away at Morillo's men while his attempt to obliterate their strongholds on the llanos were frustrated: just as the patriots could not break through on the highlands, the royalists could not prevail on the lowlands. When the rainy season stopped, Morillo risked being bogged down on enemy territory and he withdrew to Calabozo in the foothills. The Venezuelan stalemate seemed set to continue.

Bolívar then made the most fateful decision of his eventful life so far. He resolved to abandon his old goal of liberating Caracas and to march straight towards New Granada across the Andes and surprise the Spaniards there. Bolívar was later to claim that this had been the object of the expedition all along, that he had been planning such a coup for years. The evidence suggested that although he may have toyed with such a strategy, his obsession was to liberate Caracas – and only as it dawned upon him that he would be leading his troops into yet another debacle like that of the year before did he change direction. If so, it was a tactical improvisation of genius – although at the time it appeared one of madness. It may conceivably have been precisely the stroke of brilliance that he had thought of during his depression after the defeat in La Puerta. The idea was certainly suggested to him privately by his old enemy, the cold, calculating and astute Santander.

The first indication of Bolívar's change of mind came in a letter to Santander on 20 May 1819:

> To carry out an operation which I am considering in New Granada, you must group all your forces in the most careful and favourable position for entering the interior. As soon as you receive the orders I will communicate when the plan is formed and the movements co-ordinated between this body and the rest who have to take part in this enterprise. I still don't know the day for certain, and have not decided on the method which I will use. I confine myself to indicate to you the direction so that you can prepare yourself, and charge you to the ultimate secrecy, without which nothing may be done. Only you must know it.

For Bolívar, obsessed with regaining Caracas, who had deserted New Granada in order to invade Venezuela from the west, who had always argued that Venezuela was the cornerstone of any move towards Latin American independence, to consider a pre-emptive strike on New Granada and an outflanking move of this kind was astonishing enough. It seemed a sign of utter desperation, an acknowledgement that the highlands of Venezuela were impregnable.

The feat appeared to be physically impossible. This time Bolívar was not proposing to cross the spur of the mountains at Ocaña, which had been difficult enough: he was intending to traverse the uninhabited south-western llanos into the foothills of the Andes and up over the top of the cordillera itself at one of its highest points – and then descend to battle with the enemy. The immediate logic for his decision was that he had learnt that the Spaniards, believing New Granada to be safe, had left only token garrisons there, but there is no historical evidence for either view. It was also a copy of General José de San Martín's amazing tactics in crossing the Andes into Chile two years earlier.

On 23 May, in a hut in the hamlet of Setenta by the Arauca, Bolívar gathered his officers and told them of the plan: to occupy the plains of Casanare – but he made no mention of crossing the Andes after that. O'Leary takes up the story:

They met in the ruins of a cabin in the deserted and destroyed village of Setenta on the right bank of the Apure. There was no table. There were no chairs on which to sit. A party of royalists, who had bivouacked there some time before, had killed several head of cattle. The rain and the sun had bleached the skulls of the bullocks, and they served as seats on which the destiny of a great country was about to be decided. Such perhaps were the chairs on which Romulus and his rude followers sat when they traced the first narrow boundaries of the Eternal City.

The President addressed the assembly [and] spoke of the state of the army – the danger of remaining in the llanos during the winter, which was about commencing, consuming their resources and exposed to the diseases of the climate. He then ordered the Chief of the Staff to read the dispatches which had been received from Casanare and finally developed his plan of surprising the enemy in that country. He indicated his intention of invading the kingdom with the division of Paez and Ansoategui by Cucuta, while Santander should cause a diversion on the side of Casanare . . . Though he charged the most inviolable secrecy to all present – a confidence which was not betrayed – he did not let his chiefs into his real designs.

His officers were at first astonished, then appalled. This was his craziest scheme yet. But the huge, logical Colonel Rooke of the

British Legion declared he would follow Bolívar all the way to Cape Horn and the others agreed.

So began one of the epic marches in human history. There were 1,600 infantry and 800 cavalry, as well as several hundred loyal women. These were drawn up in four battalions of infantry and one rifle battalion, as well as a force of Páez's men and the British Legion. Many Indians were among them, some dressed, among them many rescued from the Caruni river settlements devastated by Piar. On 27 May they left on rafts and canoes up the Arauca in rain so dense it was difficult to breathe. They travelled this way for eight days until they reached Guasdualito, where many of Páez's men refused to continue so far from their traditional lands. They moved on to the plains of Casanare, the higher llanos, which were completely flooded, and under torrential rains and dense fog.

The penetrating gloom and dampness depressed their spirits to the bone. Most still had no idea where they were going. The water on these flooded plains came up to their waists, rendering their guns and supplies damp. Their feet were encased in mud and they were unable to stop or rest in the floodwater. They were attacked by caribe fish – tiny flesh-eating pests – as well as leeches. Their sodden clothes literally rotted away on their bodies. They rested at night on grassy mounds just above the floodwaters, most of which were a sea of mud. They could not cook and ate only raw beef. All the time the rains pounded unceasingly and the mists shut off the view.

When they crossed the Arauca river on 5 June, rafts were used to move their goods and animals. They had to traverse several more such rivers, indistinguishable from the floodwaters only by their depth. Bolívar was everywhere on his horse during these crossings, splashing and swearing, organizing and encouraging his men, help-ing them, assisting people and animals with his seemingly indefati-gable energy.

The British Legion suffered most, because of the climate and the terrain. As the land at last began to rise, the oppressive mist began to lift and they glimpsed green jungle-covered hills and the humpback mountains of the lower Andes, with, in the distance, snow-capped, jagged peaks. Nonetheless Rooke, the Englishman who had now become a kind of adopted son to the man with so many lovers but no child, frantically urged the soldiers forward.

The llaneros had never seen mountains before. At Tame they liaised with the New Granadan army of Santander, 1,200 strong, consisting of two infantry brigades and one cavalry contingent and rested for three days on dry land after their ordeal. The troops began to regain their health, only to discover with dawning horror that they were expected to climb the awesome mountains before them. Bolívar had first told them that this was only an exploratory mission into the foothills; Páez and Anzoátegui were horrified at the deception, plotting to overthrow Bolívar, but no one else supported them. Nonetheless, at Páez's instigation, the hussars deserted: the men were finished and desperate; they had been already ordered to eat horses, for fear that they would eat each other. Bolívar himself now appeared quite mad; he wore the helmet of a Russian dragoon, a blue tunic with gold buttons and red epaulettes, and on his bamboo lance carried a banner with a skull and crossbones inscribed in blood red with the slogan, 'Liberty or Death'.

Bolívar had to choose between three routes into the Andes: the Páramo (moor or plateau) de Peña Negra, which led to the Tensa valley; the Páramo de Totilla, which led to the lakes of Tota; or the Páramo de Pisba, the highest and most difficult at 12,000 feet, which would lead to the towns of Socha and the valley of the River Chicamocha. Bolívar chose Pisba because he guessed it was least likely to be defended by the Spaniards. Because of its height, the Spaniards would never believe he would attempt to cross it with an army.

The troops which had so recently been wading through ankle-deep mud were now ascending steep hills, and then traversing crags. Bolívar sent forward an advance guard under Santander to attack a garrison of 300 Spanish troops at the Paya pass. Santander destroyed the enemy and, four days after leaving Tame, Bolívar's exhausted forces arrived having only just averted another mutiny. The soldiers from Angostura and the llanos had rebelled at the steep and exhausting trail up the lower slopes of the Andes through torrential rains.

From there Bolívar reported back to Angostura:

For an entire month we marched through the province of Casanare, every day overcoming new disasters which seemed to double as we made our way through them . . . I thought this would be the main obstacle, and, once overcome, the rest seemed easy, when you speak of the obstacles which only willpower can overcome. But the harshness of the mountains is impossible to describe to anyone who doesn't know them. To give an idea of this, it is enough to know that in four marches we lost almost all the horses carrying our arsenal and almost all the cattle we had in reserve. The rigour of the season has helped make the journey more exhausting: there is hardly a day or night when it has not rained.

The worst part still lay ahead: the climb to the Páramo de Pisba. At this stage Bolívar, engulfed by the complaints of his officers and men, seriously considered calling off the whole project and retreating. Santander seems to have come up with the decisive argument: he said he was prepared to die 'a certain death in the planned operation against the royal enemy of New Granada [rather than] retreating to the llanos'. Indeed, the prospect of marching back across Casanare was worse than going on.

On 2 July 1819, Bolívar elected to press on; his only animals now were Santander's mountain horses, a handful of mules and a very few cattle. A contemporary historian sketched the scene:

At this height of the Andes there are no paths. The land is rocky and rough with no sign of vegetation other than obscure lichens. The trail can always be found, because the bones of men and animals who perished crossing the Paramo in bad weather mark it. There are on the rocks a multitude of little memorials left by pious hands in memory of those who fell there and on the ground can be seen fragments of their equipment.

The situation was really frightening: over their heads rose huge blocks of granite, and at their feet huge abysses. Nothing broke the silence, except the cry of the condor and the murmur of distant streams; the blue sky seemed close to us, and although the sun was not veiled by a cloud, it seemed to have no heat and gave out a pale light, like a full moon.

The path led upwards across the barren wilderness, past boulders and rocks. Men and horses frequently fell from the scree ledges, often thousands of feet, noiselessly. When ravines had to be crossed, crude and terrifying bridges were fashioned out of woven vines, while the cattle and mules were carried across in slings. Streams were forded by the soldiers in twos with their arms around each other's shoulders to keep them steady; if one slipped, he would be carried away by these torrents.

They climbed and climbed, and the vegetation soon grew more sparse, the path more vertiginous, the white, snow-capped peaks closer and more impregnable still. They presented a terrible spectacle. Even the best equipped were now half-naked, their clothes in tatters after they had been rotted by the waters now far below. Santander's units and the British Legion proved to be the hardiest at these heights. Accompanying them were the dark-skinned, leathered desperadoes of the llanos, their bravado on the plains having evaporated now that they were entirely out of their element, their legs, so accustomed to horses, numbed with fatigue from the climb.

Moving behind this spectral procession were the women – the indomitable loyal wives and girlfriends who would not abandon their men and nursed the wounded and the ill on that awesome ascent, most of them also half-naked from the rigours of the swamps below. The procession was single file, along the narrow path that led ever on and up.

When they had started the climb, the growing coldness had been a merciful relief from the oppressive, steaming Turkish bath of the sodden llanos far below. Now the cool had turned into cold on their sweat-drenched skins, and the rain that punished them remorselessly was an icy and unwelcome shower. As the cold began to numb the troops and their women, a new enemy loomed: altitude sickness, *soroche*, the lassitude that devours those accustomed to life at lower contours.

They began to pant, their hearts to pound, the thinning atmosphere barely able to sustain their efforts. Their movements slowed, and a metallic taste formed in their mouths; many were constantly sick. On their wretched diet of chopped raw meat they grew thin and emaciated, some falling by the wayside through sickness and lack of nutrition. As the winds screamed down and the hard rain turned to hail, sleet or snow, more and more members of that thin, naked army simply fell to the ground, their comrades beating them mercilessly to induce them to stand up again and continue. It was easy, with so little to eat, their bodies racked by the cold, to lose consciousness. They climbed six days in this manner, spending their nights huddled together for warmth on the frozen ground. As the climb continued with no signs of easing, it must have seemed that the insane Liberator had taken them on a mass suicide with no precedent in history.

When they reached the Páramo itself, they were well above the snowline on a huge rocky plateau, with spectacular peaks towering on one side. Some 13,000 feet up, the army was exposed without shelter to the freezing winds. They spent the night on that terrible plateau, scores dying of starvation, altitude sickness, lack of oxygen, exhaustion and exposure, the impact of sub-zero temperatures on unclothed bodies. Fifty members of the British Legion alone died of altitude sickness.

There was no wood for them to make fires. The lucky ones sheltered in what remained of the greedily eaten carcasses of the few animals that had survived for so long. That terrible night on the Páramo most were close to death. The stars, in their half-delirious state, at these heights, shone with unnatural brightness, while the cold moon, according to O'Leary, shone with a 'metallic luster'.

Shrieks suddenly pierced the terrible, crowded desolation: a woman had given birth. A day later, said O'Leary, 'I saw the mother with her newborn in her arms apparently in the best of health, and in the rear of the column.' The officers pushed the column forward in the first light after that dreadful night, leaving countless huddled, frozen bodies behind as fodder for the condors.

At last the journey was downward, and the cold began to ease, the oxygen to invigorate the survivors, the sickness to go. To their fevered eyes the pretty, flower-strewn valley of the Sogamoso must have seemed like a vision of paradise. Two thousand men and women had perished on the journey, along with every single horse, mule and cow. Only 1,200 of Bolívar's companions remained.

It had been the work of a madman who cared nothing about the lives of his men, a demonic imitation of San Martín's achievement two years before, an event far surpassing Hannibal's crossing of the Alps. It was also a brilliant military coup and, although no one could have foreseen it, the turning point in the hitherto appallingly bloody and seemingly futile war for the liberation of northern South America.

When this ragged, half-starved, sore-ridden army of desperate men emerged on the far side of the impregnable mountains to step into the Swiss-style prettiness of the village of Socha, the inhabitants were at first terrified, then tried to accommodate them with food and clothing. Bolívar, for all the suffering endured on the journey, knew that he had no time to waste after crossing the Andes and travelling 750 miles in four months, if he was to maintain the element of surprise necessary to succeed.

Between his army and Santa Fé de Bogotá, seat of the viceroyalty, a force of 3,000 Spaniards under General José María Barreiro was stationed at Tunja. Bolívar promptly sent out Colonel Lara to forage for horses and recruits in preparation for the imminent battle for which he and his men were so ill-prepared. Lara returned with 800 men and 1,000 horses. Bolívar now knew that he was among friends: 'Hardly had I taken my first steps on this side of the cordillera . . . when I heard resonate in front of me the blessings of men who were awaiting my arms with all the enthusiasm of liberty.' His huge gamble had proved amazingly justified; the people of New Granada, unlike those of his native Venezuela, were ready for freedom.

The main Spanish forces were at the time still concentrated on the Venezuelan highlands, several hundred miles away, ready to fend off attacks from the llanos where the partisan armies were believed to be. Bolívar had completely surprised Morillo by a flanking movement across a seemingly impassable barrier. By attacking where the Spanish troops were least concentrated and where he was least expected, he had pulled off another masterstroke.

The people of the New Granadan uplands had experienced little fighting; they were overwhelmingly white, and reasonably prosperous. They had been affected by very little of the barbarous racial and class conflict that had ignited Venezuela. But Morillo's sudden revenge against the last revolution's leaders had shocked opinion. Tunja was ripe for insurrection and the heart of the country's experiment in independence. Bolívar himself was well known for his leadership in the Magdalena, and everywhere the ragged army went, it was clear that it had popular support.

After just three days' rest, Bolívar proposed to do battle with his exhausted but hardened troops, with the hope of goading Barreiro into battle before he could summon reinforcements from the capital. The Spaniards played into his hands. On 5 July Bolívar sent his vanguard towards the River Gameza, forcing Barreiro to respond, sending forces to the town of Topaga to block the path. There the royalists inflicted a sharp defeat on the patriots, who were forced to flee back to Corrales. This was offset by a cavalry attack which wiped out a Spanish force of 300 patrolling the Sogamoso Valley.

The two armies skirmished for a few days, the royalists holding their line at the head of the Sogamoso Valley, the rebels in Tasco. Bolívar's main aim was to lure Barreiro into battle quickly, and then take the main road to the capital. The problem for the Liberator was that he needed to cross the rain-swollen River Chicamocha, which would substantially delay him and provide an opportunity for the Spaniards on the other side to pounce on him and make him fight on their own chosen ground.

He moved his main force forward, turning the enemy's right flank, but as predicted was held up by the river crossing. Barreiro moved fast, securing the rocky hills covering the road at the narrow choke-point of Paso La Balsa. The patriots now had no choice but to advance down the road under the fire of the well-armed Spaniards from above and in front of them, while on the other side there lay a swamp called Pantano de Vargas. They appeared to be walking into a trap.

When Santander attempted to occupy a hill in front of the heights, Barreiro counterattacked, and forced him back. Bolívar thereupon ordered the crack British Legion to storm the heights. This they did with magnificent bravery in three charges, in which both Rooke and O'Leary were wounded. However, reinforcements had arrived for the Spaniards and Barreiro attacked the patriot forces on the road from behind, while launching another attack to regain the heights.

Bolívar's army was now surrounded. His only chance lay in marching towards the weakest enemy point – the troops holding the road in front of him – before the British Legion was forced off the heights. This he did, ordering the llanero cavalry forward, followed by the infantry, up the steep pass where the Spaniards were waiting to massacre them. Made grim and desperate by their recent terrible ordeal in the Andes, the patriot troops stormed forward: enemy fire was nothing compared to the conditions they had experienced.

The Spaniards, caught by surprise by the recklessness of the patriots under withering fire, fled before them, and substantial losses took place on both sides. A tropical thunderstorm illuminated the scene with vivid flashes, as Bolívar's main force arrived. The Spanish commander reported, 'The destruction of the rebel army seemed inevitable and should have been so complete that not a single one should have escaped death. Desperation inspired in them resolution without parallel. Their infantry and cavalry, surging from those chasms in which they were trapped, hurled themselves against the heights with fury. Our infantry, which became confused by their excessive ardour and the difficulty of the terrain, could not resist their force.' However, as the patriots scrambled up the rocks, a large part of the Spanish army was able to slip away. The patriots had broken through but not destroyed the Spanish forces.

Afterwards, Rooke, the giant Englishman adored by Bolívar, lay wounded and his arm had to be amputated. With his other hand he took the severed limb and cried 'Viva la Patria!' The surgeon asked him which – Ireland or England? Rooke was half-Irish and had fought for both. 'The one which is to give me burial' was the reply – meaning Gran Colombia. He died a few days later, leaving his beautiful bride a widow. Bolívar had lost his adopted son and he wrote generously to Mrs Rooke: 'To Rooke I owe all my good fortune in New Granada, and Venezuela is indebted to him for the preservation of its president and will hereafter have to attribute her liberty mainly to him.'

The two armies withdrew to watch each other warily. Barreiro's priority was no longer to block Bolívar but to avoid an open battle until reinforcements could be brought up by the Spanish Viceroy, Juan de Sámano. Bolívar's aim, conversely, was to force Barreiro's army of 3,000 into battle before reinforcements could arrive. On

4 August 1819 he staged a feint, crossing the River Sogamoso, apparently to occupy the town of Paipa, then recrossing after dark to take a backroad that took his men behind the royalists, camped on the road between him and Bogotá, and allowed him the huge coup of seizing the garrison and arsenal at Tunja.

Barreiro decided to escape the trap by marching along a circuitous backroad which bypassed Tunja and rejoined the main road just behind a hill a short way from a narrow bridge that crossed the Boyacá river 10 miles further down. Bolívar's scouts spotted the Spanish army and the patriot leader himself climbed the hill separating the two roads to see the Spanish army strung out below, its advance guard about a quarter of a mile in front of the main force, the artillery in the rear.

He scrambled down to order his own troops along the easier main road in a bid to get to the bridge first. Santander led his advance guard of cavalry at a cracking pace, while the Spanish vanguard, not knowing that the patriots had spotted their secret march, rested at a farm under some trees on a hill in front of the bridge. Suddenly, to their astonishment, they spotted the cowboy cavalry and hurriedly remounted, pursuing the llaneros. They imagined this to be merely a scouting party, but when they saw the fleeing cavalry regrouping with the full support of Santander's advance troops, they realized their mistake and in turn retreated, hurrying to capture the bridge before Santander got there.

This was a fatal mistake: for the bulk of the Spanish army was a quarter of a mile away and could be cut off. Meanwhile, Bolívar ordered most of his forces to stage a march across the rough few miles that separated the two roads, and to fall upon the strung out Spanish lines. Santander's advance troops reached the river just after the Spanish vanguard had crossed it, and the two sides blazed away from opposite sides, while Santander launched several vigorous charges across the bridge.

Simultaneously the British Legion, just behind Santander, pushed forward and captured the road, cutting off the Spanish advance guard and beginning an encircling movement. Meanwhile Colonel Juan José Rondon, the hero of Pantano de Vargas, and his llanero horsemen were performing the same manoeuvre to the north of the

Spanish army. General Anzoátegui was ordered by Bolívar to launch a bayonet charge with his infantry at the centre.

Soon the British Legion and the llanero cavalry had completely encircled the depleted Spanish rump, separated from its vanguard of crack troops – the dragoons and Numancia battalions – which were pinned down by Santander's forces across the river. It was two battles rather than one. When Bolívar threw his reserves – a battalion of lancers and two of raw recruits – at the trapped Spanish force, Barreiro surrendered his sword to a patriot private. Meanwhile, Santander, after fierce fighting, had got across the bridge and some 50 Spaniards fled south to Santa Fé de Bogotá.

The battle of Boyacá was a magnificent and brilliantly improvised triumph, with Bolívar taking quicksilver advantage of his opponent's mistakes and not making a single one of his own. The patriots had killed around 500 men and captured 1,600 including the commander, along with the horses and artillery. Two officers despatched by Barreiro to seek reinforcements reported the catastrophe when they reached Santa Fé de Bogotá in the middle of the night of 8 August.

The impact of the reports of the military disaster at Boyacá was dramatic. The Spaniards believed that Bolívar's old 1813 order for a 'war to the death' was still in place, and did not know that it had been rescinded. They had heard reports of the fearsome army of scarecrows that climbed up across the Andes from the llanos. Fearing vengeance, the Spanish garrison and governing class simply fled into the night, never thinking of defending the city in the mountains.

On hearing of the Spanish abandonment of the capital of New Granada, Bolívar pushed forward with speed in order to prevent looting and destruction. Among the huge contingent of prisoners, a man was brought to him: Francisco Vinoni, whom Bolívar believed to be the traitor responsible for handing over the fort at Puerto Cabello to the Spanish prisoners in 1812. He was summarily hanged, his body dangling before the crowd in the plaza of the small town of Ventaquemada. 'How horrible,' said Barreiro as he passed. The officer escorting him explained, 'He's the Italian traitor Francisco Vinoni, whom Bolívar promised to hang if he fell into his hands, and he's fulfilled his promise.' The memory of that failure, which had led to the tragedy with Miranda, still continued to haunt the Liberator.

On 10 August 1819, the 36-year-old Bolívar, dressed in a jacket with no shirt underneath, because he had lost it in the campaign, arrived in Santa Fé de Bogotá. The reception was an emotional, nervous one, the people fearful of being put to the sword. Flowers and pretty girls greeted the shambolic, shoeless army.

A woman ran up to Bolívar on San Miguel Street and grovelled at his right foot. 'God bless you, ghost!' she exclaimed. The small, emaciated Liberator grinned and patted her on the head. In the main square, according to an eyewitness:

> Bolívar dismounted and climbed the steps of the government palace rapidly. His memory was remarkable, for he greeted with their names and surnames all the leading citizens he had known since 1814. His movements were easy and gentle . . . His skin was toasted by the sun of the llanos, his dark hair carefully groomed and combed. His penetrating black eyes had an electric mobility. His questions and answers were rapid, concise, clear and logical. He asked about the whereabouts of Dr Camilo Torres and Don Manuel Bernardo Alvarez. Of the second he said that he had foreseen he would be shot by the Spaniards. His restlessness and mobility were extraordinary.

Bolívar was looked upon by the people of Bogotá as superhuman, almost a demigod, while his triumph had, indeed, been extraordinary. In one bold stroke, followed by a dazzling military triumph, he had seized the capital of Spain's richest province while the bulk of its forces were hunting him in Venezuela. He now controlled all of the Viceroyalty of New Granada, with a population of 1 million people. But he was at pains to emphasize that the war was just beginning.

Morillo, on learning of the victory, concluded that Spain's hold on Latin America was irredeemably lost. The Marqués de la Puerta and Commander of Spanish forces in Northern Spanish America wrote to Madrid that:

> The seditious Bolívar has occupied Santa Fé (Bogota), and the fateful result of that battle has placed at his disposition the whole kingdom and the immense resources of a very populated country,

rich and abundant, from which he will plunder what he needs to continue the war in these provinces, because the insurgents and least of all this caudillo don't have any rules or inhibitions. This disgraceful attack hands to the rebels, in addition to New Granada, many ports on the southern coast, where they will gather their pirates: Popayán, Quito, Pasto and the whole interior of the continent as far as Peru remains at the mercy of whoever governs Santa Fé, to whom, at the same time, are available banks, arsenals, arms factories and everything that the King possesses in the viceroyalty. Bolívar in one day has finished the efforts of five years of campaigning, and in a single battle has reconquered what the King's troops have won in many fights.

He was exaggerating: the patriots had held Bogotá before, as well as much of Venezuela, and still lost them all. The large Spanish army in Venezuela remained undefeated, but the patriots had received an immense moral and psychological boost for what had seemed a lost cause.

Chapter 17

VICTORY AT CARABOBO

Bolívar wasted no time. Fatefully, he appointed Santander his vice-president. Of good family, trained as a lawyer, Santander was cold, calculating, imbued with a strong streak of cruelty, money-obsessed and avaricious. He also had a brilliant mind. Soublette and Anzoátegui were ordered to mop up Spanish resistance to the north – which they did with the exception of the coast. The latter soon died of an infection contracted while crossing the Andes. Sámano, the brutal departing viceroy, had descended the Magdalena and embarked for Spain. Bolívar made a triumphal provincial tour and went to Pamplona to supervise the recruitment and training of the hundreds flocking to join his new army.

Bolívar decided to return to Angostura – not in a display of gratuitous hyperactivity, but wanting to show that he still placed high priority on the liberation of Venezuela, and also prompted by disturbing reports of how things were going in his absence. Zea, the well-meaning but weak constitutionalist that Bolívar had left behind as president, had been deposed by Arismendi, the ruthless former boss of Margarita, working with the ever-disloyal Mariño, who had become army commander.

He left Santander in charge of New Granada and enjoined him to take no reprisals against royalists, but as soon as Bolívar departed, Santander had 38 provincial royalists executed, including Barreiro, apparently as a reprisal for atrocities committed by the Santa Fé garrison commander, Calzada, on his flight from Bogotá to Quito. The real reason was that after Bolívar's departure Santander feared there could be a popular uprising and wanted to stamp his authority. Santander's executions were chillingly cold-blooded:

Shortly before midday, marching in lines of four, they were led to the opposite side of the square. Barreiro, Jiménez and two other officers bound to him by friendship and duty, despite the heavy irons they dragged, had to walk all the way across the square. As he arrived on the spot where his sufferings were to end, Barreiro who was accompanied by a priest, called Colonel Plaza who commanded the troops, spoke a few words to him and, taking from his chest the portrait of the young woman he had meant to marry, begged him to deliver it to her brother, who was serving under Plaza's orders. An instant later he was ordered to kneel and was shot in the back [the 37 others were also shot, as was a protesting spectator]. Santander, preceded by some musicians, rode through the chief streets singing the refrain of a song referring to the event.

Bolívar furiously rebuked him but could take no action.

The Liberator galloped towards Angostura like a man possessed, accompanied only by a couple of guards along the main roads through New Granada, changing horses at every village, riding from dawn to dusk. At Barinas he met Páez, and they discussed tactics through the night, then he was off by fast canoe along the tributaries of the Orinoco to join the main river.

On the way he met Antonio José de Sucre coming the other way in a canoe. He was an astonishingly good-looking officer with a sincere expression, promoted to general by Zea at the age of 25. He had been born in Cumana and educated in Caracas. As a 17-year-old he had fought under Mariño and broken with him to go and serve Bolívar in Angostura.

Bolívar was furious when he learnt of Sucre's appointment as general, which he insisted Zea had no right to make. However, when the young officer promptly offered to give up the post, Bolívar personally promoted and forgave him. The young man was to replace the martyred Rooke in his affections as his adopted son – and was to become the second most famous figure in the history of the liberation of northern south America, after only Bolívar himself. O'Leary described him:

General Sucre seemed to me the best general of Colombia. He had personal bravery, an excellent *coup d'oeil*, and was indefatigable. He did every thing himself, wrote his own despatches, examined every thing, conducted the espionage, reconnoitred, visited by day and night the outposts, saw even the rations delivered. And still he was not much liked in the army. Sucre had read but little and, though he had a brilliant imagination, he wrote badly. Notwithstanding, he was a man of talent and good sense.

Bolívar later remarked of him: 'That is one of the best officers in the army. He has the professional knowledge of Soublette, the kindly character of Briceño, the talent of Santander and the activity of Salóm. For some reason I didn't know of nor suspect his aptitudes before. I intend to bring them into the light; for some day he is going to rival me.'

On arrival at Angostura after only five weeks' travelling, Arismendi, astonished, handed over power and Mariño feted Bolívar at a huge ball held in his honour. The Liberator proclaimed the creation of a huge new nation – Colombia, made up of Venezuela, New Granada and Quito. Bolívar was to be president of the whole and Santander vice-president in New Granada. Santander had opposed the merger, but had no choice but to go along with it.

After just a fortnight in Angostura, Bolívar returned to New Granada – the third time he had made the journey in a year, covering some 2,500 miles altogether. His aim was to consolidate his gain, travelling to raise and train troops. He knew what was coming. Morillo had written to Ferdinand VII of Spain:

> Nothing can compare with the untiring activity of that leader. His fearlessness and his talents entitle him to his place at the head of the revolution and of the war; but he possesses as well, from his noble Spanish strain and his education, also Spanish qualities of elegance and generosity which elevate him far above all who surround him. He is the revolution . . . Bolívar is an indomitable soul whom a single victory of the smallest nature is enough to make master of 500 leagues of territory.

The king needed little prompting. The empire was about to strike back for the second time: a colossal punitive expeditionary force of 20,000 infantry, 3,000 cavalry and 100 artillery pieces was being prepared on 47 warships, many supplied by Russia.

It was not to be. The Russian ships turned out to be unsuitable for crossing the Atlantic. As another fleet was prepared, the soldiers, idle for more than a year, began grumbling about pay and conditions and showed little eagerness for fighting in the fever-ridden tropics against the notoriously savage South Americans. Ferdinand's cruelty and absolutism had also made him deeply hated. On 1 January 1820, Rafael del Riego, commander of one of the supply points for the expedition, mutinied against the government of Madrid and outside Cádiz announced the restoration of the liberal 1812 constitution, which the despot had dissolved after the French had been driven from the peninsula. A large part of the army and the population joined him: the expeditionary force had largely turned against its king.

Ferdinand VII, unable to send the expedition, instead sent a letter: he urged negotiations between Morillo and the rebels on the basis that the patriots should agree to reincorporate themselves into the empire on the basis of a new, liberal Spanish constitution. Morillo was appalled. He told one of his officers, 'They are mad. They do not know what they order, they do not know the country, nor the enemy, nor the developments here. They want me to go through the humiliation of entering into these exchanges. I do so only because my profession is subordination and obedience.'

Morillo wrote to Bolívar proposing an armistice and asking the rebels to accept the new Spanish constitution. In Santa Fé, the news of the collapse of the Spanish expedition, before it had even been sent, had been received with a tremendous sense of relief by Bolívar. For the first time events were turning his way, a tremendous stroke of fate had played into his hands. It was possible, after all, that he was on the verge of achieving his goal.

With perfect tactical sense, he accepted the proposal for an armistice, which would give him more time to train and swell his armies while the Spaniards would receive no reinforcements, but he also contemptuously rejected the idea of submitting to the crown, as Morillo had predicted. Bolívar's forces in Venezuela now surged forwards, in a poorly organized offensive along the cordillera, occupying Mérida and Trujillo. The area, where dreadful Spanish reprisals had taken place seven years before, was racked by terrible misery, poverty and ancient blood feuds. These uprisings were said to have made a strong impression on Bolívar and reinforced him in the conviction that the war should be brought to a speedy end. In Trujillo on 26 November 1820, Bolívar sought a treaty to regulate the conduct of the war with the Spaniards – an attempt to humanize the conflict from the very city in which he had pledged a 'war to the death' with the Spaniards. An armistice was also signed.

Morillo sought to meet the foe he had once despised as a bandit, but who was now recognized as the president of New Granada. A parley was fixed at Santa Ana and Morillo appeared in a magnificent uniform accompanied by a regiment of hussars. When O'Leary arrived to tell him the general was approaching, Morillo asked him what the size of his escort was:

> I replied: 'Only ten to twelve officers and the Spanish emissaries' [sent to organize the ceasefire]. Morillo replied, 'I thought my own escort was small. But my old enemy has trumped my generosity. I will order the hussars to retire.' This he did immediately . . . shortly afterwards the Liberator's party could be seen on the hill dominating the town of Santa Ana. As the riders approached, Morillo wanted to know which was Bolívar. Pointing him out, he exclaimed: 'What, that little man with a blue tunic, a forage cap and mounted on a mule?' He had hardly finished talking when the little man was at his side, and on greeting each other the two generals dismounted and embraced warmly.

Bolívar had played every psychological trick in the book; the showman in him had once again upstaged the Spanish general. By coming so underdressed to so important a meeting, he was both expressing contempt for Spanish authority and exuding the simplicity of the truly great man. He was telling Morillo that he had no need for pomp and display, he was Bolívar – although he was a great lover of both when he wanted to impress ordinary people. After a frank exchange of views, they laid a stone to mark the spot, then had a sumptuous banquet – those two fierce old enemies whose armies had shed tens of thousands of lives fighting each other.

Afterwards Bolívar crowed:

> Never in the course of my life have I displayed more political or diplomatic energy than on that important occasion; and in this I can say without vanity, I defeated General Morillo, as I had in all his military operations [an exaggeration, to say the least!]. I was armed, moreover, with my politics and diplomacy, well covered with an appearance of frankness, good faith, confidence, and friendship, although it's obvious I could have felt none of this towards the Count of Cartagena – nor could any of these emotions have been inspired by a meeting of a few hours.

Morillo was more generous about the bandit:

> I spent one of the happiest days of my life in the company of Bolívar . . . No one could imagine the interest that interview held nor the cordiality and love which reigned between us. All of us committed absurdities of happiness. It seemed like a dream, reunited there as Spaniards, brothers and friends. Bolívar was carried away with delight and we embraced a million times. We determined to erect a monument as an eternal memorial to the beginning of our reconciliation on the spot where we had first embraced.

A witness provides an amusing recollection of the encounter:

> After their healths had been successfully proposed by each other, they, as if by mutual desire, arose to embrace, according to the custom of the country; and the men who, for years had been the most inveterate enemies, and had each essayed to surpass his antagonist in the slaughter of their respective countrymen, now hugged and kissed each other in the warmest and apparently most cordial manner . . .
> Finally, each being completely intoxicated, a briezo [toast] was given to the healths of both Generals at once, by their order, and according to the custom the glasses were dashed to pieces on the

table, which they then severally mounted again to embrace each other. Unfortunately, their motions not being very steady in a sort of *pas de deux* which they were dancing on the table after the embrace was over, it suddenly gave way, and they abruptly descended to the floor, where they rolled for some time, until picked up, still embracing each other with the greatest vehemence.

The chiefs being carried to a bed-chamber, they slept in the same room, and all retired till the next morning, when the second part of this friendly compact was made known.

Bolívar was delighted that he had at last been treated as an equal by Spain.

Two weeks after meeting the Liberator for the first and last time, his enemy of seven years of bitter fighting, the Pacifier left La Guaira knowing the royalist cause to be lost and determined not to preside over its funeral. His successor was La Torre. His departing words were: 'Defend Puerto Cabello at all costs' – the last port of evacuation for Spanish forces in the event of retreat. Of the Spanish commanders against Bolívar he was much the most intelligent, although his earlier humanity had been warped quickly by the animal ferocity of the war in Venezuela. It was hardly an inspiring legacy for La Torre.

Bolívar was pleased that Morillo had been succeeded by La Torre. The armistice, he said:

discouraged Morillo and caused him to leave the country, to be replaced by La Torre – an officer less active, less capable, less a soldier . . . I was convinced I could dominate Morillo in a personal encounter . . . It was an excuse for time to regulate the war and was adopted exactly as I had written it. It was a sane, humane and politic treaty which put an end to that horrible butchery of slaying the conquered, of giving no quarter to prisoners of war – Spanish barbarism that the patriots were forced to adopt them- selves in reprisal, that had pushed back civilization, made the soil of Colombia an abode of cannibals and soaked it with innocent blood until all humanity shuddered. It was an advantage to us, fatal to the Spaniards. Their forces could only diminish, mine augment and organize.

The armistice lasted until 28 April 1821, when the city of Maracaibo rose in revolt against the royalists, and Bolívar chose to close the trap he had so meticulously prepared. In the east, Bermúdez passed the Unare river and crushed a royalist garrison at El Guapo; in the west, Urdaneta marched from Maracaibo, defeated the royalists at Casiglia and took Coro. Mariño and Manuel Cedeño also attacked from the south east. By 15 May Bermúdez's forces had reached Caracas, taking most of the city. Meanwhile, Urdaneta's forces were threatening Puerto Cabello, the Spaniards' main line of evacuation.

La Torre began to panic; he deployed part of his large army to San Carlos to try to block Urdaneta's advance, and to another part of the capital, where Spanish inhabitants were pouring in yet another exodus down the 50-mile road to La Guaira. Páez, who had so long hesitated to send forces up into the Venezuelan highlands, also despatched his army to ride up the cordillera.

As these advanced, La Torre decided to abandon San Carlos and defend instead a line near the Lake of Valencia, with the plains of Carabobo behind him. On 7 June, Bolívar and Páez rode up to San Carlos: their combined armies now numbered 6,500 compared to 5,000 Spaniards. Their forces advanced on the Spanish position at the centre of the Carabobo savannah, straddling the main road between Caracas and Valencia.

Bolívar's forces approached in three columns, one under Páez, another under Cedeño and the third under Colonel Plaza, through narrow ravines that cut northwards across the hills to the south of the plain, in an effort to outflank the Spaniards and engage them on both sides. La Torre and his army failed to block Bolívar, but his path led upwards on to the plain where the Spaniards, from a superior position overlooking a ravine, engaged him. After three charges, the llaneros were dispersed.

A British Legion battalion held firm behind them, blasting away with precision in a disciplined line several men deep. A British officer vividly tells the heroic story:

> We halted at dusk on the 23rd at the foot of the ridge. The rain fell in torrents all night and reminded us of the night before Waterloo. Next morning the sky was cloudless when we stood to arms, and

presently Bolívar sent us the order to advance. We were moving to get round the enemy's right flank, where his guns and infantry were partly hidden by trees and broken ground. Bolívar, after reconnoitring, ordered us to attack by a deep ravine between the Spanish infantry and artillery. The enemy's guns opened fire and our men began to fall. Meantime the Bravos de Apure had advanced within pistol shot of the Spaniards, and received such a murderous volley from 3,000 muskets that they broke and fled back in disorder upon us.

It was a critical moment, but we managed to keep our ground till the fugitives had got through our ranks back into the ravine, and then our grenadier company . . . formed up and poured in their fire upon the Spaniards, who were only a few paces from them. Checked by this volley, the enemy fell back a little, while our men, pressing eagerly on, formed and delivered their fire, company after company.

Receding before our fire and the long line of British bayonets, the Spaniards fell back to the position from which they had rushed in pursuit of the Apure Bravos. But from thence they kept up a tremendous fire upon us, which we returned as rapidly as we could. As they outnumbered us in the ratio of four to one, and were strongly posted and supported by guns, we waited for reinforcements before storming their position. Not a man, however, came to help us, and after an hour passed in this manner our ammunition failed. It then really seemed to be all over with us. We tried as best we could to make signals of our distress . . .

Our commanding officer apprised General Páez of our situation and called on him to get us a supply of cartridges. It came at last, but by this time many of our officers and men had fallen . . . You may imagine we were not long in breaking open the ammunition boxes; the men numbered off anew, and after delivering a couple of volleys we prepared to charge. At this moment our cavalry, passing as before by our right flank, charged, with General Páez at their head. They went on very gallantly, but soon came galloping back and passed again to our rear without having done any execution on the enemy, while they themselves had suffered considerably.

Why Bolivar at this time, and indeed during the period since our first advance, sent us no support I have never been able to guess. Whatever the motive, it is certain that the second and third divisions of the army quietly looked on while we were being slaughtered, and made no attempt to help us. The curses of our men were loud and deep, but seeing that they must not expect any help they made up their minds to carry the enemy's position or perish. Out of nine hundred men we had not above six hundred left . . . the colours of the regiment had seven times changed hands and been literally cut to ribands and dyed with the blood of the gallant fellows who carried them.

But in spite of all this the word was passed to charge with the bayonet, and on we went, keeping our line as steadily as on a parade day and with a loud 'hurrah' we were upon them. I must do the Spaniards the justice of saying that they met us gallantly, and the struggle was for a brief time fierce, and the event doubtful. But the bayonet in the hands of British soldiers, more especially such a forlorn hope as we were, is irresistible. The Spaniards, five to one as they were, began to give ground, and at last broke and fled.

Then it was, and not till then, that two companies of the Tiradores came to our help, and our cavalry, hitherto of little use, fiercely pursued the retreating enemy . . . The remains of the corps passed before the Liberator with trailed arms at double quick, and received with a cheer, but without halting, the words, '*Salvadores de mi Patria!*'

The stand by the British Legion proved decisive to the battle. La Torre sent the cavalry to the infantry's aid, but Páez despatched his fast-wheeling llanero horsemen to intercept them, and others to cut off the retreat of the infantry. In the course of this battle, Páez's loyal giant, El Negro Primero, was mortally wounded and galloped off to say goodbye to his master, before falling to the ground. He who had so often scooped up the llanero general from the field of battle could not now be saved by Páez.

Along the main road the bulk of the patriot force was now advancing, pressing back the Spanish artillery and the crack Valencey Battalion. La Torre, under serious pressure, ordered the battalion back

and the cannon were abandoned. Moving in perfect square formation, under impeccable discipline, the Valencey Battalion, under
attack from three sides, retreated with great dignity. The battalion
offered protection to La Torre and his staff before withdrawing
towards Puerto Cabello in a famous and heroic retreat under torrential rain and constant harassment. Nearly half the Spanish army had
been killed, wounded or taken prisoner in the Battle of Carabobo.
Bolívar had won the most brilliant and decisive victory of his career,
liberating Venezuela for the last time.

Despatching Páez to follow the retreat to the coast, Bolívar entered
Caracas on 28 June, seven long years after he had left on that terrible
exodus to the east. Again, he was feted wildly, but at nearly 39 years
old, he was too wise to let it go to his head. He was, indeed, curiously sombre.

After exchanging cordialities with La Torre – unprecedented
throughout the civil war – and granting safe conduct to those who
had fled to La Guaira while forbidding his troops from carrying out
reprisals, he sought out his destitute old protector, Francisco Iturbe,
and gave him back his properties, before withdrawing to the war-
battered estate of San Mateo. There he found just three of his 1,200
former slaves, and freed them.

In the ruins of his hacienda, he contemplated the dangers ahead,
which he saw as arising from the conflicting ambitions of his subordinates. He spoke of 'the terrifying chaos of patriots, fat cats, egotists,
whites, blacks, federalists, centralists, republicans, good and bad aristocrats and the whole mass of hierarchies which subdivide into different parts'. Now that the unifying oppressor, Spain, was removed, he
feared above all the new state's disintegration into civil war, faction
and anarchy.

He tried to divide and rule, giving Páez control of the central region,
Bermúdez the west and Mariño the east. He wrote despairingly:

> You can have no idea of the spirit which animates our military
> officers. They are no longer the men you knew. They are men who
> have fought for years and believe themselves superior; and yet they
> are humiliated and impoverished, with no hope of enjoying the

fruits of the work of their lances. They are often resolute llaneros, ignorant men who think themselves superior to those of greater accomplishments. Even I, who have always been at their head, cannot say of what they might be capable. I trust them with the greatest consideration, but it doesn't seem to inspire them with the spirit which ought to exist among comrades and fellow-citizens. Believe me, we are over a volcano about to erupt. I fear peace even more than I fear war.

A lesser problem was that the Congress of Cucúta, which Bolívar had summoned to draw up the constitution of the new super-state of Colombia, had ignored many of his recommendations. He complained that the constitution had been 'very much amended and was very bad in some parts'.

Worse still, he was seriously beginning to fall out with Santander, his proconsul in Santa Fé de Bogotá. Venezuela, bled dry by a decade of war, was in no position to provide the money for the next stage of Bolívar's colossal liberating mission: to repel the Spaniards from their last and most entrenched stronghold in South America, the Viceroyalty of Peru. Only prosperous, newly peaceful New Granada could do that.

Santander, reflecting the opinion of most of his countrymen, was reluctant to be drawn into the liberation of another land, preferring that his country should safeguard its own peace and prosperity. A skilful politician with a legalistic brain, Santander was a cold fish, calculating and down to earth. Bolívar wrote to him wryly: 'There is a good exchange between you and me; you send me specifics and I send you hopes. In ordinary parlance one would say that you were more liberal than me, but that would be a mistake. The present has already passed, the future is the property of man, because he lives in the land of illusions, of fictitious appetites and desires.'

It was a shrewd point, but cut little ice with the hard-headed Santander. Bolívar asked for Santander to give him 4,000 to 5,000 men to fight the great liberation battles in Peru. Santander, who considered himself the real ruler of New Granada, and Bolívar merely as a convenient ally, had to bow to *force majeure*, but privately seethed. Meanwhile, Bermúdez had driven the last Spaniards in eastern Venezuela from Cumana; and after 14 months' siege, Mariano Montilla had taken the stubborn holdout of impregnable, walled Cartagena.

La Torre fled to Cádiz, leaving Morales, Bolívar's vicious old enemy, in control of the last stronghold of Puerto Cabello. In the city of Panama, a revolution had broken out against the Spaniards, and the Panamanians asked to join Colombia. Bolívar now controlled a territory as large as two-thirds of all western Europe. Some 260,000 people had been killed in Venezuela alone – around a quarter of the entire population.

Part 2

THE LIBERATION OF PERU

(MODERN ECUADOR, PERU AND BOLIVIA)

Chapter 18

TOWARDS THE SILVER MOUNTAIN

Bolívar now turned his attention to the greatest powerhouse of Spanish wealth and authority, the Viceroyalty of Peru. It was the source (along with Mexico) of the mineral wealth that had financed the Spanish empire for 30 years, with its capital of riches and decadence, Lima, its huge military strength and its vast near-slave population. As long as this remained loyal to the Spanish crown, Gran Colombia could never be safe from a major expedition by the empire to regain its possessions; security would come only if the Spanish were driven out of all of Latin America. Moreover, Bolívar was acutely aware that the 'Protector' of Argentina and Chile, General José de San Martín, had embarked on his own rival enterprise to liberate the richest jewel in the Spanish crown from the south, and if successful could himself threaten the newly freed northern colonies.

Already Bolívar had despatched Sucre along with the British Legion into the mountains south of New Granada. On this occasion the once motley mercenary army was brilliantly commanded and battled its way down the main Andes cordillera, across some of the most spectacular and rugged country in the world, marked by towering peaks and gorges several thousand feet deep, against a bitterly hostile and fierce local population, down as far as the city of Popayán. From there Sucre was ordered by Bolívar to go by sea to Guayaquil, the tropical, disease-ridden port which he arrived at from Buenaventura without a fight, and to take the major city of Quito.

On 13 December 1821, Bolívar himself rode at the head of a column of 3,000 troops commanded by General Bartolomé Salom, his chief of staff, along the 1,500-mile trek to Peru down the second

greatest mountain range on earth. The first phase of Bolívar's expedition to the south was surprisingly easy, down the huge valley of the
Cauca. Most of the area had already been cleared of royalists by Sucre,
and at Popayán the commander of the Spanish garrison surrendered
without a fight. However, the presence of a Spanish fleet made it
impossible for Bolívar's army to embark at Popayán for Guayaquil as
he had intended. He had no choice but to travel overland.

The rough country now began: perched on rope bridges across
gaping chasms, climbing precipitous trails up the sides of mountains,
and struggling over icy ledges and ridges, it was like another version
of the march across the Andes again, less fearsome, but longer. Lack
of oxygen, altitude sickness and falls from the great heights all took
their toll: by the time they reached the royalist stronghold of Pasto,
carefully avoiding a fight with the more locally experienced enemy,
they had lost 1,000 men.

It had been another of Bolívar's forced and ruthless marches. He
described the position thus:

> Pasto is inhabited by men who have made a tenacious defence
> of a territory they know and whose natural resources they take
> advantage of . . . The liberating army suffered from the climate,
> from a shortage of provisions, from the gruelling marches [from
> the terrain] and had to fight, on their own territory, against fresh
> men acclimatised and used to those places. The liberating army,
> from the day it undertook its march, could not count on anything
> but casualties, loss of men, horses, mules and baggage; and the
> immobile enemy suffered nothing.

Pasto was a region of rugged mountains rising to 18,000 feet,
almost entirely cut off from the outside world, dominated by the
clergy, inhabited by a closed, hard, suspicious people, many of whom
considered the king of Spain divine. It was bisected by fast-running
rivers, with enormous waterfalls: the Juanambu and, further south,
the Guaitara. The success of Bolívar's small and exhausted column
among the great peaks in hostile territory harassed by hardy, experienced mountain men was far from assured. As Pasto, the centre of
the region, came closer, the enemy was concentrating on blocking

the southern path of the Liberator. Bolívar, realizing that he had no alternative except to find a circuitous route of hundreds of miles to avoid them, decided to confront the Spaniards at last.

Arriving in the valley of Bomboná in April 1822, Bolívar and his officers could hardly ever have witnessed a more hopeless or spectacular battleground: the Spaniards were above them, overlooking the gorge that Bolívar was ascending. On their left flank ran the steep slopes of the huge Pasto volcano, the centre protected by dense forest and on the right a rocky precipice along the Guaitara river, a thunderous torrent coursing down the bottom of the ravine. The Spaniards proceeded to raid Bolívar's camp, leaving 800 dead and 1,000 wounded, and destroying 15,000 rifles.

Bolívar believed he was beaten, and it seemed madness to proceed. He commented, 'The task seems impossible. But we must conquer, and we will.' He ordered his men forwards at three in the afternoon, with just three hours before darkness, which is always at 6 p.m. on the Equator. As the troops clambered up the slopes to the centre, they were met by withering fire. They had no cavalry to charge the entrenched enemy positions, having lost all of their horses en route, while artillery on the left ripped into them.

Suddenly Bolívar noticed that Jeronimo Valdez, one of his commanders, had started leading his men in a climb directly up a cliff, using their bayonets for holds and footholds. The cliff provided shelter from enemy fire, while Bolívar gave them covering fire and prevented the enemy positions above being reinforced. The astonishing spectacle of the column climbing the almost vertical cliff face became shrouded by mist for a nail-biting hour. When the mist lifted just as the sun began to fade, the patriots had seized the unguarded top of the cliff and were charging down several hundred feet with their bayonets fixed, having reversed the Spanish advantage over the terrain; the Spaniards beneath them had run out of ammunition and were fleeing before the unexpected offensive.

Bolívar ordered all his remaining forces to attack the centre, and the Spanish lines broke. As the patriots climbed over the rough ground to secure the Spanish positions, darkness fell, but a full moon allowed the patriots to pursue the Spaniards until eventually they melted away into the mountains. Bolívar had secured a breathing space, although he had not won a decisive victory because much of the royalist army had escaped. He waited for reinforcements to come from Santa Fé de Bogotá. He had the satisfaction of knowing that he had pinned down Spanish forces that might otherwise have gone to the relief of Quito, now under siege from Sucre's army. But his road southward remained blocked, and he had not conquered Pasto.

Sucre had meanwhile been fending off a series of crises in that yellow-fevered sink of contraband and piracy, Guayaquil, with its stilt slums extending over lethal fetid sea-marshes. He was negotiating with the elders of the city, who were likely to join whichever of the patriot commanders – Bolívar from the north and General San Martín from the south – would pay them better.

In that sultry city on the Equator, a group of Sucre's soldiers mutinied and boarded six ships, proclaiming allegiance to the king of Spain. Sucre set off with members of the British Legion in pursuit, caught them and brought them back. Having secured the co-operation of the town council he and his 1,000 defenders then found themselves under siege. From August to November 1821, he fought a series of indecisive engagements in defence of the city, before signing a three-month armistice with the Spanish commander, Melchor Aymerich. During this crucial truce, he was reinforced by several hundred Peruvians under General Andrés de Santa Cruz (the future president of both Peru and Bolivia), who had been despatched by San Martín from the south.

This gave Sucre sufficient strength to march out of the city and towards Quito in the mountains. At Riobamba he defeated a small force of Spaniards, and Aymerich fell back towards Quito. Largely thanks to a vigorous frontal assault by the British Legion that divided the enemy at Pichincha in May 1822, three companies of Spaniards were crushed and the rest of the army fled into the city, where they soon surrendered. Sucre captured 2,000 men, 1,700 muskets, 14 cannon, and a huge amount of ammunition and stores.

Once news of the surrender of Quito reached Basilio García, the Spanish commander at Pasto, he surrendered to Bolívar, followed by Aymerich, the Viceroy, who surrendered the whole territory to the Liberator and was permitted to leave, along with García, for Spain.

The modern country of Ecuador had suddenly crumpled before him and been added to Bolívar's trophies – largely through the work of Sucre, following Bolívar's strategy of attacking on two fronts.

On 16 June 1822, Bolívar entered Quito, a city dominated by spectacular volcanoes. The city, with a population of 500,000 and a thriving multicoloured textile trade, was in the heartland of Indian-populated territory, very different in racial makeup to the mulatto- or black-dominated Venezuela or white-dominated New Granada. More than half the population were pure-blooded Indians, about a third white and the rest of mixed blood. For 300 years the Indians, a proud, independent race with their fabulous civilizations, had lived under the tyranny of Spanish rule. Now Bolívar, although a white man, came as Liberator; and they worshipped him as a virtual god. Triumphal arches, flags and pennants, flowers and garlands were strewn in his path. Large crowds repeatedly broke through the line of soldiers to touch him and his great white charger as he rode into town.

In front of the bishop's palace 12 beautiful young Quito girls, dressed as nymphs, crowned him with laurels. As this was happening, another laurel crown fell upon him, thrown from a balcony. He looked up and saw a captivatingly beautiful young woman and he smiled, before returning to the reception in the streets. Manuela Sáenz was the illegitimate daughter of a minor Spanish business-man who had moved from New Granada to Quito in 1790. Her father, Simón, married with four children, had kept a beautiful white woman, María de Aizpuru, as a mistress in the apartment into which Manuela was born in 1797. In this little space, shared only with her mother most of the time, Manuela grew up as a lively, strong-willed, cheerful girl.

In 1809 a revolution broke out in Quito, and Sáenz was arrested along with other Spaniards. Shortly afterwards, the Spanish returned, her father was freed and the girl witnessed the grisly spectacle of the heads and limbs of the rebel leaders displayed around town. Her mother decided to spirit her away from these barbarities to a farm where she learnt to ride, shoot and use a lance. In 1814, as Manuela became too much of a handful, she was sent to the convent of Santa Catalina. There, a Spanish hussar officer, Fausto d'Elhuyar, took her off before, a few months later, dumping her. She returned to her mother, herself an abandoned mistress, in floods of tears, with a burning dislike of Spaniards.

On this rebound, she met a middle-aged English doctor, James Thorne, who was attracted by her beauty and vitality, and in 1817 she married him. Newly respectable, she set up home as one of Quito's best known hostesses. When the apparently forgiven d'Elhuyar reappeared at some of the parties and Dr Thorne became aware of his wife's renewed intimacy with him, he decided to move the household to Lima.

She was delighted to leave stuffy, provincial Quito, albeit leaving her handsome hussar as well. In Lima her intelligent, rebellious nature soon turned the staid Dr Thorne's house into one of the principal salons of political intrigue against the Spaniards. Manuela acquired a fixation for the romantic figure of the patriot leader, José de San Martín, who had just landed further down the Peruvian coast.

She was deeply disappointed when she finally met the aloof, shy, ascetic San Martín, who awarded her a Cross of Horsewoman of the Sun for her services to the patriot camp. She became a close friend of the only woman believed to have been San Martín's mistress, Rosita Campuzano, the vibrant society beauty of Lima. Dr Thorne now decided to return to Quito to help Manuela's father, himself endangered by the patriots in the city. And there this attractive, socially and politically ambitious and probably bisexual young woman of 22 saw the Liberator of her dreams.

She made a bee-line to him at the dance on the night of his arrival in June 1822, and he invited her to partner him. He was enormously attracted to her beauty as well as her strength of character – she was a keen horsewoman and fencer – and her political outspokenness and courage. According to a French doctor, Jean-Baptiste Boussingault:

At times she was like a great lady, at others a half-breed; she danced with equal grace the minuet or the *cachucha*. She was inseparable from a young and beautiful *mulata* slave, who was always dressed like a soldier, and encouraged Manuela's sensual and licentious tendencies. She was the shadow of her mistress, and possibly her lover, a vice very extensive in Peru. She performed dances that were highly lascivious. She had no lovers: her only love was Manuela.

More than any previous woman in Bolívar's life, Manuela shared common political interests and was prepared to subsume her personality to his own remote and selfish one, whose glory, and the cause of independence, always took precedence over merely human relationships. She had an oval face, large dark eyes, long dark hair and a stunning complexion. Those first few nights in Quito were openly and scandalously passionate. Although no one woman after his deceased wife could claim to be the sole love of the sexually incontinent liberator, it was Manuela who was to have the best claim to the title, as the most enduring, persistent and genuinely caring of his partners, and also the most spirited and remarkable. Their passion was to evolve into a loving, if often tempestuous, relationship.

Bolívar was on route to the most crucial encounter of his career as well as the chapter of South American history that has caused most controversy over nearly 200 years. Following the annexation of Quito, he also seemed to be on the verge of megalomania; at a banquet of his officers he spoke of liberating Latin America all the way down to Cape Horn.

The Chimborazo volcano had him in its spell, too: he wrote an extraordinary passage of lyrical prose that can be seen as the ultimate and eloquent romantic expression, or a superb piece of mysticism, or the effusions of a mind warped, at least temporarily, by the terrible combination of struggle and triumph down the Andean spine – or all three. In 'My Delirium on Chimborazo', he wrote, 'I came wrapped in the mantle of the rainbow from whence the rushing Orinoco pays tribute to the god of waters. I had visited the enchanted fountains of the Amazon and had longed to climb to the very watchtower of the universe.' He described how he reached the summit 'as if driven forward by the genius that moved me', and there fainted. Time spoke to him saying: 'I am the father of the centuries, the arcanum of fame and of the secret, and my mother was eternity. Infinity marks the boundaries of my empire. There is no tomb for me, because I am more powerful than death. I look upon the past and the future, and the present moment trickles through my hands.'

Chapter 19

SHOWDOWN WITH SAN MARTÍN

Bolívar was now ready to execute the most ruthless coup in his life. He had destroyed Miranda eight years before and condemned him to four years' living torment in jail followed by an ignominious death, and pitilessly had his rival Piar shot. Now he was to crush entirely, and without remorse, the second greatest figure in Latin American history, a man whose career had rivalled his own and even threatened to overshadow it.

José de San Martín, liberator of Argentina and now trying to be so of Peru, represented an exactly opposite personality to the Liberator. He had freed the remote regions of northern Argentina, then led an army across the Andes into Chile, which his ally, Bernardo O'Higgins, had liberated, before sailing north up the Pacific coast with thousands of Chilean and Argentinian troops in a fleet commanded by the daring and eccentric British captain, Lord Cochrane. But San Martín's campaign in Peru had stalled. As a man, his successes were accompanied by a selflessness and devotion to duty that was in contrast to the frenzied histrionics, and fevered and sometimes murderous determination, of the Liberator. When the guerrilla chieftain encountered this pillar of military rectitude, not in battle but at a two-day conference, the results were shocking. It was Bolívar who was to emerge from this clash of titans the victor, the most famous figure in Latin American history. But it was San Martín who by his dignity and self-abnegation was to retain the real affection of much of the continent. A British traveller, Captain Basil Hall, described San Martín at the time:

There was little, at first sight, in his appearance to engage the attention; but when he rose up and began to speak, his superiority was apparent; he received us in a very homely style, on the deck of his vessel, dressed in a large surtout coat, and a large fur cap, and seated at a table made of a few loose planks laid along the top of some empty casks.

He is a tall, erect, well-proportioned, handsome man, with a large aquiline nose, thick black hair, and immense bushy, dark whiskers, extending from ear to ear under the chin; his complexion is deep olive, and his eye, which is large, prominent, and piercing, is jet black; his whole appearance being highly military. He is thoroughly well bred, and unaffectedly simple in his manners; exceedingly cordial and engaging, and possessed evidently of great kindliness of disposition: in short, I have never seen any person, the enchantment of whose address was more irresistible.

In conversation he went at once to the strong points of the topic, disdaining as it were, to trifle with its minor parts; he listened earnestly, and replied with distinctness and fairness, showing wonderful resources in argument and a most happy fertility of illustration. Yet there was nothing showy or ingenious in his discourse.

Latin American historians endlessly pore over the significance of the famous meeting because so little is known of what was actually said. There are, broadly, three views: those who sympathize with Bolívar argue that San Martín was a pompous, priggish reactionary who favoured the reimposition of a string of monarchies on South America; those who side with San Martín view him as a shining example of one who put his duty before his personal interests, surrendering his forces and abandoning his command and his future to Bolívar in the common interest of defeating the Spanish forces; and finally those desperate to paper over any idea that the two greatest figures in the wars of liberation detested each other, who argue that reports of a division were much exaggerated, and that the agreement reached was a logical and cordial one.

This last view, however convenient to revisionists, can be dismissed at once: the bitterness evident in San Martín's letter to Bolívar after the meeting, however rational the tone, cannot be concealed. In fact, the evidence points towards a modified version of the second view, in spite of Bolívar's attempts to portray himself in the best and San Martín in the worst possible light afterwards. Bolívar's prime and burning objective, in moving south so speedily after liberating New Granada and Venezuela, had been to get to Peru before San Martín, to steal from him the mantle of principal liberator of the continent. He had already re-proposed his idea of a Hispano-American union with its capital in Panama, which he now controlled. From the pathetic republic in Angostura two years before, he had created a great Colombian empire the size of western Europe.

Incorporating the Viceroyalty of Peru (which embraced both modern Peru and Bolivia) would nearly double its size and dwarf the southern peoples of Chile and Argentina. If he could achieve his ambition of annexing these as well, he would be emperor of virtually all of Spanish America, perhaps the largest dominion under the rule of one man in the history of the world, exceeding Napoleon's in size, if not in population. Only the large Spanish forces still holding out in Peru and San Martín stood in his way. The rise from utter failure to dizzying power and success after two years seems to have unhinged Bolívar.

On 10 January 1821, Bolívar had written to San Martín in response to his letter of congratulation for creating Colombia in flattering terms. Eighteen months later, after San Martín had conquered Lima, Bolívar was equally fulsome. After San Martín had despatched 1,600 men under Santa Cruz to help Sucre, turning the tables when the latter was under siege in Guayaquil and contributing to the great victory at Pichincha that liberated Quito, Bolívar warmly thanked the 'liberators of the south . . . who, for so many reasons, we must rate as our best friends and brothers in arms'. In June 1822, Bolívar wrote to San Martín offering to allow his men to help him in his campaign in Peru. It is hard to believe that Bolívar was being anything other than cynical.

By the time they met, in late July 1822, their fortunes had been remarkably inverted. Bolívar had felt a surge of new confidence after capturing Quito; by contrast, San Martín's campaign in Peru had stalled. Bolívar, no sentimentalist, prepared to take advantage of this abrupt change not just to negotiate from strength, but politically to eliminate his rival. He staged this as effectively as any military campaign. Meanwhile, the lordly San Martín believed he was on his way to embrace the services of a slightly inferior gentlemanly ally in delivering the coup de grâce to the Spaniards in Peru. The irony was that Bolívar, much more aristocratic by birth than San Martín, turned out to be a far tougher streetfighter. The latter was to receive a shock that ended his career: Bolívar, in effect, was to point a pistol at his head.

Bolívar, on hearing that his rival was preparing to set sail to Guayaquil, had rushed at his usual speed down the mountain trail from Quito to get there before him. Guayaquil had, in fact, secured its 'independence' under José Olmedo as an historic port of the old Inca Empire, having been supported against the Spaniards by both San Martín and Admiral Cochrane. A majority of the population of the port probably favoured a connection with San Martín before Sucre had arrived in 1821.

Now with Bolívar reaching Guayaquil a fortnight earlier than San Martín, he promptly annexed the tropical port, the people 'voting' to do so in the presence of his troops. O'Leary describes the coup:

> General Bolívar, who consented to the convocation of this assembly [of local delegates] for form['s] sake, became impatient at the length of its session and, when informed of what was going on, made his secretary write to the assembly to say that he understood that points were being discussed which he esteemed as foreign to the question, that he insisted upon an immediate decision. The hint was taken, Guayaquil was declared a province of Colombia, and the flag of the republic displayed and saluted at 5 p.m.

Bolívar's entry into Guayaquil had been as triumphal as usual, with an arch bearing the words 'To Simón Bolívar – the Lightning of War, the Rainbow of Peace. From the people of Guayaquil.' Bands played and cannon thundered in tribute.

Aboard the schooner *Macedonia*, sailing from Lima's port of Callao, San Martín reached the huge estuary of the Guayas river at the most temperate season in this equatorial region, sailing up through dense tropical vegetation. He received a letter of quite breathtaking unctuousness from Bolívar:

> With the utmost satisfaction, most respected friend, I give you for the first time the title which my heart has granted you. I call you friend, and this is the name we should carry through life, because friendship is the only bond that should unite brothers in arms, in enterprise and in opinion. I would regret as much your not coming to this city as the loss of many battles; but you will not leave unsatisfied the wish I have of embracing on Colombian soil the foremost friend of my heart and my country.
>
> How would it be possible that you should come from so far away without letting us in Guayaquil see the great man that all are anxious to know, and if possible to touch? It is not possible. I am waiting for you and will meet you wherever you indicate; but without desisting from the honor of having you visit this city.
>
> A few hours, as you say, are enough for a discussion between soldiers; but they would not be enough to satisfy the passion for friendship, which is going to begin to enjoy the happiness of knowing the dear object of its affection, which it loved only through opinion, only through fame.

When the ship reached Guayaquil, San Martín was astonished to be welcomed to 'Colombian soil'. One of the main purposes of his trip was to settle the status of Guayaquil, but Bolívar already had annexed it as a *fait accompli*. San Martín was so taken aback that he refused to come on shore that evening, which would mean recognizing the Colombian coup. He relented the following morning and was rowed from his ship to the quayside, to be greeted by Bolívar.

Trumpets sounded out over the port and cannon boomed as this odd couple embraced. They rode into the city: Bolívar, smiling, the consummate showman, nervous, small, thin, his glittering eyes darting about him; San Martín, tall, grave, dignified, distant, aristocratic in appearance. San Martín was guided by his host to the house he was to lodge in, and then received a succession of local worthies and prominent officers from Bolívar's army. A beautiful girl representing the women of Guayaquil placed a crown of laurels on San Martín's head. The ascetic and honour-hating general was embarrassed, wanting to remove it, as though to emphasize he had never sought a crown for himself. He did not want to snub the girl or the goodwill of the people of the port, and merely said with his customary diffidence: 'I do not deserve this demonstration. There are others more worthy of it. But I shall keep this souvenir because of the patriotic feeling that inspires it and because of the hands whence it comes, since this is one of the happiest days of my life.'

At 12 noon Bolívar and the dignitaries took their leave. After resting, at 4 p.m. San Martín went to the government house to meet Bolívar, and the two men were closeted alone for several hours. The following day they met again for four hours in the afternoon. Because the discussion was held without a single witness being present, it is impossible to know exactly what the Liberator and the Protector discussed. The only immediate record was a second-hand one, and biased at that. Bolívar's chief adviser, José Gabriel Pérez, wrote a confidential memorandum to the Colombian foreign minister:

> The Protector spoke only of what had already been the subject of their conversations, raising vague and unconnected questions on military and political matters without going deeply into any, shifting from one theme to another and mingling the serious with the trivial. If the character of the Protector is not as frivolous as appears in conversation, it must be supposed that he acted thus with a certain purpose. His Excellency is inclined to disbelieve that the Protector's character is what it appeared, but neither does it seem to him that he was calculating his words and behaviour.

In fact Bolívar himself later claimed to be more impressed: San Martín appeared to be 'very military in character, and he seems energetic, quick, and not dull. He has the kind of correct ideas that would please you but he does not seem to be subtle enough for sublimity either in ideas or practice.'

According to this untrustworthy account, San Martín talked vaguely about the issue of Guayaquil – as well he might; he had just been cheated out of the port by Bolívar. Then, according to the same source, San Martín declared that he had decided to return to

Mendoza once the war against the Spaniards had been won; but he added that before retiring he would leave the foundations of government well established; and that this should not be democratic in Peru because it would not suit the country. Finally, that a prince from Europe must come and govern the nation.

Bolívar is said to have replied nervously, pacing the room, that the conditions did not exist for the return of the monarchy and that any political system required the participation of the masses, although not a revolution against the existing social order. San Martín is said to have expressed profound concern at the radical turn taken by the revolution in Colombia, and to have predicted that chaos and civil war beckoned there; only under a monarchy could social order be restored.

Bolívar was said to have replied, on this occasion:

Democracy, which has flourished even in the polluted soil of Europe, would certainly thrive in the virgin soil of America. Here there is no real element of aristocracy, nothing but a sorry caricature. There are not then, my dear general, elements of monarchy in this land of God. Let a republic be formed here and dignity will grow in men, the necessity and habit for work for social benefits will be created and these will produce territorial wealth and commercial industry which will attract immigration from Europe where the proletariat lack lands and can find them here. It is impossible to hold back the progress of the human race. A monarchy established here would be of short duration, for an idea, once implanted in the people, is impossible to extinguish; and the idea of democracy has been firmly rooted here during twelve years of glorious struggle, full of examples of abnegation and patriotism.

He ended with a flourish: 'Neither our generation nor the generation to follow ours will see the brilliance of what we have founded. I see America in chrysalis. There will be a metamorphosis in the existence of its inhabitants, and at last a cast of all the races will produce a homogeneous people. We cannot stay the march of human progress with outmoded constitutions which are foreign to the virgin soil of America.'

According to this account, dictated by Bolívar at second hand, the scene was reduced to a clash between the enlightened, democratic and republican Bolívar, and the stuffy defender of the status quo and supporter of imported monarchies, San Martín. It is impossible to say how much of this is true: to support monarchism, which virtually equated with Spanish rule, was almost treason at the time in patriot ranks. For Bolívar it made sense to taint San Martín with this sin.

San Martín vigorously denied the stain. For his part Bolívar was to be suspected of harbouring monarchical ambitions himself during at least two later stages in his career. San Martín's supporters alleged that in the whole discussion between the two men, the subject of monarchy never came up at all. Given Bolívar's penchant for embroidery in his own interests, this is indeed possible yet it seems unlikely that Bolívar invented the whole exchange. More probably, the subject was discussed in passing. One lie put about by San Martín's detractors was that he coveted the throne of Peru for himself; he never publicly suggested this and, being of a retiring disposition and hating ceremony, it seems unlikely.

It is now known that San Martín had earlier entered discussions with the Spanish Viceroy of Peru, José de la Serna, aimed at avoiding further bloodshed, and that the possibility of a European monarch taking over was mooted as a compromise which might be acceptable to Spain. San Martín also once told Commodore William Bowles that he favoured 'dividing South America amongst principal European powers, and providing a number of kingdoms as might provide for a prince of each royal house'. San Martín may have raised some such idea with Bolívar, who wholeheartedly rejected any compromise with Spain. Whatever the exact truth, Bolívar's supporters have always put it about that the conference foundered on San Martín's preference for a monarchy to a republic – which shows Bolívar in a favourable historical light.

It seems clear that the discussion was not about forms of government at all – or only as a side issue. It was a naked power struggle between the two men as to who should command in the final phase of the struggle against Spanish domination, thus earning the coveted title of principal liberator of Spanish America. San Martín had assumed that Bolívar would offer to give him the support of his army in the final battle against the Spaniards, just as the Chileans had backed his earlier efforts along the coast. Bolívar flatly refused to allow the two armies to merge under San Martín's command.

He had decided to play on the Protector's weaknesses. Bolívar knew that San Martín's forces were heavily outnumbered by the Spaniards; that the Marqués de Torre Tagle, the former royalist aristocrat whom San Martín had left behind him to govern, was at that moment holding secret talks with the Spaniards; and that he was deeply unpopular in Lima. By denying San Martín military support, Bolívar was dealing a death blow to his chances of survival.

San Martín had exaggerated his strength: he had weak cards and Bolívar had strong ones. The latter played them to devastating advantage. Feigning sincerity, Bolívar offered to send 1,800 of his troops to help San Martín – an insufficient quantity to tilt the balance against the Spaniards. Now it was San Martín's turn to try and wrongfoot Bolívar: he offered to serve under the Liberator in the forthcoming campaign, along with his army. Bolívar presented lame excuses for not agreeing to this. Bolívar intended to lead the campaign himself and was determined that there was no place for his rival liberator.

Bolívar then delivered the coup de grâce, informing San Martín that a conspiracy to oust him was being hatched at that very moment among the patriots in Lima. It is even possible that Bolívar and his agents were behind the conspiracy. When San Martín returned he found that his chief minister had been deposed. Thus, while San Martín desperately needed Bolívar's troops, the latter considered that he did not need those of San Martín. Worse, it must have appeared to the latter that the glamorous Bolívar could appeal over the head of the unpopular San Martín to his troops and to the backers of the patriot cause in Lima. San Martín faced the possibility of being ousted by his own supporters.

The deciding factor was that most of his troops were Chilean, while he was Argentinian, and the Chileans lacked the stomach to continue the war under his command. San Martín had appealed for help from his native Argentina, but this was denied him by his political opponents. He was a general with no clothes or, rather, no troops: it had been an extraordinary combination of hauteur, bluff and luck that had got him this far in charge of an army consisting largely of foreign troops, but the luck had run out, and Bolívar was too ruthless not to exploit this. San Martín was too proud a man to be publicly humiliated, and too selfless and public-spirited to force a confrontation. He had been crushed and, good soldier that he was, accepted defeat with dignity. He agreed to hand over control of his forces to Bolívar and withdraw from the scene.

The humiliation of South America's second greatest son was poignant. Afterwards Bolívar held a glittering banquet and ball, of the kind that San Martín most disliked, in honour of his dispirited rival. While Bolívar's tone was egocentric, San Martín's was dignified. Bolívar toasted 'the two greatest men in South America – San Martín and myself'. San Martín instead drank to 'the early end of the war, the organization of the various republics of the continent, and the health of the Liberator of Colombia'. In this public skirmish between the prima donnas, San Martín effortlessly won on style.

As Bolívar plunged frenetically into the dancing, San Martín watched in distaste and decided to leave. Seeing this, Bolívar accompanied him into the warm night and gave him – typically for Bolívar – a portrait of himself as a farewell present. San Martín was later to despatch, with pointed dignity, his pistols and his horse in reciprocation. Victor and vanquished took their leave of one another. 'The Liberator has won this hand,' said the Protector sadly to his aide as the *Macedonia* slipped away from its moorings. It had been another ferocious demonstration of Bolívar's power, helping to inspire the respect which assured his survival at the top – until the very end.

The only report of the meeting from San Martín's side was expressed in a letter he sent Bolívar from Peru:

My dear General:
  I shall write you not only with the frankness of my nature, but also with that which is demanded by the high interests of America.
  The results of our interview are not those which I foresaw for a quick end of the war. Unfortunately, I am completely convinced that either you have not deemed sincere my offer to serve under your orders with the forces at my command, or that my person is embarrassing for you. The reasons you advanced, that your tact would not allow you ever to give me orders, and that even if that

were the case the Colombian Congress would not authorize your separation from the territory of Colombia, have not seemed very plausible to me.

The first one refutes itself. As far as the second one is concerned, I am convinced that if you expressed your wishes you would find unanimous approval, since the object is to end this campaign, which we have started and in which we are engaged, with your co-operation and that of your army, and that the honour of bringing it to an end would fall upon yourself and the Republic over which you preside.

Do not indulge in any illusions, General. The news which you have about the Royalist forces is wrong: they number, in Upper and Lower Peru, more than 19,000 veterans, who may unite within two months. The patriot army, decimated by illness, will not be able to send to the front more than 8,500, and of these a great part are raw recruits. General Santa Cruz's division (the casualties of which, this general writes me, have not been replaced despite his insistence) on its long march overland must experience a considerable loss, and it will not contribute anything to this campaign.

The division of 1,400 Colombians which you are sending will be needed to garrison Callao and keep order in Lima. Consequently, without the backing of the army you command, the operation which is planned by way of the Intermediate ports will not have the advantages which could be expected unless powerful forces could draw the enemy elsewhere; and in this way the struggle will be indefinitely prolonged. I say indefinitely because I am deeply convinced that, be what may the difficulties of the present war, America's independence is irrevocable; but I am also convinced that the prolongation of the war will be the ruin of its peoples, and it is a sacred duty for the men in whose hands lies [America's] destiny to prevent a continuation of such evils.

Be it as it may, General, my decision has irrevocably been made. I have called the First Congress of Peru for the 20th of next month, and on the day after its installation I shall embark for Chile, satisfied that my presence is the only obstacle which prevents you from coming to Peru with the army at your command. For me it would have been the acme of happiness to end the war of independence under the orders of a general to whom America owes its freedom. Destiny orders it otherwise, and one must resign oneself to it.

Having no doubt that after my going the Peruvian Government that may be established will request the active co-operation of Colombia, and that you will not be able to refuse so just a demand, I shall send you a list of all the officers whose conduct, both military and private, may commend themselves to you.

General Arenales will be left in command of the Argentine forces. His honesty, his courage, and his knowledge, I am sure, will make him deserving of your every consideration.

I shall say nothing to you about the annexation of Guayaquil to the Republic of Colombia. Allow me, General, to say that I did not believe it behoved us to decide this important matter. At the end of the war the respective governments would have decided it, without the troubles that now may result for the interests of the new states of South America.

I have spoken to you, General, with frankness; but the feelings expressed in this letter will be buried in the deepest silence. If they were known, the enemies of our freedom could take advantage of the fact to our sorrow, and the intriguers and the ambitious would sow discord.

With Major Delgado, the bearer of this letter, I am sending you a shotgun and a pair of pistols, together with my personal horse, which I offered to you in Guayaquil. Accept, General, this souvenir from your foremost admirer.

With these feelings and with the hope that you may have the glory of ending the war of independence of South America, I am,

Your affectionate servant,

José de San Martín

To O'Higgins in Chile he wrote bitterly, 'I am tired of hearing men call me tyrant, that I wish to make myself King, Emperor, the Devil. On the other hand my health is broken, this climate is killing me. My youth was sacrificed to the service of Spain, my manhood to my own country. I think I have now the right to dispose of my old age.'

He explained privately to his chief aide, Colonel Guido:

Bolívar and myself cannot be in Peru at the same time. I have penetrated his thoughts; I have understood his annoyance at the glory that could be mine for ending the war. He would use any means to enter Peru and perhaps I could not avoid a conflict, giving a scandal to the world, and the only ones who would profit by it would be the enemy. That, never! Let Bolívar come into Peru, and if he makes safe what we have gained, I will be happy, because America will win in any event. It will not be San Martín who will give a day of joy to the Spaniards.

In public, to pave the way for Bolívar's campaign against the Spaniards, San Martín maintained a brave face and, in September 1822, he announced his abdication to the Peruvian Congress:

When I return the insignia of the Supreme Ruler of Peru, I only carry out my duty and the dictates of my heart. If the Peruvians have anything to thank me for, it is the exercise of the powers which circumstances placed in my hands. Today, on resigning, I pray to the Supreme Being for the wisdom, the enlightenment, and the prudence which are needed for the happiness of the governed. From this moment the Sovereign Congress is installed and the people reassume the power in all its manifestations.

Congress replied by appointing him to the post of commander-in-chief of the Peruvian forces; but he declined. On 20 September 1822, he boarded the brigantine, the *Belgrano*, dressed in black civilian clothes for the long sea journey to Chile. The field was left open for Bolívar.

Chapter 20

TRAPPED IN LIMA

After his immense efforts, the Liberator could at last be forgiven a peaceful interlude and he was now to enjoy the nearest he ever came to a honeymoon and years of married life. He arranged for friends to lend him a magnificent hacienda known as El Garzal on the banks of the Guayas river. It was a slice of paradise with a temperate climate, abundant vegetation and flowers, and tropical birds wheeling around it. William Miller, who first met him at this time, gave a vivid portrait of the Liberator:

His temper, spoiled by adulation, is fiery and capricious. His opinions of men and things are variable. He is rather prone to personal abuse, but makes ample amends to those who will put up with it. Towards such his resentments are not lasting. He is a passionate admirer of the fair sex, but jealous to excess. He is fond of waltzing, and is a very quick, but not a very graceful, dancer. His mind is of the most active description . . . His voice is loud and harsh but he speaks eloquently on all subjects . . . Although the cigar is almost universally used in South America, Bolívar never smokes, nor does he permit smoking in his presence . . . Disinterested in the extreme with regard to pecuniary affairs, he is insatiably covetous of fame.

Bolívar invariably speaks of England, of her institutions and her great men, in terms of admiration. He often dwells with great warmth upon the constancy, fidelity, and sterling merit of the English officers who have served in the cause of independence, under every varying event of the war. As a collateral proof of his predilection towards England, he has always had upon his personal staff a number of British subjects.

Manuela was, for Bolívar, a more serious love than any in his life. His letters to her displayed real passion, as distinct from the more empty protestations of ardour to his other women. He wrote when they were apart, as on so many occasions, 'You want to see me with your own eyes. I too want to see you again and again, to touch you and hear you and taste you and unite you to me with every kind of touch. Why do you not love me as I you? For that is the most pure and clear truth. Learn to love and don't even go with God himself.'

Manuela, unlike Bolívar's other lovers who surrendered themselves without a struggle to the great man, knew how to tease him, how to deny herself to him and excite his jealousy, knowing that this aroused his passion all the more. Like only Fanny de Villars, his early sexual tutor, and Julia Cobier, his consoler in Jamaica, Manuela was unafraid of him, prepared to answer him back, threw tantrums and treated him as an equal, and Bolívar adored this. She was nothing if not strong-willed: she would dress in the uniform of a dragoon, mount a white horse and carry a lance like a man. They enjoyed long weeks of intimacy at the ranch together.

Bolívar was in no hurry to engage in the campaign in Peru, partly in order to rest after his efforts, partly because he felt he had to consolidate Quito before the next great challenge, and largely because he wanted the feuding elites of Lima, with San Martín's departure now deprived of a ruler, to plead for his entry into the city to save them. He also needed authority from Colombia before proceeding into Peru. This was slow in coming. Santander, enjoying ruling in his own right in the absence of the Liberator, was slapped down for his tardiness. Bolívar rounded on him with ferocity, 'The Constitution of Colombia is sacred for ten years. It will not be violated with impunity while blood flows in my veins and the army of Liberators is under my orders.'

More immediately, the royalists in the mountain stronghold of Pasto suddenly rose again in revolt. Sucre was despatched to quell them, and succeeded after two bloody battles, the second of which ended in vicious street-fighting in the city itself. Meanwhile in Venezuela there were also uprisings when Morales, in the last royalist stronghold of Puerto Cabello, had succeeded in embarking with a force to another point along the coast and raising the standard of revolt. The ever-restless Bolívar decided to return to Venezuela, but was saved the trouble when Páez drove the Spanish forces into the hothouse of Maracaibo and blockaded their fleet inside this huge inland sea. He had also assembled a patriot fleet of 22 ships and 1,300 soldiers, mostly North American volunteers. One night in July 1823, the squadron's second-in-command, the English Captain Walter Chitty, entered the lake with a few ships and drifted unnoticed into the middle of the Spanish fleet, boarding ten ships and sinking one. Morales, the longest surviving fighter for the Spanish cause, at last gave up and was permitted to sail for Cuba. A further general uprising broke out in Pasto, and the indomitable mountain men moved on Quito and seized it.

By that time Bolívar had sent the bulk of his army to Callao, Lima's port, under Sucre's command, to prepare for his arrival. Consequently, he had to raise a new army of raw recruits to restore Quito and, through a series of small skirmishes and guerrilla victories, defeated the Pastistas once again, killing 800; his chief of staff, Salóm, had to fight two more battles before crushing them. Determined to break their spirit for good, he exiled their clergy – who had been instrumental in stirring up the dissent – and marched hundreds of the fighters down to Guayaquil. These fanatical mountain people exacted a fearful moral revenge. Many threw themselves off cliffs or into streams on the long march back, while many others refused food and died of starvation by the roadside rather than submit.

On arrival Bolívar received an embassy from the government of Peru imploring him to fill the vacuum of power vacated by San Martín. The Peruvians were at last demonstrating their need of him, and he decided to leave.

Manuela begged to go with him, but he refused, because after a year of her domineering, clinging love, he wanted to reassert his freedom. Manuela was compelled by social pressures and by Bolívar himself to return to Dr Thorne at Quito, her irrepressible nature groaning at this new enslavement. Bolívar wrote a pompous letter renouncing her:

My beautiful and good Manuela, each moment I am thinking of
you and the fate which touched you. I see that nothing can unite us
under the auspices of innocence and honor. I see well and deplore
the horrible situation for you. You must be reconciled with one
you do not love and I must be separated from one I adore. Yes,
I adore you today more than ever before. Tearing myself from
your love and your possession has multiplied in me all the sentiments which bound me to your soul and heart, that heart without
equal. When you were mine I loved you more for your enchant-
ing nature than for your delicious attractions. Now it seems to me
that an eternity separates us. My own determination has put me
to torment . . . In the future you will be alone, even at the side of
your husband; I will be alone in the midst of the world. Only the
glory of having conquered ourselves will be our consolation.

It seemed that the most tempestuous love affair of his life was over,
conquered by their own impossible natures and his lust for glory and
destiny.

On 1 September 1823, nearly a year after he had destroyed Peru's
protector, San Martín, Bolívar landed at the port of Callao for his last
great effort in ridding the American continent of the Spaniards. It
promised to be the most difficult of all, for Peru, along with Mexico,
had been the corrupt heart of the Spanish empire, the source of most
of the silver and mineral wealth that had fuelled the motherland for
300 years. There the greatest Indian nation, that of the Incas, had
been defeated by one of the most barbarous of the conquistadors,
Francisco Pizarro. The city of Lima had grown up as a byword for
wealth, inequality, corruption and immorality.

The greatest force of Spanish oppressors had been concentrated
there. They remained undefeated, for San Martín had occupied
only the coastal strip between Lima and Trujillo, while Spain's best-
equipped and best-trained army of some 18,000 men was posted in
the mountains, their stronghold the ancient Inca capital of Cuzco.

Only a minority of the Peruvian criollos, it seemed, were revolutionary: the two sources of the viceroyalty's fabulous wealth were
minerals and a huge Indian and mestizo underclass, outnumbering

the whites by four to one. The existence of this wretchedly crushed majority meant that the settlers – unlike Venezuela or even New Granada – had never had to turn their hands to work. They simply employed the Indians in a vast workhouse to dig for the minerals and farm their crops. Peru had developed no indigenous industries of its own; it was just regarded as a repository of minerals with an agriculture sufficient to sustain it. It was a slave labour camp, in which the whites had for centuries lived in shimmering prosperity and the overwhelming majority of Indians in a state of feudal submission.

Not only were the whites thus privileged under the Spaniards and without the desire to overthrow the political system, but there were acute fears that any revolution against the monarchy might induce rebellion among the overwhelming Indian majority which could result in a genocidal bloodbath, of the kind that Tupac Amaru II had seemed to foreshadow with his rebellion in 1781. An Indian leader, Mateo Pumacahua, who had helped to suppress Tupac Amaru's rebellion, had recently revolted in Puno, La Paz and Arequipa before he was captured and executed in 1815. San Martín had understood the danger, and had sought to placate the fears of the privileged classes with his ideas for an independent state – one even possibly under a monarchy which respected the traditional social structures.

The Peruvian oligarchy was intensely distrustful of the revolutionary figure of Bolívar, whose programmes of social reform and equality for all races had secured him the support of Venezuela's llaneros and mestizos. They feared he would attempt to do the same in Peru. Accordingly, many were unenthusiastic about seeking his help against the Spaniards, and as soon as San Martín had departed, had determined to show that they were capable of resisting the Spaniards alone. Bolívar, for his part, had no wish to go to Peru until they realized that they could not survive by themselves.

On San Martín's departure, a collective leadership of aristocrats under the arrogant Marqués de Torre Tagle had been set up, which had then ordered San Martín's recently recruited armies into action against the superior Spanish forces. The patriot army of 8,000 was split into two, one of which, under General Juan de Arenales, was deemed necessary to maintain order in Lima, while the other half, under General Rudecindo Alvarado, set off to do battle against the royalists entrenched in the mountains.

Even by the standards of the rest of Latin America, Peru's geography is awesome. It consists of a long, narrow strip of one of the world's most arid deserts, the Atacama, running some 1,500 miles north-south into Chile. Out of the desert sheer, barren mountains, implacable and inhospitable, rise to peaks of up to 15,000 feet, before falling away to a system of more or less fertile upland river valleys – of which the central one is the Valley of the Apurimac, at the top of which Cuzco is sited.

The military theory elaborated by the generals in Lima was that as long as the viceroy's huge army was spread along the vast interior it would be relatively easy to concentrate one's forces and attack a single outpost before the Spaniards could bring up reinforcements quickly from somewhere else. The flaw in this theory was that any assault from the coast into the uplands would have to cross appalling country. An army's approach would be slow and easily detectable, permitting reinforcements to be brought at leisure to its obvious destination. This was how a contemporary observer put it: 'It's true that the enemy's military line was very extended; but because it was in the mountains, separated from the coast by a belt of sand of an average of 10–20 leagues, and by a lower line of hills of up to 1,200 feet, the Spanish line should be considered as a fortified position. To reach it, you had to cross the desert of the coast and climb the cordillera.'

Exactly that occurred: Viceroy La Serna ordered his second-in-command, José de Canterac, to Cuzco and reinforced General Valdez at Arequipa. Alvarado's patriot forces moved to Arica on the coast, from which they ascended the mountains in December 1822: there Valdez descended, trapped him, and inflicted an appalling defeat. This setback resulted in a revolt in Lima and the seizure of power by a dictator, José de la Riva Agüero, the tough-minded, devious and thoroughly unpleasant head of Lima's own circle of criollo nationalists. Riva Agüero, pronouncing himself President of Peru from February 1823, promptly despatched calls for help to Argentina, Chile and the Colombians to stage a final offensive against the Spaniards. The Argentinians, who had not been prepared to support their own commander, San Martín, showed no interest in helping the Peruvian nationalists. The Chileans said they had no troops to spare.

That left only Bolívar's Colombians to come to the rescue from nearby Quito. But Riva Agüero was determined not to cede control of the enterprise to Bolívar, and said that he would accept Colombian help only in a subordinate capacity. As had happened with San Martín, who sought to lead the patriots while controlling virtually no forces of his own, Bolívar was determined to call this upstart's bluff. He instructed Sucre, who had arrived in Callao, 'not to commit his forces to any political action with a doubtful outcome. I told the president that you would not come except with the dignity and character due to the Liberator of Colombia, with the necessary faculties to direct the war and with the full agreement of the provinces in the [Peruvian] assembly.' Riva Agüero then invited San Martín to return to serve him, and received a witheringly contemptuous reply. The dictator decided to embark on his own expedition against the Spaniards, and set off with most of his troops. Canterac, the royalist commander, on hearing of this, knew that Lima was left virtually undefended and decided on a bold attack upon the capital with 9,000 men.

Sucre, appalled by Riva Agüero's stupidity and following Bolívar's instructions to the letter, ordered the remnants of the patriot forces away from the city, which could not be defended. Meanwhile, the city's governing council, under Torre Tagle, deposed the disastrous Riva Agüero in his absence. Canterac arrived at the head of his huge army, seized Lima, imposed a tribute on the city and then, hearing that the able General Santa Cruz's army was attacking royalist posts in the south, departed to fight him.

Sucre was able to ride back into the city at the head of his small band. Riva Agüero had meanwhile fled to Trujillo where, incandescent with rage at being deposed, he treacherously initiated contact with the royalists and ordered Santa Cruz not to obey Sucre. But the order was redundant: Santa Cruz, with 6,000 men, had set off into the impassable sierra and had been driven back by the Spanish forces. In a truly terrible retreat across desolate mountains and baking, barren desert, his army of 5,000 was reduced to just 800 men without a battle being fought.

Peru could ill afford to lose any men against the powerful Spanish army. The defeated Peruvian government desperately begged Bolívar to come and, at last, he did, arriving on 1 September 1823 aboard the brig *Chimborazo* after nearly a month's journey from Guayaquil. His reception was tumultuous: fireworks, balls, operas and a bullfight were held in his honour. He was given San Martín's old villa, the Magdalena, a sumptuous residence where the dinner service was of solid gold.

Lima was the most architecturally lovely of all Latin American cities, peppered with delightful palaces, of which the most distinguished were the Archbishop's palace, next to the cathedral, and the Torre Tagle palace. Bolívar rode through streets with elaborate, ornately carved wooden balconies on the first floor, protruding over the streets so that women might witness the scene there without being seen.

Not that the women of Lima at the time had the reputation of being discreet: they were permitted to gamble, drink and smoke and were notoriously free in their sexual favours. The fashions of Lima were more eye-catching still: the women would wear white trousers with their dresses, and sport the famous hats – little bowlers, cocked to one side, or tall ones like men's top hats – that to this day the Indian women of Peru wear as the height of fashion.

Bolívar's first impression was favourable:

Lima is a very big city, agreeable, which used to be rich; it seems very pro-independence; the men seem to be very much in favour of me and say they want to make sacrifices. The women are very beautiful and good girls. Tonight we have a ball in which I will see them all . . . I am everyday more content with Lima because I go down well with everyone: the men admire me and the women love me. The food is excellent, the theatre good, adorned with beautiful objects and a fine carved door. Coaches, horses, walks, bulls, Te Deums – nothing is missing.

The city boasted a staggering 8,000 coaches, and was a constant whirl of social life and competition, the noblemen often sunk in the fug of chewing coca leaves, the ubiquitous narcotic of the city. Bolívar delighted Limeños, in contrast to the dour and austere San Martín, by throwing himself into social activities with his usual frenzied dancing and dalliances with women. The much-feared wild revolutionary of the north turned out to be a cultivated and polite aristocrat. But Bolívar wasted no time in making clear that he was not fighting the Spaniards in order to impose a new monarchy. At the official banquet in his honour he raised the toast that, 'The American people should never consent to raise a single throne in all their territory; just as Napoleon was submerged in the immensity of the ocean [in St Helena] and the new Emperor Iturbide has been deposed from the throne of Mexico, may the usurpers of the rights of the American people fall, so that not a single one remains triumphant in all the huge extension of the New World.' Bolívar's second judgment was more sombre and accurate:

The country receives us with enthusiasm but gives us nothing. We have need of much tact and great moderation to prevent this nation from becoming entirely reactionary. Money is needed but we ought not and cannot demand it of these unfortunate people, for here the era of home government has been one of crime and pillage. The inhabitants are sound but they are disinclined to military service and it is difficult to organize an army. The natives are what they were at the beginning of the world . . . The country is patriotic but unadapted to military service; it is good, but apathetic. There are provisions and transportation but no will to furnish them . . . the difficulties are immense, there reigns a disorder that appals the most determined. The theatre of war is equatorial America; our enemies are everywhere, our soldiers are men of all parties and all countries, of different dialects, colour, laws and interests. Only Providence can bring order out of this chaos.

In Lima, the liberator of Chile, Bernardo O'Higgins, met Bolívar for the first time and was deeply impressed. 'Bolívar is the greatest man in Latin America,' exclaimed the sincere, slightly naive Irish Hispano-American. O'Higgins, ironically the illegitimate son of the Viceroy of Lima had, with San Martín's support, staged a brilliant military campaign to free his own land of Chile.

★　　★　　★

It was not long before it became apparent that Bolívar, far from coasting towards a final victory over the Spaniards, had placed himself and his men in extreme peril. Dangers crowded in on all sides, as they had when he had first seized Caracas, believing himself in control of Venezuela. He wrote to Santander desperately seeking reinforcements of 12,000 men, but received no answer.

Meanwhile, the Marqués de Torre Tagle, head of the provisional government in Lima, was secretly negotiating with the royalists to rid them of the 'common enemy', as he defined Bolívar. The Liberator himself rushed off to Trujillo to put down the 'independent' government set up by Riva Agüero. The commander of the garrison there surrendered and handed over the inept dictator, whom Bolívar put aboard a boat for Europe to spare him Torre Tagle's order to have him executed.

A further disaster struck. In February 1824, the garrison of Argentine soldiers at Callao, the port of Lima, mutinied, disgruntled ever since the departure of their hero, San Martín. They freed the Spanish prisoners in the garrison jail and went over to the king's side. Meanwhile, Bolívar himself, who had long suffered from malaria as well as a variety of fevers, went down with a ferocious illness, tabardillo (a form of typhus), at a small village north of Lima, from which he was unable to move. There, stricken, he heard of the total collapse of his hopes. Torre Tagle and most of the Peruvian forces had followed the Argentinians in defecting to the Spaniards. Even the crucial Argentine Grenadiers, who had been personally trained by San Martín, went over. Lima had returned to the royalists and the Spanish army entered the fickle capital in triumph to a reception greater than that accorded Bolívar a month earlier. Torre Tagle declared in a proclamation, 'The tyrant Bolívar and his indecent supporters sought to annex Peru, and place this rich country under the control of Colombia, but he has made a mistake. The Spaniards are the only alternative who can avert our ruin.'

The Liberator, after his spectacular campaign down the spine of the Andes had, it seemed, walked into a trap. With just 5,000 Colombian troops at his disposal – he had ordered Sucre to rush all his forces up to Trujillo and destroy all guns and equipment that he could not carry from Lima and Callao – he now occupied only an enclave along the northern coast of Peru. The rest of the country was back in the hands of royalists and their allies.

The Spanish forces were awesome: the army of the north, under General José de Canterac in Huancayo, consisted of 8,000 men: some 1,000 men were based in Cuzco, the capital of the mountainous centre; Valdez had 3,000 men in Arequipa and Puno. General Pedro Antonio de Olañeta had 4,000 men in Peru's southern highlands (most of modern Bolivia). Another 2,000 men were a mobile force, moving between the various headquarters.

Through treachery and his own overambition – for Lima and Callao might not have been lost if San Martín had stayed as his second-in-command, as he had offered – the wretchedly ill Bolívar had seen the triumphs of the previous year transformed into his most dangerous predicament yet. There was no help to be had from Argentina or Chile or even from Colombia, where Santander was still hesitating to send in more men to defend what seemed a hopeless position – and even, possibly, was secretly hoping for Bolívar's defeat. Now that he was down, Bolívar was being kicked from all sides.

Visiting the sick man, Joaquín Mosquera, his ambassador to Buenos Aires, was both appalled and impressed:

I found the Liberator no longer at risk of death from tabardillo, which was past its worst; but so thin and emaciated that his appearance caused me real pain. He was sitting on a ragged cowskin, propped against the wall of a small garden with a white scarf on his head wearing cut-off riding breeches which allowed me to see his pointed knees and fleshless limbs, his hoarse and feeble voice and his cadaverous appearance.

I had to make an effort to conceal my tears and not let him know my pain and fear for his life. 'What do you think of doing now?' Raising his hollow eyes, with a firm voice he replied, 'Win! . . .' 'How will you triumph?' In a calm and confident voice he told me: 'I have given orders to raise a force of cavalry in the Trujillo region. I have ordered all the good horses of the country to be requisitioned by my army, and I have requisitioned all the alfalfa grasses to make them fat. When I have recovered my strength I will go to Trujillo. If the Spaniards descend the cordillera to take me, I will inevitably defeat them with my cavalry; if they don't descend within three months I will have a force strong enough to attack them. I will climb the cordillera and defeat the Spaniards at Jauja.'

They talked of the sad situation in Peru:

of which he charged me to inform Santander. As you know, to cross this sandy desert, night travel is preferable. It was six o'clock in the evening, and the sun set on the Pacific and gave me the sad thought that the Peruvian sun was saying goodbye to us. The majestic silence of the ocean, the view of the desert which I was going to cross, the solitude of those coasts and the cries of the seagulls oppressed my spirits on leaving my companions to embark on so arduous an enterprise in which the lives of the Hero and our army were at risk.

When my baggage arrived, the Liberator still stretched on the ground, told me: 'Tell our compatriots over there how you left me moribund on this inhospitable beach, having to fight with my hands tied, to conquer the independence of Peru and the security of Colombia.'

This was the message Bolívar wanted desperately to get across to Santander, whom he could by no means trust to come to his aid: the Spaniards had to be defeated everywhere on the continent. He was fearful that Colombia's security depended on the defeat of the large Spanish army in Peru. The defeat of the Liberator there would mark the beginning of a new Spanish offensive to reconquer the lost territories.

Even in his fever, Bolívar laboured to keep his hope alive. When Sucre and all the commanders of his depleted forces arrived to advise him that he must conclude an armistice with the Spaniards, Bolívar was contemptuous. He issued a proclamation to the Peruvians. 'The circumstances are horrible for the fatherland. You know it, but don't despair of the Republic. It is expiring, but it has not yet died. The army of Colombia is still intact and invincible. We are waiting, moreover, for 10,000 good men from the heroic fatherland of Colombia. What more do you want?' He wrote that he would even have retreated if he did not believe that with the loss of Peru, the collapse of southern Colombia was inevitable. 'We must die or win in Peru.'

He was probably right: to the north, Quito and Pasto were royalist hotbeds yearning to overthrow the patriots, which only fortified his old ferocity. He told Sucre: 'I am ready for anything. I am possessed of the very demon of war and am in the mood for putting an end to this struggle . . . the enemy will come with 8,000 and we shall go to the battlefield with as many. Victory must be ours.' He appointed a Peruvian general, José de La Mar, to raise an entirely new local army in a matter of months:

Don't spare yourselves in anything, display a terrible, inexorable character. Discipline the forces at your command, both cavalry and infantry. If there are no guns, there are lances. Moreover, I am expecting 3,000 guns from Colombia any moment; a third or fourth line of lances are not useless in a fight and will replace the casualties which are terrific in a newly recruited army. Raise 5,000 recruits so that 2,000 or 2,000 remain alive. Equip yourselves with many supplies, many fortifications throughout the region. Every tree, every man, serves some purpose.

It was brutal, basic soldiering; but it was effective. The Colombian forces simply pressganged all they could into joining the new army. They helped themselves to any food and supplies they could get their hands on and destroyed everything they could not bring in as part of a scorched earth policy to delay a royalist attack.

It is not known whether atrocities were committed during this desperate phase; but one must suppose considerable coercion was exercised upon those among the local people who did not support the patriots – although Bolívar issued no proclamation on the matter. At last reinforcements arrived from Santander, though much fewer than hoped for: some 2,500 men under a startlingly young commander, José María Córdova. It was clear that while Santander could not refuse Bolívar's plea for help, he was leaving him to wither on the vine, investing in the hope of his defeat. The cold, punctilious ruler of New Granada had disliked Bolívar from the day when, as a young captain, the Liberator had threatened to have him executed and then treated him as a coward.

Chapter 21

LANCES IN THE MOUNTAINS

In April 1824, Bolívar heard an astonishing piece of news that heralded the last great gamble of his amazing career. The army of Upper Peru (now Bolivia), under the command of the conservative General Olañeta, had rebelled. Following the liberal-constitutionalist coup in Spain against the reactionary Ferdinand VII in 1820, the diehard Olañeta would not obey the orders of the Spanish viceroy, La Serna, and his generals, Canterac and Valdéz.

In that highest and most remote of all Spanish possessions, the tiny white minority ruled the vast Indian population with feudal brutality. The mutiny came out of the blue. La Serna decided that the threat of insubordination from one of his armies in the mountains was more dangerous than that posed by Bolívar's depleted forces far down on the coast. He was certain that Bolívar was still weak and would not move until significant reinforcements arrived from Colombia. The viceroy despatched Valdez to fight Olañeta with an army of 14,000 men. Canterac, his other general, ignored Valdéz's order that he should descend to fight Bolívar with his 6,000-strong army in the Jauja valley, and decided to stay put in the security of the mountains. To the Spaniards it seemed inconceivable that they could be threatened there.

On hearing the news of the mutiny and the division of the main force into two, Bolívar responded with alacrity: his scorched earth war in a defensive enclave was suddenly transformed into an offensive one. He proposed to march straight up into that colossal mountain range and attack while the Spaniards were divided, before they had a chance to regroup. It was too good a chance to miss.

In vain Bolívar's officers, including Sucre, entreated him to wait for Colombian reinforcements; Bolívar shrewdly judged that Santander, who was becoming ever more difficult, would send none. They would march in May, he proposed, and fight in June. If they had not succeeded by July, they would retreat to defend their coastal enclave by Trujillo. The Liberator was his old self again. It was another throw of the dice, another brilliant improvisation to take advantage of a situation that might not recur, and another epic march into the mountains. The target and rendezvous point for his different forces was Cerro de Pasco, not far from the Spanish headquarters of Jauja. Bolívar, in a frenzy of activity, rode the 300 miles down from Trujillo with a handful of men on a scouting mission.

On the way he billeted at the mountain town of Huaylas and was treated to a warm reception. He told them movingly, 'All the armies of the world armed themselves for kings, for powerful men. Be the first to arm yourselves for laws, for principles, for the weak, for the just.' A beautiful, dark-skinned girl of 18, dressed in white, gave Bolívar a crown of flowers. He noted: 'She was a beautiful and very sweet girl of eighteen pursued by all the young men in town and even by older men, but hardy in rejecting all those suitors, desiring something more than a simple country husband.' Bolívar had a passionate affair with Manuela Madroño. The two of them would go for long walks into the spectacular countryside during the days he stayed in the town.

On 4 July, Bolívar, after several days' hard riding, reached Cerro de Pasco and saw in the distance the extensive plains upon which he hoped to lure the enemy to do battle upon; his strategy was to draw the enemy out of their stronghold and attack them with cavalry, where they would lose their advantage. His troops were following a long way behind: there were 3,500 Colombians under Sucre, 3,000 Peruvians under General La Mar, and some 1,500 Argentinian cavalrymen under General Mariano Necochea accompanied by that capable British commander from Buenos Aires, General William Miller; and 500 artillery men from Chile under Pedro Juan Luna. The marches, converging like some giant gathering of the clans from distant starting points to the same destination, were themselves a remarkable feat of human endurance.

Miller's division had tramped 600 miles down the cordillera, all of it on foot, with the horses being led, so that they were fresh for battle, accompanied by 6,000 head of cattle. They marched along narrow trails along the precipitous sides of mountains, with Miller setting up rudimentary supply depots along the way:

> Some of these depots were established within the line of coun-try nominally possessed by the royalists . . . The entrance of the cave was in the perpendicular side of a cliff fifty or sixty feet from the ground and as many from the top. The only way to get up was by a rope fixed in the cave, and by notches cut in the rock to give foot-hold. Indian corn, salt, charqui (jerked beef), potatoes, and barley, were hoisted up by means of the rope. A few men were sufficient to defend these cavern-depots against any numbers.

> The shelving ledges, which offered the only foothold on the rugged sires of the Andes, are so narrow as to render the passage indescribably harrassing. The troops could advance only one by one. The single file was sometimes lengthened out to an amaz-ing extent by the mal pasos, formed by deep gullies or breaks in the tracks by projecting rocks, or by numerous waterfalls; all of which required great caution, and made time to pass in safety. It became necessary for every man to dismount, and to lead the two animals in his charge, to avoid going astray, or tumbling down the most frightful precipices. But the utmost precau-tions did not always prevent the corps from losing their way. Sometimes men, at the head of a battalion, would continue to follow the windings of a deafening torrent, instead of turn-ing abruptly to the right or left, up some rocky acclivity, over which lay their proper course . . . One party was frequently heard hallooing from an apparently fathomless ravine, to their comrades passing over some high projecting summit, to know if they were going right. These would answer with their trumpets; but it often occurred that both parties had lost their road. The frequent sound of trumpets along the broken line; the shouting of officers to their men at a distance; the neighing of horses, and

the braying of mules, both men and animals being alike anxious to reach a place of rest, produced a strange and fearful concert, echoed, in the darkness of the night, from the horrid solitudes of the Andes.

[Snowblindness was another problem.] A pimple forms in the eyeball, and causes an itching prickling pain, as though needles were continually piercing it. The temporary loss of sight is occasioned by the impossibility of opening the eyelids for a single moment, the smallest ray of light being absolutely insupportable. The only relief is a poultice of snow, but as that melts away the tortures return. Later in the campaign, a whole division was blinded in this way, and the long files of sightless soldiers were led into the nearest village by Indian guides, but not before a hundred stragglers had been lost along the line.

The temperature, according to Miller, rarely rose above zero. Historian Gonzalo Bulnes described the march of the Peruvian army under La Mar:

Often after climbing a dangerous trail, exhausted, without more vegetation than the little mosses which served as food for the llamas, or the lichen from which the Indians made thread, without seeing anything living other than a condor or a flock of vicuña which stopped to look at the travellers, the soldiers found themselves suddenly on the edge of a valley, at the steep bottom of which they would see a small white house with an orchard of the richest fruits. The army would ascend the valley to rise up to a new height, and this continually. When the army stopped the cold froze their weary limbs and in the evening the soldiers had to sleep close to the fires not to freeze.

An immense human line followed the indented contours of the range, like a huge snake which enveloped, with its coils, in spirals, the indentations in the mountains. In certain places the soldiers had vertigo and needed the help of their companions; in others the thinness of the air prevented them marching, and entire battalions fell to the ground, victims of *soroche* which seems to be the jealous guardian of [the mountains'] eternal solitude.

Before reaching the mountains, Sucre's own divisions further south had crossed about 300 miles of desert along the fierce Atacama plateau to the south, freezing at night and frying by day. Some 300 died of exhaustion.

On 2 August 1824, all the divisions assembled on the great plateau beneath the Cerro de Pasco, some 12,000 feet above the sea. Bolívar reviewed them: 'Soldiers, you are going to finish the greatest task which heaven can charge to a man: to save a whole world from slavery . . . Soldiers, Peru and the whole of America are waiting for you to deliver peace, the child of victory. Even free Europe looks upon you with favour: for the freedom of the New World is the life of the universe.' The combined army set off for the Lake of the Kings, at the other end of which lay the Jauja valley leading to the plains of Junín.

Canterac's forces, meanwhile, astonished by the appearance of this large army at the very gates of its supposedly impregnable mountain headquarters, marched down the left side of the lake to intercept them. Too late, Canterac learnt that Bolívar's forces were marching down the right-hand side of this immense inland sea in the mountains, towards the head of the now unguarded Jauja valley. Canterac ordered a hurried countermarch to avoid being cut off from his headquarters.

When Bolívar learned of this, he spurred his men frantically forward. However, the Spanish infantry was now winning the race. He detached his cavalry to try and prevent Canterac's forces from reaching the neck of the Jauja valley where they could easily fend off a patriot attack. His mounted troops galloped forward to the southern end of the lake, on to the plains of Junín, but only two cavalry brigades made it out to the open country in time – to find themselves facing the whole enemy army on 6 August 1824.

Canterac, delighted to catch them out in the open with overwhelmingly superior forces, spurred his glistening, highly trained hussars forwards, himself leading the charge. The only patriot footsoldiers in the vanguard, the Argentinian grenadiers, were quickly overwhelmed. But the magnificent half-naked llanero cavalrymen held firm, wheeling about to reform in charge after charge, while

Bolívar hurried the rest of his army forward. The Colombian hussars and the grenadiers at last buttressed the faltering lines of cavalry, whose commander, General Necochea, had been wounded and taken prisoner. With these reinforcements, the patriots surged forward and rescued Necochea.

The royalist army threw in their cavalry reserves, which charged forward at full gallop. Miller, using an old trick he had learnt from the llanero riders, ordered their retreat towards the line of partisan infantry, which was waiting in reserve. Defeat seemed certain as the royalist cavalry charged. 'About turn!' yelled Miller and his cavalry wheeled about, charging straight into the astonished enemy cavalry, their lances spearing the enemy horses to deadly effect.

This charge broke the Spanish lines, and they began to fall back into a headlong retreat. They had at least made it to the head of the valley. Bolívar called a halt to the pursuit to allow his rearguard to catch up. Canterac, terrified of being caught out on the plains again, took advantage of nightfall to initiate one of the longest retreats in history: within two days he had crossed 120 miles to his headquarters in Jauja, abandoning that again to keep ahead of his opponents by retreating a further 300 miles to the sacred Apurimac river.

The Battle of Junín had been spectacular under the blue skies of that remote mountain plain by a lake 12,000 feet up. It had lasted barely an hour and not a shot had been fired, the only sound being the surreal one of the crunch of opposing lances and the cries of the injured and dying. An almost purely cavalry battle, it had the flavour of a medieval jousting tournament. The uniformed and helmeted Spanish dragoons, their uniforms reflecting in the cold sun, had been routed by the long-haired llaneros in their jaguar caps, bare torsos and breeches, by the disciplined Argentinian horsemen, and by the Peruvian regiments in their ponchos. The Spaniards had lost 1,000 killed or taken prisoner, along with 700 muskets and a huge quantity of supplies.

Once again, Bolívar had astonished. He had climbed a seemingly impregnable mountain range, assembled three armies there, surprised the enemy and lured his opponents out to fight on his chosen ground: the plains of Junín, where the brilliant horsemanship of his llaneros had been deployed to best effect, achieving the miracles of cavalry attack, dispersal and regrouping that they had perfected on the Venezuelan llanos. He had moved with characteristic speed of reaction and improvisation to wrongfoot Canterac.

He paused, showing the caution of a seasoned commander. He had won a magnificent victory, but Canterac had preserved most of his army intact. The royalist commander had fled all the way to Cuzco, where the news of the decisive defeat had reached the Viceroy, La Serna, at the same time as reports of a brilliant victory gained by General Valdéz against the rebellious Olañeta in Upper Peru.

La Serna, horrified by the outcome of Junín, promptly ordered Valdéz back to Cuzco, and there assembled the full Spanish complement of 12,000 men. Bolívar, learning this, decided not to fight until the end of the rainy season which was just beginning and, leaving Sucre in charge of the forces in the mountains, galloped down to his coastal enclave at Trujillo. Urdaneta had taken charge there, and at last a force of 4,500 men had been despatched by Páez to Bolívar's aid.

In spite of the victory at Junín, the Liberator was pessimistic about the chances of his forces in the mountains prevailing against such a large Spanish army, and he wanted to create a virtually impregnable 'liberated' state in northern Peru. Descending to Huancayo in October 1824, he was received by his passionate girlfriend, Manuela Madroño.

He also had a rude shock. Unlike Páez, Santander, the de facto president of Colombia, had been dragging his feet about reinforcing him. 'Without the consent of congress, I can do nothing, because I lack the discretionary power, which I require to be in accordance with the laws, even if disaster comes to the republic.'

Santander and the New Granadan leaders, once so grateful to the Liberator, now bitterly resented the union with Venezuela. They disliked having a Venezuelan as their president. They were unimpressed by the argument that the defeat of the patriots in Peru would threaten the very survival of Colombia and resent having to send their expensive armies down to help Bolívar. They were also jealous of men such as Sucre winning their spurs as Bolívar's commanders in Peru, fearing that these men would later take over as rulers of

Colombia when Bolívar returned. While the cat was away, the mice were playing.

Santander himself was engaged in a duplicitous power play. While arguing that Congress was tying his hands, he used the excuse that he had to obey the law – he had always been known as a legal pedant – for not sending help to Bolívar. In fact, this was just a pretext; throughout the desperate circumstances of the wars of liberation laws had been ignored where the need was urgent enough. It was Santander himself who now asked Congress to consider whether the appropriations requested by Bolívar for Peru had legal force. Congress replied, as he had anticipated, not just by disavowing them, but by stripping Bolívar of his title as commander-in-chief of Colombian forces in Peru. The Liberator now had no official military status and he could no longer order his troops.

Furiously, Bolívar wrote back. 'I ask you to forward my prior resignation to congress and I shall write to everyone exposing your secret manoeuvres against me. Instead of rendering thanks for my services they [congress] question my abilities.' In his absence, a coup had in effect been staged against him. In response Sucre and his officers immediately refused to accept his dismissal.

Bolívar now had to bid goodbye to Manuela Madroño as he set out for the coast. He descended to Trujillo to fortify his armies, yet learnt from Sucre in the mountains that the Spanish armies were considering a surprise attack down the sierra through Arequipa on to the coastal enclave. Bolívar considered this unlikely – and indeed it proved to be a feint.

Instead, the royalist armies had decided to march from Cuzco across Sucre's rear, cutting him off from retreat to the north. As soon as Sucre realized this, he pulled back with such speed that he escaped the flanking movement and, pursued by the much bigger Spanish army that was trying to force battle upon him on unfavourable mountain territory, he began a cat-and-mouse retreat across the cordillera – on one occasion marching at dead of night to escape a massive ambush. The Spaniards, as they trekked across higher ground, suffered from hunger. La Serna would not send detachments in search of cattle, for fear men would desert, so they were reduced to eating their horses, mules and asses.

The Spanish troops, accustomed to the altitude, proved the faster force and Sucre, although instructed by Bolívar to avoid a fight at all costs, nonetheless decided he no longer wished to run. 'Defensive war is so disagreeable and appears to me so disadvantageous that I confess I am tormented when I have to display a tranquil response to the movements of the enemy, as are my troops who want to go on the offensive'. On 6 December 1824 the patriot army camped in the village of Quinua, near the plain of Ayacucho, while the royalists seized the overlooking heights called Condorcunca – Worthy of the Condors. Battle seemed inevitable, and this was a relief to Sucre and his officers, although they were heavily outnumbered and fighting on territory of the royalists' choosing.

Down on the coast, Bolívar, made newly confident by his victory at the Battle of Junín, decided to march on Lima. On his approach, the Marqués de Torre Tagle and other treacherous pro-Spanish grandees fled to the safety of the fort at Callao, Lima's port, leaving Bolívar to enter the once glittering capital that he now found in a dreadful state. Prey to raids by marauding bands of partisans, it had been presided over by the wretchedly sadistic Brigadier Mateo Ramírez, the Spanish commander, who amused himself by decapitating young Limeños for wearing 'republican hats'. Grass grew on the streets, which were largely deserted for fear of being seized by patrols of Spanish soldiery. Ramírez had become known as the 'Robespierre of Peru' for his cruelty. Bolívar was greeted with relief by its depressed and cowed population, who begged him not to take his coastal army into the mountains, but to stay and restore order.

At 10 a.m. on 9 December 1824, the patriot armies under Sucre and the Spanish armies under the overall control of the Viceroy, La Serna, met for the battle which was finally to decide the fate of Spanish America. If the Spaniards lost, their last great army would be defeated and their position on the continent all but eliminated. If they won, they might yet recover all of Peru and carry the fight to Colombia in the north.

The Spaniards, in much the stronger position, decided to take the offensive and grouped together in the hills to the north of the plain of Ayacucho. Valdez, the best of their generals, commanded the right flank; General Juan Antonio Monet, positioned on slopes descending to the plain, commanded the centre; on the left were the Spanish reservists under Marshal Alejandro González. Facing them, respectively, were the Peruvian troops of General La Mar, the cavalry and infantry divisions of Sucre's youngest general, the 24-year-old New Granadan Córdova, and the reserves under the orders of General Jacinto Lara. Reckoning that La Mar's Peruvian forces were the weakest, Valdéz decided to attack him with his crack troops. As the 11 cannon of the Spaniards blazed away, the battle between 5,800 patriots and 9,300 Spaniards was joined, Sucre declared, 'on your efforts today will depend the destinies of South America. Another day of glory will crown your admirable efforts.'

Valdéz, with his usual ferocity, was leading a frontal attack on La Mar's troops, who began to panic as cannon and rifle fire played havoc in their ranks. The Peruvian general tried desperately to calm them, while sending urgently for reinforcements from the centre. The Spaniards had calculated he would do just this and once the reinforcements had been despatched, weakening the centre, they intended to launch a frontal attack there.

However, Monet, carried away, ordered his Spanish force down the slopes before the reinforcements were despatched. Sucre, seeing the centre under attack, ordered the men to stay put and told the beleaguered La Mar to fight to the death with the troops at his disposal. The young Córdova, commanding the infantry and cavalry in the centre, descended from his horse theatrically and killed it, declaring he wanted no means of escape. Then he issued a famous order: 'Soldiers, fire at will, Paso de Vencedores' (March of Victors).

The charging Spanish cavalry, nearly upon them, was astonished to see the patriots not just standing firm but advancing towards them bearing the long lances which had proved so deadly in Junín. Thrusting at the horsemen, these weapons turned the tables in a long half-hour of hand-to-hand fighting. As the confusion began to clear, it became apparent that Córdova was still advancing and the Spaniards retreating. Soon he had gained the crest of the hill, where he disarmed the Spanish artillery.

La Mar, meanwhile, had somehow managed to hold the right flank, and Sucre now felt able to transfer reserves to him and push back the exhausted soldiers of Valdéz. The courageous Spaniard, realizing that the tide of battle was turning, attempted to get himself killed in action but was saved by one of his colonels, who forcibly dragged him from the field. The viceroy tried to save the day by sending his reserves up to try to retake the hill from Córdova but they were driven off and their commander, Canterac, was wounded. Córdova's cavalry, on the crest of the hill, galloped down from the heights to seize La Serna in his camp at the rear. Monet, however, managed to escape to the mountains with 500 men.

But it was over. The Spanish force surrendered when Sucre offered the defenders safe passage to Spain. When the battle was over, Sucre had captured two lieutenant-generals, La Serna and Canterac; four field marshals, including Valdéz and Monet; two brigadier-generals, 17 colonels, 78 lieutenant-colonels, 484 majors and junior officers, 2,500 soldiers and a huge quantity of munitions. Some 1,900 Spaniards lay dead and 700 wounded, compared to 310 patriot dead and more than 600 wounded. It had been a crushing victory against superior odds, a triumph worthy of the Liberator himself. It was the last great battle in the liberation of the Americas from Spanish rule, one of the bloodiest and most savage wars in history.

The day after the battle Sucre invited Valdez, whom he admired, to lunch with his senior officers and toasted him: 'I drink to one who, had he been born in America, would have been the best defender of its independence.' Sucre wrote to Bolívar, presenting him 'with the whole territory of Peru submitted to your authority after five months of campaigning'.

The victory was all the sweeter for its being unexpected; Bolívar had doubted that Sucre's inferior forces could win any confrontation with the well-equipped Spaniards in the mountains. Bolívar is said to have received the news in his luxurious villa of Magdalena outside the capital by throwing his sword and his uniform jacket to the ground and promising never to use them again.

To Sucre he wrote in glowing terms:

The Battle of Ayacucho is the climax of American glory and the work of General Sucre. His dispositions for it were perfect and their executions flawless. Quick and skilful movements destroyed in an hour the victors of fourteen years – an enemy perfectly organized and expertly commanded . . . General Sucre is the father of Ayacucho; he is the redeemer of the Children of the Sun; he has broken the chains with which Pizarro bound the Empire of the Incas. Posterity will picture him with one foot on Pichincha and the other on Potosí, bearing in his arms the cradle of Manco Capac and contemplating the chains broken by his sword.

Bolívar appointed Sucre Grand Marshal and gave him the title of Liberator of Peru. He ordered him to proceed to the heights of Upper Peru to put an end to the resistance of the reactionary General Olañeta, who had refused to obey La Serna's order to surrender. The general's men deserted in droves as Sucre successively took Cochabamba and La Paz with speed and efficiency, and Olañeta was killed after a skirmish, his army surrendering.

The port of Callao under the Spaniard Rodic held out as the last enclave of Spanish military power on the continent. A siege was mounted which, astonishingly, lasted a year, the Spanish garrison suffering from appalling malnutrition until its surrender in January 1826. Bolívar was generous to the survivors and allowed them to depart for Spain.

The Liberator was begged by the Peruvians to stay on as dictator and keep order. Acceding to this for the moment, he invited Manuela Sáenz at last to come down from her frustrating life in Quito and set up home with him. She became a striking figure by his side, riding around the city in a uniform of tight red trousers, long boots, a black cape and plumed hat, riding and fencing with Bolívar's officers and presiding as hostess over innumerable social events in the Liberator's residence. Her pet bear cub became as famous as her black maid, who was a fine mimic of the country's top politicians.

Bolívar's achievement in Peru had been as staggering as any in his career. In the space of a year, from holding a strip on the country's north coast while himself nearly moribund, he and Sucre had taken on and defeated an army of 18,000 men and secured a country the size of nearly all of western Europe to add to the vastness of Colombia. He could now claim to be the ruler of one of the greatest empires of any military leader in history, some 1 million square miles in extent. He was on a par with Tamerlane, Genghis Khan, Alexander the Great and Augustus Caesar, far eclipsing Cortés, Pizarro and Clive of India in the extent of his conquests. The investment of personal energy, the distances covered and the four army expeditions across supposedly impassable mountain ranges – west to east across the Andes, back the other way, down the central Andes to Quito, and up again to Cerro de Pasco – had qualified him for superhuman status.

In ten years he had personally covered around 16,000 miles of territory on horseback – most of it across extremely inhospitable land – and fought some 300 battles and skirmishes. His stamina and military achievements put him at the forefront of the global heroes of world history. He was now about to embark on his lap of honour before attempting to secure his claim to immortality and greatness, by laying down the basis for effective and lasting constitutional government for his beloved South America. He wanted to go down in history as a statesman, as well as a military conqueror and liberator; and he still entertained the further dream of uniting all of South America under his rule. Nothing seemed impossible for this extraordinary figure and on 31 December 1824, the British foreign secretary, George Canning, in the teeth of the opposition of King George IV and the Duke of Wellington, formally recognized Colombia.

On 15 April 1825, the liberator set out from Lima, with a huge party of his most trusted cronies, which included O'Leary and even his old tutor, Simón Rodríguez, on a triumphal progress around his new dominion, the ancient empire of the Incas. Manuela, to her fury, was left behind.

He was faced with an immediate problem as he travelled: his faithful lieutenant Sucre, sent to cleanse the Spanish army from Upper Peru, had understood the passionate desire of the overwhelmingly Indian population for independence from the Viceroyalty of La Plata (Argentina), and on 9 February 1825 proclaimed the self-government of Upper Peru. Bolívar was furious with his favourite, as this action threatened to anger both the Argentinians and Peruvians, but accepted it as a *fait accompli*. He wrote in paternal tones to Sucre, who wanted to abdicate power:

My dear general, fulfil your destiny, yield to the good fortune that courts you, do not imitate San Martín and Iturbide who threw away the glory that sought them. You are capable of everything

and should not hesitate to let yourself be drawn by fortune . . . I
am not ambitious, but I see that you ought to be a bit ambitious, to
equal or excel me. Remember that you have in me a living father
who will always rejoice in the glory of his son.

Bolívar travelled up into the mountains to be greeted with delirium
by the overwhelmingly Indian population. He was their Liberator
from 300 years of Spanish oppression, and the fact that he was an aristocratic white man – albeit with some mixed blood – mattered not
at all. Bolívar, described as 'El Zambo' by the sneering upper class of
Lima, was a national hero to the Indians: 'It is difficult to describe the
reception which the towns gave the Liberator on his whole journey.
His voyage was a triumphal march. The inhabitants would emerge
from the towns to greet him as he approached. The Indians were
enthusiastic, dressing in rich and colourful dresses handed down by
their ancestors.'

These receptions were no mere indulgence. Traditionally they
were staged to try and placate conquerors or the authorities and
stave off punishment and pillage. This time, there could be little
doubt that the demonstrations were genuine, a relief and welcome
for a conqueror who exacted no vengeance, but had come to liberate them. On 25 June 25, two months after leaving Lima, Bolívar's
procession reached Cuzco.

There, another welcome awaited. O'Leary described it:

The fronts of the houses were adorned with rich hangings and ornaments of gold and silver. The triumphal arches in the streets boasted
the same rich adornments, beautifully arranged, and from the windows
and balconies there fell a rain of flowers and laurel crowns which the
delicate hands of pretty Cuzcan girls threw as the cavalcade passed
by, along with medallions from the people. As in Arequipa, the city
fathers presented him with a horse with a bridle and a saddle of gold
and the keys of the city made from the same metal. After listening to
a solemn Te Deum which was celebrated in the cathedral, he went to
the municipal palace, where the principal ladies of the city presented
him with a civic crown of diamonds and pearls.

Bolívar now successfully occupied the seat of the Inca empire, the very city where in 1781, less than half a century before, Tupac Amaru II had staged his rebellion against the Spanish empire and been dismembered in fearsome punishment. Like an Inca emperor, Bolívar promptly issued a decree that favourably astonished his millions of subjects and appalled the old ruling classes of Lima.

The Andean cordillera of Peru was characterized by mountains so precipitous and valleys so narrow and steep that the Incas had been able to create their civilization by two methods: cutting an extensive network of trails across them, and creating terraces halfway up the sides of steep mountain slopes, where they cultivated a variety of crops, channelling water and soil to their best advantage. Below, in the deep valleys and chasms, the tropical climate made cultivation impossible; higher up, the intensity of the sun, the coldness of the nights and the thinness of the air made life equally unbearable for farmers and crops alike. The Inca system was necessarily a communal one, founded on strict principles of hierarchy and co-operation, as was essential for a people that could only survive through the collective effort of maintaining and harvesting the terraces.

On to this special pyramid the Spaniards had grafted their own colonial control, which was also ruthlessly hierarchical, using Indian overseers – *caciques* – to impose virtual slavery upon the Indians. While continuing to exploit agriculture, the Spaniards also created a large class of Indian forced labour to work the gold, silver and tin mines. The coca leaf was also extensively cultivated by the Spaniards to give to the miners to ease their hunger and suffering; this in turn had to be cultivated in the deep tropical valleys by Indian labourers, who died in their thousands.

The Liberator had inherited this system of exploitation and near-slavery and to his great credit he lived up to his name, even if his decrees in the event were to prove largely unenforceable. First, he announced the abolition of the hated *caciques*. He went on to insist that all labourers must be paid in cash, at fair rates established by the market, not in kind; all forced labour was banned; and all employment had to be freely and fairly contracted. Bolívar wrote privately from Cuzco: 'The poor Indians find themselves in a state of submission that is really appalling. I want to do them all possible good; first for the good of humanity; and, second, because that is their right.'

He also announced a programme of land reform, under which Indian farmers assumed possession of the land they cultivated, and all communal land was divided up among landless peasants. Although in practice many of the reforms were to be trampled upon in later years, they earned Bolívar the loyalty of the overwhelming majority of Indians. The actions were those of Bolívar the reformer, the romantic revolutionary, harking back to his enlistment of the dispossessed of Venezuela in his cause, still inspired by his early reading of Rousseau.

While in Cuzco, the libidinous liberator had yet another romantic dalliance – this time with the most formidable woman of the city. Francisca Zubiaga de Gamarra, wife of Augustín Gamarra the prefect of Cuzco – who was later to become president of Peru – was nicknamed La Mariscala – the Marshalless – for her commanding manner. Large-boned and masculine, she was deprived of all personal affection in her youth, and trained as a nun. She confided to a friend, 'I have to supplement the weakness of my sex by making use of men. I have loved and lied. I have done everything, I have resorted to everything. Oh glory, how costly you are!' She told a young officer courting her, 'Be gone, with your sighs, your sentimental words and your romances with little girls. I am vulnerable only to the sighs of the cannon, to the words of congress and to the applause and acclamation of the people as I pass through the streets.'

The first lady of Cuzco was bewitched by the aura surrounding Bolívar, but the liaison proved to be unusually short, even by his standards: he quickly cooled towards her cold character and naked ambition. She was furious at the rejection, and revealed details of the affair to her powerful husband, who from that moment on joined the aristocrats in Lima as a sworn enemy of Bolívar. Sucre later wrote to Bolívar warning him that Gamarra had become 'his bitterest enemy'.

Bolívar was now to be offered the chance of even greater glory: he was to be called up the highest mountain, and have a vaster territory laid at his feet. While in Cuzco, and about to embark on the next stage of his triumphal procession across the highlands of Upper

Peru, he learnt that Brazil, now under the control of the independent emperor, Dom Pedro I, had taken advantage of the virtual anarchy prevailing in Argentina to move in and occupy the so-called East Bank of the River Plate (now Uruguay).

What was left of the government in Buenos Aires had despatched a mission to seek help from the Liberator in resisting Brazil's imperialist aims, which were seen as monarchical, aristocratic and against the spirit of Bolívar's democratic and reformist aims. Bolívar was on the verge, it seems, of realizing his ultimate dream: of marching down to annex Argentina to his dominions. More dramatic still, the continent seemed on the brink of war between Spanish-speaking America and the vast outback of Portuguese-speaking Brazil.

Bolívar wrote to Santander, who must have thought him mad, seeking authorization to commit his troops to the Argentinian cause: 'Caesar in Gaul threatened Rome, and I in Upper Peru threaten all the conspirators of America and, consequently, can save all its republics. If I lose my position in the south the conquest of Peru is worthless and the emperor of Brazil will devour the River Plate and Upper Peru.' With Spain defeated, it seemed Bolívar had found another enemy: Brazil's imperial pretensions. At the same time Bolívar shrewdly suggested an alliance of neutrality with the British, whom he rightly suspected of backing Brazilian expansionism. From the heights of Upper Peru, Bolívar was now proposing to descend on the plains of Argentina as a defending angel.

He and his huge entourage hurried across the extensive, empty landscapes of the central Andes to the barren high plain bordered by serrated mountain peaks alongside the vast 13,000-foot high Lake Titicaca. On the lake's deserted shores on 19 August 1825, Bolívar met his dashing young protégé, General Sucre, and after close embraces, the two rode together into the city of La Paz, dramatically sited in a canyon between the plain and the mountain range. There he assented to the announcement that the country's Congress had decided to call the new independent state of Upper Peru after the Liberator himself: Bolivia. Sucre had chosen a shrewd way of reconciling himself after insubordination and the violation of his master's orders. Bolívar accepted this supreme accolade, and refused the office of president of the new state, conferring it on Sucre.

After a month in La Paz, he resumed his journey to the most fabulous name of all in Spanish America, the city of Potosí, whose mountain of silver had provided much of the wealth of the Spanish empire for 300 years. Another splendid welcome awaited him there, as Indians danced around him, their children were lowered triumphant from a giant triumphal arch in a cloud of smoke to impress him or to pour flowers upon him, and fireworks cannonaded across the upland remoteness of the mountain. At this pinnacle of wealth and corruption Bolívar delivered one of his most famous speeches, comparable to Lincoln's Gettysburg address:

> We have come victorious from our Atlantic coasts and in 15 years in a battle of the giants we have toppled the edifice of tyranny built calmly over three centuries of usurpation and violence. The miserable subjects of these people were condemned to the most degrading slavery. How great must be our joy at seeing so many millions of men regain their rights through perseverance and effort.
>
> As for me, with my feet on this mountain of silver called Potosí, whose enormously rich veins were for 300 years the treasury of Spain, I regard this opulence as nothing when I compare it with the glory of having carried victoriously the standard of freedom from the burning shores of the Orinoco to fix it here, on the peak of this mountain, whose breast is the wonder and envy of the universe.

It was striking that at this intoxicating moment he chose to highlight his credentials as liberator and revolutionary, not as continental dictator, much less emperor, although there can be little doubt that at times he saw himself as the indispensable sole guarantor of Latin America's freedom. He was torn between his belief that he, and only he, could continue to rule and maintain the interests of the countries he had liberated, as well as those like Argentina which needed his protection as well as his repugnance for tyranny and monarchical rule.

Unlike Napoleon, he refused to take action to assert his control, through for example establishing an empire, taking advantage of his godlike status and the devotion of millions, knowing full well that that road would lead to tyranny and the end of his real glory as

Liberator. It is impossible to say whether he took this decision for purely idealistic reasons, or whether he recognized that in Spanish America, as was not the case in Europe, the power of the ruling elites was such as to be able, probably, to crush any attempt by him to found a truly revolutionary empire, based on one man and the support of the continent's millions.

He toyed with the idea of proclaiming himself, like the ill-fated Tupac Amaru II, 'Inca', and of waging a civil war against privilege around the continent; and it is to his credit that he decided not to do so. He came down off the mountain, proclaiming instead the ideals of freedom and constitutional rule which he had sought to establish across the continent. He had wrestled with the dark side of his own nature, where megalomania and ruthlessness had sometimes taken control, and the passion for freedom and rationalism had won.

The downside was that he failed to take on the old elites who continued to dominate the continent. His revolutionary detractors believe that he alone could have initiated a real social and economic revolution in the land he had conquered. But he had spared his people the upheaval, bloodshed and almost certain failure that would have accompanied such a revolution. In this he was both humane and justified.

He was just 42, impelled still by his lust for glory and political liberty. Now new tasks and lands beckoned. The huge expanse of Argentina lay thousands of metres below him to the south. At Potosí he received General Carlos María de Alvear, the senior Argentinian leader seeking his intercession against Brazil, who told him that war between Argentina and Brazil was inevitable, that the former lacked the forces to win, and that it desperately needed help from Chile and Peru. He begged Bolívar, with his immense prestige, to act as Protector of all of Spanish America.

Bolívar had learnt that Brazilian troops had already moved to occupy a province of Bolivia and, furiously, he threatened war. He also wrote to Santander again begging for authorization to come to Argentina's aid, only to be told that it was legally impossible for Colombian troops to be used to such effect. Bolívar angrily declared he would march forward with Peruvian troops instead. Santander retorted that, as president of Colombia, Bolívar would still require authorization from the Colombian Congress to do so.

The Liberator showed no signs of paying any attention. He prepared to march down to La Plata, the Argentine city at the head-waters of the River Plate, without permission. He was in high good humour once again: he was off on another great adventure.

Before leaving he even wrote to Manuela Sáenz, neglected for the best part of a year in Lima, inviting her to join him. She wrote back with a mixture of mischief, histrionic pique and alluring charm:

> I am very good and very ill. Long absences extinguish love and stimulate even greater passions. The little love you extend to me has been killed by long separation. I have conserved my passion for you, to preserve my well-being and my health, and it exists and will exist as long as Manuela lives. I leave on December 1st (and I go because you called me). But don't tell me afterwards to return to Quito, because I had rather die than go there in shame.

She was trying to insist that Bolívar end his request that she should stay married to Dr Thorne, who still pleaded with her to return from Lima. To the doctor's entreaties she wrote:

> Do you believe me to be less honourable for [Bolívar] being my lover and not my husband. Ah: I don't live for social considera-tions, which were invented to torment us matually. Leave me, my beloved Englishman. Let us do something else: in heaven let us marry again, but on earth not. Do you think this argument a bad one? Then you must be very discontented. In the celestial father-land we will spend an angelic life in full spirituality (because as a man you are heavy). Then, all will be English-style, because the manotonous life is reserved to your nation (in love, I say, because as far the rest, who is more able in commerce or shipping?) [The English] prefer love without pleasure; conversation without grace; and walking slowly; greeting with reverence; getting up and sitting down with care; conversation and without laughter.

Manuela was an irrepressible spirit, but occasionally, it seems, too irrepressible even for a man of Bolívar's energy. Nevertheless, after several deliberate separations, he was never to lose his addiction to her and their affair endured to his death. It was one of the greatest of Latin American love stories: he had found at last a sort of maniacally unstable emotional stability. His stormy eight-year passion for Manuela outlasted every previous love by many years.

Meanwhile, he was riding upon the town of La Plata for his next rendezvous with destiny. He learnt that Argentina had declared war on Brazil and that his enemy, Bernardino Rivadavia, the leader of the aristocratic party in Argentina, had been elected head of its government.

Rivadavia moved swiftly, summoning Woodbine Parish, the British ambassador in Buenos Aires, to urge his government to restrain the Brazilians. If that did not happen, Rivadavia warned Parish, Bolívar would widen the war into a general one aimed at spreading republicanism and overthrowing aristocratic and monarchical forms of government, including the British empire. Parish was astute enough to inform the British foreign secretary, George Canning, that he considered these arguments purely 'personal resentments' towards Bolívar. The British nonetheless replied to the Argentinians that Brazil would only be satisfied with setting up an independent buffer state on the east shore of the Plate – Uruguay – which Rivadavia grudgingly agreed to, provided it was guaranteed by Britain.

War was averted, and Bolívar's mission left hanging.

His ambitions were now shattered by a new blow: news came of tumultuous events in Colombia in his absence: it seemed that the two parts of the country, the former New Granada and Venezuela, were breaking apart and civil war beckoned. Páez, who ruled Venezuela, begged him to return. Bolívar wrote haughtily back: 'The title of Liberator is superior to every other that human pride has conceived; it is unthinkable that I should degrade it.'

He returned swiftly to the Bolivian capital of Chuquisaca (later to be renamed Sucre) to another tremendous reception and copious gifts, including that of a sword, a hilt of gold and a scabbard inset with 1,433 diamonds weighing 73 carats. A month later he rushed to Tacna from the high plains in just four days' hard riding and sailed for Lima, arriving there in February 1826. He settled down again in splendour, quarrelling ferociously with Manuela.

Part 3

DOWNFALL

Chapter 22

THE IDEALIST

Bolívar had been inspired, through Simón Rodríguez, by Rousseau's quintessentially romantic ideals of the goodness and perfectibility of mankind, although like Rousseau he saw no contradiction in sometimes using tyrannical means to achieve this – but he had already nobly turned his back on tyranny itself, the lure of absolute power over a vast dominion, the capture of further territories. He was now to be confronted with the further Rousseauian goal of creating a social contract that would ensure lasting good government over the vast lands he had freed – but in this he was to prove the classic romantic failure. The social contract was, baldly expressed, that the governor derives his authority from his responsibility to deliver good government and stability to the people he governs; if he fails to do so, he forfeits his right to rule. Try as hard as he might, Bolívar could not establish good and stable government over the lands he had captured – and was toppled by lesser men. The romantic hero and conqueror was thus led inexorably to his equally romantic, perhaps inevitable, downfall.

The third phase of Bolívar's career – the first being that of the ruthless and frenzied aristocratic fighter defending his own class interests, the second his conversion to ensuring the wellbeing of all classes, and to more humanitarian and subtle military tactics – now occurred. Power, said Lord Acton pompously, corrupts. Absolute power corrupts absolutely. Given absolute power over a domain larger than those of Alexander the Great, Augustus Caesar, Attila, Genghis Khan, Tamerlane and Napoleon, would Bolívar inevitably succumb to hubris and megalomania?

He had dominion over six provinces of the Spanish empire, soon to become nations. Another, Argentina, was vying for his support. Even in Portuguese Brazil, Argentina's rival, he had his partisans. He had been urged to take a crown and don an imperial mantle. Deeply tempted, he considered doing so before his own sense of realism brought him down to earth and he refused, preferring the title of Liberator. Far from spurning such glory, the aforementioned leaders and emperors had desperately pursued it, but Bolívar's course and instinct, in spite of his love of glory and vanity, was to turn away his flatterers. In the end, his domain was to dissolve into ruins anyway, although he could not have foreseen this.

During the previous couple of years he had changed. He had developed as a military commander: on top of his prowess in commanding small armies and as a guerrilla leader, he had shown he could organize, provision and lead armies across high mountains, an incredibly difficult military discipline rarely attempted by conventional commanders, and triumph. The piteous poverty of the indigenous peoples fed his growing humanism (although it also engendered in him the view that they were too easily manipulated to be trusted with the vote). He insisted he wanted to give them land rights – which although well-meaning turned out, as we shall see, to be counterproductive. The hard, formidable commander of the 'war to the death' had become a humanitarian, if realistic, social reformer.

Nonetheless, his empire was under threat in its heartland. The Bolívar dream was beginning to fragment where it had begun, in Venezuela and New Granada. He had penetrated as far south as he ever would on the continent and from now on the achievement was to crumble inexorably, in spite of his frantic efforts to save it. The career that had started with such difficulty and then taken off like a rocket to the stars was sputtering at last and beginning to fall back to earth. From now on its trajectory would be downwards, accelerating at a speed few can have foreseen. The vast and glittering expanse of Bolívar-led Spanish America, extending in a giant crescent from the Atlantic to the Pacific, from the Orinoco river to the Atacama desert, from Caracas to Potosí, was to shrink and curl up into charred pieces, as though a paper empire set on fire.

Before Bolívar returned to Colombia, he wanted to set the seal on the republic he and Sucre had created in Peru and Bolivia, and he lingered to do so. The constitution he drew up for Bolivia, which was also the model for Peru, represented the final refinement of his political thinking. Indeed, Bolívar toyed with the idea of using this constitutional model as a single one for a confederation of all the liberated territories. Although impossible to enforce over such a disparate area, Bolívar was historically farsighted in considering this as he sought to emulate the example of the United States and create a strong federation, so avoiding the deep fractures which have plagued Latin America ever since.

The constitution prepared for Bolivia and, in slightly modified form, for Peru, contained many of Bolívar's old ideas – which had already been rejected by the congresses of Angostura and Cucúta. It was based on an elected assembly drawn from men of property, a powerful president-for-life around which the system would revolve, and a college of 'censors' composed of the great and the good – a kind of supreme court.

He outlined his plan to Santander, leader of New Granada. This was a fatal mistake, for his proposal was to set himself up as president-for-life of the newly liberated confederation – with Sucre, not Santander, as his vice-president and anointed successor. Overnight, from political rival, the latter, who had always privately disliked Bolívar, was turned into a bitter enemy. The cold, legalistic, scheming Santander was prepared to go along only with a confederal constitution that designated him as Bolívar's successor; otherwise he preferred to carry on as boss of New Granada.

Bolívar, apart from preferring the valiant young Sucre as a man, reasoned that he was respected in Bolivia, Peru and Ecuador as one of their liberators and was thus much more capable of binding those countries to the confederation. Once again Bolívar was right, but wildly impractical and the confederation was to be stillborn. All he did achieve was to make a mortal enemy of Santander, with whom relations were already fraught.

The idea of a president-for-life – and even vice-president-for-life – was controversial and surely illiberal. In fact, it represented a compromise between the radicalism of eighteenth-century liberals

who sought to dispense with the need for a powerful executive altogether – with disastrous results wherever the experiment had been
tried, as in Venezuela's first republic and Argentina, leading to anarchy, civil war and, usually, the reimposition of an iron hand – and the
old Bourbon concept of absolute monarchy.

Bolívar, always a republican, vigorously opposed the idea of an
hereditary monarchy as a reaction against the tyranny of the Spanish
empire, yet he was a believer in firm central government and considered that only a president-for-life, above the fray, could deliver this:

> The President of the Republic in our constitution will be like the
> Sun which, firmly in the centre, gives life to the universe. The
> supreme authority must be permanent because in non-hereditary
> systems one needs, more than in others, a fixed point around
> which circle the magistrates and citizens, men and things. For
> a people to be free it must have a strong government which
> possesses sufficient means to free them from popular anarchy and
> the abuse of the powerful. The savage vastness of this continent
> by itself rules out monarchy; deserts conduce to independence
> (of spirit).

It was a formulation of good sense around a probably indefensible
institution.

Bolívar was not always consistent in his approach to this subject.
In a document from Captain Thomas Maling to Viscount Melville in
March 1825, Bolívar was reported as saying:

> You may say I never have been an enemy to monarchies upon
> general principles; on the contrary, I think it essential to the
> respectability and well being of new nations, and if any proposal
> ever comes from the British Cabinet for the establishment of a
> royal government, that is, of a monarchy or monarchies in the
> New World, they will find in me a steady and firm promoter of
> their views, perfectly ready to uphold the sovereign England may
> propose to place and support upon the throne.
>
> I know it has been said of me I wish to be a King, but it is not
> so. I would not accept the Crown for myself, for when I see this

country made happy under a good and firm government, I shall again retire into private life . . .

The title of King would perhaps not be popular at first in South America, and therefore it might be as well to meet the prejudice by assuming that of 'Inca' which the Indians are so much attached to. This enslaved and miserable country has hitherto only heard the name of King coupled with its miseries, and Spanish cruelties . . . Democracy has its charms for the people, and in theory it appears plausible to have a free government which shall exclude all hereditary distinctions, but England is again our example; how infinitely more respectable your nation is, governed by its King, Lords and Commons, than that which prides itself upon an equality but with little temptation to exertion for the benefit of the state; indeed, I question much whether the present situation will continue very long in the United States . . . If we are to have a new government, let it be modelled on yours.

This may have been no more than diplomatic feint, to ingratiate himself with the British; or it may have represented a genuine hankering after British-style constitutional monarchy. There were those who believed he intended to set himself up as just such an Inca, but the despatch suggested otherwise and made clear what he meant by the term.

Certainly, his constitutional proposals for Bolivia and Peru represented his fullest and final view of the subject. In the senate he sought to enshrine the hereditary principle through the nomination of a kind of House of Lords. However, he would not entertain the idea of hereditary monarchy, and yet failed to understand that a presidency-for-life was equally capable of degenerating into tyranny, and that the idea was a recipe for dictatorship.

He had in mind the experience of good Spanish kings like Charles III being succeeded by degenerate ones like Charles IV and he believed the idea would reassure those who equated republicanism with anarchy. By enshrining the concepts of legislative power and the censors in the constitution, sufficient checks would exist to control the presidency. In retrospect the idea looks absurd; but it must be remembered that with the exception of the British and American constitutions, his ideas were still way in advance of the absolutisms that prevailed almost everywhere else in Europe.

Where Bolívar was radical – to the extent of upsetting the very creole aristocracy and ruling class that he came from and which had backed him – was in his concept of equality and rights. As has been seen, Bolívar in the end secured the liberation of Venezuela through harnessing the very forces that had been the bulwark of the monarchy against the creole aristocracy – the dispossessed, the poor, the llaneros, the blacks, the slaves and the freemen, the Indians and the mulattos. In Cuzco again he had sought to emancipate the wretched Indian masses, providing them with elemental rights and property. Even his president-for-life would have no power to override the rights of these people, under Bolívar's constitution.

His belief in the rights of the individual derived in part from his concept of natural rights derived from Rousseau (as taught by his old tutor, Simón Rodríguez, who had accompanied him on his visit to Bolivia, more eccentric than ever, and was to be rewarded with the post of minister of education there, at which he proved a disaster, appearing naked in class as an extension of his theories of natural education); in part from his natural affinity with the dispossessed; and in part too because these had been the people that supported him, fought for him, achieved his revolution and welcomed him across a continent.

Bolívar's position on these matters was unequivocal. He identified the freedom of the individual with the minimal rights of the masses: equality of rights even for the lowest was his principle. He wrote: 'I am setting up a constitution . . . which revokes the slavery of the masses and all privileges'. And again: 'I have kept intact the law of laws: equality [of rights before the law – not economic equality]. Without it all guarantees perish, as do all rights. We must sacrifice everything for this.' His sometime lieutenant, Louis Peru de Lacroix, explains his thinking in a passage worth quoting at length:

> I heard him repeat several times that the state of slavery in which the people find themselves must be done away with; as must the fact that they were not only beneath the yoke of the mayors and the parish priests but of the two or three magnates in each parish.

In the cities it was the same, with the difference that there are many more masters because there are many more clerics and doctors.

Freedom and guarantees were only for these men and for the rich, and not for the people, whose slavery is worse than that even of the Indies; that slaves remained beneath the constitution of Cucúta and slaves would remain under the most liberal of constitutions; that in Colombia there was an aristocracy of rank, work and riches equivalent, through its pretensions, influence and weight upon the people, to the most despotic aristocracy of titles and birth in Europe. That in that aristocracy there were also clerics, doctors, lawyers, soldiers and demagogues.

Because even if they talk of freedom and guarantees, these apply only to those who want them and not to the people who, they believe, must continue under the oppression. They want equality to raise themselves and become equal to the most powerful but not to level themselves with individuals from the inferior classes of society. These they want always to consider as servants, in spite of their pretensions at demagoguery and liberalism.

In these quasi-Marxist views – certainly in their scorn for the middle classes – Bolívar was setting himself up as Latin America's foremost revolutionary: these incredibly radical sentiments for the times were an outright attack on the bourgeois backbone of society. Even in Latin America today they align him on the centre-left of the political spectrum – and in all too many countries the people remain treated as servants.

Yet the equality he preached was never of a Marxist economic kind: he was talking about rights and freedoms, not money or property. It was small wonder that Bolívar was to become a hero of the oppressed who, through race or economic circumstance, were treated as slaves throughout Latin America – and worshipped with almost godlike veneration on a mass scale. Nor was it surprising that he was to incur the wrath and hatred of a large section of the vested interests there – which again helped towards his undoing.

Bolívar was a passionate social reformer, way ahead of his times, although he was not an extremist or preacher of class warfare. Rather, he sought to reconcile the classes on the basis of unequal incomes

and status, but equal rights. He was always an elitist: he believed the
state of ignorance of the masses made them incapable of governing
themselves. But that did not mean that they lacked personal rights or
that they should be condemned to slavery: indeed, one of the prime
purposes of government was to protect those rights. It was a view at
least as enlightened as those of the radical English and French social
reformers of the time.

Bolívar's social reforms were soon dashed like waves on the rocks
of entrenched interests. After his victory the 10,000 criollo elite reas-
serted itself in Venezuela over the nearly 1 million others. The landowners sought to tame the llaneros and in 1828 issued a law making
ownership of the region's vast cattle herds dependent on ownership
of the land, which they held. Very few of the owners of haciendas
followed Bolívar's example in liberating slaves. In 1827, he introduced laws to improve the conditions of slaves, but could not secure
abolition – although he considered the practice a negation of law and
an outrage to reason as well as to justice, equality and human dignity
– a view which made him more enlightened than the United States
politicians of the time.

Bolívar was sometimes cynical about the Indians of both the
lower and upper Andes: 'In general the natives contribute nothing to
production and this race has suffered less from the war than others'.
In 1821 the harsh tithe and labour laws were abolished – but by
now they constituted a recognition of entitlement to land, so these
well-meaning measures were not welcomed even by the indigenous
people. *Resguardas* – reservations – were returned to the indigenous
people, in little parcels, but this in practice meant that the great white
landowners moved on to these lands and the Indians were pushed on
to more marginal land. They actually preferred the communal system
to individual landholdings (which linked the Peruvians in particular
to their Inca roots), and lacking either capital or equipment, they
were forced to mortgage their land to the bigger landowners to obtain
these, becoming debt slaves. Bolívar was also forced to hand out huge
estates to his leading caudillos, in particular Páez, to keep them quiet.

The constitution that Bolívar drew up for Bolivia – which
included civil liberty, freedom of speech, the press, work, movement and equality before the law, as well as abolishing slavery and

providing for due process of law and trial by jury, was to be described as the most liberal constitution in the world and 'the most notable philosophic-political speculation of South American history'. It was carried in a famous journey across 1,800 miles of Andean trails from Lima to Chuquisaca in 19 days by two Englishmen, Colonel William Ferguson and Belford Wilson. There it was adopted and Sucre was elected president (although self-deprecatingly only insisting on a two-year term).

Bolívar's second great venture into statecraft in Lima was the convening of the Congress of Panama, which met in June 1826. Bolívar had urged continental co-operation as far back as the constitution of Angostura (although he never believed in a unified Latin American state). Instead, he sought the resolution of disputes and joint declarations of support for independence and democracy by Latin American states, as well as overseas recognition. The project was already in a sadly reduced condition by the time the Congress met. Argentina refused to attend, both because of the loss of Bolivia and because it objected to the proposal to support the Monroe Doctrine recently promulgated by the United States (stating that European colonization or interference in the Americas would be treated as acts of aggression); Chile also declined. Fatuously, Brazil replied that it would only attend a congress that was neutral, such as between Latin America and the Spanish empire. The proposed Congress was thus reduced to Colombia, Peru, Central America and Mexico, the latter rather doubtfully.

However, both the United States and Britain, the second of which had recently recognized Colombia, sent delegates (recently Bolívar had received a gold medallion and a tuft of George Washington's hair from the adopted son of the first American president, together with a letter from the Marquis de Lafayette). The Congress largely neutralized Bolívar's ambitious plan for joint Latin American armed forces, but it did adopt six elemental principles of collaboration: first, a pledge to neutrality and coexistence among the members; second, adoption of the Monroe Doctrine; third, acceptance of international arbitration in disputes between member states; fourth, the abolition of slavery; fifth, the recognition of the national sovereignty of member states; and sixth, guarantees of these principles. The basic six points continue to govern relations between Latin American states today and have proved remarkably effective and durable at composing differences between them. However, there was no commitment to common democratic and republican goals, largely owing to Mexican objections.

The Congress was a manifest failure in Bolívar's terms, consisting as it did of only half the countries he wanted and falling short of his objectives, although he defended the attempt, saying it set a marker for the future. It did more than that. Subtly, it exposed the new reality of power that the nascent Latin American countries were about to face. For with the failure of Napoleon to establish a foothold on the continent and the defeat of the Spanish empire, only two nations were left to contend in the power vacuum: Britain and the United States. Britain, with a policy so inept that it almost beggars belief, had failed to take advantage of the almost universal goodwill prevailing towards it among Latin America's new masters. The view of most of the independence fighters was that Britain had the perfect combination of freedoms and stability that they sought to emulate in Latin America.

Moreover, the British had been at war with Spain; they had huge contraband trade links with Latin America, undermining the Spanish empire; and Britain had both tolerated and on occasion encouraged the Latin American independence movement. Grafton Street had been the focus of the patriots' early plotting; Miranda had taken refuge there; and Bolívar, San Martín and O'Higgins had all conspired there. A Briton, Cochrane, could reasonably be considered one of the fathers of Latin American independence. The great subplot of the revolutionary wars was that British and Irish soldiers had become the best fighters, the right-hand men and some of the most effective officers of the Liberators. Finally, George Canning had led the world in recognizing the independence of Spanish America.

Possessed of these formidable credits and reserves of goodwill, the craven opportunism of successive British governments – with the notable exceptions of Grenville and Canning – threw these advantages away. Miranda was initially provided backing, then abandoned in favour of the Peninsular War, and subsequently written off, self-defeatingly, as a natural-born loser. Bolívar was treated as an outcast and a joke in British Jamaica and had to secure support from a Haitian despot. In Argentina two military expeditions, one covert, one openly backed by the British, which amounted to little more than naked attempts at colonial annexation, failed – whereas expeditions to booster the independence cause would have succeeded and given Britain preferential trading rights.

Only in its policy towards Brazil did Britain reap dividends – at the risk of infuriating the newly independent Spanish American countries which regarded the 'empire' there with deep suspicion. In spite of all the disappointments, Bolívar continued to look upon Britain as a kindred spirit. He argued that British and South American citizens be given equal rights on the continent, and even that Spanish America should join the British Commonwealth of countries as a group of independent nations.

C.M. Ricketts, Britain's representative in Lima, wrote to George Canning after an interview with Bolívar that:

His Excellency at the same time requested me to state to you that on this occasion he could not withhold the expression of his anxious hope that Great Britain would not be a silent observer of the discussions which would arise in the Congress, since he was satisfied that they could not terminate in any practical good unless aided by your judicious and impartial counsels. The several States required to be upheld by the power and influence of Great Britain, without which no security could be expected, no consistency preserved, and no social compact maintained. All would be alike subjected to destruction by disputes with each other and by internal anarchy. Different interests were already propelling them; wars which might have been prevented unfortunately raged . . . The respective classes of inhabitants began to feel that they had equal rights, and as the coloured population so far exceeded the white, the safety of the latter was threatened.

Under the protection of Great Britain, the South American States would learn the measures most advisable to adopt for the general preservation and tranquillity.

Bolívar's pro-Britishness was not shared by everyone. The Mexican leader, Carlos María de Bustamante, wrote in 1825 to Bolívar that:

> We should work for ourselves, without taking into account that England exists; the manoeuvres of that cabinet are tortuous. Let us remember that the Minister of that Nation excited the deputies of the Madrid Cortes to continue opposing the French army when it was on the point of passing the Bidasoa. They did so, counting Britain's help. And what happened? The promises were broken. England opted out and left them in the lurch.

Sadly, Bustamante's assessment was to prove the more accurate.

Bolívar's passion for Britain was not merely sentimental. He saw Britain as the hub of the civilized world against the dark forces of the Holy Alliance of reactionary nations in Europe led by Prince von Metternich, which included, apart from the Austro-Hungarian empire, France and Russia. But he may also have understood – as Argentina, even more closely aligned with Britain, had – the dangers represented by President James Monroe's historic speech before Congress on 2 December 1823:

> the occasion has been judged proper for asserting as a principle in which the rights and interests of the United States are involved, that the American continents, by the free and independent condition which they have assumed and maintain, are henceforth not to be considered as subject for future colonization by any European powers . . . We owe it, therefore, to candour, and to the amicable relations existing between the United States and those powers, to declare that we should consider any attempt on their part to extend their system to any portion of this hemisphere as dangerous to our peace and safety. With the existing colonies or dependencies of any European power we have not interfered and shall not interfere

Bolívar had opposed inviting the United States to the Panama Congress, but was overridden by Santander who was in charge in Colombia. The Monroe Doctrine, ostensibly aimed at Spain and other continental European powers, was in fact specifically targeted against Britain: John Quincy Adams, who formulated it, was determined that Britain should be denied the chance – as seemed possible after Florida was ceded to the United States – of occupying Cuba and Puerto Rico.

By 1823 the United States had formulated the ambition of occupying Cuba, and therefore blocked another ambitious Bolívar plan to liberate the island from Spanish rule. The Americans even threatened war with Britain should the latter seek to back Bolívar's designs on Cuba. At the Congress of Panama, the United States also sought to impose its economic hegemony on the hemisphere, arguing that no American nation should grant favourable commercial or navigational rights to any foreign power that were not extended to all American countries – an effort to attempt to secure a veto over trading relations between Latin America and Europe.

The British, by contrast, sought to retain navigational rights and to support Bolívar's ambitions in Cuba. For a moment it seemed Bolívar would be the spearhead for British ambitions in the Caribbean, leading to war with the United States. But it was too late: the British had disappointed their friends and acted with opportunism and timidity. The United States was henceforth to exert its sway over the southern hemisphere and, 20 years later, to seize Texas from Mexico. Britain had been crowded out.

The irony was that, with the exception of the pathetic support offered to Miranda's quixotic expedition nearly two decades earlier, the United States had done almost nothing to help the cause of independence for its fellow Americans in the south. In the end it was humble mercenaries in the British Legion (as well as the many Britons and Irishmen who fought with San Martín) who deserved the credit as the freedom fighters' only foreign supporters. This they at last received at the Pan-American Centennial Congress of 1926 which noted:

> That Great Britain lent to the Liberty of Spanish America not only the support of its diplomacy, represented by Canning, but also an appreciable contingent of blood, and it may be asserted that there was no battlefield in the War of Independence on which British blood was not shed.

That the heroic collaboration is made more brilliant by the decisive bravery of the British Legion in the battle of Carabobo; by the admirable loyalty of the British aides of Bolívar, whose model was Ferguson, killed in defence of the Liberator, at the post of duty; by the actions of MacGregor, Rooke, Brown, Guise and a hundred more; by the intrepid bravery of Cochrane and the battling constancy of William Miller of Peru.

That later on the British heroes who survived the apogee of liberty incorporated themselves in the life of our democracies and also set through their austerity and love for order and institutions the highest civic examples.

That finally it was such Britishers as O'Leary, Miller, O'Connor and Stevenson who laid the basis of the history of Spanish America by collecting for posterity the first fragments of the immense Bolivian legend.

It is resolved that the Bolivarian Congress, commemorative of the Congress of 1826, gratefully pays tribute and homage to the memory of the British Heroes who gave their lives or fought without compensation except their love of Liberty and Glory, in favour of the Independence of Spanish America.

Bolívar's dream of a pan-American congress had ended in a flop which signalled the growing shadow of the United States' intention to dominate the southern hemisphere. He had drawn up model constitutions for Peru and Bolivia, but he had no way of knowing how long they would last. He knew now that he was needed urgently elsewhere, in Colombia, to shore up his disintegrating achievement there. He wrote a letter pregnant with foreboding to Páez at the unravelling of his dream in August 1826. Then he announced he would leave Lima.

The carping, sneering aristocracy of the city, which had so long laughed at the Liberator, was astounded by the announcement. Bolívar represented stability at the very least, and they entreated him to stay. A large demonstration was staged outside his residence at the Villa Magdalena, begging him to reconsider. The women of Lima made their own plea, to which Bolívar replied:

Ladies! Silence is the only answer I ought to give those enchant-
ing expressions . . . When beauty speaks, what breast can resist it?
I have been the soldier of beauty, because Liberty is bewitchingly
beautiful; she diffuses happiness, and decorates the path of life with
flowers.

Bolívar delayed his departure only a few days, attending the approval
of his constitution, but declining the presidency of Peru. On 4
September he set sail from the former jewel of the Spanish crown
with the words, 'Beware the horses of anarchy'. He was on his way to
Guayaquil, leaving Manuela behind, but receiving a poignant letter
from the 51-year-old Fanny de Villars, who had helped initiate him
in love:

Twenty-one years ago today you left Paris . . . Now, in Europe,
all the world proclaims you the first man of the century . . . do
you remember the tears I shed, how I begged you not to go away?
Your will resisted all my entreaties. The love of glory had already
possessed you and you belonged to us only superficially, conceal-
ing your real purpose, which only time has brought to light.

I remember with pride the confidences you made me about
your plans for the future, the sublimity of your thoughts and your
exalted feeling for liberty. I had some value at that time, for you
found me worthy of your secrets. Your determination to leave
wounded me profoundly but today your resolution raises you in
my estimation and I place you easily above all men.

I have had, and still have, confidence that you love me sincerely
and that in your moments of triumph as well as of danger you
knew that Fanny's thoughts were upon you and were invoking
Divine Providence to watch over you . . .

Goodbye, dear friend. I love you . . . It is not impossible that this
is farewell forever; only God and yourself can know that.

Keep my picture. It will be happier than I because, sending it
to you, I cannot put my soul into its face. If I could, perhaps you
would forget my years.

Chapter 23

THE DIVISION OF COLOMBIA

The trouble in Colombia arose primarily from the fusion of two completely different states into one. The overwhelmingly white-dominated state of New Granada, with its substantial and sophisticated middle class lording it over prosperous uplands, was a world apart from much more tropical, lawless and largely non-white Venezuela. New Granada was ruled by the fussy, legalistic, scheming Santander; Venezuela was divided into a set of fiefdoms dominated by Bolívar's old commanders – with Páez as first among equals, but including Mariño, Arismendi, Bermúdez and Urdaneta. New Granada was a state in which politics flourished and Congress was tetchy, assertive and difficult; Venezuela was, essentially, a territory carved up among regional warlords.

Santander, as Bolívar's vice-president, was nominally in charge of both regions and clumsily attempted to exert his authority over Venezuela. One of his first acts in this respect was to have one of the most brutal of the warlords, the black Venezuelan colonel, Leonardo Infante, one of the butchers in the 'war to the death' in Venezuela, sentenced to death as a deterrent to others. Santander, at the head of his troops, personally attended the execution.

This incensed the Venezuelan leaders and when Santander issued an order that all men between the ages of 16 and 50 be called up for military service, few Venezuelans obeyed. Páez, seeking to obey his nominal chief, then forcibly pressganged thousands, his troops breaking into people's houses – which in turn appalled the legalistic Santander. Seizing his chance, he ordered Páez to abandon his command and come to Santa Fé de Bogotá to face charges.

The disorganized, rough-hewn, but canny llanero chieftain wrote to Bolívar imploring that he return to rescue the country from its divisions – and implicitly from Santander's misrule. As the Liberator rode northwards again across the Andean passes, receiving tumultuous welcomes in such places as Quito and even Pasto, he threatened to turn against Santander unless the latter agreed to a revision of the Colombian constitution to allow the Bolívarist stamp of firm government to be imposed upon it. Santander, realizing that he would need Bolívar's support in any confrontation with Páez, was forced to back down. Bolívar was determined at last to impose his will upon his own creation, knowing that while Santander and the fractious constitutionalists of Santa Fé de Bogotá might resent this, they could not resist him.

Santander rode out to meet Bolívar on his approach to the capital at the town of Tocaima and after a few chilling moments between these two men, Santander made a series of diplomatic concessions. He accepted Bolívar's demand for constitutional revision provided that the latter rejected Páez's call for Bolívar to become dictator, and ruled out Sucre as vice-president of Colombia. Bolívar unwisely agreed to all of this, thus failing to win over the scheming Santander but incensing his two principal allies, Páez and Sucre.

After the agreement, the devious Santander returned to the capital, where he continued to stir up anti-Bolívar sentiment. He put it about that the Liberator was coming to seize power; and instead of triumphal arches to welcome him, slogans were put up declaring 'Viva la Constitucion!' Bolívar was so incensed when an official rode out from the city to let him know of these events that he spurred his horse onwards and rode into the capital in pouring rain in the middle of the night, his first entry there for five years. In the face of opposition Bolívar suppressed his anger and, standing in his stirrups, yelled 'Viva La Republica! Viva its distinguished vice-president [Santander]! Viva la Constitucion!' Within a few days Bolívar was beginning to win over the city's leading politicians; and Santander was forced to submit to the idea of a confederation between Colombia, Peru and Bolivia.

When news of the agreement reached Páez, who had the backing of the ever-rebellious Mariño, the old llanero chief raised the standard of open rebellion against not just Santander but Bolívar as well. In Puerto Cabello, Cumana and Valencia there were revolts, while the old rogue shed his glorious general's uniform and donned his old llanero garb, riding from Caracas to the llanos, raising the spectacle once again of a cowboy racial war against the privileged white castes. Bolívar had few illusions about Páez in 1827: 'General Páez is the most ambitious and vain man in the world: he has no desire to obey, only to command . . . I regard him as the most dangerous man for Colombia.'

Páez, who had suggested that Bolívar should take the crown of Napoleon in the first place, now accused his old chief of seeking it for himself and suddenly another civil war loomed over the land that had shed so much blood over the past 15 years. Bolívar showed that he had lost none of his old ferocity in his first declaration to his former comrade-in-arms:

> You have conquered with me. You have won glory and fortune with me, and you have been able to hope for everything with me. On the contrary, General Labatut lost against me; General Castillo lost; General Piar lost against me; General Mariño lost against me; General Riva-Aguero lost, and General Torre Tagle lost against me. It seems that Providence condemns my enemies to perdition, whether they be Americans or Spaniards. And you see to what Generals Sucre, Santander and Santa Cruz have been elected to.

Bolívar rode down towards Lake Maracaibo. On crossing the border he offered Páez an olive branch: he could take part in the new constitutional assembly. Páez grasped at it, and declared that Bolívar, far from coming to wage war against the llaneros, was coming as a simple citizen: 'The Liberator, from the center of Peru, heard our clamors and has flown to our aid . . . he comes for our happiness – not to destroy the civil and military authority that I have received from the people, but to aid us with his counsel, with his wisdom and experience; to perfect the work of our reforms . . . Venezuelans! Forget your troubles: The Great Bolívar is with us.'

Bolívar replied acidly:

I shudder when I think, as I am always thinking, of the horrible calamity that endangers Colombia. I see clearly our work destroyed and the maledictions of the centuries falling on our heads as perverse authors of such lamentable mutations . . .

Your proclamation says that I am 'coming as a simple citizen'. And what could I do as a citizen? Who has dissolved the laws of Colombia? . . . Who shall tear the reins from my hands? Your friends! The infamy would be a thousand times greater for the ingratitude than for its treason. I cannot believe it. I shall never believe that you carry the ambitions of your friends and the dishonor of your name to this point. It is not possible, General, that you want to see me humiliated for the sake of a handful of deserters whom we have never seen in battle . . . What do not all owe me in Venezuela? Do not even you owe me your existence? . . .

I have come from Peru to spare you the crime of civil war. I have come that Caracas and Venezuela may not stain themselves with precious blood. And you want me to come without any legal authority? . . . There is no other legitimate authority in Venezuela but mine. I mean supreme authority . . . You have your command from municipalities, born from three assassinations. There is nothing glorious in this, my dear general . . .

I want to set myself right. I want to know if you obey me or not and if my patria recognizes me as its chief. May God forbid that my authority is questioned on my own hearth . . . I will yield everything for glory; but I will also combat everything for it . . .

Dear General, you will be everything to me, everything, everything. I want nothing for myself. Thus you will be everything, without taking it at the cost of my glory, which has been founded on duty and public good . . . Be assured of the affection with which I love you from my heart.

The Liberator rode to Puerto Cabello, the port of Páez's headquarters in Valencia. On New Year's Day, 1827, he announced a pardon for Páez's men and recognized the old warrior as supreme military and civil authority in Venezuela, in exchange for Páez's acceptance of Bolívar's authority as president of Colombia. Bolívar took the road to Valencia, where, in the mountains of Naguanagua, the two old comrades met in a fiercely emotional embrace, before riding back to Caracas, where it had all started, in triumph.

The Liberator had come home at last. Bolívar and Páez rode together in an open coach, with flowers poured upon them and cannons, bells and bugles sounded. It was a fitting climax to another incredible journey: in four months, since leaving Lima, Bolívar had travelled 1,356 leagues on horseback. Now he had defused a civil war. The climax of his reconciliation with Páez was a ceremony in which Bolívar entrusted to him the jewel-encrusted sword he had been given at Potosí in Bolivia. Páez wept with gratitude:

> He has given me the sword which has liberated a world . . . How can I preserve its laurels, its glory, its honour? It demands of me strength which only Bolívar possesses. It bewilders me. The redeeming sword of humanity! . . . In my hands this sword shall never be other than Bolívar's. His will shall direct it, my arm shall carry it. I shall perish a hundred times and all my blood shall be spilled before it shall leave my hands or ever attempt to shed the blood it has liberated . . . Bolívar's sword is in my hands . . . For him I will go with it to eternity.

However, Bolívar had broken all his pledges to Santander: sent to put down Páez's insurrection, he had ended up by recognizing it; sent to assert the authority of the government of the two states that comprised Colombia, he had recognized Páez's unchallenged authority in Venezuela, subordinate only to the Liberator himself, and had virtually acknowledged the independence of Venezuela. Bolívar, who had created Colombia, was now presiding over its dissolution. For Santander it was the last straw: Bolívar had abandoned his side of the bargain. The politician and legalist who had just, in spite of his deep dislike, managed to remain on speaking terms with Bolívar, now became his implacable enemy.

Bolívar's excuse was that his actions were justified to save Venezuela from bloodshed, but he had blundered appallingly for he should never have taken Santander's side in the first place. Santander's view was that, if the newly liberated lands were to prosper, the law had to take precedence over the sword; and Bolívar, himself a man of the sword, had elevated its status above that of the rule of law.

Bolívar was to pay a personal price for his accommodation with Páez. His old touch had deserted him at last. Santander now openly joined the ranks of Bolívar's enemies in Santa Fé de Bogotá, spurring on demonstrations against his deal with Páez. In hindsight, the episode marked the turning point for Bolívar's fortunes. In substituting compromise for his old fire, accommodation in place of determination in the cause of what was right, he for the first time displayed weakness – which Páez and the other warlords were quick to seize upon. The grim determination that he had practised in the war against Spain was missing in his attempt to enforce constitutional rule upon the tough old warrior who had confronted him.

Henceforth his attempt to keep New Granada and Venezuela in the same union were doomed – if they were ever practical at all – as were his attempts to impose his own constitutional settlement. Where Spanish butchers had quailed before Bolívar, the fractious politicians of New Granada and Venezuela shrugged him off. To the simple-minded, Bolívar continued to rule half a continent; to the politicians just below him, he had been the vehicle of their deliverance from Spain, certainly, but otherwise merely an interfering soldier whose grandiose schemes kept butting into their own comfortable parochial ambitions. He was trying to bridge two irreconcilables, although his aim of avoiding fresh civil war was admirable. Perhaps the blame did indeed lie with him for trying to forge a unitary state out of two completely different countries.

A few days later word reached Santander of a rebellion by a New Granadan officer, José Bustamante, against the patriot garrison in Lima (which Manuela, dressing as a soldier and infiltrating the garrison, had tried to avert before being seized and put on a ship to Guayaquil where she tried unsuccessfully to seduce Córdova, the hero of Ayacucho). Andrés Santa Cruz put down the insurrection, but Bustamente fled to Guayaquil where he instigated another revolt, successfully this time. Santander, if he did not actually instigate the revolt, celebrated with parties in Santa Fé de Bogotá.

In Lima, the old Peruvian aristocracy used the pretext of the revolt to block the Bolívarist constitution only six months after it had been promulgated and Marshal La Mar was elected president of Peru in place of Bolívar's nominee, Santa Cruz. The radical had been blocked by the old guard. Santander's support of the revolt incensed Bolívar. 'Santander is perfidious . . . I have no confidence in either his morality or his heart,' he declared. Bitterly he wrote to Santander that he sought no more help from him; and Santander, 'in the serenity inspired by innocence' promised to send none.

The colossal empire created by Bolívar was now beginning to crumble on all sides. He had temporarily arrested its decay in Venezuela; but Peru was now shrugging off his control and New Granada was openly disloyal. In the country and capital of his birth, meanwhile, where his bloodiest victories had been won, Bolívar knew that his achievement was beginning to disintegrate. He distracted himself with his assiduous attention to family affairs, which was one of the more endearing traits of this most promiscuous of men. He had adopted the orphaned children of his dead brother, Juan Vicente. He was not particularly close to one of his sisters, Juana (although he adored her daughter, Benigna), but very fond of the other, María Antonia. She, who had managed the family properties in his absence, was plagued by a feckless son, Anacleto, who had abandoned his wife and children, immersed himself in shady political activities and piled up huge gambling debts. To him, Bolívar played the stern uncle:

> It pains me to be forced to address thus one to whom I have always written so affectionately. I am tired of hearing the complaints of your mother and family. If you cannot provide for that family, at least you needn't discredit it as you are doing in Bogotá. I tell you for the last time, if you don't leave Bogotá at once and give up these vices, I shall disinherit you . . . Doesn't it shame you, considering that you are my nephew, having for a mother a woman of the finest character, to be inferior to so many poor guerrillas who have no other family than the fatherland?

Less admirably he forced his ward Felicia, daughter of his deceased older brother, to marry one of his mulatto officers, General Laurencio

Silva, possibly because he wanted to show that race was of no consequence to his bloodline, for political purposes. Even in that era of arranged marriages his threat to disinherit her was brutal in an attempt to force her into what she regarded as a shameful union. She submitted to what was to prove a deeply unhappy marriage.

On 5 July 1827, Bolívar, having learnt of an abortive rebellion in Bolivia stoked up by La Mar in Lima and General Gamarra – whom he had cuckolded when in Cuzco – left La Guaira in the British frigate *Druid* accompanied by Sir Alexander Cockburn, the British ambassador. It was the anniversary of the Venezuelan declaration of independence. He was never to return to the city of his birth, to which he had given its freedom.

Chapter 24

SHOWDOWN WITH SANTANDER

Bolívar was on his way to his final showdown with Santander, his old comrade, rival and now hated enemy. To those who had seen him in Caracas it was apparent that a change had come over the Liberator. He looked prematurely aged for his nearly 44 years. His eyes were sunk in his colourless, cadaverous face, his cheeks were hollow. He was still capable of sudden bursts of immense energy and charm; but he often fell into lassitude and irritability. His incorrigible optimism was exhausted.

Yet he still had unmatchable style. Arriving at Cartagena, he travelled up the Magdalena, where he had staged his first successful military campaign. As he approached Santa Fé de Bogotá, Santander, panic-stricken, considered fleeing the capital and leading a rebellion. But when Bolívar appeared, he embraced the fearful and embarrassed Santander, and took charge as president, in spite of the hostility of the leaders of the capital.

He summoned Manuela, who from Guayaquil had travelled to Quito, with his usual warmth. 'Your goodness and graces reanimate the ice of my years. Your love animates a life which is expiring . . . Come, come, come.' She came without further prompting, taking up residence in a house in front of the Church of San Carlos. She also used Bolívar's country estate outside the capital at Quinta de Portocarrero, entertaining the leaders of New Granadan society. Just under the mountains, this was a delightful, spacious retreat with extensive gardens and trees.

Latin Americans have tended to gloss over Bolívar's relationship with women as though this was an example of testosterone-fuelled

Latin American men at best, and at worst merely an embarrassment in such a great man. Yet his sexual behaviour was unusual even for his time – offensive and unconventional in a lesser man, it flouted even the low standards permitted of great, rich and powerful men. The commonly accepted version is that, after the death of his first love, his beloved wife María Teresa, whom he knew for less than three years and was married to for only eight months, his heart never mended – he became married to his cause of liberating Venezuela and Spanish America. He supposedly embarked on his remarkable string of sexual conquests to indulge his frisky nature while he did great things.

Needless to say, this is not a satisfactory explanation, either of the callous way he behaved towards many women (he was, though, always as courteous in dumping them as in seducing them) or of a sexual odyssey which in some ways mirrored his complex, intellectual, political and military journeys. Even in contemporary Latin America, male machismo was to some extent harnessed to at least a few rules: it was acceptable, even expected of a married man of Bolívar's class to have a mistress or two, and to resort to prostitutes for entertainment, provided this was carried out discreetly. Marriage by contrast was a financial and dynastic commitment. It was unusual for an aristocratic young man of immense fortune not to wed at all again after so brief a marriage, if only to produce heirs: a man like Bolívar, descended from one of the top families, extremely rich, well educated and soon a military hero and a superstar, who was also good-looking and charming, would have been immensely desirable for any aristocratic young woman and her family.

He defied convention in this as in everything else. Bolívar had clearly inherited a powerful sexual urge from his father, who was notorious in pursuing young girls, dependants and even servants. But after María Teresa's death Simón seemed to prefer to keep his sexual relations at a purely superficial level, avoiding commitment, consorting with women of pleasure and with women attracted by his fame. His explanation that he was so in love with María Teresa he could betroth no other is the stuff of juvenile romantic pulp, not the hard-headed man that Bolívar soon became, and simply does not ring true. The worldly, maternal and perhaps somewhat blasé Fanny de Villars was his first serious confidante, but he spurned her fairly abruptly on leaving Paris (he may have had a child by her, which suggests he was not impotent, although given the frequency of his relationships he should have had many more). After that it was just short-lived dalliances until he encountered Josefina Machado.

The much overlooked Josefina Machado, although not upper class nor particularly beautiful, but obviously sexy, was the first real commitment in his life since María Teresa, as the Venezuelan novelist Gladys Revilla Pérez has observed in her masterpiece *Bolívar y Josefina*. Bolívar's desperate cruise along the coast following the terrible flight from Caracas to Barcelona and his subsequent ignominious expulsion from Venezuela show that he pined for her as for no one else since his wife – earning him the contempt of his own men, who thought he was putting love for a woman above his duty. Tough, bossy and impulsive, although attractive, she was in a sense Bolívar's first real wife – and she set something of a pattern.

While he passed through countless girlfriends, groupies and prostitutes in assembly-line fashion, it was the ones that stood up to him, that were stronger, that interested him and were to prove the more lasting. He seemed to crave a fighter, an equal, even a superior who could give him the maternal embrace he felt he was denied after his mother's death when he was aged seven; he had also been intensely spoilt as a youth and craved affection and admiration. His lover, protector and benefactor in Jamaica, Julia Cobier, was intelligent, older and maternal and possibly not so alluring as many others. He may have had a mercenary motive in courting her; but she lasted longer than most for the usually fly-by-night Bolívar. He had a relationship with the ugly, formidable and bossy Francisca Zubiaga de Gamarra in Cuzco, Peru: he was clearly attracted to powerful women alongside beautiful, undemanding ones such as his voluptuous girlfriend Anita Lenoit in the Magdalena region and Manuela Madroño in the Peruvian Andes. It was not until he encountered Manuela Sáenz that he met his match – a combination of lithe sensuality with firmness of character.

What in his makeup made him indulge in fleeting pleasures most of the time, and shun long-term relationships, and above all marriage, to seek out stronger and often older women for medium-term ones? This must be a fount for speculation alone: but it is not uncommon for powerful, driven men to seek strong partners, nor for men who have lost parents at an early age to seek substitutes. A man of his wealth, initially, and fame later, could satisfy his sexual needs easily in those days. At the same time as he seemed addicted to fleeting female companionship, though, he was desperate to avoid commitment. Why? Possibly the loss of his parents, possibly the loss of María Teresa, which a romantic like him could not afford to endure again, possibly because he enjoyed sexual variety for its own sake, and possibly because his lust for glory militated against getting tied down to a family and children – although it was astonishing that he never felt the urge for dynastic succession to consolidate his own greatness, as virtually every other great historical figure has done throughout history. It was probably a mixture of all these.

Was there any link with his manic, unstoppable personality, his drive to succeed? He wanted sexual relationships but he wanted to be unencumbered by the burden of commitment and a family. His quasi-clinical attitude to women was at one with his indifference to human suffering and ruthlessness to win a war. Yet he was capable of great tenderness, at least for relatively short spells, and even submitted to the two principal – and strongest – women in his life, Josefina and, even more so, Manuela. The great puzzle in his psyche remains his ferocious drive to succeed, given that he could have led the life of an immensely wealthy man tending his estates (Miranda's drive is easy to understand, as an immigrant 'Canary Islander', regarded as from a lower caste originally by the Spanish and the Venezuelan criollos). The answer, perhaps, lies in his formidable vision and intellect: like George Washington, another man who succeeded to wealth early, money was not enough – he realized he could use that wealth and his abilities to secure a place in history. With such ambitions, wives and family were mere encumbrances. Perhaps it was as simple as that.

The old glamour of Simón and Manuela that had so illuminated Lima still shone briefly in Santa Fé de Bogotá. An eyewitness describes a reception at their house:

The dining-room, between two gardens with wide bay windows, was an elegant room in the shape of an ellipse; and had the four seasons painted *al fresco* on its walls. At the head, a portrait of Bolívar crowned by two genii and this inscription: Bolívar is the God of Colombia. The Libertador sat alone, that is with no one right or left, at the head of the table which was set for thirty persons. Some of those present drank toasts to Colombia and to Bolívar without excess flattery but fully expressing their feelings towards their hero.

Bolívar heard them all with his usual indifference but with that mobility of eyes and body which was so typical of his character. And as champagne was served, he raised his glass and answered them all in short sparkling phrases which aroused general enthusiasm. As soon as he sat down, he was surrounded by his guests who, full of admiration, were eager to come close to him and touch his glass; they acclaimed him loudly and embraced him effusively. He, seeing himself mobbed, nearly smothered, stepped on to a chair and then on to a table and with long paces walked from one end to the other breaking plates and cups and upsetting bottles. The tumultuous crowd seized him at the other end and carried him in triumph to the reception hall.

But there were rumbles of distant thunder. In October 1827 there were reports of fresh fighting in western Venezuela and Bolívar toyed briefly with travelling there. In February 1828, a squadron of Spanish warships went from Puerto Rico to the Venezuelan coast and royalist sympathizers rose in the region. Bolívar set out for the Venezuelan border, but the uprising was suppressed before he got there. In Cartagena there was an uprising by Admiral José Padilla and Bolívar set out once again, but the revolt was quickly quelled.

The final journey in Bolívar's life passage had now begun: after being a formidable and spirited fighter for the interests of his own class, after acquiring the common touch and becoming a man of the people leading a guerrilla army, after occupying a vast empire and then renouncing absolute power, as well as commanding great mountain armies, he embarked on a career as a politician and administrator – and was found wanting. This does not detract from his career as a statesman: he was a profound visionary who had formulated the ideals which govern Latin America today – the need to reconcile different races, to balance decisive government with popular rights and extreme wealth with extreme poverty, and to promote Latin American co-operation so as to create an authoritative and powerful voice for the continent to match those of the United States and Britain. In all of these he was far ahead of his time, which was probably the reason why they failed.

No previous great leader possessed such global vision – certainly not Napoleon, whose cynical protestations of idealism were surely a mask for his own self-aggrandizement, promotion of the interests of himself and his family, and further, ever-expanding conquest. Bolívar was no cynic, but a highly intelligent and progressive idealist blessed, as very few such men are, with the precious abilities as a commander to attempt to fulfil his ideals: it was as though More, Locke, Rousseau or Kant had been superb generals as well as philosophers.

However, as a day-to-day, election-winning politician and administrator – the very mundane ordering of peaceful states that his own republican ideals had ushered in – he was simply no good. In part this was because he was too bright a star, too controversial a figure, dwarfing his opponents, and inviting them to combine against his otherwise effortless domination. Also, he represented the military power in the state – which had won the wars of liberation against Spain, but would bedevil the development of plodding democratic principles in Latin America for a century and a half. Finally, this restless, energetic, brilliant man of action simply did not have the patience for vote-grubbing, deal-making and administration necessary to govern a peaceful, well-ordered society.

He was overturned by two opposites: Francisco de Paula Santander, skilled in the low arts of politics and administration, who had appealed to local political interests in defiance of Bolívar's grandiose pan-American visions; and Antonio Páez, a crafty, illiterate country thug who had to be taught how to eat with a knife and fork. Against these a man reared on the Enlightenment, philosophy and the great salons of Madrid, London and Paris could not prevail. Confronted by the parochial scheming of these two lesser men, Bolívar could fall back only his military reputation and dwindling band of supporters.

His idealism fell on stony ground and his great creation of a liberal and loosely confederated Latin America fell apart. As we shall see, he found himself forced into the most abject decision of his life, like

Oliver Cromwell, of intervening as a dictator backed by military force against the decisions of an elected parliament – the very negation of everything he had stood for. He had no stomach for it, and ruled with a light hand – thereby exchanging his old reputation as a ferocious and indomitable strongman for an image as a hen-pecked, ailing weakling. He was nearly killed in an assassination attempt, before abdicating power after just two years. If he had resorted to repression, he could have survived in power many more years, but that would have been to betray what he believed in. It would have represented an inglorious end to a career which had blazed across the heavens. Instead, he bowed out of his own accord, to die with honour almost intact in great disillusion, although it would be decades before he was recognized as a father to his people and the demi-god of his continent.

Having, in the end, rejected ruthlessness and ambition, he fell victim to political hacks equipped with the peculiar small-minded ruthlessness and ambition of their nature. This was to be the final irony, yet perhaps it was also his ultimate glory that after a career steeped in blood, he decided not to perpetuate his power through shedding even more, but to bow out as a meek constitutionalist, providing a shining example for Latin America – which it was not to follow for a century and a half.

In early 1828 in Ocaña, the convention he had so long sought to implement his new constitution was assembling, and Bolívar, on his way back from Cartagena, decided to stay in the town of Bucaranaga, some 90 miles from the city. The struggle between him and Santander had now become a fight to the finish.

At the Convention of Ocaña, there were 23 supporters of Santander, 21 of Bolívar, and 18 independents. Santander stood for federalism and decentralization, Bolívar for a strong, if democratic, central government. Santander, addressing the Convention insisted he had 'the heart of a tiger', but as O'Leary commented caustically, he took this to mean arrogance, a fierce nature and a thick skin. For once, though, Bolívar was not fighting on his chosen ground. Santander, with unceasing energy and astuteness, had travelled the land securing the election of his 'federalist' supporters. He had considerable support throughout New Granada and in Venezuela, too, which ought to have been loyal to Bolívar. Santander, with the archness of the seasoned politician pronounced: 'In my profession one avoids fighting a powerful and well entrenched enemy in the field when there is hope of destroying him with skirmishes, surprises, ambushes and all kinds of hostilities.'

The Convention of Ocaña began its deliberations on 9 April 1828. Its president, casting a beady eye on Bolívar camped just a couple of day's ride away like some predatory eagle, intimidating the delegates, counselled pointedly that, 'I hope seduction and terror cannot penetrate these walls.'

Bolívar despatched a moderate appeal to the delegates. 'Colombians [the last congress] busied itself with its rights, not its duties. We have made the legislature alone the sovereign government, when it should be no more than a member of the sovereign government ... We subordinated the executive to it and gave it a much greater part in the general administration than legitimate interests allow.' Agriculture, industry and commerce, he said, were in a deplorable state. 'A firm, powerful and just government is the call of the nation. Put it on its feet over the ruins of the desert which despotism has left pale with fright, 15,000 heroes weeping who have died for her, whose blood sown in the fields gave birth to its rights. Give us a government in which the law is obeyed, the magistracy respected and the people are free.'

He argued that a strong constitutional government was the best guarantee of freedom. He was deeply reluctant to intervene directly to close down the congress, and it is to his credit that he resisted the temptation: the army was on his side, as were the ordinary people, but the deputies represented the upper and middle classes, and Santander pandered to what they sought: power for themselves as petty local potentates, resistance to strong central control from Bogotá – a message even more effective in Bolívar's native Venezuela than in the scattered provincial centres of New Granada. Santander rejected any attempt to invite the Liberator to attend the proceedings: 'The man has a blinding and hypnotic presence. I myself have experienced it. Many times, going into his presence, angry and with well-formed and just proposals, I have left disarmed and full of admiration. No man living can oppose Bolívar face to face.'

As the Convention adopted a federalist, congress-dictated constitution, Bolívar could only wring his hands in frustration. Peru de
Lacroix, his military aide at the time, described him as increasingly
solitary and irritable, losing his temper when he lost at cards. He
remained as driven as ever, rising early, going to bed late, eating
little, drinking only two glasses of wine at meals, fastidious as ever in
personal hygiene, exercising conscientiously.

In a bid to secure the support of New Granada's powerful clergy he
showed a pronounced religious streak, attending Mass every morning. O'Leary for one was surprised: 'Bolívar was a complete atheist. Notwithstanding, he thought religion necessary for government.
His indiscretion, which was very great at all times, knew no bounds
when he spoke of religion, which he used to ridicule in a disgusting
manner. At mass he was sure to have some book or other in his hand
and sometimes a gazette.' He also asserted his civilian credentials by
shedding his uniform, wearing white trousers, a blue coat, a broad-
brimmed cap and his familiar cavalry boots.

He seethed with impatience and resentment towards Santander:

> They are all in my hands. A mere signal from me would exter-
> minate them all. Yet, in my place, they would not only give the
> signal to kill me but also all my friends, partisans and anyone who
> doesn't hold their opinions. Such are our so-called liberals – cruel,
> bloody, frenetic, intolerant and covering their crimes with the
> word 'liberty'! They believe themselves as justified in their crimes
> as the Inquisitors and all who have shed human blood in the name
> of God and religion believed themselves justified in theirs.
>
> Individual interests, ambitions, rivalries, necessity, provincial-
> ism, thirst for vengeance and other miserable passions animate our
> demagogues and unite them now to overthrow existing form; but
> afterwards they will only separate, and establish their partial sover-
> eignties, and govern the people as slaves and with the old Spanish
> system.

Like Cromwell, he watched in horror as the elected government he believed in so manifestly failed in its task, knowing that if
he moved against it he would be substituting constitutional chaos

for a dictatorship – something almost as abhorrent to him. But he responded to the inevitable. Almost certainly on his orders, the delegates faithful to him walked out of the assembly, depriving it of a quorum. The old constitution lay dead, and the new one was thus strangled at birth.

In the vacuum, both the army and leading citizens called on Bolívar to take power, as he knew they would and he did so as dictator, pending the summoning of a new constitutional convention two years later. The great republican and champion of liberal reform, albeit administered by a strong central government, was now briefly a tinpot military dictator, overriding the wishes of the people, one of the first to plague the continent. The Liberator had metamorphosed into autocrat and his reluctance was heartfelt, for he feared that the bearer of freedom would now go down in history as a despot: 'Remember what I say. Colombia will be lost because of the lack of ambition of its leader. He has no love for command and nearly any inclination for glory and abhors more the title of ambitious man than death and tyranny . . . Under a dictatorship, who can talk of freedom? Let us pity both the people who obey and the man who rules alone.'

It was hardly a stirring call; but it was genuine enough. The man who had experienced the glory of having a continent at his feet at Potosí hardly craved the pleasure of ruling a small part as dictator. His ambition now was to consolidate the surviving part of his achievement and endow it with good government.

At first, Bolívar ruled with a light hand. Santander was appointed ambassador to Washington, although he delayed his departure. There was no suppression of the press and his opponents were free to continue their political activities. Old Culo de Hierro – Iron Bottom – was not, it seemed, made of stern enough stuff to suppress his fellow countrymen. In any event more pressing problems loomed. In another mortal blow to his dream of a free America, the reactionary government of General La Mar in Peru had now seized its opportunity not just of throwing off the Colombian yoke, but of asserting its own ambition of a greater Peru by invading Upper Peru, now Bolivia.

Sucre, Bolívar's protégé and surrogate son, a fine and steely commander in battle, was an extraordinarily merciful and generous commander in peacetime. When an assassination attempt was made upon him, he pardoned the would-be killer from the death penalty, and gave him the money to go into exile. He was compassionate, but hardly a man to inspire fear. Faced by this threat and conscious of the inferiority of his forces, Sucre announced that Colombian 'occupation' forces would be withdrawn from the country. But, at the Peruvians' instigation, an insurrection broke out in the barracks of Chuquisaca in April 1828, and Sucre was badly injured by a bullet that hit his right arm and another that grazed his head.

Using this as a pretext, Augustín Gamarra sent troops over the border to 'protect the precious life of the Marshal of Ayacucho [Sucre] and free the country from factions and anarchy'. Shortly afterwards Sucre resigned as president and departed. This most romantic of Bolívar's lieutenants now married a beautiful girl from Quito, María Carcelén y Larrea, the Marchioness of Solanda, and left for 'retirement' in his early thirties. O'Leary sheds light on this strange man:

> Sucre was a very vain man, but he had reason to be so. He was superior to most public men that I have met with in America. In his principles he was liberal, but no republican. The last words he ever said to me were: 'Tell the Liberator to concentrate all the troops he can dispose of and not to allow himself to be dictated to by anyone. Tell him that now is the time to save the country and, if he thinks that the monarchic form is what Colombia wants, let him say it and he shall not need men who will support him.

Bolivia was now to have two presidents murdered and a third installed in the space of five days – an unstable tradition that endures in Bolivia to this day, retaining its record of having more presidents than years of independence.

Tensions grew alarmingly between Peru and Colombia, as Bolívar moved his forces to the frontier and La Mar assembled his troops. Bolívar was also beset by other minor rebellions – one in Popayán, another in Venezuela. In Cartagena, José Padilla staged a black revolt aimed at installing Santander, but this collapsed. Most woundingly General Córdova, the young hero of Ayacucho, also raised the standard of revolt against the dictator in Antioquia, but was killed by a British legionnaire – although almost certainly not on Bolívar's orders – and O'Leary crushed the rebels there. O'Leary wrote of Córdova: 'His vanity was unbounded and his knowledge of the world limited . . . fighting like a lion, he fell and expired sternly, proud and unrepentant'.

The cobbled, steep streets of Santa Fé de Bogotá, under a towering 1,000-foot cordillera at the far end of an extensive saucer-like fertile plain 9,000 feet up in the Andes, were deserted after nightfall on 28 September 1828. But in the house of one Luis Vargas Tejada, a large number of men had gathered, in concert with the commanders of an artillery battalion, the adjutant-general of the armed forces, Lieutenant Colonel Pedro Carujo, and two civilian leaders, Agustin Horment and Florentino González, leading lights of 'committees of public safety' that had been set up in opposition to Bolívar.

The committee had been tacitly approved by the army chief of staff, Colonel Ramón Guerra, and by Santander himself, who took no active part and wanted a coup to take place after he had left to take up his post in the United States. As González put it: 'It was necessary that blood should flow, as had occurred in all the great insurrections of people against tyrants. I find myself in a critical position to carry out that hard resolution.' The plot was hurriedly brought forward when one of the conspirators, blind drunk, revealed the plot to a loyal officer. Twelve civilians and 25 soldiers, under the orders of Carujo, went at midnight to break into the government palace and seize Bolívar dead or alive. They killed two guard dogs outside, stabbed the sentries and forced their way upstairs, badly injuring Ibarra, Bolívar's personal bodyguard. A young British legionnaire, William Ferguson (who had previously ridden from Lima to Chuquisaca to deliver Bolivia's constitution), was stabbed to death defending the door to Bolívar's room against the conspirators.

Manuela Sáenz, who was with the Liberator, takes up the story:

It was midnight when the dogs of the Liberator started barking furiously and I heard a strange noise which must have been the killing of the sentries. I woke the Liberator, and the first thing he did was to take up his sword and a pistol and try to open the door. I held him back and made him dress, which he did calmly and quickly. He said, 'Good. Now I am dressed. What shall we do? Fight back?' He tried to open the door and I prevented him.

Then something he himself had told me occurred to me. 'Didn't you say to Pepe Paris that this would be a good window to jump from?' (The room was on the first floor.) 'You're right,' he told me, and went to the window. I prevented him from jumping because people were passing, but I gave him the signal when there were no people and because the door was being forced.

I went to intercept them to give him time to flee, but I didn't have time to see him jump, nor to shut the window. When they saw me they seized me. 'Where is Bolívar?' I said he was in the council chamber, which was the first thing that came into my head. They searched the outer room carefully, went into the bedroom, and seeing the open window, exclaimed, 'He has escaped. He has saved himself.'

I told them, 'No, gentlemen, he has not escaped. He is in the council room.' 'And why is this window open?' 'I have just opened it, because I wanted to know what the noise was.' Some believed me, some didn't. They went back into the other room, felt the warm bed, and became more dejected still, although I told them I had been resting there, waiting that he should emerge from the council chamber to give him a bath.

One rebel wanted to kill her. Instead, she was beaten so badly with the flat of a sword she spent the next 12 days in bed. Bolívar, carrying his pistol and his sword, was joined by his loyal chief retainer, José Palacio, and the two men made their way through the dark streets, past the sounds of fighting and running men, to the Carmen Bridge across the San Agustin River, where they took refuge under the arches. There he ruefully repeated Miranda's bitter words on being betrayed: 'Hubbub, hubbub, all is hubbub.' After four hours Palacio went to reconnoitre and returned to accompany Bolívar to the headquarters of the loyal Vargas regiment. Order was meanwhile restored.

Bolívar commandeered a horse and with his soldiers went to the plaza, where Manuela, still just on her feet, went to find him and bring him home. 'You are the liberator of the Liberator,' he told her, as he had once told Bermúdez. On the way he prevented the summary beheading of one of his assassins, who had been captured.

He was told: 'These men were going to kill you.' He replied, 'It was the power they were going to kill, not the man.' General Rafael Urdaneta, his most loyal commander, was determined, however, that the ringleaders be executed.

Bolívar insisted on sparing Santander who, although not a plotter, knew of the conspiracy and had taken refuge in Urdaneta's house during the night to avoid a pro-Bolívar lynch mob. Bolívar's bitterest enemy was sent into exile in France, from which he was to return in 1832 to serve a controversial term as Colombia's president. Bolívar seemed to have been rid of his bane at last: his most subtle foe had been vanquished, as had all the others previously.

O'Leary writes this bitter epitaph on Santander's career:

> Santander was one of those men who, of mediocre talents and much daring, but without any morality, raise themselves in the political tumult to distinguished positions ... False, ungrateful, mean, vengeful, cruel, to the extent of attending executions and delighting himself with seeing the blood shed by his orders. His soul was perverse, without value or merit. As a soldier his career was undistinguished; he was despised by his enemies and sneered at by his comrades. Administratively gifted and very hardworking, he was assiduous at his desk, and with these qualities he could have done good for his country, but his vices weakened his actions and he has not left a single monument of public usefulness behind him.

Bolívar, already half the man he was, had been badly shaken by the assassination and coup attempts. He was demoralized and, suffering badly from the damp and chill of spending four hours in the river, his chest and lungs were in a poor state.

The French ambassador went to see him shortly afterwards. His face was 'long and yellow ... of gaunt appearance, with a cotton cap, wrapped in his cloak, with his legs protruding from wide canvas trousers'. He told the ambassador:

> It is not the laws of nature which have put me in this state, but the burdens that weigh upon my heart. My fellow countrymen, who

could not kill me with knives, are now trying to assassinate me morally with their ingratitude and calumnies. When I stop existing, the demagogues will devour each other like wolves, and the edifice I built with superhuman effort will sink into the mud of revolution.

It was a startlingly accurate assessment.

Indeed, in spite of the failure of the insurrection, he was sitting on a tinderbox. Although the people remained with him, the New Granadan oligarchy was against him, deeply hating the Venezuelan soldiery that carried out his orders. His great dream of uniting the two countries had utterly failed and he resorted to desultory repression, banning public gatherings and curbing the hostile press; yet his could hardly be called an intolerant regime, to those who remembered Spanish rule. Of those who had attempted to murder him, only a handful were executed. Nonetheless, he could not conquer his own mortality, nor control what would come after him. He had no sway over the destiny of the countries he had liberated. Yet the glory was not quite over yet. His southern dominions had collapsed with breathtaking speed. Bolivia and Peru were now in hostile hands. But New Granada and Venezuela remained united – just.

With the news that the Peruvian leader La Mar was approaching the frontier with a large army and that New Granadan armies down south had rebelled against Bolívar and were backing the Peruvians, the Liberator exerted himself one last time to protect his achievement. Once more he took to the saddle to march southwards, appointing Sucre, retired in Quito, his commander there. The 8,000-strong army of La Mar had invaded Loja and was advancing on Cuenca.

Sucre, with a force a third its size, moved to intercept him and the Peruvians withdrew to defend positions across the River Saraguro and here Sucre and La Mar initiated negotiations. The latter treacherously took advantage of these suddenly to seek to outflank Sucre's forces by marching on Girón, cutting his communications with Bogotá. Sucre, learning of this in time, moved swiftly towards the same city and despatched two companies to seize the lightly defended Peruvian positions on the Saraguro, which they did easily.

The two armies shadowed each other, each trying to do battle on favourable terrain, as far as Portete de Tarqui, which La Mar occupied on 26 February 1829. There the following day Sucre's small but ordered army advanced on the enemy trenches and, after a brief battle, the Peruvians fled. When the weary and ailing Bolívar reached Quito, his adopted son was able to hand him the lances of the enemy seized in battle. However, they learnt that La Mar was raising a new army in Piura.

This proved too much for the Peruvian general's colleagues to stomach. Fearful that Bolívar and Sucre would seize upon this as a pretext to reinvade Peru, Gamarra deposed La Mar and concluded an armistice with the Liberator, over the protests of his scorned, Bolívar-hating wife. More good news reached the Liberator on this, his last campaign: his other faithful lieutenant, Santa Cruz, had seized power in Bolivia, throwing off the Peruvian yoke and restoring the Bolívarist constitution. Santa Cruz is regarded by Bolivians as their greatest president. Meanwhile, General Juan José Flores, another loyalist, had arrested the rebel Bustamante, and regained control of Guayaquil and all of Ecuador.

Rumours were buzzing around Colombia that the Liberator (and dictator) had taken a step backwards: he was said to be contemplating placing a European prince on the throne of Colombia as his successor. The truth was somewhat different, representing another throw in the superpower rivalries for influence in Latin America. With Bolívar's physical powers visibly waning, Urdaneta, his strongest and most loyal general, had summoned the leaders of the country to consider a proposal by the British ambassador to install a constitutional monarchy in Colombia after Bolívar. Urdaneta and the others believed that no other form of government would ensure legitimacy and continuity after Bolívar had departed the scene.

It was intended to solicit the approval of the French and British cabinets. A Bavarian prince was considered the most eligible, as not being closely allied to any of the principal potentates of Europe, though the heir of the House of Orléans would be preferable on account of his wealth. Páez had been consulted and, though he did not openly oppose the project, he recommended its being laid aside for the present. Briceño Méndez and Soublette both opposed it, predicting that it would be the cause of a revolution in Venezuela, where Bolívar's enemies would lay hold of it as a pretext. It never was meant that General Bolívar should take the crown, but to have him elected chief magistrate *ad vitam* under the popular title of Libertador. After his death the foreign prince was to succeed.

The British plan was designed to increase their own influence at the expense of the United States, who supported Santander's loose republicanism. But Urdaneta and his allies believed such a prince should be Latin, Catholic and non-Spanish – which pointed towards France – something which held little appeal for the British.

Bolívar, in distant Guayaquil, with some of his old optimism restored by events in the south, was also far from enthusiastic about espousing the principle against which he had laboured all his life, even in constitutional form. He replied with a diplomatic but firm 'no' to the British ambassador, Patrick Campbell:

I do not know what to say to you about this notion, which is fraught with innumerable difficulties. You must know that there is no objection on my part since I am determined to resign at the next congress. But who is to appease the ambition of our leaders and the fear of inequality among the common people? Do you not think that England would be jealous if a Bourbon prince were chosen? Would not all the new American nations oppose it, and also the United States which seems destined by Providence to plague America with torments in the name of freedom? I already seem to detect a general conspiracy against poor Colombia, which is too much envied by all the American republics.

The whole Press would call for a fresh crusade against those guilty of treachery to freedom, of supporting the Bourbons, and of betraying the American system. In the south the Peruvians, on the Isthmus the Guatemalans and Mexicans, and in the Antilles the Americans and the liberals of all parties would kindle the flame of discord. Santo Domingo would not remain passive but would call upon her brothers to make common cause against a prince of France. Everyone would become our enemy, and Europe would do nothing to help us because it is not worth sacrificing a Holy Alliance for the New World.

To the last he had not betrayed his republicanism, as some of his enemies were later to allege from this episode. The idea was quietly shelved. William Henry Harrison, the American envoy in Colombia, went so far as to charge that Bolívar himself aspired to the crown, and unwisely lectured him against the dangers of tyranny; he had to leave hurriedly, before Bolívar expelled him. The Liberator's anger had switched from Britain, which had done little to help him, to the United States, which had done nothing at all.

To his people, Bolívar asserted humorously that no foreign prince would wish to rule so anarchic a land or one so unable to sustain a rich court.

Much has been made by historians about Napoleon and his marshals: the key to the relationship was that, although they obeyed him, they were the only men in that absolutist, dictatorial and imperialist system capable of standing up to him, arguing with him and – as happened in the end – deposing him after military defeat. Many were able military officers, and although subordinate after he obtained absolute power, shared the barrack-room camaraderie of peers. They judged him by the standards of his profession, as Napoleon was essentially a brilliant soldier and administrator, not a visionary, still less a politician.

Bolívar, like Napoleon, lacked the authority of an hereditary divine right of kings which up to then had been the fount of authority in most countries: to begin with, at least, he was one of many tough, determined and intelligent men determined to seize power from the crumbling Spanish empire. Much more so than in already highly centralized France, he had to vie for authority with his counterparts, first with Francisco de Miranda who looked down upon him until he was venomously removed from the scene by Bolívar.

He had to compete with another aristocratic criollo, Santiago Mariño, who regarded himself as Bolívar's military equal and for a long time dominated eastern Venezuela; with José Bermúdez, a canny thug of a man; with the formidable Manuel Piar, who had tried to ignite racial war in the llanos and seize power, and whom Bolívar despatched with firmness and ruthlessness; with the brutal ruler of the island of Margarita, Juan Bautista Arismendi, whom

Bolívar alternately flattered and contained; with his decent and loyal ally Rafael Urdaneta, his chief of staff, who briefly abandoned him towards the end in anger after his nomination of another, Sucre, as his successor; with the militarily brilliant José María Córdova, who also turned against him at the end; with his own favourite, the intelligent and martial Antonio José Sucre, with whom however he argued about the independence of Bolivia and who (like Bolívar himself) sometimes put his own vanity first; and with his two wily allies-turned-enemies, the devious and scheming lawyer-soldier Francisco de Paula Santander and the cunning and fierce José Antonio Páez. These men were his supposed friends.

On the other side there were some of the most formidable and brutal enemies ever faced by a fighting general – Domingo de Monteverde, José Tomás Boves, Francisco Tomás Morales, Pablo Morillo, General Miguel de La Torre, General José de La Mar (eventually), Colonel José Bustamante – a small legion of enemies. Bolívar was never master in his own house, having to assert his authority over the overmighty caudillos on his own side as much as his Spanish enemies: it was a measure of his determination that he did, right until the end.

Bolívar remained in Guayaquil until the summer of 1829. In August he had suffered an attack of 'nervous bile' and for the first time spoke with apparent sincerity of resigning. This was no mere gesture. Bolívar wanted to hand over authority while he was still alive and capable of influencing events from behind the scenes. As he wrote to O'Leary, 'Would it not be better for Colombia and for me, and still more for public opinion, if a president was nominated and I remained a simple general? I would circle around the government as a bull around a herd of cows. I would defend it with all my forces and those of the republic.' He had Sucre in mind.

He wrote to Sucre: 'You fell in love with freedom, and were dazzled by her potent charms. But, since freedom is as dangerous as beauty in women, whom all seduce and desire out of love or vanity, you have not kept her as innocent and pure as when she descended from Heaven. Power, the born enemy of human rights, has excited personal ambition in all classes of the state.'

To his astonishment the young man declined the vice-presidency abandoned by Santander, criticizing Bolívar for summoning the prospective congress of 1830, a reply which bitterly disappointed Bolívar, who chided his protégé for failing to understand that the norms of government must be respected. To some extent revived, after signing a peace treaty with Peru, Bolívar took to the saddle again along the bone-jarring journey from Guayaquil via Pasto to Bogotá. He was comforted by a charming letter from his old comrade-in-arms, Páez, effective dictator of Venezuela, suggesting the two of them return to live at his hacienda in Apure, 'like simple Roman citizens'. Bolívar replied: 'I remain, my beloved general, your grateful friend. The idea has moved me greatly. Would to God I could enjoy the rest of my life in your companionship.'

But the old rogue was even then plotting another shock for the ailing Liberator as he bumped sorely and uncomfortably along the mountain trail from the now pacified southern frontier and the scene of his last triumphs. In November 1829, on the road, he learnt that Páez had insisted that as the New Granadan Santander had held the vice-presidency for so long, now it was the turn of the Venezuelan Páez for the post.

Bolívar temporized, and Páez replied by threatening that Venezuela would break away from the union with New Granada. He vigorously denounced Bolívar for seeking to reimpose the rule of 'absolute kings, conniving with the Holy Alliance; planning to re-establish the Inquisition and slavery; and introducing dukes and counts, marquesses and barons, all of them white, destroying the equality of rights conceded to Indians, blacks and mixed races'. Like Brutus, Bolívar's oldest and best lieutenant had betrayed him: he had put his trust in a fierce, cunning and ultimately unreliable comrade. Páez was making his grab for the succession. The regime of Páez had become ruthless: the vicious Arismendi was the chief of the secret police which penetrated the very huts of the peasants. It was rumoured that the British were backing Páez to forestall plans to impose a French monarch on Colombia.

Chapter 25

PLOUGHING THE SEA

On 15 January 1830, Bolívar re-entered Santa Fé de Bogotá for the last triumphal welcome of his life. An eyewitness described the occasion:

> The streets were decorated as never before. All the regiments of militia of cavalry of the savannah, 3,000 men in all, paraded on the avenue from Santa Victoria towards the palace. You can be sure that anyone who had a horse or could obtain one came out to meet him. The balconies, windows and towers were full of people.
>
> But in this great multitude sad silence rather than animation reigned. The bursts of artillery, the church bells sounded without producing happiness. The instinct of the masses was that they were witnessing the solemn funeral of the great republic rather than the entry of its glorious founder. Almost certainly even his bitterest enemies were moved, patriotism overshadowing the illegitimate feeling of party rancour.
>
> When Bolívar appeared, I saw tears being shed. Pale, emaciated, his eyes, shining and expressive in his good days, were now extinguished. His voice was hollow, barely audible. The profile of his face – all in the end, suggested the imminent collapse of his body and the approaching beginning of eternal life, which excited real sympathy.

His final long journey had almost wasted him. He told Manuela, who had ridden out to meet him after yet another long separation, 'I seem an old man of 60!' On 20 January, as he had promised, the new Congress met and Bolívar resigned his dictatorship.

> Fearing that I am regarded as an obstacle to establishing the Republic on a firm base of happiness, I remove myself from the high office to which you were good enough to elevate me ... Never, never, I swear to you, has the ambition for a monarchy soiled my mind. My enemies have invented that idea to destroy me in your good opinion. Undeceive yourselves. My one desire has been to contribute to your liberty ... The Republic will be happy if, accepting my resignation you name a president beloved of all the nation ... Hear my prayers. Save the Republic. Save my glory, which is Colombia's.

He had been as good as his word. He returned to his hacienda outside Bogotá, learning there that his last major family property, the mines at Aroa, had been confiscated by Páez. The house of his sister, María Antonia, had been daubed with doggerel, no doubt by Páez's agents: 'Maria Antonia, don't be stupid, and if you are, don't be too much. If you want to see Bolívar, go and walk to the graveyard.'
One of Bolívar's supporters reported:

> He walked slowly and with effort, his voice nearly extinguished, and had to make an effort to be intelligible. He walked the banks of the stream that slowly wound through that picturesque countryside and with his arms crossed contemplated its flow, an image of life. 'How long,' he said, 'will this water take to flow into the immense ocean, as men in the darkness of the grave flow into the earth from which they come? A large part will evaporate and disappear, like human glory, like fame. Isn't that true, Colonel?'
> Suddenly he beat his breast with his hands, exclaiming in a tremulous voice, 'My glory! My glory! Why do they take it from me? Why do they insult me? Páez! Páez! Bermúdez insulted me indignantly in a proclamation. But Bermúdez was like Mariño, always an enemy, and he was offended: I was unjust to him in 1826. Santander became my rival to replace me, he wanted to kill me after having waged a cruel war of calumny and defamation ...'

In this conversation the agonised breathing of Bolívar, the languor of his gaze, the deep sighs which emerged from his anguished breast – all indicated the weakness of the body and the anguish of the soul, inspiring compassion and respect. How terrible it is to be a great man!

As Bolívar had feared, the new Congress adopted the kind of loose federal constitution which he had always resisted. His dictatorship had failed to influence the parochialism of the New Granadans. He exclaimed bitterly, 'Wretches! I gave them the very air they breathe and they suspect me [of acting from personal ambition, not patriotism]'. Bolívar decided to stand down, as promised, after two years, half expecting to be recalled. Instead General Joaquín Mosquera, a supporter of Santander, was elected president by the Congress. Many feared Bolívar's army supporters would mount a coup, but none materialized. Others feared he would be assassinated. His last expression of a political settlement was that:

The Constituent Congress must choose one of two courses, the only ones available in the present situation: 1) The separation of New Granada and Venezuela. 2) The creation of a strong life-term government . . . Colombia must forget her illusions and make her decisions, for I cannot rule any longer. These are the facts and we must face the difficulties. What will Congress do to appoint my successor? Will he be New Granadan or Venezuelan? An army man or a civilian? . . . Are the military always to rule by the sword? Will not the civilian population complain of the despotism of the soldiers? I admit that the existing Republic cannot be governed except by the sword, and at the same time I must agree that the military spirit is incompatible with civilian rule. Congress will be forced to return to the question of dividing the country, because whoever they select their choice of a president will always be questioned.

The fight had gone out of the Liberator. Bolívar decided to leave, to keep Colombia united. He told neither of the two closest to him, Manuela, who was always left behind, nor Sucre, of his decision, to prevent them from dissuading him. Yet he was certain he would revive, and return; he would not have abandoned Manuela if he believed he was dying, but they were never to see him again.

On 8 May he left Santa Fé de Bogotá while officials and citizens, many openly weeping, waved him farewell. Colonel Patrick Campbell, the British ambassador remarked: 'He is great – the greatest gentleman of Colombia.' As Bolívar reached the outskirts, youths jeered and shouted 'Longanizo' ('Sausage') after a well-known idiot of the city who wandered the streets dressed as a soldier.

When he reached Honda he learnt of another disaster: General Flores, who together with Sucre had beaten off the Peruvians, had proclaimed the independence of Guayaquil, Quito and the southern province of Colombia as the republic of Ecuador. Sadly, Bolívar remarked that 'posterity has not seen a picture more frightening than that offered by America, more for the future than for the present because who would have imagined that an entire world would collapse in frenzy and devour its own race like cannibals?'

On 16 May he embarked on a boat down the Magdalena river, along which he had ascended on his first triumphs. The strong currents bore him down past the scenes of his glory. Arriving in Cartagena on 24 June, he suffered the worst blow of his life. He had left Bogotá early, deliberately, so as not to say goodbye to his adopted son and chosen successor, Sucre. The latter, deeply disappointed at not accompanying him to the coast, as planned, had decided to return to Quito to rejoin the wife and young son he idolized.

Near Barruecos, Sucre was ambushed and shot dead by the hirelings of the local bandit chief, under the orders of anti-Bolívarists from Bogotá, General Miguel Santamaría and Bolívar's enemy, José María Obando. There is a possibility that Ecuador's Flores or Bolívar's oldest colleague, Urdaneta, Sucre's bitter rival for the succession, may have been the instigator. Bolívar exclaimed, 'God almighty. They have spilt the blood of innocent Abel!' A couple of days later, by terrible irony, Sucre's letter of farewell, written before his departure from Bogotá, reached Bolívar.

My general, when I went to your house to go with you, I found you gone. Perhaps it is well, for it has spared me the sorrow of a last farewell. Right now my heart is empty. I do not know what to say to you.

I have not the words to tell you easily the sentiments of my soul regarding you. You know them well, for you have known me a long time and you know that it has not been your position but only friendship which has inspired in me the deepest affection for your person. I shall conserve it no matter what the fate which befalls us and I beg of you to conserve for me the appreciation you have always bestowed upon me. I shall try in every circumstance to deserve it.

Good-bye, my general. Receive as a token of my friendship the tears which I am shedding at this moment. Be happy, wherever you are going, and be sure always of the devotion and gratitude of your most loyal and passionate friend.

Bolívar was devastated but he remained convinced he was staging a strategic retreat. He spoke of returning to public life in his letters; and he kept in touch with Urdaneta – who, either believing Bolívar spent or seeking to replace him, became steadily less communicative.

Bolívar's health soon took a sharp turn for the worse, and he insisted on being carried first to Soledad, then to Barranquilla in a desperate search for a more agreeable climate. His intention had been to take a boat to Trinidad, then to somewhere in Europe, probably Britain, but he had no strength left. He wrote a testament to the creator of Ecuador, Flores, in November 1830, with tragic, bitter and brilliant humour:

I have arrived at only a few sure conclusions: 1. For us, America is ungovernable. 2. He who serves a revolution ploughs the sea. 3. The only thing we can do in America is to emigrate. 4. This country will eventually fall into the hands of the unbridled mob, and will proceed to almost imperceptible petty tyrannies of all complexions and races. 5. Devoured as we are by every kind of crime and annihilated by ferocity, Europeans will not go to the trouble of conquering us. 6. If it were possible for any part of the world to revert to primordial chaos, that would be America's final state.

News reached him that his enemy in Bogotá, Mosquera, had been forced to resign, and that faithful Urdaneta had seized power and pleaded with him to return to power. His sister, María Antonia, cheered him by writing that the people were clamouring for his return against the tyrants. He told Urdaneta that although he might still serve his country, a return to power needed firmer foundations. He was not quite closing the door; at this point even he did not realize how ill he was.

Desperate for relief from his suffering, he took a boat to Santa Marta, further along the coast. He had conceived the idea of despatching a force to fight Páez, and Santa Marta would be the jumping-off point. He arrived there on 1 December 1830, to take refuge – ironically enough – in the home of the gracious Spanish consul there, Joaquín de Mier, a magnificent *quinta* of white villas in the village of San Pedro Alejandrino. He wrote:

I am about to die. My cycle is completed. God calls me. I must prepare to give an account and my account will be terrible, for the agitations of my life have been terrible . . . I have scarcely strength enough to support the last days that remain of my miserable life . . . I see no salvation for the country. I believe everything is lost forever. If there were a single sacrifice I could make – my life, my happiness or my honour – believe me, I would not hesitate; but I am convinced the sacrifice would be useless. Since I am unable to secure the happiness of my country, I refuse to rule it. Further, the tyrants have taken my native land from me and therefore I have no longer any country for which to make a sacrifice . . . All who have served the Revolution have ploughed the sea.

There he was attended by a French doctor, Prospero Reverend. Bolívar remarked half-deliriously on his arrival: 'The three great killers of humanity have been Jesus Christ, Don Quixote and myself.' Killers, presumably, because they had been idealists and misled the people. Racked by alternate hot flushes and shivering, he could still walk about briefly and he complained that Urdaneta had not written to him. Next door, his officers noisily played cards and sang.

On 9 December, having lost all hope of living, he dictated his last proclamation:

> Colombians! You have witnessed my efforts to plant liberty where tyranny reigned before. I have laboured with disinterest, sacrificing my fortune and my own peace. I resigned from command when I saw that you had no faith in my disinterest. My enemies took advantage of your credulity and trampled upon what is most sacred to me – my reputation and my love of liberty. I have been the victim of my persecutors, who have led me to the gates of the sepulchre. I forgive them. On disappearing from among you, my affection tells me that I should declare my last wishes. I aspire to no other glory than the consolidation of Colombia. All of you must work for the inestimable good of the Union: the people obeying the government in order to avoid anarchy; the ministers praying to Heaven for guidance; and the military using its sword in defence of social guarantees.
>
> Colombians! My last wish is for the happiness of the fatherland. If my death contributes to the end of partisanship and the consolidation of the Union, I shall be lowered in peace into my grave.

This was read before his loyal attendants, his nephew and adopted son Fernando, Belford Wilson and the faithful José Palacio, as well as a crowd of weeping villagers. He now drifted increasingly into half-consciousness and delirium. His last words were: 'Let's go, let's go, these people do not want us here.' At around midday on 17 December 1830 he died, aged just 47.

It is said that a day later the French girl he had seduced 17 years earlier on the Magdalena arrived – too late. Manuela Sáenz, so cruelly left behind once again, heard the news of his death when she was already journeying down the Magdalena to join him. Santander, who returned to seize power immediately after the news, promptly had her exiled. She refused the defunct Dr Thorne's estates and lived in poverty, faithful to Bolívar's memory at Pasto in Peru. Giuseppe Garibaldi met her there in 1858 and after listening to her tales of the Liberator, described her as the most gracious lady he had ever met. She also met the half-crazed Simón Rodríguez once more, and the novelist Herman Melville. She died of the plague aged 59.

On the twelfth anniversary of his death, Bolívar's remains were shipped back to Caracas, to be received by his two elderly black nurses, Hipolita and Matea – although sadly not by his sister María Antonia, who had just died. Páez, now president of his independent Venezuela, presided over the return of the hero he had betrayed. He wrote of his master posthumously:

> Simón Bolívar belongs to the band of modern men whose equals are to be found only when we reach back to the republican times of Greece and Rome . . . In the midst of people who had no more tradition than the respect for an authority sanctioned by the acquiescence of three centuries of ignorance, superstition, and fanaticism, not any political dogma but submission to an order of things supported by might and force, Bolívar succeeded in defying that power.

Simón Bolívar is a quasi-deity in Spanish America today. To the educated and propertied classes, his radicalism has long since been quietly forgotten. In the terrible history of most of Latin American countries to date, he is the one continental leader, the man who freed millions of people from tyranny and did not enslave them himself. The bitterness of modern Latin American divisions – between left and right, between militarists and democrats, between oligarchies and revolutionaries – does not apply to Bolívar. He overthrew the common enemy, the Spanish empire, and predated these struggles, transcending political division.

To hundreds of millions of ordinary South Americans, many of them illiterate, he was the leader who had tried to overcome class and racial divisions, who had tried to give rights to that vast swathe of humanity that remains downtrodden and without rights. After the terrible litany of tyrants, demagogues and corrupt politicians of the nearly 180 years that have laid waste to that astonishing continent since he died, he and his fellow liberators remain unsullied as hero figures. They liberated, and left the scene before enslavement began anew.

Faced with this continent-wide hero worship, which extends from the prosperous university student to the slum-dweller, it is hard for the outsider not to wish to debunk the myth. This is not difficult, considering the flaws, some of them colossal, in the man.

His amazing career was littered with them: from the wastage of his youth to his Shakespearean betrayal of Miranda; from the descent into darkness with the 'war to the death' to the relentless failure of his early attempts at Venezuelan independence amidst horrific suffering for his people; from the unstinting ferocity with which he drove so many of his own men to their deaths to the cold-blooded murder of 800 prisoners of war; from the apparent madness of trying to stitch together three very different nations against their will, and then add three more, to the vainglory of his posturing and preening as he liberated countless cities and towns; from his assembly-line appetite for women to the hubris with which he stood on the silver mountain at Potosí beholding new vast lands to conquer in the south; from the grandiose dream to the eventual reckoning – his whole vast empire, three times bigger than western Europe, crumbled away within the space of five years, leaving him impoverished and an outcast on his way to exile.

While the achievement lapsed into savage alternation between tyranny and left-wing extremism, from which it has only precariously emerged today, it is not difficult to find fault with the Liberator, or even to portray him as a figure of Macbeth-like megalomania and evil, another Napoleon with an added demonic quality, one of the monsters of history. O'Leary mentions one revealing episode: 'Doctor Salazar, having mentioned to Bolívar that his friends complained of his apparent insensibility, that he saw his partisans and friends fall in battle without eliciting from him the tribute of a tear or a sigh, "Good God," replies Bolívar, "were I to weep for every friend I have lost or am to lose in future I would be called General Jeremiah not General Bolívar."'

His very title, to the cynics, reeks of the emptiness of his achievements: he liberated his people from what, for what? What more did he do than 'liberate'? And what, even today, does liberation mean for most people, steeped in backwardness, poverty and ignorance? How diminutive this strutting little man, with his uniforms and grand gestures, looks beside the simple, towering gravitas of a George Washington or a Thomas Jefferson.

Yet men must be judged by their achievements within the context of the societies and times they lived in, not by some artificial historical absolute, much less by modern standards. Those who see him as a quasi-mystical figure are almost right, because he lived a life and achieved things that are, by any standard, nearly superhuman. He had the good fortune to live at a time when the historical tide was turning: the Spanish empire was buckling under the weight of its own contradictions. But as an individual, at a time when few dared challenge its overwhelming military might, he overcame a succession of appalling setbacks that would have deterred anyone else and tried, and tried, and tried again until the spark of revolution at last ignited.

His first campaign to reconquer Venezuela was won virtually single-handed. His landings on the Venezuelan coast were triumphs of determination over adversity, his return to the Orinoco was a leap of the imagination. His march across the Andes was a terrifying feat of endurance and his final conquest of Venezuela was a triumph of strategy. His taking of Quito, Peru and Upper Peru was a string of victories in strange landscapes of almost dreamlike implausibility.

He overcame terrible odds and, when on a winning streak, wherever he went he won. More than that, the superhuman energy needed to cross the thousands of miles of the most murderous terrain in the world continues to astonish anyone who knows that land. In terms of stamina alone, he showed powers that few statesmen in history have possessed. His energy, combined with an appearance that was cheerful and intense, gaunt and alive, charming and fierce all at the same time, endowed him with a demonic quality that transcends mere mortality, although in the end his very efforts may have burnt him out and led to his tragically early grave – if the reason for his death is not solely that he was suffering from the tuberculosis of the lungs that killed so many in his day, including his mother.

If his energies were superhuman, so was the military feat – to have beaten off the most formidable and feared army of his day, after the British and French, with his ill-trained irregulars across not one but six countries spanning the crown and side of a continent. Judged by his military achievement alone he deserves to be placed in the front rank of soldiers in history: Cortés and Pizarro took on empires with comparatively small armies; but their opponents lacked horses and firearms. Clive of India similarly secured an empire in Bengal – but largely through guile not force of arms, and against ill-equipped local armies rather than a well-armed European foe.

Bolívar's generalship vies with those of Julius and Augustus Caesar, Alexander the Great, Tamerlane and Genghis Khan: he was a fighter on a continental scale, his enemies if anything were more formidable, his friends fewer, and the terrain arguably the harshest in the world. As a warrior he rises to mythical proportions. In modern terms he was the first and greatest guerrilla leader in history, vastly overshadowing Fidel Castro and Che Guevara in recent day.

Yet soldiery was only half of Bolívar's achievement. The fact that he was, ultimately, a political failure (or only half a success – he liberated his peoples from Spanish rule, but did not succeed in putting anything permanent in their place) should not obscure the value or enormity of what he was trying to do. If the judgment of this narrative is at least a quarter right, it becomes obvious that Bolívar, in spite of lapses in times of great stress, was as close to being a political idealist as any actual practitioner of politics can get. He tried to set up representative assemblies in the countries he freed; only in the last resort did he rule by force, and then only briefly and reluctantly, with a light touch.

He genuinely tried to formulate and grant his huge domain enlightened, representative and paternalist rule. None of the charges that he was a covert monarchist, imperialist or one-man ruler stand up to scrutiny. He had an obsessive belief in his own abilities, certainly, but everywhere he sought to leave ordered constitutional rule behind him. He had a clear idea of what that rule should be. It is easy to laugh today at some of the absurdities of the Bolívarist constitutions – the idea of a president-for-life, for example, or an hereditary senate. Yet these were not illiberal ideas in the context of his time, by comparison with the absolutisms holding sway over continental Europe.

Bolívar had two great guiding principles. He believed in the need for a strong central state to guarantee the freedom of the weak against the strong, although he argued that such an executive must be checked by parliament and had no power to override the inalienable rights of all the people. Secondly, he argued relentlessly, knowing that his dream was almost certainly quixotic, for a confederal South America, albeit divided into different countries.

Who, looking at the history of the continent since his death, can say he was wrong? The absence of a tradition of effective democratic government spawned a murderous alternation between strong dictatorship and weak and populist democratic governments usually undermined by left-wing extremists. The division of Latin America into some 20 republics, some in Central America barely the size of a small city in the United States, has made the continent globally irrelevant and fissiparously parochial.

The fact that Bolívar was, in his phrase, ploughing the sea – no man could perhaps have prevailed on either count against the social and political realities of his time – should not detract from his attempt. His vision was a noble one and most, although not all, of his successors, lacking his vision, have shown far less ability even in day-to-day government than the visionary did. He at least set down a standard, a marker for strong representative rule, constitutional government and pan-Americanism that is a long way from being met to this day. It is hard to quarrel with any of the underlying values he sought to embody in his constitutions: equality before the law; the rights of even the poorest; the abolition of slavery; strong central government checked by elected institutions. It was a noble vision.

Why did he so singularly fail when the North American colonists succeeded in creating both a united and constitutional federation of states? Perhaps because the British empire in America was primarily an economic one overthrown for these reasons by a trading class. The Spanish empire was primarily a military construct, overthrown by force of arms, leaving a deep divide between landowners and the poor. The trading classes played little or no part in its downfall. The United States' revolution was a middle-class one, while the revolution of the Spanish colonies was an aristocratic-militarist one harnessing undercurrents of class and racial war.

In another respect, too, Bolívar was something altogether unique for his times: he was a compassionate figure, a radical if not a revolutionary. He genuinely believed in the rights of the poorest and the equality of races to the point of pressganging his adopted daughter into marrying a mixed-race officer. He was no egalitarian – he believed in an ordered society, with those of property and education at the top, and despaired of the ignorance of the masses – but he recognized the land, legal and human rights of even the poorest of the poor, the most illiterate peasant, the freed slave or the broken-backed Indian worker in highland Peru.

In this he was way in advance of thinking on his continent, and in the forefront of that in the rest of the world, including most of Europe. It was this that so disturbed most of the Spanish American oligarchies of his time, although now they embrace Bolívar as one of their own; it was this that gave him appeal to the masses of Latin America and qualified him as a genuine popular leader, much more so than Napoleon or twentieth-century demagogues. He was a liberal populist in the best senses of both words, espousing almost Anglo-Saxon values. His admiration for Britain's constitutional balance was no mere coincidence.

Bolívar displayed other, lesser political skills: as a superb orator; as an inspired crafter of words; as a devious diplomat; as a brilliant showman; as an intelligent political thinker; and, often, as an attractive personality and warm human being. The defects ranked alongside them: the occasional descent into manic cruelty; the vanity; the sexual predatoriness (although this was regarded as a virtue by many Latin Americans, rather than a sin); the lust for glory beside the passion for liberty.

Yet as soldier, statesman and man of common humanity he stands head and shoulders above any other figure that Latin America has ever produced and amongst the greatest men in global history. Small wonder that the Liberator remains a figure of hope to millions of Latin Americans seeking liberation from poverty, ignorance and disease. He deserves to be rescued from the obscurity in which western historians have until recently relegated him.

'But what good came of it at last?' asks little Peterkin in Robert Southey's poem 'The Battle of Blenheim'. Did Simón Bolívar's achievement matter in view of the suffering that the continent has endured since his day? The answer must be an unequivocal yes. It did matter that Latin America was freed from the yoke of a crushing, cruel and parasitic empire. It should not be held against him that after its release from those crippling chains, the continent has taken nearly two centuries to stand on its feet.

In Latin America, and even in the Iberian peninsula, Simón Bolívar is revered as a demi-god, the man who wrenched a continent from the grip of imperial rule. In the United States and most of Europe, people know of Bolívar the name, if at all, as applying a brand of cigar and a type of hat. Why this dichotomy? Partly because Latin America, since independence, has widely if unfairly been seen as a disappointment, even a failure, marginalized from the stage of global power politics (although now the strength and culture of the continent are beginning to assert themselves); partly because of simple ignorance as to the nature of these astonishing wars of independence, and the man who primarily drove them. He was one of the greatest soldiers in history, a huge political thinker, and a lousy politician. He was the embodiment of the superman conjured up by Friedrich Nietzsche – yet a man of profoundly liberal and constitutional ideals, in spite of his martial prowess. He died at the age of just 47, having accomplished more in a short lifetime than most could in a dozen.

Bolívar has been blamed for many of the ills that befell Latin America after independence. His left-wing critics say that he instituted *caudillismo*, the military domination over civilian life, the *pronunciamento* or coup, the cult of the individual leader and of centralized presidential authority. Some left-wingers condemn him for being in thrall to his own class, the criollo feudal landowners, and for failing to change the whole hierarchical structure of the Spanish empire based on oligarchs, a few traders, and labourers and slaves. Others on the right condemn him for overthrowing an entire social order, espousing the working and slave classes. Venezuela's president, Hugo Chávez, who has renamed Venezuela as the Bolívarian Republic of Venezuela, commends him for doing just that from a left-wing standpoint. If so, Bolívar was singularly unsuccessful, with the achievements of his revolution being frustrated even while he was still alive. Yet the remembrance of what he tried to do continues to make him venerated among almost all classes, including the indigenous and black populations, mestizos, mulattos and zambos. Modern Latin Americans admire him hugely, both as a general and as a political visionary.

But the question remains as to why this beautiful, abundant and immensely cultured continent is still a developing one while its neighbour the United States – much poorer at the time of liberation – has become the most industrious and prosperous on earth. In his brilliant book, *Forgotten Continent*, Michael Reid addresses these questions without coming to an entirely satisfactory conclusion: for while Latin America's economic backwardness, and immense pockets of poverty, are not in dispute, the continent has nevertheless – not everywhere but in many places – managed to carry on a way of life, culture, familial relations, interracial tolerance (along with profound inequality between races) and community that is largely absent from the United States. The challenge is to raise levels of prosperity without endangering those treasures in what is perhaps the world's most geographically beautiful continent. Precariously, in the past 20 years the legacy of *caudillismo*, populism and left- and right-wing extremism has almost, not quite, been stamped out.

The last dream of Simón Bolívar, who had briefly succeeded in welding together what are now six countries into a single state, was of a League of Southern American Nations to represent the continent's interests in a world dominated by major, exploitative powers. That perhaps is more pertinent than ever today, as the 'new great powers', the United States, the European Union, Japan, Russia, China and India, carve up the globe between them. The dream remains perhaps a little in advance of its time, even today.

BIBLIOGRAPHY

Francisco de Miranda

Atkinson, William Christopher, *Miranda: His Life and Times*, Canning House Lecture, London, 1950

Becerra, Ricardo, *Vida de Don Francisco de Miranda*, Madrid, 1927

Bohórquez, Carmen, *Francisco de Miranda: Précurseur des Indépendences de l'Amérique Latin*, Paris, 1998

Carr, Raymond, *Spain 1838–1939*, Cambridge, 1966

Carrasco, Ricardo, *Francisco de Miranda, Precursor de la Independencia Hispano-Americana 1750–1792*, Buenos Aires, 1951

García, Lautico, *Francisco de Miranda y el Antiguo Régimen Español*, Caracas, 1961

Grases, Pedro, *El Regreso de Miranda a Caracas en 1810*, Caracas, 1957

Grases, Pedro, *La Biblioteca de Francisco de Miranda*, Caracas, 1966

Jane, Cecil, *Liberty and Despotism in Spanish America*, Cambridge, 1929

Miranda, Francisco de, *Archivo del General Miranda*, Caracas, 1930

Nucete-Sardi, José, *Aventura y Tragedia de Don Francisco de Miranda*, 1956

Parra-Pérez, Caracciolo, *Paginas de Historia y de Polemica*, Caracas, 1943

Parra-Pérez, Caracciolo, *Miranda-Bolívar: Lectures*, Paris, 1947

Parra-Pérez, Caracciolo, *Miranda et Madame de Custine*, Paris, 1950

Parra-Pérez, Caracciolo, *Historia de la Primera Republic de Venezuela*, Caracas, 1959

Parry, J.H., *The Spanish Seaborne Empire*, London, 1966

Pendle, George, *A History of Latin America*, London, 1963

Picón Salas, Mariano, *Miranda* (4th edition), Caracas, 1972

Pueyrredón, Carlos Alberto, *En Tiempos de los Virreyes*, Buenos Aires, 1932

Rippy, J. Fred, *Latin America: A Modern History*, Ann Arbor, MI, 1959

Rojas, A., *Miranda dans la Révolution Française*, Caracas, 1889

Rumazo González, Alfonso, *Miranda, Protolider de la Independencia Americana*, Los Teques, 1985

Rydjord, John, *Foreign Interest in the Independence of New Spain*, Durham, NC, 1935

Verjerano, Jorge Ricardo, *La Vida Fabulosa de Miranda*, Bogotá, 1945

Villoro, Luis, *El Proceso Ideologico de la Revolucion de Independencia*, Mexico City, 1967

Webster, C.K., *Foreign Policy of Castlereagh, 1812–1822*, London, 1934

Webster, C.K. (ed.), *Britain and the Independence of Latin America 1812–1830*, 2 vols, London, 1938

Simón Bolívar

Abreu y Lima, José Ignacio de, *Resumen Histórico de la Última Dictadura del Libertador Simón Bolívar*, Rio de Janeiro, 1922

Academia Nacional de la Historia, *Archivo Santander*, Bogotá, 1932

Acosta Saignes, Miguel, *Acción y Utopía del Hombre de las Dificultades*, Havana, 1977

Altuve Carrillo, Leonardo, *Genio y Apoteosis de Bolívar en la Campaña del Perú*, Barcelona, 1979

André, Marius, *Bolívar y la Democracia*, Barcelona, 1924

Andrien, Kenneth J. and Johnson, Lyman L. (eds), *The Political Economy of Spanish America in the Age of Revolution, 1750–1850*, Albuquerque, 1994

Angell, Hildegarde, *Simon Bolivar, South American Liberator*, New York, 1930

Arias, Harmodo, *The International Policy of Bolivar*, New York, 1918

Arocha Moreno, Jesús, *Bolívar Juzgado por el General San Martín*, Caracas, 1930

Austria, José de, *Bosquejo de la historia militar de Venezuela*, 2 vols, Caracas, 1960

Balch, Oliver, *Viva South America!*, London, 2004

Barbagelata, Hugo, *Bolívar y San Martín*, Paris, 1911

Barnola, Pedro Pablo, *Por Qué Bolívar*, Caracas, 1960

Bayo, Ciro, *Bolívar y sus Tenientes*, Madrid, 1929

Bazan, Armando, *San Martín y Bolívar: Paralelo de sus Vidas*, Buenos Aires, 1949

Belaunde, Victor Andrés, *Bolívar and the Political Thought of the Spanish American Revolution*, Baltimore, 1938

Beltrán Avila, Marcos, *El Tabú Bolívarista, 1825–1828*, Oruro, 1960

Berruezo León, María Teresa, *La Lucha de Hispanoamérica por su Independencia en Inglaterra, 1800–1830*, Madrid, 1989

Blanco, José Felix and Azpurua, Ramón (eds), *Documentos para la Historia de la Vida Pública del Libertador de Colombia, Perú y Bolivia*, 14 vols, Caracas, 1875–8

Bolívar, Simón, *Cartas, 1799–1830*, 4 vols, denotes by R. Blanco-Fombona, Madrid and Paris, 1912–22

Bolívar, Simón, *Papeles de Bolívar. Publicados por Vicente Lecuna*, 2 vols, Madrid, 1920

Bolívar, Simón, *Proclamas y Discursos del Libertador*, ed. Vicente Lecuna, Caracas, 1939

Bolívar, Simón, *Decretos del Libertador*, 3 vols, Caracas, 1961

Bolívar, Simón, *El Libertador: Writings of Simón Bolívar*, trans. Frederick H. Fornoff, ed. David Bushnell, Oxford, 2003

Brading, D.A., *Classical Republicanism and Creole Patriotism: Simón Bolívar and the Spanish American Revolution*, London, 1983

Brice, Angel Francisco, *El 'Bolívar' de Marx Ampliado por Madariaga*, Caracas, 1952

Bulnes, Gonzalo, *Bolívar en el Perú*, 2 vols, Madrid, 1919

Bulnes, Gonzalo, *Historia de la Expedición Libertadora del Perú*, 2 vols, Santiago, 1888

Bushnell, David (ed.), *The Liberator, Simón Bolívar: Man and Image*, New York, 1970

Bushnell, David, 'Independence Compared: the Americas North and South', in A. MacFarlane and E. Posada-Carbó, *Independence and Revolution in Spanish America*, London, 2002, pp 69–83

Carrillo Moreno, José, *Bolívar, Maestro del Pueblo*, Caracas, 1971

Cova Maza, J.M., *Mocedades de Simón Bolívar*, Barcelona, 1924

Cuervo, Luis Augusto, *La Monarquía en Colombia*, Bogota, 1916

Dalencour, Francois, *Alexandre Pétion devant l'Humanité; Alexandre Pétion et Simon Bolívar; Haiti et l'Amérique Latine; Et l'expedition de Bolívar par Marion Aine*, Port-au-Prince, 1928

Ducoudray-Holstein, H.L.V., *Memoirs of Simón Bolívar*, 2 vols, London, 1830

Elliott, J.H., *Imperial Spain, 1496–1716*, London, 1963

Espinosa Apolo, Manuel (ed.), *Simón Bolívar y Manuela Sáenz: Correspondencia Intima*, Quito, 1996

García Márquez, Gabriel, *The General in His Labyrinth*, London, 1991

Gil Fortoul, José, *Historia Constitucional de Venezuela*, Caracas, 1930

Goenaga, José Manuel, *La Entrevista de Guayaquil*, Bogotá, 1911

Gómez Picón, Alirio, *Bolívar y Santander: Historia de una Amistad*, Bogotá, 1971

González, Juan Vicente, *Biografía del General José Felix Ribas*, Madrid, 1918

Gott, Richard, *In the Shadow of the Liberator*, London, 2002

Graham, Robert Cunninghame, *José Antonio Páez*, London, 1929

Grisanti, Angel, *Bolívar, su Idilio y Matrimonio en Madrid*, Caracas, 1959

Guevara, Arturo, *Historia Clínica del Libertador*, Caracas, 1948

Gutiérrez, Alberto, *La Iglesia que Entendió el Libertado Simón Bolívar*, Bogotá, 1981

Halperin Donghi, Tulio, *Reforma y Disolución de los Imperios Ibéricos 1750–1850*, Madrid, 1985

Harvey, Robert, *Liberators*, London, 2000

Harvey, Robert, *The War of Wars*, London, 2007

Hasbrouck, Alfred, *Foreign Legionaries in the Liberation of Spanish America*, New York, 1928

Herring, Hubert, *A History of Latin America*, New York, 1961

Hildebrandt, Martha, *Los Peruanismos en el Léxico de Bolívar*, Lima, 1960

Hippisley, G., *A Narrative of the Expedition to the Rivers Orinoco and Apure . . .* , London, 1819

Hispano, Cornelio, *Historia Secreta de Bolívar, su Gloria y sus Amores*, Medellin, 1977

Humboldt, Alexander von, *Cartas Americanas*, ed. Charles Minguet, Caracas, 1980

Humboldt, Alexander von, *Personal Narrative of a Journey to the Equinoctial Regions of the New Continent*, trans. Jason Wilson, London, 1995

Humphreys, R.A., 'British merchants and South American Independence', in *Proceedings of the British Academy, Vol. 51*, London, 1965

Izard, Miguel, *El Miedo a la Revolución: La Lucha por la Libertad en Venezuela (1777–1830)*, Madrid, 1979

Izquierdo, José, *Simón Bolívar: Reseña Histórica*, Buenos Aires, 1967

Jane, Cecil, *Liberty and Despotism in Spanish America*, Oxford, 1929

Jaramillo, Juan Diego, *Bolívar y Canning, 1822–7: Desde el Congreso de Verona*, Bogotá, 1983

Lafond, Georges and Tersane, Gabriel, *Bolívar et la Libération de l'Amérique du Sud*, Paris, 1931

Langley, Lester D., *The Americas in the Age of Revolution, 1750–1850*, New Haven, 1996

Larrazábal, Felipe, *La Vida y Correspondencia General del Libertador Simón Bolívar*, New York, 1878

Lecuna, Vicente, *Historia de la Casa de Bolívar*, Caracas, 1924

Lecuna, Vicente (ed.), *Cartas del Libertador*, 10 vols, Caracas, 1939

Lecuna, Vicente, *Crónica Razonada de las Guerras de Bolívar*, New York, 1950

Lecuna, Vicente, *La Casa Natal del Libertador*, Caracas, 1954

Lecuna, Vicente, *Proclamas y Discursos del Libertador*, Caracas, 1939

Lecuna, Vicente, *Simón Bolívar, Obras Completas*, 3 vols, Havana, 1950

Lecuna, Vicente, *Simón Bolívar, Selected Writings*, 2 vols, New York, 1951

Lemboke, Jorge Bailey, *La Verdadera Manuela Sáenz*, Caracas, 1927

Lemly, Henry, *Bolívar, Liberator of Venezuela, Colombia, Peru and Bolívar*, Boston, 1928

Liévano Aguirre, Indalecio, *Simón Bolívar*, Caracas, 1971

Llorens Casani, Milagro, *Sebastián del Toro, Ascendiente de los Héroes de la Independencia de Venezuela*, 2 vols, Jaén, 1998

Lofstrom, William L., *La Presidencia de Sucre en Bolivia*, Caracas, 1987
Lombardi, John V., *The Decline and Abolition of Negro Slavery in Venezuela 1820–1854*, Westport, 1971
López, Ismael, *Las Amadas de Bolívar*, Lima, 1924
Lynch, John, *Simón Bolívar and the Age of Revolution*, London, 1983
Lynch, John, *Caudillos in Spanish America 1800–1850*, Oxford, 1992
Lynch, John, *Simón Bolívar: A Life*, London, 2006
McFarlane, Anthony, *Colombia before Independence: Economy, Society, and Politics Under Bourbon Rule*, Cambridge, 1993
Madariaga, Salvador de, *Bolívar*, Madrid, 1951
Marschall, Phyllis, *Bolívar*, Santiago de Chile, 1949
Masur, Gerhard, *Simón Bolívar*, Albuquerque, 1948
Mijares, Augusto, *El Libertador*, Caracas, 1983
Miller, John, *Memoirs of General Miller*, 2 vols, London, 1828
Moses, Bernard, *The Intellectual Background of the Revolution in South America, 1810–24*, New York, 1926
Mosquera, Tomás Cipriano de, *Memorias sobre la Vida del Libertador Simón Bolívar*, New York, 1853
Muñoz, Gabriel E., *Monteverde: Cuatro Años de Historia Patria 1812–1816*, 2 vols, Caracas, 1987
Navarro, Nicolás, *La Cristiana Muerte del Libertador*, Caracas, 1930
O'Leary, Daniel Florencio, *Memorias del General O'Leary*, 6 vols, Caracas, 1952
Olmedo, José de, *La Victoria de Junín*, Lima, 1974
O'Phelan Gody, Scarlett (ed.), *La Independencia del Perú: De los Borbones a Bolívar*, Lima, 2001
Páez, José Antonio, *Autobiografia*, 2 vols, New York, 1867
Palma, Ricardo, *Bolívar en las Tradiciones Peruanas*, Madrid, 1930
Parra-Pérez, Caracciolo, *Paginas de Historia y de Polemica*, Caracas, 1943
Parra-Pérez, Caracciolo, *Miranda-Bolívar: Lectures*, Paris, 1947
Parra-Pérez, Caracciolo, *La Monarquia en la Gran Colombia*, Madrid, 1957
Pérez Díaz, Dr M., *Estudio Medico-psicologico de Bolívar*, Caracas, 1915
Pérez y Soto, Juan Bautista (comp.), *Defensa de Bolívar*, Lima, 1878
Pérez Vila, Manuel, *Bolívar y su Época: Cartas Testimonios de Extranjeros*, Caracas, 1953
Pérez Vila, Manuel, *La Biblioteca del Libertador*, Caracas, 1960
Pérez Vila, Manuel, *Documentos Apocrifos Atribuidos al Libertador 1809–12*, Caracas, 1968
Pérez Vila, Manuel, *Simón Bolívar, el Libertador: Sintesis Biografia*, Caracas, 1972
Pérez Vila, Manuel, *La Formacion Intelectual del Libertador*, 2nd edition, Caracas, 1979
Pérez Vila, Manuel, *Simón Bolívar, His Basic Thoughts*, Caracas, 1980
Peru de Lacroix, Louis, *Bolívar Jugé par un Officier de Napoléon*, Paris, 1913
Peru de Lacroix, Louis, *Diario de Bucaramanga*, Caracas, 1935
Petre, Francis Loraine, *Simón Bolívar 'El Libertador'*, New York, 1910
Pike, Frederick, *The Modern History of Peru*, London, 1967
Pineda, C. Manuel Antonio, *Bolívar ante la Historia*, Cartagena, 1930
Piñeyro, Enrique, *Biografías Americanas: Simón Bolívar*, Paris, 1906
Pinilla, Sabino, *La Creación de Bolivia*, Madrid, 1917
Pividal, Francisco, *Bolívar, Pensamiento Precursor del Antiimperialismo*, Caracas, 1977
Polanco Alcántara, Tomás, *Simón Bolívar: Ensayo de una Interpretación Biográfica a Través de sus Documentos*, Caracas, 1994
Ponte, Andrés, *Bolívar y Otros Ensayos*, Caracas, 1919
Ponte, Andrés, *La Puebla de Bolívar*, Caracas, 1919
Porras Troconis, Gabriel, *Campañas Bolívarianas de la Libertad*, Caracas, 1953

Pradt, Dominique de Fourt de, *Congres de Panama*, Paris, 1825

Racine, Karen, *Francisco de Miranda: A Transatlantic Life in the Age of Revolution*, Wilmington, Delaware, 2003

Ramos, Demetrio, *España y la Independencia de América*, Madrid, 1996

Reid, Michael, *Forgotten Continent*, London, 2007

Revérénd, Alejandro Próspero, *Diario Sobre la Enfermadad que Padece S.E. El Libertador*, Caracas, 1930

Revilla Pérez, Gladys, *Bolívar y Josefina*, Caracas, 2000

Rio, Daniel A. del, *Simón Bolívar*, New York, 1965

Rippy, J. Fred, *Latin America: A Modern History*, Ann Arbor, MI, 1959

Rivas Vicuña, Francisco, *Las Guerras de Bolívar*, Caracas, 1921–2

Robertson, William Spence, *France and Latin American Independence*, Baltimore, 1939

Robertson, William Spence, *History of Latin American Nations*, New York, 1925

Robertson, William Spence, *Rise of the Spanish American Republics*, New York, 1918

Rodríguez, Simón, *Defensa de Bolívar*, Caracas, 1916

Roig, Arturo, *Bolívarismo y Filosofía Latinoamericana*, Quito, 1984

Rojas, José María, *Simón Bolívar*, Paris, 1883

Rojas, Ricardo, *La entrevista de Guayaquil*, Buenos Aires, 1950

Rourke, Thomas, *Simon Bolivar*, London, 1940

Rumazo González, Alfonso, *Manuela Sáenz: La Libertadora del Libertador*, 6th edition, Caracas, 1972

Saénz, Vicente, *Morelos y Bolívar*, San Salvador, 1956

Salcedo-Bastardo, J.L., *Bolívar, Un Continente ye un Destino*, Caracas, 1972

Salcedo-Bastardo, J.L., *Un Hombre Diáfano: Vida de Simón Bolívar para los Nuevos*, Caracas, 1976

Salcedo-Bastardo, J.L., *Vision y Revision de Bolívar*, Caracas, 1977

Salcedo-Bastardo, J.L., *Bolívar: A Continent and its Destiny*, Richmond, 1978

Santander, Francisco de Paula, *Archivo Santander*, 24 vols, Bogotá, 1913–32

Santander, Francisco de Paula, *Cartas Santander-Bolívar*, 6 vols, Bogotá, 1988–90

Santana, Arturo, *La Campaña de Carabobo*, Caracas, 1921

Saurat, Gilette, *Bolívar le Libertador*, Paris, 1979

Sherwell, Guillermo Antonio, *Simón Bolívar (El Libertador)*, Washington, DC, 1921

Sociedad Bolivariana del Perú, *Testimonios Peruanos sobre El Libertador*, Lima, 1964

Soler, Ricaurte, *Cuatros Ensayos de Historia*, Panama, 1985

Sucre, Antonio José de, *Cartas de Sucre el Libertador*, 2 vols, Madrid, 1919

Sucre, Antonio José de, *Archivo de Sucre*, 15 vols, Caracas, 1973–8

Tejera, Humberto, *Bolívar, Guía Democrático de América*, Caracas, 1944

Trend, J.B., *Bolívar and the Independence of Spanish America*, New York, 1946

Trompiz, G., *Bolívar, Autentico y Actual: Ensayos sobre la Armonia*, Caracas, 1977

Urdaneta, Rafael, *Memorias*, Madrid, 1916

Uribe White, Enrique, *Iconografía del Libertador*, Bogatá, 1967

Uribe White, Enrique, *El Libertador: Campaña de 1819, Episodios en su Vida*, Bogatá, 1969

Urrutia, Francisco José, *El Ideal Internacional de Bolívar*, Quito, 1911

Urueta Insignares, Raúl, *Bolívar: Estudio y Antología*, Madrid, 1973

Vallejo, Carlos María de, *Romancero del Libertador Simón Bolívar*, Caracas, 1942

Vargas Ugarte, Ruben, *Historia del Perú. Emancipation, 1809–1825*, Buenos Aires, 1958

Vásconez Hurtado, Gustavo, *Cartas de Bolívar al General Juan José Flores*, Quito, 1976

Vaucaire, Michel, *Bolívar, the Liberator*, Boston, 1929

Verna, Paul, *Robert Sutherland: Un Amigo de Bolívar en Haiti*, Caracas, 1966

Verna, Paul, *Pétion y Bolívar: Una Etapa Decisiva en la Emancipación de Hispanoamérica 1790–1830*, Caracas, 1980

Von Hagen, Victor Wolfgang, *The Four Seasons of Manuela: The Love Story of Manuela Saenz and Simon Bolivar*, London, 1966

Webster, C.K. (ed.), *Britain and the Independence of Latin America 1812–1830*, 2 vols, London, 1938

Ybarra, T.R., *Bolívar, The Passionate Warrior*, New York, 1929

INDEX

Note: Simón Bolivár is abbreviated to SB in parts of index.